BALLOTS AND BIBLES

A volume in the series

CUSHWA CENTER STUDIES OF CATHOLICISM
IN TWENTIETH-CENTURY AMERICA
edited by R. Scott Appleby, University of Notre Dame

A full list of titles in the series appears at the end of the book.

Ballots & Bibles

*Ethnic Politics
and the
Catholic Church
in Providence*

EVELYN SAVIDGE STERNE

Cornell University Press *Ithaca & London*

First published 2003 by Cornell University Press
Printed in the United States of America

Portions of this book are reprinted, with changes, from: Evelyn Sterne, "All Americans: The Politics of Citizenship in Providence, 1840–1940" (Ph.D. diss., Duke University, 1999); Evelyn Savidge Sterne, "Bringing Religion into Working-Class History: Parish, Public and Politics in Providence, 1890–1930," *Social Science History* 24, no. 1 (2000): 149–82, by permission of Duke University Press; and Evelyn Savidge Sterne, "Beyond the Boss: Immigration and American Political Culture, 1880–1940," chapter 1 in *E Pluribus Unum? Contemporary and Historical Perspectives on Immigrant Political Incorporation,* ed. Gary Gerstle and John Mollenkopf (New York: Russell Sage Foundation, 2001), by permission of the Russell Sage Foundation.

Library of Congress Cataloging-in-Publication Data

Sterne, Evelyn Savidge, 1967–
    Ballots and Bibles : ethnic politics and the Catholic Church in Providence / Evelyn Savidge Sterne.
        p.   cm.
    Includes bibliographical references (p.   ) and index.
        ISBN 0-8014-4117-X (cloth : alk. paper)
        1. Catholic Church—Rhode Island—Providence—Political activity—History.
2. Immigrants—Rhode Island—Providence—Political activity—History.   3. Catholics—Rhode Island—Providence—Political activity—History.   4. Christianity and politics—Rhode Island—Providence—History.   5. Christianity and politics—Catholic Church—History.
6. Providence (R.I.)—Politics and government.   7. Providence (R.I.)—Church history.
I. Title.
    BX1418.P76S74 2003
    322′.1′09745209034—dc21

                                                                                              2003011983

Cornell University Press strives to use environmentally responsible suppliers and materials to the fullest extent possible in the publishing of its books. Such materials include vegetable-based, low-VOC inks and acid-free papers that are recycled, totally chlorine-free, or partly composed of nonwood fibers. For further information, visit our website at www.cornellpress.cornell.edu.

Cloth printing   10 9 8 7 6 5 4 3 2 1

To the memory of my father, Michael Lyon Sterne,
whose passion for history and the written word was infectious

CONTENTS

ILLUSTRATIONS

ACKNOWLEDGMENTS

This book had its unlikely origins in an aging Connecticut mill town called Stafford Springs. It was while covering Stafford as a reporter for the *Manchester Journal Inquirer* that I became interested in the politics of ethnic, working-class communities. This interest led me first to graduate school at Duke and then back to New England, where Providence proved an ideal city in which to study the questions that interested me. Along the way I incurred innumerable obligations.

The Center for Religion and American Life at Yale demonstrated exceptional generosity by awarding both a dissertation and postdoctoral fellowship. I will always be grateful to the Center, and especially to its directors Jon Butler and Harry Stout, for support that meant more than I can say. Grants from the John Nicholas Brown Center for the Study of American Civilization at Brown, the American Historical Association, and the University of Rhode Island (URI) Council for Research supplied invaluable assistance at critical moments, and Duke University provided years of deeply appreciated support during my graduate studies.

At Duke I had the good fortune to find a remarkable group of mentors. Susan Thorne helped me frame the questions I needed to ask about religion and politics, and Peter Wood exposed me to the complexities of early American history and enriched my thinking through his creative insights. William Chafe sparked my interest in social movements through a series of stimulating seminars, shared his sound advice whenever I needed it, and served as a model of professionalism. Nancy Hewitt helped me incorporate gender into my analysis more gracefully, edited with an expert eye, and sustained me with her warm encouragement and unflagging good spirits.

My greatest intellectual debt goes to Alex Keyssar, who constantly challenged me to do better work. Alex taught me to write more clearly, strengthened my analysis through his ability to recognize its major flaws, and always mixed cogent criticism with an endearing sense of humor. He also reminded me to keep the succinct yet valuable "so what" question in mind as I worked. I am deeply grateful to him for guiding me through graduate school and beyond, and for reading more drafts of this project than anyone has a right to expect.

Duke provided a supportive community of colleagues as well as committed mentors. I am particularly grateful to Robert Angevine, David Carter, Kirsten Delegard, Karen Ferguson, Paul Husbands, Rhonda Mawhood, Paul Ortiz, James Shiffer, and Mary Wingerd for making those years such special ones. When I left this nurturing environment to begin my research in Rhode Island, a welcoming network of scholars provided an intellectual home away from home. The John Nicholas Brown Center furnished both a spectacular space and a stimulating community. I thank Joyce Botehlo and her wonderful staff for making my time there so pleasant and productive, and the Center's interdisciplinary group of fellows for broadening my perspective. Elsewhere at Brown, Joanne Melish was kind enough to invite me to join her writing group. There I met Janice Okoomian, Kristen Petersen, and Miriam Reumann, three fine scholars and wonderful friends whom I cannot thank enough for their moral support and insightful critiques over the years. I also benefited from the enormous generosity of two local scholars. Father Robert Hayman of Providence College allowed me to use his personal archives on Rhode Island Catholicism and never hesitated to share the fruits of his labors. Scott Molloy of URI's Labor Research Center has been a supportive mentor, thoughtful reader, and good friend, graciously giving of his scarce time and copious resources. My colleagues in URI's Department of History provided a stimulating and exceptionally collegial working environment, and my students there taught me as much as I them.

Over the years, a number of scholars were kind enough to offer feedback on this project as it developed. Mara Berkley, Joyce Botelho, Nancy Cook, Peter D'Agostino, Kirsten Delegard, Kathleen Franz, Karen Markin, Helen Mederer, Joanne Melish, Robert Orsi, Joelle Rollo-Koster, Andrea Rusnock, Nick Salvatore, Catherine Sama, Susan Thorne, and audiences and copanelists at conferences too numerous to name commented on various excerpts. William Chafe, James C. Garman, Nancy Hewitt, Alex Keyssar, Maureen Moakley, Scott Molloy, Janice Okoomian, Kristen Petersen, Miriam Reumann, Marie Schwartz, and Peter Wood went the extra mile by reading entire drafts. These generous readers deserve much of the credit for what merits this book has.

A researcher is only as good as the archivists who guide her to needed sources, and here too I have accumulated many debts. At the Rhode Island Historical Society, Allison Cywin, Dana Signe K. Munroe, Meredith Sorozan, and most of all Rick Stattler provided invaluable assistance. Many thanks also to Veronica Lima at the Providence Catholic Diocesan Archives, whose generosity and good humor made my time there so pleasant, Tim Meagher and John Shepherd at the Catholic University of America Archives, Diana

Zimmerman at the Center for Migration Studies of New York, and Kenneth Carlson at the Rhode Island State Archives.

As this project neared the home stretch, it benefited immeasurably from the support of Cornell University Press and the Cushwa Center for the Study of American Catholicism at Notre Dame, cosponsor of this series. I am deeply grateful to series editor R. Scott Appleby for his commitment to my book, Christopher Shannon for his advocacy early in the process, Sheri Englund for her unflagging support and cheerful guidance, and the anonymous reviewers at Cornell University Press for their extraordinarily thoughtful feedback. Many thanks also to the Lilly Foundation for helping to underwrite the series.

My last and most important debt is to my family. My husband, James C. Garman, motivated me through the example of his own scholarship, offered advice at so many crucial moments, kept me grounded with his wit and sense of perspective, and strengthened me with an enduring love which has meant more than words can express. Jim also kept the home fires burning during the push to finish the book, demonstrating infinite patience and a flair for gourmet cooking. My sister, Christie Sterne, kept my spirits high with her sense of humor and unceasing encouragement. My mother, Geri Savidge Sterne, provided a bottomless supply of moral support throughout the process and lent expert proofreading skills at the end. My mother and my father, Michael Lyon Sterne, inspired me to become a scholar by providing me with the best possible education, creating a home environment that encouraged intellectual inquiry, and always letting me know how much they believed in me. I deeply regret that my father did not live to see this book completed, and I dedicate it to his memory.

ABBREVIATIONS USED IN THE TEXT

AFCS   American Federation of Catholic Societies
AFL   American Federation of Labor
AOH   Ancient Order of Hibernians
APA   American Protective Association
CPI   Committee on Public Information
CTAU   Catholic Total Abstinence Union
ERA   Equal Rights Association
IWW   Industrial Workers of the World
KOC   Knights of Columbus
NCCM   National Council of Catholic Men
NCCW   National Council of Catholic Women
NCWC   National Catholic Welfare Conference
NWLB   National War Labor Board
PCFU   Providence Central Federated Union
RICLU   Rhode Island Central Labor Union
RILWV   Rhode Island League of Women Voters
RISA   Rhode Island Suffrage Association
RISFL   Rhode Island State Federation of Labor
RISFWC   Rhode Island State Federation of Women's Clubs
RIWSA   Rhode Island Woman Suffrage Association
SLP   Socialist Labor Party
USJB   Union Saint-Jean-Baptiste
UTW   United Textile Workers

BALLOTS AND BIBLES

INTRODUCTION

Patrick J. McCarthy was born in County Sligo, Ireland, in 1848. At age two he fled the potato famine with his Gaelic-speaking parents and six older brothers, only to lose both parents to typhus shortly after their arrival in Boston. McCarthy's early years were a story of marginality and mobility as he shuffled between relatives and orphanages and worked as a farm laborer, peddler, foundry worker, printer, carpenter, mason, painter, and brass finisher. In between he acted in dramatic societies and theatrical troupes and attended a night school for working boys organized by Harvard professors Charles Eliot Norton and Charles W. Eliot (later president of the university), who took a personal interest in his academic development. In 1868 he moved to the booming industrial city of Providence to live with his brother John and seek better opportunities.[1]

McCarthy, like so many Irish immigrants, looked to politics as a means of upward mobility when good private sector jobs proved elusive. Relatively few of the Irish arrived with industrial skills, but they spoke English, were familiar with Anglo-American governing institutions, and had a strong activist tradition as a result of their struggles with the British. The problem McCarthy faced was that Rhode Island did not allow immigrants to vote unless they owned real estate, an acquisition difficult for newcomers, who tended to hold poorly paid jobs. Lacking easy access to electoral politics, McCarthy and others like him turned to Catholic networks to gain experience and build constituencies.

Always pious, McCarthy became an active layman when he moved to Providence and began to worship at the Cathedral of SS. Peter and Paul, the city's oldest Catholic parish. There the ambitious young man taught Sunday school, sang in the choir, and joined the Christian Doctrine Society, where he received his first taste of government. "Parliamentary Law governed the proceedings with much exactness," he recalled. He also joined the Brownson Lyceum, a "literary and debating society composed of Catholics only" and a base of agitation for immigrant voting rights, and served as its president for three years. McCarthy eventually left Cathedral for St. Michael's. There he met his future wife, Annie M. McGinney, who died five years after their 1875 wedding. More enduring was his relationship with the parish's Catholic Total Abstinence Union (CTAU), which lasted more than twenty-five years and nurtured his political aspirations. McCarthy served on the union's constitution and by-law committee and traveled around the state to promote temperance. "The society afforded scope for ambitious young men to study and practice Parliamentary Law relating to procedure, to business of the organization, public demonstrations, and conventions in Providence and elsewhere," he wrote in his memoirs. "As one of the Board of Directors of the Rhode Island Union, I came prominently before the Catholic people of the State."[2]

Armed with his Catholic contacts and the Harvard law degree he earned in 1876, McCarthy rapidly ascended Rhode Island's political ladder. He served three terms on the city council beginning in 1890, followed by two terms in the General Assembly (Rhode Island's state legislature), but his crowning achievement came when he was elected Providence's first foreign-born mayor in 1906. McCarthy's success reflected his reputation as a witty speaker and committed reformer who campaigned for good government and against special interests, as well as his ability to use religious networks to promote his political career. As a young man, McCarthy had used the church to develop contacts, learn parliamentary proceedings, and become an accomplished speaker. As a rising politician, he courted coreligionists by speaking to parish societies and joining such fraternal and charitable groups as the St. Vincent de Paul Society, Catholic Club, Holy Name Society, and Knights of Columbus (KOC). As the diocesan newspaper later noted, "His strong faith won the admiration of his ecclesiastical superiors as well as the esteem of the Catholic people."[3]

Catholicism provided not only an organizational base but also a set of principles that informed McCarthy's public agenda. In the 1907 inaugural speech that laid out his plan to improve city services and undermine corporate influence, he reminded listeners that "the civil law is based on God's law." He elaborated on this theme in a 1912 diary entry: "Religion is the strongest force for good in the world. . . . It trains heart and conscience and qualifies for true citizenship." By the time McCarthy died of pancreatic cancer in 1921, he had fulfilled the prayer he made on the eve of his first mayoral inauguration, to "leave a record worthy of a Catholic gentleman." The church had played a critical role in his career, training him in the democratic process, honing his speaking abilities, providing a constituency, and furnishing a value system that informed his record as an upright public servant.[4]

McCarthy was one of hundreds of Providence immigrants who used Catholic parishes as political vehicles in the late nineteenth and early twentieth centuries. In Providence, as in many other industrial communities, the church was the institution most accessible to an ethnic population overwhelmingly Catholic in faith, blue-collar in status, and underrepresented in other organizations. Providence had been founded in 1636 as a haven for Protestant dissenters, but its emergence as an industrial center at the turn of the nineteenth century made it a magnet for immigrants. By 1905 almost 70 percent of residents were first- or second-generation immigrants (the majority from Ireland, French Canada, and Italy), and just over half were Catholics. In that year Rhode Island earned the distinction of being the first state with a Catholic majority.[5] Many of these Catholic newcomers did not participate in electoral politics because of citizenship and language barriers and rules that restricted voting on the basis of class, ethnicity, and sex. Lacking political clout, they could not elect pro-labor candidates or lobby effectively for worker-friendly laws. As a result the city's unions were relatively weak, and only a minority of the working class (mostly skilled workers of Irish, British, or German heritage) was organized. Some new Americans came together in taverns or mutual aid societies, but these institutions seldom welcomed women and thus were limited in their ability to mobilize entire communities. In short, the places traditionally recognized as ethnic organizational spaces—unions, political machines, mutual aid associations, and saloons—were, while valuable to their members, restricted in their scope. The church was the only institution to which every Catholic could, theoretically, belong.[6]

In this book I argue that Catholic parishes were the most accessible and important institutions in ethnic neighborhoods in the late nineteenth and early twentieth centuries, and that as such they played critical roles in politicizing new Americans. It was at church that the largest proportion of immigrants (first-generation) and ethnics (second- and third-generation) congregated on a regular basis. At this time parishes had few social service providers to compete with, and most priests enjoyed a community status and moral authority untarnished by the scandals of later years. In this context parishes functioned not only as sources of spiritual solace but also as dispensers of charity, promoters of upward mobility, and centers of neigh-

Patrick J. McCarthy was elected mayor of Providence in 1906, the first foreign-born Catholic to hold the office. McCarthy honed his political skills and built his constituency at church. Photograph, courtesy of the *Providence Journal*.

borhood life. Parishioners had access to a vast array of recreational activities, and many joined the lay societies that organized them. Priests promoted these societies to foster congregational loyalties, but the groups also served as political organizing spaces for Catholic women (who generally lacked other formal means of self-assertion) and men. Active laypeople like McCarthy learned to be leaders, fund-raisers, and public speakers by participating in groups like the Christian Doctrine Society and the CTAU. They educated themselves about current events by participating in parish study groups and debating societies, and they learned democratic processes by writing constitutions and holding elections. In coming together at meetings, they also forged alliances, traded information, and devised solutions to their problems. The church thus functioned in a Habermasian sense as "a mediator between society and state," an arena in which information was exchanged and public opinion developed.[7] Participants turned lay societies into activist groups, launching lobbying campaigns, organizing voter registration drives, and using religious rhetoric to argue for social justice. Some Catholics used parish resources to lobby for goals that would benefit their communities: improved access to the vote; better treatment at the workplace; and a redefinition of Americanism that recognized ethnic Catholics as full members of the nation. Others, like McCarthy, drew on church networks to build political careers.

By no means was Providence unique as a city where parishes served as organizing centers and religion informed public debate; yet too often religion remains on the margins of modern American history. Scholars have been quick to grasp the ways in which African Americans used religion for inspiration and churches as mobilizing sites, but most studies of white workers ignore religion or dismiss it as a negative influence that distracted from more "radical" or "political" forms of activism. Labor historians have argued, justifiably, that employers used religion to promote industrial discipline, that faith could encourage an otherworldly focus instead of attention to immediate problems, and that church membership brought working people under the influence of clerics and middle-class laypeople who might discourage strikes and radical unions. It is only quite recently that American labor historians have begun to seriously consider that religion could inspire as well as detract from working-class protest. A rich new scholarship examines the positive as well as negative influence of Protestantism on antebellum labor activism. Disagreeing that religion was no more than a tool to discipline workers and instill bourgeois values, these studies prove that religion also inspired workers, legitimated their struggles, and even informed their process of class formation.[8]

With a few exceptions, twentieth-century American labor history lacks the nuanced treatment of religion devoted to the pre–Civil War era. A few scholars have made steps in this direction by exploring alliances between unionists and Protestant ministers, the formation of Catholic worker movements, and the influence of faith on workplace activism and political strategies.[9] For the most part, however, labor historians have not considered the multifaceted roles churches played in the daily lives and politics of working-class immigrants. Notably absent from their accounts is the Catholic Church, at least nominally the religious home of a majority of immigrants. If the church enters the story at all, it usually does so as a conservative villain that discouraged parishioners from joining the Socialist Party or Industrial Workers of the World (IWW). Disapproval of priests' antiradical politics have prompted most labor historians to forget that parishes were community centers and organizing spaces where working people spent enormous amounts of time. As such they deserve more attention.

Immigration scholars have been more likely to treat religion in a balanced fashion. Studies of ethnic Catholics and Jews, focusing on older immigrants as well as recent arrivals, recognize that faith had complex and sometimes contradictory influences on national identities, political initiatives, and relationships with the state.[10] Even these accounts, however, pay little attention to places of worship as physical spaces where new Americans organized. The study of ethnic activism still tends to focus on two institutions: the labor union and the political machine. To be sure, these institutions effectively politicized the new Americans they served. Union members had ready-made forums to discuss injustices and develop solutions, and many went to the polls together to promote labor-friendly laws and candidates. As Michael Kazin writes, "Whether they lived in Sydney, Winnipeg, or Chicago, skilled workers tended to thrust themselves into politics behind their growing unions." For other immigrants, a boss like Providence's Charles Brayton, Boston's James Curley, or New York's Charles Francis Murphy introduced them to American politics by literally walking them through the process of becoming citizens and voters. Bosses made themselves indispensable to ethnic neighborhood life by doling out jobs, providing food baskets, and attending weddings and funerals, as well as helping immigrants secure relief and negotiate problems with the law. Grateful recipients, in return, became naturalized and delivered up their votes.[11]

Machines and unions thus played critical roles in politicizing new Americans; yet many immigrants, especially women and recent arrivals, had little or no connection to these mobilizing institutions. The American Federation of Labor (AFL), which dominated the American labor movement from 1886 to 1935, admitted only skilled workers and thus effectively limited its membership to white men of native birth or "old" immigrant stock. As immigration intensified and demand for skilled laborers declined, the AFL served a shrinking proportion of the working class. Even after the rise of the more inclusive Congress of Industrial Organizations (CIO), unions never enrolled more than a third of the nonagricultural workforce.

Machines, for their part, were neither capable of nor interested in mobilizing large sectors of the foreign-born population. Scholars have begun to question whether urban machines were ever as powerful or omnipresent as had been assumed. Challenging the image of bosses as urban potentates who ruled American cities with iron fists, they have demonstrated that many bosses were no more than small-time operators who restricted their limited resources to the community's dominant ethnic group (often but not always the Irish) and did not serve even that group terribly well. Moreover, they catered only to those immigrants able and willing to vote. This was a limited pool, given that less than half the foreigners listed in the 1910 and 1920 federal censuses were citizens and that, between 1908 and 1923, 35 percent of the nation's immigrants returned home.[12] Even those intending to stay and wishing to vote confronted language barriers, illiteracy, inexperience, and a host of electoral restrictions designed to keep foreign-born (as well as poor and black) citizens from casting ballots. The "new" immigration, in fact, coincided with a period of sharp and deliberate electoral contraction. Voting restrictions and complicated registration rules coincided with reduced party competition, the rise of interest group politics, and a resulting decline in popular interest to seriously depress turnout after the turn of the twentieth century.[13]

New Americans who lacked access to unions and electoral politics had to find creative ways to become political, and community institutions offered an indirect yet effective entrée. Mutual aid societies, saloons, social clubs, charitable organizations, neighborhood networks, and most of all places of worship were sites where newcomers discussed problems and raised challenges. Immigrants barred from other institutions by gender, language, citizenship, or skill level could join these civic associations, situated in their neighborhoods and run by compatriots. It was at these institutions that many newcomers became aware of the problems and possibilities of American politics, and from them that they entered public life and influenced, directly or indirectly, electoral politics and the state.

For men, the ethnic mutual aid society or fraternal order was particularly valuable. Before Americans had access to employer- or state-funded social insurance, immigrants formed groups that paid for funerals and helped members survive periods of illness and unemployment, as well as organizing street festivals and family gatherings. Although settlement houses run by native-born Protestants offered more extensive resources, many immigrants preferred to seek help from indigenous institutions. In many cases mutual aid societies acted as bridges between neighborhood and polity, encouraging members to Americanize even as they preserved elements of their native culture. Belonging to a mutual aid society was an exercise in self-government, and some members applied these lessons by becoming citizens and voters and lobbying on matters of importance to the community.[14]

Female immigrants, who rarely belonged to mutual aid societies, formed their own networks of assistance and used them to become political actors. Even after the Nineteenth Amendment, women faced institutional barriers and social proscriptions against entering the male preserve of electoral politics. Recognizing this, women's historians have expanded definitions of the "political" and written creative accounts of female ethnic activism. Rather than focusing on male-dominated institutions like unions, machines, and mutual aid associations, they have shown that middle-class ethnic women, like their native-born counterparts, used civic clubs to carve out roles as "social housekeepers" by running nurseries and health care clinics. Working women, for their part, drew on neighborhood networks to organize strikes and consumer boycotts. While sons and husbands congregated in saloons, wives and daughters formed bonds by exchanging recipes on street corners and helping one another with childcare and housework. When a community crisis arose, they relied on these networks to rally support, convey information, and exert pressure. As the historian Paula Hyman argues, foreign-born women "were not apolitical. They simply expressed their political concerns in a different, less historically accessible arena—the neighborhood." Women's networks and men's mutual aid societies thus served important roles in politicizing new Americans, as did unions and machines. None of these institutions, however, could rival the Catholic Church in the size and inclusiveness of its constituency (crossing lines of class, gender, and ethnicity), the extent of its resources, or its potential to politicize; yet places of worship figure prominently in very few studies of ethnic activism.[15]

It is primarily scholars of religion who have recognized how critically Catholicism, as well as Judaism, shaped ethnic and working-class politics in late nineteenth- and twentieth-century America. On the one hand, religion could discourage participation in public life by fostering a separatist mentality and stressing individual salvation instead of social reform. On the other, Jews brought with them traditions of reform and radicalism inspired by faith and years of persecution. Catholics, for their part, entered politics through lay societies or at the urging of priests to protect parochial schools, defend workers' rights, oppose immigration restriction, influence foreign policy, resist communism, censor "indecent" films and literature, restrict divorce and birth control, and enforce racial boundaries (even as others campaigned for racial justice). As Leslie Woodcock Tentler argues, "immigrants honed their political skills in the parish as well as the local machine." Although not focused on the political implications of faith, these social histories of immigrant religion offer valuable starting points for research.[16]

This book seeks to explain how an immigrant like McCarthy started life in a Catholic orphanage and ended as chief elected officer of a major American city, and it does so by bringing religion from the margins to the center of the story. In explaining McCarthy's meteoric career, and the quieter accomplishments of many of his coreligionists, I focus on parishes as grassroots political vehicles that incorporated Catholic immigrants into American public life. I document the roles churches played as mobilizing institutions for men like McCarthy, as well as discussing ways in which activists invoked religious rhetoric and faith informed political choices. I find this evidence in newspapers (Catholic, labor, Socialist, and mainstream), parish records and histories, papers of local and national Catholic organizations, union records, and government documents. My goal is to integrate religion into the history of ethnic politics in late nineteenth- and early twentieth-century America, without dismissing the importance of other vehicles such as unions, machines, and ethnic associations.

Providence is an ideal location for such a study. By the turn of the twentieth century, a majority of residents were Catholics and first- or second-generation immigrants. As a result, ethno-religious rivalries played out in bold relief and the Catholic Church assumed a crucial role in civic life. Access to the vote followed sharp class and ethnic (and thus religious) lines, leaving new Americans little choice but to assert their interests through mechanisms other than the ballot. In Providence, as in so many other cities, Catholics used the resources of their parishes and authority of their faith to influence electoral politics and engage with public life. Because the city's three major Catholic ethnic groups—the Irish, French Canadians, and Italians—arrived with very different political backgrounds, relationships to the church, and ideas about how parishes should function, they drew on religion in a variety of ways. Collectively, therefore, they offer a comparative perspective on ways in which immigrants used religion as a political tool. This history begins by examining their largely abortive attempts to achieve change through electoral politics between the Dorr Rebellion of 1842, an armed conflict over voting rights that reflected nascent ethno-religious tensions, and the Progressive Era. The second section of the book explores the process by which immigrants began to use parishes as organizing spaces during the first two decades of the twentieth century. The final section explores the blossoming of this Catholic brand of politics in the 1920s and 1930s. It was during this period that immigrants and ethnics successfully used the resources of religion to demand their rights, prove themselves full-fledged Americans, and integrate themselves into the nation's public life.

I

THE LIMITS OF ELECTORAL POLITICS

1

"GIVE US OUR RIGHTS, OR WE WILL TAKE THEM"

The Dorr Rebellion of 1842

All men are created equal, except in Rhode-Island.
—Seth Luther, *An Address on the Right of Free Suffrage*, 1833

THE DORR INAUGURAL

On May 3, 1842, the narrow streets of Providence were filled with excitement. Thousands of Rhode Islanders had flocked to the capital city to celebrate the inauguration of Governor Thomas Wilson Dorr. Artisans, shopkeepers, mechanics, and armed militia companies (including the sixty-member Dorr Troop of Horse, the governor's personal guard) assembled in front of Hoyle Tavern in the city's west end. From there they marched through the downtown streets to the festive accompaniment of the Providence Brass Band. The procession ended at the State House on Benefit Street, but the marchers did not enter. Instead they assembled in a drafty and unfinished foundry building. There they sat on crossbeams and rafters, dodging the raindrops that leaked in as their new leader assembled his government.[1]

The humble setting for Dorr's inaugural gathering was testimony to the unconventional nature of his position, for he was one of two governors claiming leadership of the nation's smallest state. In the spring of 1842 Rhode Island was divided into two camps, with citizens agitating for a broader suffrage locked in battle with those who believed only landowners should vote. Frustrated in their attempts to achieve reform through traditional means, suffragists had taken matters into their own hands by writing a more liberal constitution and forming a separate government with Dorr at its helm. The suffragists claimed to represent the people, a majority of adult white males having approved their constitution in a referendum the reformers had called, but this argument did not sit well with the Landholders' government that was the state's elected authority. It was this stalemate that prompted Dorr and his followers to form their administration in the shadow of the State House, which was carefully locked to keep the rebels out.[2]

SETH LUTHER AND THE EARLY MOVEMENT

The drama of 1842 followed decades of agitation over the state's antiquated government. Rhode Island had been the first American colony to declare its independence and the first state to industrialize and attract a population of Irish Catholic factory workers; yet it clung to the outlines of a royal charter that catered to an agricultural society. The House of Representatives was so poorly apportioned that by 1834 Providence controlled barely 5 percent of the seats, although it housed almost 17 percent of the state's population and produced two-thirds of its taxes. Even more striking were limits on the right to vote. Since colonial days Rhode Island had limited the franchise to men who owned real property—at a value adjusted to $134 in 1798—and to their eldest sons; and in 1822 it further restricted the vote to white real estate owners. The system was fairly equitable for white men as long as land was widely available and most residents worked as farmers. Before the Revolution, between one-half and three-quarters of white males could vote. But as available land and the proportion of residents engaged in agriculture dwindled, a shrinking proportion of Rhode Islanders qualified as voters. The freehold requirement affected not only workers but also merchants and professionals whose work did not require land. It fell with particular severity on Providence, the state's commercial and immigrant center. About 43 percent of men could vote statewide by 1840, but closer to 30 percent qualified in the capital city. Disproportionately affected was the city's small but growing community of working-class Irish Catholics. By 1840 more than 7 percent of the city's 23,171 residents were Catholic; and by 1845, the first date for which such statistics are available, about 19 percent were foreign-born, most from Ireland.[3]

The restrictive franchise had been a topic of contention since the Revolution, and by the 1820s demands for reform grew louder as a series of competitive presidential races aroused interest in politics. The suffrage movement found an eloquent spokesman in Seth Luther, an iconoclastic carpenter who represented the workers and artisans of Providence and the northern mill towns. Born into a family of Providence tradesmen in 1795, Luther spent his young adulthood exploring the frontier before coming home to work as a carpenter and mill hand. The industrializing New England to which he returned did not square with the egalitarian ideals he had absorbed in his travels and from his father, a Revolutionary War veteran. Luther himself served time in debtors' prison in the early 1820s. Tall, lean, well read, and possessed of a rapier-like wit, Luther brought his skills to the Northeast's nascent labor movement. He served as traveling agent for the *New England Artisan,* a labor paper, and his 1832 *Address to the Working Men of New England* quickly went through three printings.[4]

For Luther, improving working conditions went hand in hand with winning workingmen the vote. He saw the ballot as a critical weapon in the struggle for goals like the ten-hour day. Rather than allowing the "mushroom lordlings" and "small potato aristocrats" who owned land to control politics, he argued, all adult males should cast ballots. Artisans and laborers agreed and organized under his leadership, holding weekly meetings to which they wore green baize jackets to distinguish themselves from the well-clad "aristocrats" who could vote.[5]

Suffragists flooded the state legislature with eloquent petitions that questioned the fairness and wisdom of limiting the vote to landowners. "Miserable indeed must be that attachment to our free institutions," stated one petition, "which depends upon the ownership of 134 dollars worth of land, and which can be the subject of bargain, sale and conveyance." Are "the principles of equitable government . . . better understood by the proprietors of the *soil*?" asked the residents of Warren, a commercial town south of Providence. At any rate, petitioners from North Providence noted, the population was increasing so rapidly that the "whole soil would not be sufficient to make voters of a majority of her actual population." Some reformers suggested militia service or tax payment should be conditions for voting, as they were in most other states. It was a major source of contention that citizens were required to serve in the militia, yet denied the vote. How, reformers asked, could land ownership better prove civic fitness than risking one's life for one's country? Luther urged the "vassals" who could not vote to refuse to pay taxes or serve in the militia until they received a voice in government. On April 1, 1833, militiamen came to their spring drill dressed in "fantastical" costumes to protest the absurdity of their disenfranchisement.[6]

Statements like these invoked the republican principles that carried so much currency in the nation's early years. The slogans "all men are created equal" and "no taxation without representation" were particularly appropriate. As Luther asked in his famous *Address on the Right of Free Suffrage* (1833), "If it was the right of British subjects not to be taxed without their consent before the Revolution, and the General Assembly now tax twelve thousand citizens of this state directly or indirectly without their consent, what has that body of men gained by the Revolution but a change of masters?" Petitioners from North Providence predicted that a second American Revolution would erupt if a majority of adult males could not vote. As Luther warned in 1836, "We will try the ballot box first; if that will not effect our righteous purpose the next and last resort is the cartridge box."[7]

If republicanism served as a political philosophy for the suffrage campaign, religion offered moral authority. Christianity provided a powerful rhetoric for the antebellum labor movement, and Luther used it effectively in his struggles for workplace reform and political equality. Luther himself had a checkered religious past. He had joined Providence's First Baptist Church during an 1815 revival but was thrown out nine years later for "disorderly walking"—an undefined charge various biographers have attributed to his penchant for strong beer, imprisonment for debt, unorthodox interpretation of Scripture, missing too many services, or selling portraits of the minister for personal profit. Luther's ignominious departure from the congregation did not stop him from articulating a religious critique of capitalism. "Ye cannot serve GOD and mammon," he charged in his 1834 *Address on the Origins and Progress of Avarice*. Luther brought his sermonizing to the suffrage battle, making the cogent argument that voting restrictions violated the principle that all humans were equal before God. "Has the great Author of our existence," he asked, "scattered blessings with a partial hand?" Echoing these sentiments, a Providence barber named William Tillinghast argued that "the principles contained in the holy Bible & the true principles of Republicanism (or liberty & equality) both came from God." Moreover, he pointed out, "No tyrant can be a true Christian, for how can he 'do as he would be done by'?"[8]

The appeals of these working-class suffragists fell on deaf ears. According to the Universalist minister Jacob Frieze, who later wrote a hostile account of the suffrage crusade, most legislators felt that "the qualification demanded by law was of trifling amount" and "the safety of the state required the voter to possess an interest in the soil." Class prejudice also conspired against the suffragists, whom state senator Benjamin Hazard of Newport dismissed as "vagabonds and renegades from other states." Frustrated by these responses, Tillinghast complained in 1833 that the suffragists "might as well petition Engine Company No. 2" as waste their time on the Rhode Island General Assembly. "Both would throw a vast quantity of cold water and in a very short time; the Engine Company to extinguish fire, and the General Assembly to extinguish the flame of liberty." It was clear that working-class radicals like Luther and Tillinghast would not make headway with a state legislature dominated by farmers and urban elites. By 1834 the movement was ready for a leader perceived as respectable and moderate. It found that leader in Thomas Wilson Dorr.[9]

THOMAS DORR AND THE 1842 REVOLT

Dorr was an unlikely rebel. Born into a wealthy Providence family in 1805, he was educated at Phillips Exeter Academy and Harvard College, where he was anything but a troublemaker. In the 1820s Harvard was seething with unrest as students resisted the university's strict discipline, but Dorr cast his lot with the administration. His position led his classmates to blacklist him and pen a sarcastic ditty about his *"gift of the gab,* though 'tis all empty sound."* After graduating, Dorr studied law, made a reputation for himself back in Providence, and was elected to the General Assembly as a Whig by the age of thirty. There he abandoned his youthful conservatism and became a champion for abolition, expanded public education, an end to debtors' prison, and a more democratic franchise. He also became a Democrat, attracted to the party's egalitarian rhetoric and commitment to suffrage reform. Dorr's liberal turn may have reflected a new appreciation of his family history. Although he was a child of privilege, his father was a self-made man and his grandfather an Irish Protestant immigrant who had served in the Revolution and accompanied Paul Revere on his famous ride.[10]

As a suffragist Dorr initially spoke for the moderate branch of the movement, calling to reapportion the legislature and extend the vote to taxpayers and militiamen. Under his leadership suffragists sought reform through traditional means such as creating their own party and calling for a constitutional convention. This strategy fared no better than the workers' petitions, however, and convinced Dorr more dramatic action was needed. He came to share Luther's conviction that the suffrage was a right all male citizens should hold, rather than a privilege to be limited to the "better" classes, and to look to more confrontational forms of protest.[11]

In 1840 the quiet campaign transformed itself into a mass movement. The turning point was the spirited Harrison–Van Buren presidential contest, which rallied enthusiasm for justice and good government and pioneered modern campaign strategies as well as intensifying the frustrations of citizens who were excited about the election but could not vote. At this point Rhode Island suffragists abandoned polite petitions in favor of mass meet-

Thomas Wilson Dorr, c. 1844, two years after he led a rebellion to liberalize Rhode Island's restrictive suffrage laws. Lithograph after a painting by J. Bailler, courtesy of the Rhode Island Historical Society, RHi X3 6683.

ings and torchlight parades. In April 1841, three thousand protesters gathered on Jefferson Plains in Providence, joined the Universalist minister William S. Balch in a moment of prayer, and marched through the city in a procession three-quarters of a mile long. According to one observer, the parade "was headed by a troupe of butchers in white frocks with blue sashes. Then came the revolutionaries in carriages, after whom on foot men of all ages and sizes, gray hairs and red, blue coats and gray, all jumbled together 'higledy pigledy' with badges on their coats giving the important information, 'I am an American Citizen.'" Marchers also bore banners with slogans such as "Worth makes the man, but sand and gravel make the voter," and the more threatening "Peaceably if we can, forcibly if we must." The parade ended with a barbecue at which marchers feasted on a roasted ox, a ten-foot loaf of bread, and several barrels of beer.[12]

These innovative tactics energized the movement. Branches of the Rhode Island Suffrage Association (RISA) formed in every town, open to citizens age twenty-one and older and attracting support across lines of class, birth, denomination, and sex. The cause was popular among native-born artisans and workers as well as Irish Catholic immigrants like Henry J. Duff. Duff arrived in Providence in 1833, found work as a block printer and became active in the Hibernian Orphans Society and parish of SS. Peter and Paul. He corresponded with Dorr during and after the rebellion and later described himself as "an old admirer." An opponent characterized him less charitably as a "rabid Dorrite." Duff believed "many evils followed the deprivation of the right of suffrage" and linked the plight of disenfranchised Rhode Islanders to that of Catholics in Ireland. As he later wrote to the Irish patriot Daniel O'Connell, "The people of this State, have suffered enough to cause them to feel for the wrongs which unhappy Ireland has so patiently endured for so many centuries." Duff was not alone in this line of thinking. "It is our own Home Rule question in Rhode Island," agreed the Irish American *Truth Teller* of New York in a commentary on the Rhode Island voting agitation.[13]

Even as Dorr's cause attracted working-class immigrants like Duff, it also won the support of ministers, professionals, Democratic politicians, and representatives of old families like the Bosworths and Allens who felt the freehold requirement was an undemocratic embarrassment to the state. Support was strong among Providence's Universalist, Methodist, and Freewill Baptist congregations, where an anti-authoritarian mindset fostered sympathy for the crusade. Balch, minister of First Universalist Church, served as chaplain for the suffrage association and gave the keynote address at a mass meeting at the Dexter Training Grounds. The support of men like Balch reinforced Luther's argument that God was behind the suffrage movement. This was a position RISA's newspaper, the *New Age and Constitutional Advocate*, firmly endorsed. "Say not," argued one editorial, "that religion has nothing to do with government. A true democracy has its roots in Christianity." Depicting the Dorr Rebellion as a divine crusade not only legitimated the struggle but also created an opening for women by placing the movement within the accepted domain of female religious activism. Perhaps hoping looser voting requirements for men would be the first step toward woman suffrage, "suffrage ladies" organized auxiliaries, corresponded with Dorr, and raised funds. RISA, fortified by the authority of religion and the power of this diverse constituency, assembled Friday evenings and sent lecturers to spread the word across the state. The speakers' message contained a new militancy. "The right of suffrage we do not ask as a favor," they declared. "We claim it as our own. We demand it." The Whig-dominated General Assembly, however, continued to ignore their demands.[14]

In August frustrated activists took more drastic action. Invoking the Revolutionary principle of popular sovereignty, they formed a People's Party and called their own constitutional convention. "Give us our rights, or we will take them," declared a broadside announcing this gathering. Opponents, clearly not intimidated, held their own assembly, and within a few months Rhode Islanders faced two competing constitutions. The Landholders' document jettisoned the freehold requirement only for native-born white men, while the People's proposal enfranchised all white males with one year's residency. The latter also instituted a secret ballot, reapportioned the legislature, called for free public education, and—in a clause that appealed to Irish Catholics in particular—denounced discrimination against any individual, organization, or religious denomination.[15]

There were limits to the reformers' egalitarianism, however. Their constitution failed to enfranchise women, Native Americans, or African Americans, skirting the last issue by agreeing to hold a referendum on black suffrage once the new constitution was in place. Dorr was a committed abolitionist and vigorously objected to this decision, but he was overruled by colleagues who feared voters would reject a constitution that included black suffrage. As the delegates put it, they were proposing "no Greek temple of ideal democracy, but rather a solid homely City Hall structure." The resulting constitution was, one critic noted, "a little too genteel for the workers who had labored in its erection."[16]

The proposal sparked an immediate outcry from African Americans (about 3 percent of the state's population) and prominent abolitionists who traveled to Rhode Island in protest. The state's black citizens had lost the vote in 1822—a move that reflected both local concerns about black economic advancement and a national trend of curtailing black suffrage—and wished to be included in Dorr's revolution. In an eloquent petition, they demanded the vote on the grounds they were native-born citizens, raised "under a Republican creed," and had contributed to the nation through their labor and military service. "Making the right of citizenship identical with color, brings a stain upon the State, unmans the heart of an already injured people, and corrupts the purity of Republican Faith," they argued. "Elevate the humblest class . . . to the duties of manhood and the prerogatives of citizenship, rather than debar them from the most efficient instrument of elevation on account of a matter beyond their control." Black and white suffragists agreed the vote was a basic right of citizenship, but for whites citizenship stopped at the color line.[17]

Tensions mounted in the next months as two constitutions competed for popular approval. In an election open to all adult white men with permanent residency, the People's constitution passed with only fifty-two dissenting votes. These results are misleading as most opponents simply boycotted the referendum; yet suffragists claimed their victory was legitimate because 13,944 of the state's estimated 23,142 adult white men (and a majority of freemen) had approved their constitution. This was the largest number of voters that ever had participated in a Rhode Island election and, not surprisingly, support was strongest in industrial and commercial towns. The Landholders' constitution failed narrowly, 8,639 to 8,013, in a referendum in which native-born non-freeholders could vote. Presumably the margin of defeat would have been higher had Irish immigrants been allowed to participate. Nonetheless, the General Assembly refused to recognize the rebels' extralegal referendum despite some precedent for calling a constitutional convention with the legislature's consent.[18]

The People's Party responded by organizing military companies, forming a separate government, electing Dorr governor, and establishing headquarters in the aforementioned foundry. The Law and Order Party, representing rural Democrats and well-heeled urban Whigs who supported the existing government, went on the attack with a propaganda campaign in broadsides and the *Providence Journal*. They depicted the rebels as a coalition of urban free-spenders, ignorant Irish Catholics, union radicals, and advocates of mob rule, and they warned that a suffrage extension would be dangerous because Rhode Island, unlike other states, did not have enough farmers to outvote urban workers. The General Assembly even enacted a measure, which opponents dubbed the "Algerine Law" after the notorious tyranny of Algiers, that made holding office in the People's government an act of treason and served to drive moderates out of the suffrage party.[19]

As the situation grew increasingly tense, Dorr concluded the only way to break the stalemate was "to strike a blow" to prove his government legitimate. The blow he chose was an attack on the Providence arsenal, probably in hope that bold action would energize his forces and intimidate his enemies. After midnight on May 18, 1842, a ragtag band of about two hundred suffragists, Luther among them, marched on the arsenal. Church bells rang to alert residents to the impending attack. As Frieze, a Dorr supporter until the attack, later described the scene, "Never perhaps had the citizens of Providence witnessed a moment so full of horror! . . . Visions of a city in flames, sacked and plundered, and its inhabitants devoted to the knife of the midnight assassin, rose up in the imagination, and struck the soul with horror!" These dire premonitions were unwarranted. The rebels were disorganized and poorly armed, and a posse of citizens that included Dorr's father and brother manned the two-story stone arsenal. When the defenders refused to surrender the Dorrites tried to set off two Revolutionary War cannons, but neither fired and the rebels retreated to their headquarters on Federal Hill.[20]

Dorr escaped arrest by fleeing to New York, where he tried to regroup his crumbling movement. Refusing to believe "right and justice" could be "overthrown by a failure of arms," he planned to reconvene the People's legislature on July 4 in Chepachet, a village in the northern mill country where working-class support remained strong. His supporters organized militia units with such colorful names as Dorr's Invincibles, the Pascoag Ripguts, and the Harmonious Reptiles, but their spirit proved no match for the state's resources. By the time Dorr made what was to be his triumphant comeback, three thousand militiamen were advancing on the rebels. With an army of only 225, Dorr disbanded his forces and went into exile, this time in New Hampshire.[21]

The state's response was swift and severe. Law and Order troops stormed Dorrite strongholds, the General Assembly declared martial law, Governor Samuel Ward King placed a thousand-dollar bounty on Dorr's head, and three hundred suspected rebels were arrested. Some (including Luther) were paraded through the Providence streets in order, Luther later wrote, "to glut the vengeance of the most cursed aristocracy that ever disgraced humanity." Many erstwhile supporters abandoned the suffragists, and public opinion turned against Dorr in the wake of his violent tactics.[22]

Even before the arsenal incident, the city's two Catholic priests had pressed their congregations to avoid involvement for fear of reinforcing negative stereotypes about disorderly Irishmen. On May 1, Elisha R. Potter Jr. of the Law and Order Party wrote to Governor John Brown Francis, "I hear a report . . . that Father Curry [sic] has interfered to prevent the Irish people

The capture of Acote Hill and the sacking of the village of Chepachet, 1842. Dorr planned to rally his supporters in Chepachet when he returned to Rhode Island in July 1842, but Law and Order forces easily routed his militia and sent him into exile once again. Lithograph after a painting by H. Lord, courtesy of the Rhode Island Historical Society, RHi X3 107.

from arming in the suffrage cause." The governor's response confirmed the rumor: "My Irishman Patrick who was boiling over with fight, came home from Chapel . . . and said that the Irish were to take no part in the quarrel, Father Curry [sic] having interdicted them. This story has been confirmed from many quarters. The Bishop put his injunction upon them." This injunction seems to have been effective, for when the rebellion was over only a handful of prisoners identified themselves as Irish. Latent support was stronger, however, and some Catholics resented the priests' proscriptions. According to a history of SS. Peter and Paul, the rebellion "caused tension between the pastor and some of its members. This rift was a dominant factor in the resignation of the pastor in 1843 and was to color all the activities of the Catholic community in Providence for a number of years."[23]

Latent support did not help Dorr, however, as residents of all stripes deserted his cause. "I can hardly find a suffrage man in the city with whom to advise or consult, so completely have we been defeated," wrote supporter Aaron White. Even though White may have had trouble finding a suffrage man, a number of suffrage ladies continued to champion the cause, rightly suspecting that state authorities would not arrest them for violating the Algerine Law. Female supporters in Providence wrote to Dorr, reminding him of their shared commitment to "Equal Rights," and the Ladies Benevolent Suffrage Association of Woonsocket, a northern mill town, organized more than one thousand marchers in an October demonstration. Catherine Williams, an influential writer and reformer, even secured Dorr an audience with President John Tyler.[24]

Despite the women's support, however, anti-Dorr sentiment was growing, and the Law and Order Party took advantage of the shift to propose a second constitution. This document differed from the party's original offer in just one important respect. Black men won the right to vote in reward for supporting the Law and Order Party and on the expectation they would be "conservative and go with the wealthy part of the community." In an important move that expanded the electorate by about 60 percent, natives were allowed to vote if they paid one dollar in property or poll taxes or served in the state militia. Women, for their part, could serve on school committees.[25]

The good news ended there. In keeping with nationwide trends, the proposal disenfranchised Narragansett Indians, paupers, "lunatics," criminals, and persons "under guardianship." The real blow to the suffragists was the restriction on immigrant voting. Under the new constitution, naturalized citizens (unlike natives) had to own $134 in real estate if they wished to cast ballots. This was an onerous burden, as land ownership was out of reach for an overwhelmingly working-class population of Irish Catholics. In addition to confronting the obstacle of poverty, aliens had to obtain permission from the General Assembly to buy real estate, and Catholics found that many landowners would not sell to them. The real estate requirement thus amounted to a virtual ban on Irish Catholic voting. As Potter noted, his party "would rather have the Negroes vote than the d—d Irish."[26]

These were only the most obvious ways in which the new constitution restricted the suffrage. All electors had to register almost a full year before Election Day, a rule becoming popular nationwide as lawmakers grew concerned that ineligible transients and immigrants were casting ballots. All men, regardless of birth, had to own real or personal property worth $134 to vote on financial questions at town meetings and for the city council in Providence, the only municipality run by a council form of government. This too was a popular requirement in antebellum America, reflecting a belief that local government dealt mostly with finances and thus only taxpayers should participate. Even the Dorrites had proposed similar restrictions on municipal elections. But although rules like these were not unique to Rhode Island, they had a chilling effect on political participation when combined with the more unusual immigrant property requirement. The state's Democrats would complain a few years later that the new constitution had created a system of "elections without voters."[27]

Worse still, the system almost defied change. The process of ratifying amendments was deliberately difficult, requiring the approval of two successive legislatures and three-fifths of the electorate, and there was no mechanism for calling constitutional conventions. This meant that power to alter the constitution was vested in a legislature that, despite some reapportionment, still was controlled by a rural minority with no interest in making it easier for urban immigrants and workers to vote. The Dorrites boycotted a referendum on this disappointing constitution, and the document became law in 1843 with the approval of just 28 percent of the electorate.[28]

Dorr was devastated by the outcome of the revolution. "All is lost save honor," he lamented. He returned to Rhode Island in 1843, intending to use the trial that would ensue as a legal test of the doctrine of popular sovereignty. He was promptly arrested and convicted of treason in a trial moved from Providence to Newport, where he was much less popular. Dorr received a life sentence of hard labor in solitary confinement in the grim Rhode Island State Prison, where he was forbidden to write and exercise under the strict "Pennsylvania" or isolated system of imprisonment. The martyred Dorr became a cause célèbre inside and outside Rhode Island, and "Polk, Dallas and Dorr" was a slogan in the 1844 presidential campaign. Thanks to the tireless efforts of his supporters, authorities released him from jail after almost two years and reversed his conviction shortly before his death in 1854 at age forty-nine. Luther, for his part, got out of jail in 1843 and spent several years traveling to promote Dorr's release, suffrage reform, and the ten-hour day. During this period he observed his "mind had been extremely impaired by my confinement," and subsequent events bore him out. In 1846 he was arrested in a strange incident in which he entered a Boston bank, brandished a sword, and demanded one thousand dollars "in the name of President Polk." He spent the remaining seventeen years of his life in asylums, dying in 1863.[29]

VOTING RIGHTS IN THE NEW REPUBLIC

The most perplexing question about the Dorr Rebellion is why it was not more successful at a time when suffrage reform was advancing rapidly across the new nation. By the 1850s Rhode Island would be the only state to require that some whites own land to vote, or to impose special requirements on foreign-born citizens. During the antebellum period, proposals to restrict immigrant voting through literacy tests failed elsewhere in the North, and aliens won the right to vote outside the Northeast.[30] Certainly some blame for Dorr's failure lies in the nature of his movement. The rebellion brought together Irish immigrants with native-born workers and professionals, a diversity that was both a signal strength and a fatal flaw. This broad-based coalition agreed on the need for reform but not on how far it should go or how it should be achieved. Moreover, its leader was a genteel lawyer who lacked revolutionary experience and made a series of tactical blunders. Equally significant, Dorr's opponents were backed by the power of the state. The question is why they opposed reform so bitterly when their counterparts in other states were liberalizing their voting laws. Why did Dorr and his followers have to resort to force to secure a right awarded to white men elsewhere in the country? The answer lies in Rhode Island's unusual economic and demographic position. As the first state to industrialize and attract a foreign-born proletariat, it harbored exceptionally strong concerns about the votes of workers, immigrants, and Catholics. In this context, maintaining the traditional link between property and voting—a link that had gone out of fashion elsewhere—was an effective way to defuse a political threat.

Economic requirements for voting drew on time-honored beliefs about the relationship between property and good citizenship. Building on a long-standing belief that only men who owned property had a stake in upholding the social order and the means to resist bribery, the American colonies generally limited voting to real or personal property owners. Although these requirements effectively limited the suffrage to white men, some colonies explicitly disenfranchised blacks and women, transients and paupers, and Catholics and Jews. In the eighteenth century Catholics could not vote in five states including Rhode Island, and Jews in four.[31]

On the eve of the Revolution close to 60 percent of white men had access to the ballot, but contraction of available farmland, rising interest in politics, and demands for "no taxation without representation" were prompting colonists to question the fairness of limiting the suffrage to property owners. By 1790 a majority of states had replaced land with tax or personal property requirements, and Vermont had dispensed with economic qualifications altogether. Restrictions on Catholics and Jews melted away; only two states explicitly limited the vote to whites; and New Jersey briefly gave the vote to property-owning women. By the late 1850s, only two of thirty-one states mandated that some voters own land (immigrants in Rhode Island and African Americans in New York), just six retained taxpaying requirements (some quite small), and it was common, outside the Northeast, to enfranchise aliens who had filed papers declaring their intention to become citizens. At the same time, however, various states disenfranchised nonwhites and the underclass by restricting the vote on the basis of race and residency, implementing formal registration procedures, and barring paupers and criminals from casting ballots.[32]

The antebellum trend toward enfranchising economically stable white men reflected pragmatic and philosophical factors. A growing population of citizens who owned little taxable property demanded the suffrage, and policymakers realized franchise extensions would help to raise militias, expand party bases, do away with electoral restrictions that were confusing and widely abused, and (in the South) create a cross-class white alliance in support of slavery. These practical concerns coincided with the rise of a somewhat more democratic political philosophy, which held that the people (or at least the white male portion thereof) should be sovereign and that popular sovereignty should not hinge on economic success.[33]

Few Americans went so far as to call the vote a universal right, a declaration that could open the polls to women, racial minorities, and noncitizens. Instead, most suffrage advocates argued that the vote was an earned right to be secured through a variety of means (paying taxes, serving in the militia, or even working on public roads) that included but were not limited to owning property. Their goal was not to institute universal suffrage but to enfranchise the "intermediate class" of mechanics, professionals, and small landholders whom President Martin Van Buren called the "bone, pith, and muscle" of the population. Few suffrage reformers heeded warnings about the dangers of enfranchising a future urban proletariat.[34]

THE EXCEPTION OF RHODE ISLAND

These warnings resonated in Rhode Island, however. In colonial days, the state had been a formidable mercantile power made wealthy by its fisheries and trade in rum, molasses, and slaves. When the British immigrant Samuel Slater opened the nation's first mechanized textile mill just north of Providence in 1790, he initiated an industrial revolution that had profound demographic and political consequences. The Providence area became the nation's first industrial center, and by 1840 Rhode Island had the highest proportion of manufacturing workers and (along with Massachusetts) was one of just two states where more workers labored in factories than on farms. Providence, which had taken a back seat to Newport during Rhode Island's maritime heyday, now emerged as the state's economic powerhouse as well as its capital. The port city boasted a superb location (sited at the confluence of three major rivers and connected to the hinterland through a network of roads and later railways), abundant waterpower, and an ideal climate for textile production. It also had access to innovative entrepreneurship, available capital, and workers and markets in the growing towns that surrounded it. Over time the city moved beyond textiles to develop a diversified economy that also produced jewelry, metals, and machinery. Its factories were magnets for Irish Catholic immigrants, and by 1845 foreigners, the vast majority of them Irish, comprised almost one-fifth of the city's population. They kept the city's economic wheels turning by accepting essential positions in its nascent industrial order, but they had no place in the polity. Fears about how they would use their votes were a powerful roadblock to electoral reform.[35]

The state's native-born Protestants raised a host of arguments for why Irish Catholics should not vote. Immigrants, they claimed, were paupers, illiterates, and criminals who placed a burden on taxpayers and debased society. Senator Hazard voiced a popular viewpoint when he observed in 1829 that the Irish were in "as degraded a condition as men can be brought by abject servitude, poverty, ignorance and vice." Few, moreover, had accumulated property and thus, in the words of a Brown professor, William G. Goddard, had failed to demonstrate "those habits of industry, sobriety and economy . . . without with no man is fitted to discharge the right of suffrage." Instead, he maintained, they were "bound to the State by ties which may, at any moment, be severed." Invoking the link between economic stability and political independence, Rhode Islanders like Goddard worried vulnerable immigrants would become "tools of crafty politicians" or manipulative employers. An anonymous pamphlet circulated in 1829 warned that a suffrage extension would "place the political power of this State in the hands of the aristocracy of wealth; to give a single manufacturer . . . the power of putting into the ballot-boxes from 20 to 300 votes besides his own." Farmers were particularly worried an employer-worker bloc would shift the tax burden from businesses to land. As Goddard charged in 1841, suffrage reform would "change the centre of political power from the country to the town; from the farm to the workshop; from the plough to the spinning-jenny." The *Journal* agreed, warning small-town voters that "foreign elements . . . would neutralize your power and effectiveness." For all these reasons the *Journal*'s Whig editor, Henry Bowen Anthony, launched a vituperative campaign against enfranchising the "foreign vagabond."[36]

Objections like these could be dismissed as self-serving, but it was more difficult to ignore the argument that immigrants were unprepared to vote responsibly. Goddard articulated widely held fears when he asserted that immigrants were "neither familiar with the practical working of democratic institutions; nor identified with our interests." Even Dorr shared this concern early in his career. In 1834 the future rebel had favored retaining the freehold requirement for foreign-born citizens on the grounds that they "have been subjects of great oppression in the countries from which they came, where they were kept in ignorance and imbued with ideas of a monarchical system. . . . They ought to become in some measure assimilated to our habits and feelings, and acquire a knowledge of our institutions and an attachment to them before being admitted to a perfect equality of political privileges." Dorr later referred to this position with embarrassment as his "former Whiggish heresy," but at the time it expressed a popular perspective. Ironically, eight years later the General Assembly employed a very similar logic in arguing against Dorr's proposal to enfranchise immigrants on the same basis as native-born Americans. A legislative committee reported in 1842 that it was not "prudent" to enfranchise the foreign-born until "by a longer residence, and a freehold qualification, there was such evidence of a permanent common interest with and attachment to the community as would render it safe to extend to them this most important right."[37]

Compounding fears about the civic fitness of Irish immigrants was the fact that most of them were Catholic. Between 1830 and 1839, the estimated size of Providence's Irish Catholic community rose from less than two hundred to almost seventeen hundred—just over 7 percent of the population. If Dorr had his way this growing population would have easy access to the ballot, a prospect that awakened long-standing fears about Catholic political participation. In nineteenth-century America, it was widely believed Catholics could not be good citizens because they were unfamiliar with democratic traditions and beholden to the Vatican. An 1842 *Journal* editorial warned, "Foreigners still remain foreign and are still embraced by mother church. He still bows down to her rituals, worships the host, and obeys and craves absolution from the priest. He cannot be assimilated." If Catholics were the dupes of pastors, it stood to reason they voted the way their pastors told them to (a perception fostered by the hierarchical nature of their church and the fact that they tended to vote in blocs). This reinforced a popular conspiracy theory that the Vatican planned to use Catholic voters to take over the U.S. government.[38]

Arguments like these abounded during the Dorr Rebellion. Dorr's opponents insisted that Catholic voters would lobby for special privileges such as state support for their parochial schools, or worse. "They will league and band together and usurp our native political power," the *Journal* claimed. One particularly strident broadside warned old stock Rhode Islanders that a franchise extension would "place your government, your civil and political institutions, your PUBLIC SCHOOLS, and perhaps your RELIGIOUS PRIVILEGES under the control of the POPE OF ROME through the medium of thousands of NATURALIZED FOREIGN CATHOLICS." Unless natives took action to prevent this, the writer warned, they would see "a Catholic Bishop, at the head of a posse of Catholic Priests, and a band of their servile dependents, take the field to subvert your institutions." The author called himself Roger Williams, the name of the man who had founded Providence in 1636 as a beacon of religious toleration.[39]

Fears like these fused with more pragmatic concerns, such as the Whigs' well-founded suspicion that the Irish would support Democratic candidates, to inform a bitterly anti-Catholic and anti-Irish response to the Dorr Rebellion. Even though priests had limited their parishioners' involvement, anti-Dorrites misrepresented the suffrage movement as an Irish Catholic plot. According to one broadside, "every Roman Catholic Irishman in Rhode Island is a Dorrite." Joshua Rathbun, a suffragist, reacted to such warnings with consternation. Nativist sentiment, he told Dorr, "has perhaps operated against us more than anything else. Men were called upon not to vote for a constitution but to vote against Irishmen." Rathbun was an astute observer. Fears about Catholic political power, combined with concerns that immigrants would vote irresponsibly and outweigh farmers at the polls, stymied Dorr's crusade. To citizens in other states, suffrage reform meant enfranchising native-born artisans and small farmers. To Rhode Islanders, it meant putting ballots into the hands of a growing population of Irish Catholic factory workers.[40]

ANTI-CATHOLICISM IN ANTEBELLUM AMERICA

The religious tensions that helped to foil the Dorr Rebellion were rooted in the broader context of anti-Catholicism in antebellum America. Many of the original colonists came from a post-Reformation England where religious rivalries ran deep and the Catholic Church was seen as a threat to the nation's political well-being as well as its spiritual health. The settlers brought this baggage to the new world, where they restricted Catholic voting and office-holding as well as religious practice. These prejudices intensified during the eighteenth century when England and its colonies engaged in a series of wars with Catholic Spain and France. Across New England, residents played a game called "Break the Pope's Neck" and held annual Pope Day parades that included the burning of papal effigies. Religious bigotry infected even Providence, created on the principle that "no man should be molested for his conscience." Privately, however, founder Williams wrote of the "Romish wolf gorging herself with huge bowls of the blood of saints." Inconsistencies like these undermined the colony's vaunted reputation for religious freedom, as did a 1719 law that citizens "of different Judgmnts in Religious Affairs (Roman Catholicks only excepted) shall be admitted Freemen, And shall have Liberty to Chuse and be Chosen Officers in the Colony both Military and Civil."[41]

Nationwide, anti-Catholicism abated somewhat in the wake of the Revolution. During the war, the alliance with France and the contributions of Catholic patriots like Maryland's Charles Carroll improved attitudes toward the church. Afterward, the Constitution's guarantee of religious freedom set a tone of toleration for the new nation. Although Massachusetts and Connecticut still barred Catholics from holding office, Maryland and Pennsylvania dismantled their old restrictions. In keeping with the egalitarian spirit of the age, Rhode Island overturned its discriminatory law in 1783 and replaced it with a new statute that gave Catholics "all the rights and privileges of the Protestant citizens."[42]

In the post-Revolutionary era, the church also improved its image by assuming a more "American" character. Under the leadership of Baltimore's John Carroll, the nation's first Catholic bishop, the church declared some independence from Rome by electing its own bishops, building its own seminaries, conducting services in English, and allowing elected lay trustees to govern temporal affairs. Many of these reforms proved short-lived, in part because a shortage of priests led to an influx of European-trained pastors committed to a more traditional model, but the lay trustee system did survive and suggested that the church was in some ways adapting to its new environment.[43]

Denominational tensions reemerged in the 1830s as concerns about a new wave of immigration coincided with a broader sense of malaise. Many Americans felt the nation was going awry—plagued by market fluctuations and financial panics (the price of a modernizing economy), a breakdown in traditional patterns of authority as merchants and industrialists rivaled the old farming aristocracy, a bewildering religious pluralism in the wake of the Second Great Awakening (which had prompted many Christians to abandon older churches and form their own sects), and a growing division between North and South. Native-born Protestants found it tempting to blame ethnic and religious outsiders for these signs of fragmentation. The cities in particular showed signs of distress, and there seemed to be a clear connection between immigration and urban decay.[44]

Natives charged, furthermore, that newcomers were undermining the independent character, democratic principles, and Protestant faith central to their concepts of Americanism. Industrialization was turning self-reliant artisans and farmers into wage-earners, a trend especially pronounced in industrial centers like Providence, and it was easy to blame foreign-born workers for facilitating the new industrial order by accepting poorly paid jobs in New England's factories. Immigrants allegedly were debasing democracy by casting ballots in blocs and selling their votes. And natives misread Catholic resistance to exclusive use of the Protestant Bible in public schools as an attack on the Scriptures and an opening wedge to secure control of the schools.[45]

As fears of Catholicism intensified, theological and political debates gave way to salacious rumors spread through a growing print culture. Protestants devoured stories about unwholesome sexual relationships between priests and nuns facilitated by secret passageways between their cloistered domiciles. These rumors spawned a confessional literature by women claiming to be former nuns. The most famous was Maria Monk's *Awful Disclosures of the Hotel Dieu Nunnery of Montreal* (1836), a lurid and utterly false exposé of nuns who were forced into sexual slavery by priests and bore illegitimate children who were promptly baptized and strangled. These wild rumors drew on fears about Catholic secrecy and conspiracy, expressed the sexual anxieties of a modernizing society, and provided a semi-pornographic outlet for strait-laced readers. The inflammatory literature led Americans to fear convent schools as places where virtuous young Protestant women were forcibly converted, kept against their will, and subjected to indignities. In 1834 a mob burned down an Ursuline convent in Charlestown, Massachusetts, on unfounded rumors that a disenchanted nun was imprisoned inside. In the wake of the Charlestown conflagration, attacks on parishes became so frequent many congregations posted armed guards and insurance companies refused to issue policies to churches built of flammable materials.[46]

The Charlestown riots marked the beginning of two decades of hysteria and mob violence. One of the worst episodes occurred in Philadelphia in 1844, when the school board's decision to allow Catholic children to use their own version of the Bible in public schools sparked days of rioting. One year later Rhode Island hanged John Gordon, an Irish Catholic immigrant convicted on circumstantial evidence of murdering the industrialist Amasa Sprague. Nationwide the most sustained unrest came in response to the 1853 tour of Vatican emissary Gaetano Bedini, whom many Protestants believed part of a papal plot to subvert democracy. The worst anti-Bedini demonstration was in Cincinnati, where two thousand citizens marched through the streets carrying a gallows, the priest's effigy, and signs with such slogans as "No Priests, No Kings, No Popery."[47]

As the Bedini controversy illustrated, by the 1850s anti-Catholicism had assumed a distinctly political tone. Overshadowing theological disputes and sexual innuendos were fears that Catholics had designs on America's democratic institutions. By this time many immigrants had been in the country long enough to become citizens and voters, and there was evidence of electoral fraud by noncitizens manipulated by unscrupulous office-seekers. In this context, the issues raised in Rhode Island during the Dorr War surfaced nationwide. Americans became convinced that Catholics were casting ballots the way their priests told them to, would vote to secure special privileges such as state funding for their schools, and were pawns in a papal scheme to control the nation. Some natives even worried émigrés from Ireland and Germany would subvert American isolationism by involving the United States in their homeland politics.[48]

By the early 1850s, these fears gave birth to the American or Know-Nothing Party. The party, which loathed immigrants and Catholics and believed that only native-born Protestants should hold office, burst onto the political scene in 1854. By the following year it controlled state legislatures in New England and the border states and had substantial representation in Congress. The Know-Nothings appealed to native-born Protestants in Providence, where immigrants (the majority of them Irish Catholics) comprised almost 25 percent of the population by 1850. A letter that appeared in the *Journal* in 1851 expressed deeply held concerns. If the Irish were given free rein, the writer warned, "Rhode Island will no longer be Rhode Island. . . . It will become a province of Ireland; St. Patrick will take the place of Roger Williams, and the shamrock will supersede the anchor and Hope." Local Whigs, for their part, encouraged Know-Nothing sentiment in hope of weakening the Democrats' Irish Catholic constituency. In 1854 the state's Whig governor circulated an unfounded rumor about an armed Catholic conspiracy, and the following year a riot almost broke out over a false report that a young woman was being held against her will in a Sisters of Mercy convent in Providence. The convent incident was defused, yet it contributed to a nativist tidal wave that enabled the Know-Nothings to capture the General Assembly in the following month's state elections. Once in office, however, they found it difficult to translate their agenda into law. Although they did make it more difficult for immigrants to naturalize by moving the procedure from state to federal court, they failed to push through a twenty-one-year residency requirement.[49]

The party's fate in Rhode Island mirrored its record across the country. The Know-Nothings proved better able to win office than to enact laws. Once the party became a legitimate national organization, it had to abandon the mysterious fraternal rituals that had attracted so many adherents, to negotiate the demands of a bewilderingly diverse constituency, and to confront the divisive issue of slavery. As the decade progressed, questions of abolition and union became far more pressing than fear of the foreigner, and the party faded away in Rhode Island and nationwide.[50]

The ethno-religious rivalries that surfaced during the Dorr Rebellion thus formed one chapter in a larger story of nativism and anti-Catholicism in antebellum America. At a time when politicians, editors, and ministers across the nation were depicting Irish Catholics as shiftless, sexually depraved, and politically dangerous, it is scarcely surprising that Dorr's opponents did all they could to keep the ballot out of their hands. Drawing on this nativist current, they stymied Dorr and produced a deeply flawed compromise. The 1843 constitution created a two-tiered polity that enfranchised natives but made it clear that immigrants, most of them Catholic, were not welcome to participate in affairs of state. This system split a nascent industrial working class between native-born (mostly Protestant) voters and foreign-born (mostly Catholic) nonvoters.

After 1842 the voting agitation fizzled despite efforts by Irish Catholics and their Democratic allies to keep it alive. Residents who had opposed Dorr's crusade continued to fear that Irish votes would lead to "Roman Catholic tyrany [sic]," as an 1846 broadside put it. "Our political rights and state institutions will be completely at the mercy of Irish Catholic voters, marshaled and drilled by Catholic Jesuits [sic] priests," the Journal agreed in 1851. In nineteenth-century Rhode Island, prevailing definitions of Americanism rejected Catholic immigrants as members of the national community and blocked their access to electoral politics. Some of them found this situation profoundly discouraging. Henry Duff, who had unsuccessfully petitioned Congress for voting reform in 1844, finally left Rhode Island in disgust. "Finding myself still politically branded below the negro—an 'Alien Citizen,' and without hope of better treatment from the reputed descendents [sic] of Roger Williams," he wrote Dorr in 1852, he moved to the more democratic climate of San Francisco. His compatriots who remained in Rhode Island had to find alternate ways of influencing public life.[51]

2

A CITY IN TRANSITION

Immigration in the Nineteenth Century

The pay is good, Basile. We work from sunrise to sunset, but on Sunday the mills are closed and it is like a church holy day. The work is not hard. . . . Some of the children are working and we make more money than we can spend.

—French Canadian immigrant in
The French in Rhode Island: A Brief History, 1988

THE IRISH

Rhode Islanders who had opposed Dorr's crusade on nativist grounds had growing cause for concern as the immigrant and Catholic communities exploded in the following decades. Thanks to successive waves of immigration from Ireland, French Canada, and Italy, by 1885 almost 60 percent of the city's 118,070 residents were first- or second-generation immigrants and more than 40 percent were Catholic.[1] By this time the city was a complex ethnic landscape, its physical structure reflecting its cultural diversity. Its political system, however, remained bound by rules that privileged a shrinking Yankee minority. The requirement that immigrants own real estate to vote prevented the growing population of foreign-born Catholics from wielding political power. With the exception of the Irish, the only group to arrive with a strong activist tradition, relatively few newcomers were equipped or motivated to challenge the suffrage restrictions. But even as many found politics unappealing or inaccessible, they built an alternative institution, the Catholic Church, that strengthened their communities and promoted their interests.

In the four decades after the Dorr Rebellion, the Irish population swelled in size and changed in character. By 1885, almost 16 percent of the Providence population was Irish-born and another 40 percent had at least one Irish-born parent. Not only were there significantly more Irish Americans than ever before, but they were more likely to be Catholic, Gaelic-speaking, and poor and, thus, to be perceived as outside the American mainstream. The Irish exodus of 1820 to 1920, which brought about 4.7 million immigrants to the United States, was a response to economic disaster. Even before the potato famine, a population explosion (the result of medical advances and a cheap source of nutrition in the potato) and a depression that set in after the Napoleonic Wars in 1815 created a crisis. As better access to public schools improved literacy and English-language skills among the Gaelic-speaking population, the Irish read about the United States and its booming economy; and cheaper and more regular passage made it easier, although hardly more pleasant, to contemplate making the journey. At the same time, modernization was challenging an Irish Catholic worldview that had discouraged leaving the old sod by valuing communalism over individualism and fatalism over optimism. For all these reasons, when the potato blight started in 1845 it was more feasible for the Irish to choose emigration as a survival strategy than it would have been several decades earlier.[2]

Most Irish immigrants who came to the United States settled in northeastern cities, although a significant minority (generally those with better personal and financial resources) pushed west. In Providence the newcomers congregated in Fox Point, the North End, Smith Hill, Olneyville, Manton, Wanskuck, and South Providence. Settlements like these were known as "Little Dublins" or "Paddy Towns," cohesive if troubled neighborhoods plagued by crime, alcoholism, and disease. When a cholera epidemic struck Providence in 1854, the highest fatality rates were in the Irish settlements.[3]

The social pathologies that ravaged Irish neighborhoods reflected the difficulty of finding decent work, for nativist prejudice limited the Irish to the least attractive jobs. As late as 1887 the *Providence Journal* was printing "help wanted" advertisements that included the notorious phrase "no Irish need apply." The immigrants themselves brought handicaps such as pre-industrial work habits, lack of relevant skills, and a communal mindset ill suited to the aggressive individualism of nineteenth-century America. Prospects were particularly poor for the famine immigrants, many of whom arrived in poor health or with very young or old relatives who could not contribute to the family economy. Many also harbored an "exile" mentality that prompted them to see themselves as involuntary immigrants, banished from the old world and ambivalent about their presence in the new.[4]

The Irish in Providence, as in other cities, had no alternative but to take the lowest-paid, least skilled, most dangerous, and least secure jobs. Whereas women gravitated toward domestic service, men worked as unskilled laborers, digging the Blackstone Canal or laying railroad lines between Providence and Boston. Entire families found work in the region's growing textile mills. By the last quarter of the nineteenth century, second-generation immigrants were beginning to achieve upward mobility. With newer immigrants taking the less attractive slots and bearing the brunt of prejudice, Irish factory workers moved into skilled or managerial positions while others became building tradesmen, streetcar drivers, police officers, or firefighters (many of these public servants appointed by Mayor Thomas A. Doyle, a native-born Protestant of Irish descent). A number advanced into the middle class, men through politics, the professions, and the priesthood and women through nursing and teaching. A small Irish American elite included Irish-born building entrepreneurs William and Thomas Gilbane and industrialist Joseph Banigan, the state's first Irish Catholic millionaire. The Irish-born Banigan helped found the Woonsocket Rubber Company and built Providence's first skyscraper.[5]

The Irish were especially well positioned to use Democratic politics as a means of advancement. As a group they were not well trained for industrial work but did arrive with activist experiences and cultural advantages that facilitated political involvement. Until 1885 only one in six adult men could vote in Ireland, but many nonvoters were seasoned organizers who had cut their teeth as members of rural secret societies or O'Connell's Catholic Association. Although a number of Irish immigrants came from insular Gaelic-speaking communities, as a group they were far more likely than other immigrants to speak English and understand Anglo-American institutions. Regular contact with natives in urban areas facilitated absorption into American life, and the devastation of the Irish economy discouraged remigration (only about 10 percent of post-famine immigrants nationwide returned home) and fostered a sense of permanence. About 26 percent of all foreign-born, voting-age men in Providence were citizens in 1885, but almost 31 percent of the Irish had become naturalized. Finally, the Irish had the good fortune to arrive in the United States in an era when a partisan, street-based mass politics encouraged electoral engagement. Most Providence Irishmen (like their counterparts in other cities) voted Democratic, attracted to the party's cultural pluralism and commitment to overturning the voting restrictions. As the future mayor McCarthy once put it, "I am a

Democrat . . . because that party has always been in favor of just and equitable laws, equal rights and good government of, for and by the people."[6]

Despite limits on immigrant voting in Providence, Irishmen like McCarthy seized on electoral politics as a means of upward mobility. Their electoral clout grew as they found better jobs and accumulated enough property to vote, their American-born children reached voting age, and nativists focused their concerns on newer immigrants from French Canada and Italy. The Irish also capitalized on having proved themselves loyal citizens by fighting in the Union Army during the Civil War. Two local men, John Corcoran and James Welsh, even received the Congressional Medal of Honor. By the 1870s the Irish were winning seats in the state legislature and city council and were well on the way to controlling the Democratic Party, which they would guard jealously against the incursions of newer immigrants. One early success story was Charles E. Gorman, a second-generation immigrant who became the state's first Irish Catholic legislator in 1870 and went on to serve as speaker of the state House of Representatives. Politicians like Gorman and McCarthy used their influence to lobby for a suffrage extension, but reluctance to share power with other immigrants undermined the unity needed to build an effective movement.[7]

Engagement in American life did not signify an emotional break from the homeland. Although few Irish immigrants remigrated, ties to the old sod remained strong. The tendency to perceive immigration as forced exile fostered Irish nationalism, and problems encountered in the new country intensified nostalgia for the old. Even as the Irish became American political operators, they joined groups like the Fenians and Clan na Gael and found the two endeavors could be mutually reinforcing. Like the Dorrite Henry Duff, many Irish Americans drew links between struggles against discrimination at home and in the new country. Dublin workers, for example, shared with their Providence counterparts a requirement that they own property to vote.[8]

The Providence Irish, like their compatriots in other cities, thus struck a balance between American citizenship and commitment to the old country. As early as 1827 they formed a Hibernian Relief Society to raise funds for the emancipation struggle, and in ensuing decades they threw themselves into the cause of home rule. The state chapter of the Ancient Order of Hibernians (AOH) sponsored fund drives to which compatriots responded generously, inspired by Irish partisans who had fled to Rhode Island. In 1880, nine Providence branches of the Irish Land League donated $1,635.50 to the cause, the sixth largest contribution of any American city. The enduring appeal of Irish nationalism was evident in the *Providence Visitor,* the city's

Catholic newspaper, which began publishing in 1875. News of Ireland filled the front page while city happenings were consigned to the inside sections, although editors made exceptions for important local events like the St. Patrick's Day parade.[9]

As the *Visitor*'s priorities indicated, many Irish Americans mingled national and religious identities and expressed ethnicity through Catholicism, but this had not always been the case. Although the Irish later were known as devout Catholics, many pre-famine immigrants arrived with a lukewarm commitment to the church. Protestant suppression of the Catholic Church had created a scarcity of priests and parishes in Ireland, so that many peasants practiced a pre-modern folk religion based on superstition and magic rather than church attendance and the teachings of Rome. According to one estimate, only 33 percent of Catholics in pre-famine Ireland went to Mass. Over the course of the nineteenth century, however, the church cemented its position through a physical expansion, devotional revolution, and renewed commitment to Irish nationalism. Abandoning a policy of accommodation with the British, the church threw itself into O'Connell's early nineteenth-century emancipation crusade. Priests headed parish branches of his Catholic Association, collected funds to prevent evictions, led boycotts of Protestant merchants, and embraced agrarian reform. At the same time, the priest-parishioner ratio improved as immigration depleted the population. These changes reestablished the preeminence of the church and the links between religious and ethnic identity. By 1900 the Irish were known as the most devout Catholics in the world.[10]

These shifts in Irish Catholicism were evident in changing relationships between Irish Americans and their church. At first many had found the American church unwelcoming—understaffed, run by non-Irish priests and bishops, and charging pew rents and even entry fees. In Providence early attempts to create a church were stymied by inadequate funding, the transient nature of the population, and the difficulty of convincing Protestant landowners to sell land. In 1832, a resident named Francis Hye secured a lot for the city's first Catholic church only through "clever maneuvering." Equally problematic were divisions within the Irish community that reflected regional rivalries, disagreements over local and nationalist politics, and disputes between priests and parishioners. Father John Corry, who later tangled with his flock when he opposed their joining Dorr's armed uprising, finally opened SS. Peter and Paul in 1838 despite funding shortages and dissension within his congregation. "It is not to be found in history that ever was a Catholic Church built with so much opposition on the part of Catholics as this," he complained. Even after the church was built, rivalries between two Irish nationalist societies—one led by Corry and the other by Duff—continued to divide the congregation. According to a parish history, "one half of [Corry's] congregation disliked him, and he returned their indifference with a cordial hatred." These parishioners ultimately left to form St. Patrick's, the city's second Catholic church.[11]

During the nineteenth century, however, the bond between Irish Americans and the church tightened in Providence and other cities just as it did in Ireland. More immigrants arrived as practicing Catholics and perceived religion as an integral part of national identity, and they found a church in which they felt more comfortable than their predecessors had. Efforts to expand the physical infrastructure and satisfy demands for Irish priests and nuns had made the church more accessible. By the 1850s, Providence boasted four parishes and 1,640 parochial school students. The 1872 creation of the Diocese of Providence (previously part of the Hartford diocese), with Kilkenny-born Thomas Hendricken as its bishop, signaled that the church was becoming an Irish American institution. Continuing the trend, Hendricken's successor Matthew Harkins was a second-generation Irish American. Anecdotal evidence from at least one Providence parish suggests that the Hibernization of the church may have boosted attendance. An 1889 census of St. Edward's, an Irish parish, reported that only five of the congregation's 431 families failed to attend Mass regularly. Of course, ethnic bonds between priests and parishioners did not always ensure harmony. In 1893 Thomas D'Arcy of St. Michael's complained to Harkins that Rev. Joseph McDonough was "an autocrat who proposes to rule the parish with a rod of iron. Already he has driven men out of the Church, made women weep, insulted and threatened some of the oldest and best supporters of the church."[12]

Despite occasional disputes like this, the parish had assumed a central role in Irish American neighborhoods. In addition to serving as a link to the old world, it was a critical source of support in the new. William Tyler, who became bishop of the diocese in 1844 and chose Providence's SS. Peter and Paul as his episcopal residence, distributed food at that parish every Monday. When a depression hit in 1851, the clergy and lay people of St. Mary's in Pawtucket rallied to provide food and shelter for needy parishioners. "Father McKenna supported my whole family for two years," one recipient later noted with gratitude. Rev. William Wiley of St. Patrick's, for his part, took no salary for two years during the economic downturn. St. Patrick's rose to the challenge again when cholera broke out in 1854. According to the parish history, the new pastor, Rev. Patrick Lambe, "though not of a very robust constitution himself, seemed equal to any amount of toil and hardship in

The original Cathedral of SS. Peter and Paul, illustrated here c. 1880 before its reconstruction, was Providence's first Catholic parish. The church opened in 1838 despite funding shortages and divisions within the Irish American congregation. Engraving, courtesy of the Rhode Island Historical Society, RHi X3 4430.

ministering to the wants of his suffering people." Over the next decades, as chapter 5 will demonstrate, parishes like St. Patrick's became backbones of Irish communities by providing an impressive array of spiritual, social, and material resources. They also maintained close links to Irish American fraternal orders like the AOH, once that organization renounced its ties to violent secret societies. For all these reasons, by the turn of the twentieth century the church had become, as the historian Kerby Miller notes, "the central institution of Irish life and the primary source and expression of Irish identity."[13]

THE FRENCH CANADIANS

By the 1860s, a new group of immigrants was swelling Providence's population and intensifying Yankee concerns about ethnic, Catholic political power. Most French Canadians who emigrated to the United States did so between 1845 and 1895, and almost two-thirds settled in New England. The land in Quebec was not well suited for cultivation, and by the mid-nineteenth century overuse had wrought further damage. The land could not support the population of a nation where it was not unusual for families to have as many as sixteen children. To make things worse, in 1846 Great Britain repealed its protective tariffs and placed Canadian farmers in competition with their American counterparts. At the same time, French Canadians were catching "migration fever" from Europeans who passed through on their way to the States, as well as from friends and relatives who wrote glowing letters home about the jobs available in New England's textile mills, foundries, quarries, and boot factories. Proximity to the United States and availability of fast, inexpensive rail travel made immigration a simple and easily reversible endeavor.[14]

The French Canadians began to enter Rhode Island in large numbers during the Civil War, lured by textile jobs in Providence and the Blackstone and Pawtuxet river valleys and undeterred by the rigors of factory life. An estimated 57,000 immigrants had arrived by 1930, when the Great Depression stemmed the flow. Those who settled in Providence congregated in Olneyville and the West End. Typically fathers and unmarried children worked in the mills while mothers took in sewing and boarders. Mill work was monotonous and exhausting, and living conditions were no better. According to an 1888 profile in the *Journal*, French Canadian tenements were "squalid and filthy in the extreme" and it was common for "sixteen or seventeen persons to crowd into four or five rooms, or for four persons to occupy a single bed . . . their conditions in many respects reminding one of the habits and manners of life of the slave race before emancipation." These conditions were no shock for people used to a hardscrabble farming life, and many felt mill work provided a better future than that available at home. Nonetheless, textile jobs were no guarantee of upward mobility. By the 1920s, a majority of French Canadians in Rhode Island were still semi-skilled factory workers. Across New England, more than 40 percent of first- and second-generation French Canadians remained in factory jobs as late as 1950, making them more blue-collar than any other ethnic group.[15]

Social discrimination and workplace rivalries contributed to the French Canadians' troubles. Native-born Protestants mistrusted their ardent Catholicism and reluctance to learn English. Fellow workers derided them as "the Chinese of the East," a reference to their reputation for stealing jobs, depressing wages, and breaking strikes. "They are servile and ready to do the bidding of their taskmasters to any extent desired," the *Journal* agreed. "They are easily controlled and avoid strikes." The real story was more complicated. Most new arrivals were indeed unfamiliar with organized labor and influenced by priests who sometimes discouraged unions; yet they probably were no more likely than other vulnerable newcomers to break strikes. There were, moreover, numerous instances of French Canadian labor militancy across New England. In some cases grievances were cultural rather than economic. In 1895, Rhode Island French Canadians walked off the job when mill owners demanded they work on New Year's Day, usually a holiday.[16]

Despite these examples of involvement in American affairs, natives were suspicious, often rightly so, that the French Canadians were sojourners hoping to make money and return home. According to the *Journal*, they had "one general and definite aim . . . to purchase a farm in Canada," and indeed an estimated 50 percent of those who emigrated to the United States before 1900 returned home with their savings. Some did so at the encouragement of the Canadian government, which in 1875 began to lure émigrés home with offers of free or inexpensive land. The propensity to remigrate reflected not only desire for land and ease of crossing the border but also fierce commitment to *la survivance*. This movement to preserve the native language, religion, and culture emerged after the 1763 Treaty of Paris, in which French Canada fell under British control and residents had to struggle for ethno-religious survival. *Survivance*—epitomized in Quebec's motto "Je me souviens" (I remember)—assumed a special imperative for people who migrated to New England and sought to maintain their heritage against the onslaughts of Americanization and urban life.[17]

Survivance and the tendency to remigrate were only the most obvious factors preventing the French Canadians from engaging with American

Silk warping machines and employees at the Royal Weaving Company in Pawtucket, pictured here c. 1910. Mills like this attracted French Canadian immigrants to Rhode Island. Silver gelatin print, courtesy of the Rhode Island Historical Society, RHi X3 875.

public life. Ease of contact with the homeland kept old loyalties alive, language barriers and illiteracy made it difficult to understand U.S. culture, and unlike the Irish they lacked a strong activist tradition. Their resulting disengagement from American politics was visible in low rates of citizenship. In Providence, fewer than 12 percent of voting-age French Canadian men had become naturalized in 1885. These numbers disappointed community spokesmen, who formed clubs to promote citizenship and build an electoral voice. As the *Providence Telegram* observed, the French Canadians were "an ambitious and energetic class, having taken a lively interest in the local business and social affairs. They do not manifest the same inclination to mingle in politics as the other nationalities."[18]

Yet immigrants could not, in the words of the historian Jon Gjerde, remain "hermetically sealed." Many found jobs outside ethnic enclaves, subjecting themselves to assimilative influences and becoming involved in American life. In 1888 the *Journal* described the French Canadians as "exceedingly clannish," but twelve years later the newspaper reported they were putting down roots in the community—"building homes, embarking in business enterprises and building churches, halls and schools" as well as becoming naturalized and learning English. Even those who entered politics to defend cultural prerogatives or promote compatriots for office exposed themselves to outside forces. French Canadians who did vote were likely to vote Republican, linking their interests with the mill owners', resenting Irish control of the Democratic Party and the Catholic Church, and appreciating the Republicans' willingness to promote French Canadian candidates like Aram J. Pothier. Born in southern Quebec in 1854, Pothier emigrated to Woonsocket at age sixteen, found work as a bank clerk, and before long was director of the Woonsocket Institution of Savings. A Republican and business booster, he became Woonsocket's first French Canadian mayor in 1894 and Rhode Island's first French Canadian governor in 1908. Pothier occupied the governor's mansion for seven terms, dying in office in 1928. He and his cohorts formed a politically active minority that urged compatriots to take more interest in politics and challenge the state's restrictive voting rules.[19]

Despite the efforts of men like Pothier, for the most part religion loomed much larger than politics in French Canadian communities. These immigrants brought with them an intense piety that had deep roots in Canadian history. Many of the earliest French settlers had perceived themselves as a chosen people on a mission to convert the Native Americans, and after the Treaty of Paris religion became even more central to Quebecois culture because the French saw themselves as an embattled religious and ethnic community. Religion was central not only to French Canadian identity but also to the rhythms of peasant life. Usually located in the center of the village, the church was the focus of neighborhood activity. The priest was the most powerful member of the community and advised parishioners on secular as well as sacred matters. Religious festivals ordered the calendar, and rites shaped the patterns of daily life. On the state level, the church controlled education and social service and pushed through laws that regulated conduct according to Catholic principles. As the historian Jean-Charles Falardeau writes, "The history of French Canada is the history of the Church in Canada and vice versa."[20]

In Rhode Island, immigrants recreated the texture of life at home by settling in "little Canadas" centered on the parish. Nearby were the school, rectory, and convent as well as compatriot-owned businesses and social clubs. Just a few blocks away were tenements housing extended families, all within walking distance of the mills. The parish was more than the physical nucleus of the neighborhood; it also stood at the center of French Canadian identity. As one observer stated, "The church meant home, the village in . . . Quebec, French-Canadian customs, relatives, friends; the church gave vent to all that complex of feelings tied up intimately with home." Religion and language were integrally linked, as evidenced by the adage "he who loses his language loses his faith." *Survivance* thus depended on the recreation of Canadian-style parishes and parochial schools where French was spoken and compatriots were in charge.[21]

This commitment fueled bitter clashes with the Catholic hierarchy. Just as pre-famine Irish immigrants had found American parishes unwelcoming, now the Irish-dominated church alienated newcomers from Canada. French Canadians were used to a democratic and localized system in which lay trustees ran the secular life of the parish with little interference from the bishop, and they resented the centralized structure of the American church. Coming from the well-endowed parishes of Canada, they were unaccustomed to paying pew rents and other fees. They also were unhappy to find that Irish priests, sensitive to charges of "popish pageantry," had toned down the rich liturgy in favor of a sparer "American" ceremony. The sharpest conflicts arose over selecting priests. A shortage of clerics in French Canada made it difficult for that country to send pastors to minister to immigrants, but expatriates would accept only one of their own; even a French-speaker from another country would not do. Tensions reached a high point at Precious Blood in Woonsocket in 1875, when parishioners hung an effigy of Rev. James Berkins, a Belgian, outside the church. This was typical of the severe and often spectacular battles that broke out in Rhode Island, and elsewhere in the region, as French Canadians resisted Irish bishops they considered dangerously assimilationist. In time the immigrants secured the right to worship in national parishes run by compatriot priests and to operate bilingual parochial schools, yet they remained vigilant about threats to church autonomy and were quick to react to perceived slights. As late as the Second World War, some retained a siege mentality and referred to their parishes as citadels.[22]

THE ITALIANS

By the 1880s a wave of immigration from Italy was eclipsing the smaller stream from French Canada. Although the first known European to set foot in the state was the explorer Giovanni da Verrazzano in 1524, Providence was home to only a handful of Italians, most from the north, until late in the nineteenth century. Then began an influx of southerners from Abruzzi, Campania, Basilicata, Calabria, and Sicily that would make the Italians the city's largest immigrant group by 1915. Poor soil, outdated agricultural methods, population pressure (caused in part by declining infant mortality), and economic policies that favored northern Italy made for widespread poverty and chronic malnutrition in the south. Families survived by putting all members to work and combining farming with industrial work, day labor, and craft production, but this last source of income declined as southern artisans found themselves competing with factory-made products from the north. The farmers' precarious economic situation worsened when an agricultural depression began around 1870. Many responded by emigrating to the United States, lured by cheap and efficient travel and the promise of higher wages.[23]

The Italians who reached Providence congregated in the North End and on Federal Hill and replaced Irish and French Canadian workers at the bottom of the economic ladder. Used to seasonal labor and juggling multiple jobs, they were in some sense prepared for the unpredictable nature of work in the industrializing United States. The employment they found reflected personal inclination, such as preference for outdoor labor, and limited opportunity. "Many of them, owing to ignorance of the language of the country and the lack of any trade or profession, have been compelled to secure any employment that was open to them," the *Journal* noted in 1887. "This has generally presented itself in the form of the hardest kind of out-door labor at a very small remuneration." Providence Italians who did not find construction jobs tended to work in textile mills or jewelry factories. As in other cities, skilled workers labored as tailors, mechanics, stonecutters, or bakers, and small entrepreneurs owned barbershops, butcheries, or grocery stores. These groceries were community centers as well as markets and, according to the *Journal*, "there is little or nothing of common interest that does not take place" there. Among the more fortunate immigrants was Michele Pastore of Sant'Arcangelo, who came to Providence in 1899. Having apprenticed to a tailor at home, Pastore found work at Paoluzzi's shop near the downtown Arcade shopping center. This set his family on the road to respectability, a path that ultimately led his son John to the governor's mansion and U.S. Senate.[24]

In most Italian American families, the labor of women and children was critical to the household economy. Wives rarely worked outside the home but contributed by taking in boarders, doing industrial homework, or assisting in family businesses. Unmarried women labored in garment factories and millinery shops. In Providence, Italian-born sisters Anna and Laura Tirocchi ran an elegant dressmaking establishment. When necessary, young daughters did piecework at home or worked in family businesses, while sons worked in the streets as newsboys, bootblacks, and organ grinders. The immediate benefits of children's wages seemed more relevant than the long-term advantages of education, and many first-generation immigrants sacrificed children's occupational advancement to satisfy family dreams of home ownership.[25]

By the 1890s the city's Italian community was divided between established immigrants from the north and newer arrivals from the south. The *Journal* reported that many among the older population were "in respectable, profitable business, and in pleasant quarters far away from the colony, are establishing and improving snug little homes of their own." Families like these, the paper noted approvingly, were "living in a manner commensurate with the best idea of American home life." The *Journal* drew a sharp contrast between these Italians and the "squalid unfortunates of Federal Hill," living in "miserable hovels" and "digging in the putrefying collection of garbage and refuse at the dumping grounds." Inside their crowded tenements, "the odor of garlic, the smell of smoke, pervades. . . . There are no means of ventilation and the air is always foul."[26]

Conditions improved, but only somewhat, by the 1920s. By this time a majority of Providence Italians had acquired skilled or semi-skilled jobs in mills, jewelry factories, foundries, and building trades. Although relatively few were organized, some had carved out niches in the barbers and building trades locals. Despite these advances, a 1921 report by the Rhode Island Commissioner of Labor found that the Italians were the lowest-paid of the state's major ethnic groups. Their limited gains reflected social prejudice, the

A reporter for the *Providence Journal* was dismayed to see poverty-stricken immigrants, like those captured on film on West Exchange Street c. 1903, digging through garbage for survival. Photograph, courtesy of the Rhode Island Historical Society, RHi X3 867.

decline of skilled jobs in an industrial economy, reluctance to allow wives to work or send children to school, and a sense of transiency. Nationwide, between 1908 and 1923, 37 percent of northern Italians and 60 percent of southern Italians went back home. Intending to return to the old country, many did not invest in businesses, learn English, or become citizens. In Providence fewer than 15 percent of Italian-born men of voting age were citizens in 1895, and as late as 1925 just over 42.5 percent of voting-age immigrants (male and female) had become naturalized.[27]

For the Italians, as for the French Canadians, impermanency combined with poverty, illiteracy, language barriers, and inexperience to discourage political involvement. In southern Italy, local elites and *mafia* middlemen ran community affairs with little popular input. Only male taxpayers who met certain educational requirements could vote, which meant virtually all peasants were disenfranchised. As a result, the average peasant had little knowledge of democratic self-government and relied on family to solve problems. Immigrants brought these traditions with them. "It has been very hard work to get the average Italian interested in either local or national politics," the *Journal* reported in 1887. "This is owing more to a lack of understanding of the intricacies of American politics than from any apathy regarding the subject." The situation had not changed dramatically by 1915, when the state Bureau of Labor reported the Italians were the ethnic group least likely to participate in electoral politics. They did become more active over time, most voting Republican (until the 1930s) and a small minority becoming active in left-wing politics. In 1913, for example, there were two Italian American representatives in the General Assembly, two on the Providence city council, and two on the city's school committee. It was not until the 1930s, however, that Italians in Providence and across the nation would begin to wield real power. This shift was evident in the career of the aforementioned John O. Pastore, who became the first Italian American in the nation to serve as governor (in 1944) and U.S. senator (in 1950).[28]

Most Italian Americans found recourse through community institutions rather than electoral politics. Particularly popular were mutual aid societies such as Providence's Unione e Benevolenza. Organized around occupational or provincial affiliations, these societies provided illness and death benefits to members and their families as well as organizing patron saint festivals. Immigrants also formed fraternal orders such as the Sons of Italy, which opened its first Rhode Island chapter in 1915 to promote both assimilation and Italian culture. These societies usually limited membership to men, although women received husbands' benefits and participated in community-wide celebrations. Providence women, like their counterparts in Buffalo and

Lawrence, Massachusetts, instead developed neighborhood networks of relatives and friends who cooperated in the daily struggle for survival. Catholic societies were the only formal organizations to which most of these women belonged, and membership in parish societies, female and male, grew over time as Catholicism became more central to Italian American culture.[29]

It took some time for the Catholic Church to assume the prominence in Italian neighborhoods that it enjoyed in other ethnic communities, for many immigrants arrived with a strained relationship to the church. Whereas the Irish and French Canadians had looked to the church as a defender in the old country, Italian peasants knew it as the ally of exploitative landowners and an oppressive state. They saw priests not as simple men of the cloth but immoral and greedy parasites, not as advocates for the people but a source of their troubles. Nor did the Italians experience the twin curses of religious and political persecution that would have forged links between faith and nationalism and made the church a center of resistance. In fact, the church's opposition to national unification in the nineteenth century made it difficult to be an Italian patriot and a devout Catholic. Alienated from the church, many peasants practiced a folk or popular religion that fused Christian and pre-Christian practices and took place at home and on the streets. Each village had patron saints whose favor was deemed essential and who were honored at annual feast days (elaborate celebrations involving Masses, parades, music, and fireworks) as well as home shrines. On a daily basis, peasants used potions and magical rites to ward off witches' spells and the evil eye. Many southern Italians entered church only on feast days and for the necessary rites of birth, marriage, and death.[30]

Many Italians, therefore, arrived in the United States with a hostile or at least unorthodox attitude toward the church. As one writer noted in the journal *America* in 1914, they came "insufficiently instructed in their Faith, and not infrequently with a hatred of the Church and the priesthood in their hearts." Initially, they found little reason to judge the American church more favorably than its Italian counterpart. American Catholicism, one observer remarked in 1888, was "to the mass of the Italians almost like a new religion." Italians disliked the austere atmosphere and disciplined worship, resented the cold stares of parishioners who scorned them as unkempt and consigned them to the back pews, and could not understand English-language services. Father Henry Conboy, of St. John's on Federal Hill, "never preaches in Italian, and this is one of the main reasons why more Italians do not go to church," the *Journal* observed in 1887. Immigrants also objected to assimilation-minded clerics, and, as chapter 9 will illustrate, bitter disputes broke out when priests discouraged cherished patron saint festivals. Even Italian

American pastors like Providence's Antonio Bove and Domenico Belliotti saw these festive celebrations as paganistic throwbacks and a waste of funds. They were still more distressed by superstitions and rituals they found barbaric. At some Calabrian weddings in Providence, the *Journal* reported in 1888, the bride would dip her handkerchief into a bowl of chicken blood just before the ceremony; if either spouse were unfaithful, the handkerchief was supposed to turn white again. Although the article noted this "relic of pagan days" did not occur "often enough to call it a custom," reports like this convinced priests and other observers that Italians were poor Catholics. They were "not a church-going people," the *Journal* agreed in 1887. Rather than gathering for Mass on Sundays, the newspaper noted, they assembled for family dinners. "It is not uncommon to see from forty to fifty persons around the festive board, all eating, talking and gesticulating at the same time, devouring immense quantities of macaroni, cooked in most excellent style."[31]

Italians who tried to form national parishes, where they could worship in their own ways, faced numerous problems. One was the unsettled nature of their neighborhoods, populated by single men who moved frequently and worked on Sundays. Even in stable communities, Italians from different villages had trouble agreeing on whose patron saint the church would honor. Finances were another problem, for the Italians, like the French Canadians, were used to government supporting the church. As a history of the Federal Hill parish of Holy Ghost notes, clergy "had to overcome the rather poor economy that prevailed amongst the faithful and the lack of responsibility that existed toward parish upkeep." Even when immigrants formed parishes, they had trouble finding acceptable pastors. This was a recurrent issue at St. Ann's in Providence's North End. "Father Bove complains he cannot find a good self-sacrificing priest to help him," Bishop Harkins recorded in his diary in April 1910. Three years later he again noted staffing problems at St. Ann's: "Father Ascoli who has been assisting cannot stay. Finds work too hard." Not only was there a severe shortage of Italian clerics, a problem that typically bedeviled communities of new immigrants, but priest-parishioner relations were rocky. Regional rivalries created tensions between priests, who tended to be from the north, and parishioners, who were overwhelmingly southern. Many Italians treated priests with contempt, accusing them of sexual misconduct and fiscal mismanagement, and at least some of these charges were grounded. In 1917 Harkins noted an assistant pastor at St. Ann's had "disappeared and taken money belonging to the church and the pastor." Because of these problems, endemic in Providence and other cities, as late as 1920 it was estimated that between one-half and two-thirds of the nation's Italian Americans were not practicing Catholics.[32]

A 1926 history of St. Ann's eloquently describes the obstacles that Bove, and priests like him, confronted in building Italian American parishes.

> Well do I remember the well-nigh hopeless days when this young priest, new to the country and to the diocese, just beginning to learn the English language, was commissioned to go among the scattered, poor, neglected, disunited Italian people of the "North End". . . . They were far from any church in which their language was spoken; and, as a result, they had become indifferent, in great part, in regard to practical religion. They possessed, indeed, the faith of Catholic Italy, but they had few opportunities to practice that faith in the land of their adoption. And it must be admitted that they were disunited. For a short time some of them, evidently misguided, were openly hostile to the priest of God who came among them.

This hostility was evident the moment Bove arrived to take over the fledgling parish in 1901. Parishioners, angry he was replacing the well-liked Father Giulio Triolo, were waiting when a moving van arrived to remove Triolo's furniture. About two hundred people (mostly women) assembled outside the priest's residence, and whenever the movers carried out a piece of furniture the parishioners took it back in. Later that night, parishioners changed the locks on the church doors so that Bove could not enter. Triolo finally convinced the parishioners to cease their obstructions, but many rebelled more quietly by refusing to attend services. The energetic Bove was "destined to work wonders," however, and in time St. Ann's became "one of the best Italian parishes in New England." In 1925, the priest's "untiring energy and unswerving purpose" earned him the rank of monsignor.[33]

The success of St. Ann's reflected more than the accomplishments of a committed cleric. Despite national statistics that suggested widespread disaffection with the church, religion was in fact critically important to the spiritual and community lives of many Providence Italians. A vibrant Catholicism was evident not only in folk practices but also in commitment to the parish. The church was, after all, the only institution that would accept virtually every immigrant as a member, and religion filled two functions in Italian American communities it had not needed to fill in Italy. First, religion helped preserve an old world identity embattled by pressures to become "American." Elaborate festivals honoring village patron saints affirmed homeland traditions on the streets of the new world. Second, the parish was an anchor for immigrants uprooted from traditional support networks and battered by urban industrial life, offering services family and village had provided in Italy. Competing with Protestants who used material incentives to induce immigrants to convert, Italian priests appealed to compatriots by

offering recreational facilities, theatrical societies, evening schools, employment offices, and nurseries. In so doing they sent the message that here the
church was the friend of the working class.[34]

Recognizing the spiritual and material value of a community church, in
1889 three hundred Federal Hill Italians attended a meeting to discuss creating their own parish. A committee of four quickly raised thirteen hundred
dollars to open a small chapel on Brayton Avenue, but before long it was
clear the growing congregation required a full-sized church. When Holy
Ghost opened in 1890, response was overwhelming. Parishioners had to be
assigned specific Masses so that everyone could attend, and eleven years later
construction began on an even larger church. In Providence as in other
cities, to be sure, the anticlerical impulse remained strong and Italians registered lower than other ethnic groups in rates of church attendance. But
many others developed a new and intimate relationship with the Catholic
Church. This relationship would serve them well at a time when unions and
electoral politics provided limited assistance.[35]

THE URBAN LANDSCAPE

As the Italians, French Canadians, and Irish flooded into Providence, they
altered its physical landscape as well as its social makeup. By 1885 the population had more than quintupled since the Dorr Rebellion. Almost 29 percent of the city's 118,070 residents were foreign-born, more than 59 percent
were of foreign parentage, and only 26 percent of the immigrants were citizens. The Irish were still by far the largest ethnic group, comprising over 55
percent of the foreign-born population, but by 1915 the Italians would over-
take them. The city founded as a haven for Protestant dissenters, moreover,
was now 42 percent Catholic.[36]

Population shifts were both cause and consequence of the fact that Providence was in its golden age. Boasting the "Five Industrial Wonders of the
World," the city was home to the largest tool, file, steam engine, screw, and
silverware factories on the earth. Among its nationally known products were
Corliss steam engines, Brown and Sharpe tools, and Fruit of the Loom cot-
tons. Eager to take advantage of the booming textile, jewelry, and machinery industries, women and men streamed into Providence from the
surrounding countryside and abroad. To absorb the growing population the
city annexed surrounding villages, nearly tripling its size in the decade after
the Civil War alone, and built streets, trolley tracks, fire stations, and electric street lamps. The trolleys facilitated travel within the city and connected
the urban center to a growing network of suburbs.[37]

A view of the upper harbor looking north toward Market Square in the city's commercial district, c. 1895. Providence's waterways were key to its economic growth. Gelatin print, courtesy of the Rhode Island Historical Society, RHi X3 4579.

A walking tour of Providence in these years might have begun on the elegant East Side. Looking over the city from the top of imposing College Hill, the East Side was the home of Brown University, the Rhode Island School of Design, and old families like the Browns and Aldriches. As one strolled along the tree-lined streets, one would have stopped to admire the stately colonial and federal-style homes as well as the Baptist and Congregational churches where their occupants worshipped. Punctuating gracious thoroughfares like Benefit Street were cultural institutions such as the Athenaeum and the Art Club. Closer to the Brown campus, professionals and businessmen mingled at the University Club and the even more exclusive Hope Club.[38]

Walking down College Hill toward Market Square, one would look west toward the Woonasquatucket River and notice the smoke-belching industrial buildings that contrasted so sharply with the East Side. Large factories lined Providence's three rivers and its railroad tracks, while smaller mills, foundries, rubber works, and jewelry shops were scattered throughout the city. After crossing the river one would enter the business district along Westminster Street and other narrow thoroughfares that comprised downtown. The business district was home to impressive new commercial structures like the Butler Exchange and Shepard's Department Store, whose brightly lit windows broadcast prosperity and tempted consumers with the latest wares. Among Shepard's patrons were the newly rich families who settled near their downtown businesses in homes that contrasted with the simpler structures of the "old money" East Side. Sharing the downtown space were the new City Hall, the lavish Providence Opera House, and the Catholic Cathedral of SS. Peter and Paul—the last a physical reminder of the city's shifting demographics. The Union Railroad's downtown depot, for its part, signified the growing importance of streetcar travel to city life.[39]

In neighborhoods surrounding downtown, newer immigrants were replacing older ethnic groups who took advantage of better jobs and an expanding trolley system to move further from the urban center. Just north of downtown lay Smith Hill, a working-class district nestled behind the site where the magnificent State House would be built a few years later. Once an Irish district, Smith Hill now was home to eastern European Jews. West of downtown, the Irish district of Federal Hill was becoming an Italian colony. Federal Hill had a distinctive ethnic flavor with street-corner gatherings, open-air markets selling traditional foodstuffs, and religious processions winding through the crowded streets. To the southwest the Irish and French Canadians mingled in the mill district of Olneyville, which would become a hotbed of union and Socialist activity in the following decades. A small settlement of Portuguese immigrants congregated near the wharves on Fox Point. In all these neighborhoods, mutual aid societies, fraternal lodges, union halls, and Catholic churches mingled with saloons and ethnic groceries. Despite its rapid population expansion, Providence was not yet overcrowded. In 1875 more than half the city was still farmland, and as late as 1900 it would remain a community of one- and two-family homes.[40]

A variety of recreations entertained the city's diverse population. Working people enjoyed burlesque shows at the Theatre Comique and exhibits at the dime and freak museums that sprang up in storefronts throughout the city. They congregated downtown at the Providence Roller Skating Rink and the Base Ball Ground, as well as in neighborhood parks and playgrounds built by reformers seeking to guide them toward salubrious forms of entertainment. On the southern outskirts of the city, Roger Williams Park, an 1871 gift from a descendant of the city's founder, beckoned to rich and poor alike with its grand lakes and impressive menagerie. During the summer, residents patronized the resorts that lined Narragansett Bay or took day trips to Crescent Park (an amusement park in East Providence) or Rocky Point. This

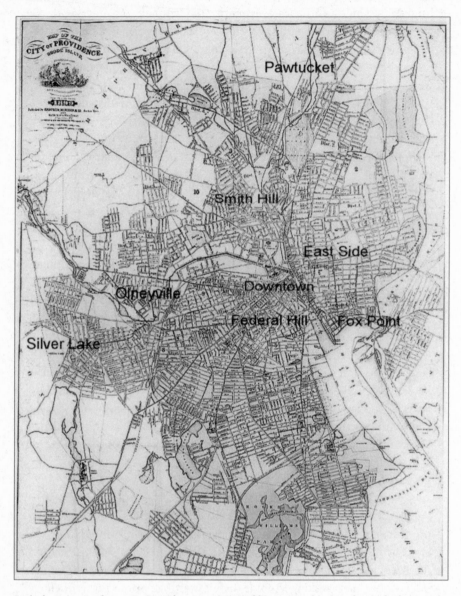

In the late nineteenth century Providence was in its golden age. By this time the city had annexed a number of adjacent towns and was home to distinct ethnic neighborhoods. Adapted from a map provided courtesy of the Rhode Island Historical Society, RHi X3 4591.

mini–Coney Island, twelve miles from Providence, boasted its own Ferris wheel, vaudeville theater, and dancing pavilion.[41]

Residents of all backgrounds traversed Providence through an extensive network of trolley routes, but the city's increasing segmentation by class and ethnicity was representative of its inequitable and sharply divided politics. Three waves of immigration had intensified the division between natives and foreigners, Protestants and Catholics, voters and nonvoters, as well as splintering the Catholic population among immigrants from different countries. Many native-born Protestants, particularly those residing in the state's rural areas, were more determined than ever to keep political power out of ethnic, Catholic hands, but a growing population of immigrants resolved to challenge the voting restrictions.

3

"A STATE FOR SALE"

Corruption and Protest in the Gilded Age

We are but a short step from . . . plutocracy, *or the rule of wealth as against the people,* dollars *against* men.
— Hiram Howard, *A Plea for Progress,* 1890

"NEARER AN OLIGARCHY THAN A DEMOCRACY": POLITICS IN THE GILDED AGE

By the 1880s a shrinking population of native-born Protestants controlled local politics, while a growing number of Catholic immigrants and ethnics found it difficult to assert themselves at the polls. The property requirement, malapportioned legislature, and divisions among immigrant groups undermined ethnic and Catholic political power and enabled the old guard to govern with little accountability. In the 1880s, a series of scandals brought these problems into relief and prompted demands for change. Once again state politics became focused on the right to vote and whether Catholic immigrants deserved to be treated as full citizens.

The voting restrictions cast a far wider net than they had in 1843, as a growing proportion of residents were immigrants and factory workers who did not own taxable property. In 1885 fewer than 15 percent of the city's foreign-born, voting-age men met the immigrant real estate qualification, and it was likely that a much smaller proportion actually voted. The rule that all residents own $134 in real or personal property to vote in Providence city council elections affected natives and foreigners alike. Of all voting-age men, two-thirds could participate in state and federal contests, but less than 20 percent owned enough property to vote in most city elections. The "registry" voters who did not meet the property requirement could cast ballots for citywide offices like the mayor, which had little clout, but not for the powerful city council. As a result four-fifths of Providence residents had very little say in municipal government, the level of administration with most bearing on their daily lives.[1]

Irish Americans never had abandoned their efforts to liberalize the voting laws, despite the disappointing outcome of the Dorr Rebellion. When repeated petitions to Congress and the state legislature failed, they turned to the Brownson Lyceum, the Catholic lecture and debating society Patrick McCarthy had headed, as an organizational base. There, the Catholic reformer Charles Gorman recalled, "the question relating to their and their fathers' disfranchisement received an early consideration, and from 1860 until 1870 such agitation as was carried on was under the auspices of its members." Irish American suffragists seized on the Fifteenth Amendment as an opportunity to do away with all biased voting restrictions, and they were bitterly disappointed when the measure became law in 1870 without a clause guaranteeing the vote to immigrants as well as native-born blacks. In 1878, eleven hundred Rhode Islanders once again asked Congress to outlaw voting discrimination on the basis of ethnicity. "The rights of naturalized citizens, though we have the misfortune to belong to the Caucasian race . . . should be not less sacred than those of persons of African origin," they argued in an unsuccessful petition. What the historian David Roediger calls the "wages of whiteness"—advantages that accrued to Irish American workers on the basis of skin color—did not buy much in Rhode Island.[2]

This situation was particularly offensive to Irish-born Rhode Islanders who had fought in the Union Army, only to see voters refuse three times to exempt them from the property rule. George C. Williams of Newport, a veteran, voiced a popular sentiment when he argued that this measure would "make us feel like men and citizens of a free land. . . . Did we not amply pay for the boon we most humbly ask for?" Despite eloquent pleas like this, it took until 1886 for immigrant veterans who did not own real estate to win the vote. Concerns about the foreign vote still outweighed appreciation of immigrants' military contributions. It was "a waste of time to argue upon the qualified suffrage for naturalized aliens in this state," the *Journal* noted in 1868. Opposition was "too deep to be easily eradicated."[3]

Despite repeated setbacks, the Irish continued to agitate and gradually broadened their constituency. By the 1880s, second- and third-generation immigrants were reaching voting age. As native-born citizens they did not

This 1882 trade card, depicting an Irish Catholic with simian characteristics, suggested immigrants were unprepared for full citizenship. Prejudice like this blocked efforts to exempt foreign-born veterans from the property qualification. Drawing by George Tropp, courtesy of the Rhode Island Historical Society, RHi X3 2282.

have to own real estate to vote in state and federal elections, but they resented the restriction as an insult to foreign-born parents and grandparents and an obstacle to ethnic electoral power. It also reminded them of civic disabilities imposed on Catholics in the old country, a parallel that often surfaced at Irish nationalist gatherings. Among foreigners, the property requirement affected prominent citizens as well as soldiers and workers. Thomas Davis, a Dublin-born Protestant who had represented Rhode Island in Congress from 1853 to 1855, lost the right to vote after his business failed. Thomas McMurrough, an Irishman who served as president of RISA, had been disenfranchised when Rhode Island annexed the Massachusetts town in which he lived. At the same time that Irish Americans like these were campaigning for a broader suffrage, French Canadians were entering politics and feeling the effects of the voting restrictions. Some went so far as to petition the General Assembly for "the rights of citizenship," by which they meant full access to the ballot. The Irish continued to spearhead the ethnic voting movement, but they were picking up support beyond their own ranks.[4]

The Democratic Party joined ethnic voters in calling for suffrage reform but was unable to do much more than complain about the undemocratic voting rules. Something was rotten in Rhode Island, where a rapacious Republican machine used electoral restrictions and corporate monies to retain an iron grip on power. The governing system put the Democrats at a double disadvantage. Republican small towns outweighed Democratic cities in the legislature. Providence, for example, contained 40 percent of the state's population and paid 47 percent of its taxes but claimed only 16 percent of state representatives and 3 percent of senators. Moreover, the biased voting restrictions disenfranchised the immigrants and workers who were likely to be Democrats. The Republicans, for their part, enjoyed a cozy relationship with business interests who filled party coffers with enough cash to buy the necessary votes. This was no small feat in an age of rampant electoral fraud. Politicians allegedly paid voters two to five dollars in a typical election year and up to thirty-five dollars in highly contested campaigns. Such abuses later prompted muckraker Lincoln Steffens to call Rhode Island "a State for sale."[5]

At the center of this Republican-business matrix was an unholy trinity of potentates known as the "*Journal* Ring." Henry Bowen Anthony, who had spearheaded nativist opposition to the Dorr Rebellion and now served in the U.S. Senate, still owned the *Journal* and used it as a party organ until his death in 1884. His cohort Nelson W. Aldrich wielded so much power in the U.S. Senate that he was known as "General Manager of the United States."

Dublin-born Thomas Davis represented Rhode Island in Congress from 1853 to 1855 but lost the right to vote when his business failed and he no longer could meet the property requirement. Gelatin print, courtesy of the Rhode Island Historical Society, RHi X3 7577.

Aldrich's local pointman was Charles "Boss" Brayton, who coordinated daily dealings with finesse and little regard for ethics. As their critic Sidney Rider quipped, "Anthony taught, but Brayton bought; and the people's rights all went to naught."[6]

Realizing their rivals controlled the corporate vote, Democrats tried to attract urban immigrants and Catholics but were unable to extend their base beyond the Irish. The party's Hibernian flavor alienated Protestants from Great Britain and Scandinavia, who felt more comfortable in the Yankee-dominated Republican Party, and Catholics from Italy and French Canada, who competed with the Irish for jobs, political recognition, and control of the church. The Republicans could nominate ethnic candidates from time to time because they controlled most offices, whereas the Democrats, in the minority and beholden to the Irish, rarely could afford to name standard-bearers from other groups.[7]

Economic considerations were as important as cultural questions in drawing new Americans into the Republican fold. Many believed Republican victories meant more jobs and higher wages. When the appeal of the full dinner pail did not suffice, Republican employers escorted workers to the polls, offered voting bonuses (some allegedly as much as one-third of a week's pay) and paid the one-dollar tax charged registry voters. In 1887 the *Journal* estimated half the state's voters had these taxes paid for them. Particularly loyal supporters received patronage jobs, which the dominant party controlled almost completely. In cities like New York and Boston, Democrats controlled machines and distributed their largesse to the Irish; but in Providence a Republican machine awarded patronage to newer immigrants.[8]

Beginning in the 1870s, however, a series of scandals undermined the Republicans' reputation and pushed residents into the reform camp. Vote-buying had grown so rampant that in 1880 the U.S. Senate agreed to investigate charges of electoral fraud in Rhode Island. In addition to uncovering widespread bribery, the Senate committee censured the Republican-run state for allowing employers to coerce workers' votes and requiring registry voters to pay poll taxes. The committee was particularly distressed to find that Rhode Island was the only state that set different voting rules for natives and foreigners, a situation its report described as "unjust, unwise, and anti-republican." As a result of these restrictions, in 1876 proportionately fewer voters had cast ballots there than in any other state. Rhode Island, the report concluded, was "nearer an oligarchy than a democracy." The Republican-controlled Congress dismissed the committee's findings, not wishing to take action against such a loyal Republican state, but in Rhode Island the report offered a legal underpinning and moral boost to the suffrage movement.[9]

Response to the Senate report revealed a schism among Rhode Island Republicans. The party traditionally had been the home of middle-class Yankees, rural and urban, but now control was passing from the "middling" sort to business interests. The small towns remained loyally Republican, largely out of cultural animosity toward Irish Catholic Democrats; but a growing cadre of reform-minded urban professionals became disenchanted as the party dismissed their campaigns for temperance, good government, and worker protections and did favors for large corporations. Old stock reformers were particularly distressed when the party granted lucrative franchises to utility companies (a symbol of corporate monopoly) and refused to enforce a popular prohibition law. More and more, these former Republicans came to believe expanding the electorate would undermine corruption and corporate power.[10]

At the same time that middle-class reformers were agitating for change, working people were demonstrating new militancy. Until the 1870s the city's workforce was barely organized, with craft unions catering to only a small minority of skilled building tradesmen. Workers became more aggressive after the 1870s depression ended, and when a series of mill strikes failed they looked to electoral politics as an alternative tactic; but they realized they had to dismantle the property requirement in order to wield power at the polls. The energetic new Knights of Labor spearheaded the working-class drive for suffrage reform. The Knights founded a Rhode Island local in 1882, aiming to attract workers of both sexes and all skill levels and ethnic backgrounds. Under the direction of District Master Workman Patrick H. Quinn, a Catholic active in parish life as well as workplace activism, the union published a local newspaper (complete with a feminist column), provided social clubs and reading rooms, and even offered day care at a Providence church. The Knights claimed 18 percent of the state's workers as members by 1886 and channeled their energies into fighting for full access to the ballot. By the mid 1880s, therefore, concerns about electoral injustice and political corruption had extended the suffrage movement beyond Democratic and Irish Catholic politicians to include unionists, middle-class reformers, and French Canadians.[11]

"EQUAL PARTICIPATION":
WOMAN SUFFRAGE AND THE BOURN AMENDMENT

A simultaneous campaign for woman suffrage overlapped with the movement to overturn the property qualifications and drew on many of the same concerns. The Rhode Island Woman Suffrage Association (RIWSA) formed in 1868 and chose as its first president Paulina Wright Davis, wife of the Irish-born congressman who had lost the right to vote. RIWSA argued on the basis of natural rights—"to every human being belongs every human right"—and women's special qualities—their inherent morality would allow them to clean up Rhode Island's murky political waters. Even as this last argument attracted middle-class reformers, it alienated office-holders who feared that female voters would undermine their lucrative relationships with big business. Although the legislature did accede to some minor requests, authorizing women to serve on boards overseeing the state orphanage and school for the deaf, it refused to consider the larger issue of woman suffrage.[12]

In March 1887, legislators finally agreed to hold a referendum on a proposal to enfranchise women under the same property restrictions as men. They scheduled the vote for April, leaving the suffragists a mere four weeks to rally support. RIWSA established a downtown Providence headquarters open every day from nine in the morning until ten at night, published a newspaper, and organized almost a hundred public meetings. Women's clubs, reformers, progressive legislators, and ministers like Providence's Frederick A. Hinckley endorsed the cause, yet the referendum was a bitter disappointment. Voters rejected the proposal by a margin of about three to one, the largest defeat a woman suffrage amendment had ever received in this country.[13]

One reason for the defeat was tensions between woman suffragists and Catholic workers and immigrants campaigning against the property rule. There were moments when the two groups came together to support electoral and workplace reform, yet the women disappointed working-class activists by refusing to challenge the property requirements. Women may have resented the fact that a man could vote on the basis of his wife's real estate, provided she had borne him a living child, while she could not. Some Catholic, ethnic, and working-class voters, for their part, opposed the referendum because they felt it improper for women to vote when so many men could not. This last objection found expression in the Catholic *Visitor,* many of whose readers were disenfranchised immigrants: "Rhode Islanders do not believe in woman suffrage—at least not for the present. After the restrictions on manhood suffrage are removed the ladies' claims may be considered with some favor."[14]

The *Visitor*'s editors were among those Rhode Islanders who took more interest in the campaign against the property qualification. This movement brought together workers (foreign- and native-born, Catholic and Protestant) who wanted better access to the vote, Democrats who expected to benefit from a franchise extension, and reformers who knew the restrictions were blocking progressive change by disenfranchising supporters. Spearheading the drive was the new Equal Rights Association (ERA), led by middle-class reformers like Dr. Lucius F. Garvin of Cumberland but working in concert with the Greenback Labor Party and the Knights of Labor. Among its prominent members were Irish American politicians like the Protestant Davis and the Catholics McCarthy and Gorman. Years later the *Visitor* would describe Gorman as one of the movement's strongest champions, claiming "no man did more to abolish the property qualification."[15]

The ERA organized Equal Rights Clubs across the state, held monthly meetings, and flooded the legislature with petitions. When the General Assembly held a hearing on a proposed constitutional convention (a first step toward extending the franchise), so many people appeared to testify that two additional sessions had to be scheduled; but in 1882 electors voted down a proposal to call a convention. A majority of voters clearly shared Anthony's feeling that it was best to keep the ballot from immigrants, "men who came upon us uninvited and on whose departure there is no restraint." They were, Anthony charged in an echo of the Dorr era, "ignorant of our institutions, unacquainted with our form of government, embittered against all government, and ready with little solicitation to become the instruments of demagogues." Most of the state's immigrants were, moreover, Catholics who might use their votes to secure public funding for their churches and tax exemptions for their charitable institutions. For all these reasons, Anthony argued, "the agricultural class is the safest depositary [*sic*] of political power."[16]

Local fears about Catholic and immigrant votes reflected nationwide concerns. The Civil War had diverted attention from the Know-Nothing crusade without destroying nativist sentiment, and once the war ended, the perplexing question of national identity reemerged. The United States had proved itself a nation, but what type of nation it was or should be remained open to debate. The postbellum years also witnessed economic and institutional developments that native-born Protestants found deeply threatening. Industrialization and urbanization disrupted traditional relationships, created a new sense of vulnerability, and intensified social pathologies in the growing cities—all blamed on Catholic immigrants who accepted factory jobs. These newcomers, moreover, were organizing themselves in ethnic institutions like the Fenians; in labor unions and radical movements, both perceived as foreign imports; in urban machines, associated with the Irish and seen as a scourge on American politics; and in the expanding Catholic Church. This last phenomenon was particularly troubling. Catholics' efforts to ban use of the King James Bible in public schools and secure tax exemptions for their schools and charities awakened old fears about their influence in public life. And the Vatican's 1870 proclamation of papal infallibility reinforced the church's reputation as autocratic and un-American.[17]

Finally dismissing such worries, in 1884 Rhode Island's Republican governor, Augustus Bourn, called for an end to the property rule. Bourn's party was losing voters to the Democrats, who styled themselves as champions of equal rights and clean government (despite considerable corruption on their own part) and pledged to enfranchise immigrants and improve working conditions. This platform appealed across class, ethnic, and religious lines and struck fear into Republican hearts. Hoping to rebuild their damaged reputation and win back ethnic and Catholic voters, Republican legislators finally agreed to hold a referendum on the immigrant voting restriction.[18]

On April 14, 1888, Rhode Islanders voted by a healthy majority—20,068 to 12,193—to repeal the property qualification. Their decision allowed naturalized citizens to vote on the same basis as natives for the first time since 1843 and had potential to transform the Providence electorate. To the 22,355 men eligible to vote in 1885, the Bourn Amendment added almost 1,500 naturalized citizens who had not met the old real estate requirement. This number was not large, but ethnic community leaders hoped the 9,679 voting-age men who had not become citizens would do so now that they could vote without owning property. At a celebratory dinner Gorman, the Irish Catholic legislator, commended voters for admitting immigrants into "an equal participation in . . . citizenship." Seeing the referendum as a sign of great things to come, he predicted "a new and better era is ready to dawn upon us."[19]

In his optimism Gorman overlooked the fact that the General Assembly had given with one hand and taken away with the other. The Republicans knew they would retain control of the General Assembly, as small-town representatives still outnumbered urban office-holders, but they worried the new voters would elect Democrats to run city governments. To avert this danger they added to the text of the amendment a clause requiring ownership of $134 in real or personal property for voting on financial questions and in most city elections. This provision, in place in Providence since 1843, now applied to other cities. All electors could vote for mayor and a few other figurehead positions, but only those who met the property qualification could elect the city councils, the real seats of municipal power. A number of complicated registration requirements, moreover, made it difficult for workers and immigrants to vote. Citizens who failed to meet the property qualification had to put their names on the voting rolls every year, to do so by June 30, long before the campaign season had heated up, and to find a way to get to the registry office during hours when most were at work. Foreigners without property worth $134 also had to present naturalization papers each time they registered. These restrictions were an effective way to keep the Republican Party in power and undermine Catholic political influence, as they affected workers and immigrants who were disproportionately members of that church.[20]

The antidemocratic tenor of the Bourn Amendment echoed across the nation as other states rewrote their voting laws in the late nineteenth and early twentieth centuries. Rhode Island, formerly behind the times with respect to electoral law, now was on the cutting edge of a new trend. In response to demographic changes wrought by emancipation, immigration, and industrialization, other states were adopting the Rhode Island model and disenfranchising citizens who were not white, native-born, or middle-class. Nationwide, poll taxes, literacy tests, residency requirements, and Asian exclusions affirmed the Rhode Island tradition of limiting the suffrage. So did the decision by Maryland, Kentucky, Vermont, Texas, and parts of New York to join Rhode Island in requiring property ownership for voting in municipal elections. These rules reflected a desire to weaken political machines, labor unions, and Socialist parties as well as betraying the kinds of social prejudice so rampant in Rhode Island.[21]

"TO EXERCISE EVERY FUNCTION OF THEIR CITIZENSHIP": PROVIDENCE VOTERS ORGANIZE

Nonetheless, there was some cause for optimism on the part of Providence's reformers, labor activists, and ethnic Catholics. It soon would become clear that the lingering voting restrictions were serious obstacles, but in 1888 the Bourn Amendment seemed an important step forward and sparked a sense of possibility that crossed social lines. Despite limits on municipal voting, a significantly larger proportion of Providence residents could and did cast ballots. The percentage of all adult men qualified to vote in state and federal contests rose from 67 percent in 1885 to 78 percent by 1895, even though foreigners comprised a growing proportion of the voting population. Less than 15 percent of the city's voting-age male immigrants met the property requirement in 1885, but ten years later 53 percent could vote in state and federal elections. As for turnout, the proportion of qualified electors (people entitled to cast ballots) who actually voted in gubernatorial elections surged from 43 percent in 1888 to a high of 70 percent in 1892 before dropping to 55 percent in 1896. Clearly the suffrage extension did more than create new voters; it encouraged old voters to come to the polls.[22]

Immigrants demonstrated particular enthusiasm. Finally admitted to the polity on an equal footing with natives, they took greater interest in electoral politics. The proportion of foreigners who became naturalized in Providence more than doubled, from 26.2 to 54.3 percent, in the decade after 1885. Newer immigrant groups joined the Irish in their eagerness to be voters. As the *Journal* observed in 1896, "The immediate effect of the passage of the Bourn Amendment was the rally of the Irish to the polls. . . . The Irish have 'shot their bolt,' and now the English and Scotch, the French Canadians, Swedes, Italians and Russian Jews are pushing them aside." Civic and religious leaders encouraged this way of thinking by organizing naturalization rallies, forming political clubs, and urging new citizens to vote. In so doing they sought to win recognition and lobby for further reforms, as well as combat a rise in nativism.[23]

French Canadian leaders were particularly eager to encourage active citizenship. In 1881, the Bureau of Labor Statistics in neighboring Massachusetts had issued a blistering report charging that immigrants from French Canada were a "horde of industrial invaders" who "manifested no interest in our institutions and assumed none of the burdens of the State." Stung by this insult, middle-class French Canadians across New England spearheaded protests. In October merchants and professionals from Rhode Island and Massachusetts held a three-day meeting in Fall River, where they resolved that "instruction in the English language was a necessity and an obligation" and strongly recommended that compatriots become citizens. In response to pleas like this, the French Canadians of Olneyville formed a naturalization club in 1890. At an organizational meeting that attracted five hundred people, H. A. Dubuque of Fall River declared that in "[holding] aloof from citizenship" his compatriots had gained a reputation as "an inferior race." Becoming citizens would enable them to "gain many desirable advantages and even concessions," he noted. This message resonated. In March 1892, seven hundred people from Olneyville and surrounding neighborhoods attended a "family soiree" that the French Canadian Naturalization Society sponsored in Dyer's Opera House. Three years later, almost ten thousand Rhode Islanders participated in a "monster" naturalization rally on "French Day." French Canadian Catholics were beginning to believe that becoming a citizen was a civic obligation, a means of upward mobility, and a way to defend their reputation as an ethnic community even as they became American.[24]

This new political enthusiasm spread to some Italian communities.

When more than 150 Italian Americans attended a naturalization meeting in November 1890, the *Journal* observed, "The Italian residents are taking an active interest in securing the rights of citizenship, and it is anticipated that a large number will avail themselves of the privilege." In the 1892 elections, Providence's Italian Political Club was expected to serve as a swing vote, and both parties, wrote the *Journal,* were "anxious to gain [its] good will." Four years later, Federal Hill's most prominent residents pledged themselves to the McKinley ticket and organized the Abraham Lincoln Italo-American Republic Club to spearhead their efforts. The club's founders included Vincenzo Bufalo and Pasquale Mastrobuono, both bankers, and Alessandro Durante, a liquor dealer. It is no coincidence that these men were solidly middle-class. Italians active in politics at this early date tended to be economically stable or part of the older immigration from northern Italy. For newcomers streaming in from the south, naturalization and voting ranked behind economic survival.[25]

Catholic priests and editors joined ethnic leaders in encouraging constituents from all nations to engage with public life. "It is the imperative duty of citizens to exercise every function of their citizenship on all occasions," the *Visitor* counseled in 1894. "Immigrants must leave behind them all the traditions and antipathies of race, creed and nationality, and must enter into our public life with . . . pure love for the flag that protects them, and a deep obligation to learn the history of the country and acquire a thorough-going knowledge of the character of our institutions." One of the most important functions of citizenship was the vote, a "precious and inestimable right . . . of too sacred a character to be indifferently exercised." It was a frequent refrain in the diocesan newspaper that voting was a sacred duty, a rhetoric that implied Catholics had a divine as well as civic obligation to cast ballots. The *Visitor*'s pronouncements echoed those of John Ireland, archbishop of St. Paul, Minnesota, and an influential voice in nationwide Catholic circles. In an 1895 address he declared, "The essence of the American republic is manhood suffrage. . . . The ballot is the pride of the true American; its proper use is his sacred duty."[26]

Catholic spokesmen like Ireland and the *Visitor*'s editors had a multifaceted agenda in urging laymen to vote. The hierarchy wanted parishioners to cast their votes on principle rather than in exchange for favors from machine bosses, thus undermining charges that Catholic immigrants were responsible for political corruption. Catholic leaders also sought to elect legislators who would promote tax exemptions for religious institutions and funding for parochial schools and oppose laws the church found offensive. Like their counterparts in other dioceses, Providence clerics resented efforts to enact temperance laws (considered an intrusion of state power into personal life) and woman suffrage (seen as disruptive of family stability). In Providence, as in Catholic areas of the Midwest, priests gave parishioners the paradoxical advice to enter politics (an assimilative gesture) to protect their agenda as a separate community.[27]

Church leaders also needed coreligionists to prove their patriotism in the face of attacks by the American Protective Association (APA). Founded in Clinton, Iowa, in 1887, the APA defended "true Americanism"—by which it meant native-born Protestantism—by seeking to reduce Catholic influence. It was based in the Midwest but attracted supporters across the country, especially in cities where residents competed with the Irish for jobs and political offices. APA publicists spoke with alarm of "Pat's Grip on the Government" and speculated, "The Society of Jesus: Will It Set the Next Pope in Washington?" When a crippling nationwide depression started in 1893, some Americans blamed the pope for their troubles and circulated rumors about an armed Catholic conspiracy.[28]

The APA held special appeal for Rhode Island Protestants, deeply concerned that theirs was the most Catholic state in the nation. In November 1893, two thousand supporters assembled in Providence's Music Hall to plan strategy and hear Protestant ministers deliver anti-Catholic speeches. The following year they campaigned to have Catholic teachers fired from the city's public schools. Another nativist organization, the United Order of Deputies, ran slates in local elections on a platform of restricting Irish political power by limiting immigration and reversing the Bourn Amendment. There was widespread concern that newly enfranchised Catholics were voting according to priestly directives. "None but good Christians voted in Rhode Island last Wednesday as all who did vote made the sign of the cross before depositing their ballots," the *Woonsocket Patriot* commented in April 1890. Capitalizing on these concerns, the APA made headway among the state's Yankees. In March 1896 a letter-writer to Boston's anti-Catholic weekly, the *American Citizen,* reported with pleasure that the group had "captured the G.O.P. in Rhode Island." The *Citizen*'s Rhode Island column printed charges that ranged from the shrill—"papist plotters" were responsible for Abraham Lincoln's assassination, convents were "places of torture and crime," and parochial schools were "hell's nurseries"—to the more reasonable—immigrant saloon keepers were undermining the social order, and destitute foreigners were burdening public treasuries. The most frequent complaint was that Catholics were taking over public sector jobs such as teaching and police work. "They have a finger in all our pies," an anonymous writer charged.[29]

THE AMERICAN-RIVER-GANGES.

Reproduced, from HARPER'S WEEKLY, for September 30, 1871.

This 1871 Thomas Nast cartoon evoked widespread concerns that the Catholic Church was taking over America's governing institutions and public schools. Fears of this nature surfaced during the Dorr Rebellion and again during the APA agitation of the 1890s. Courtesy of the Rhode Island Historical Society, RHi X3 8959.

Particularly troubling was the 1895 election of Democrat Edwin McGuinness, former secretary of state, as Providence's first Catholic mayor. McGuinness, a native of Irish ancestry, was elected by Irish supporters as well as Yankee reformers who applauded his reputation as an upright public servant and good government advocate. Although the mayor was little more than a figurehead, the *Visitor* welcomed his election as a triumph for "that liberty-loving principle which every Rhode Islander claims as the birthright of the State." Bishop Harkins evinced less confidence in that principle when he declined an invitation to say a prayer at the new mayor's inaugural, no doubt fearing his presence would ignite fears about Catholic designs on government. A letter-writer to the *Citizen* expressed these very concerns: "On Tuesday last Bishop Harkins was elected mayor of Providence. . . . Over seven hundred Irishmen have already put in applications to be appointed to the police force."[30]

Old stock women who were worried about Catholic politicians like McGuinness joined the Loyal Women of American Liberty, a nativist group that formed in Boston in 1888 and opened a Providence chapter the following year. Mrs. Isaac C. Manchester—a Baptist, former teacher, and founding member of the Providence Woman's Christian Temperance Union—coordinated the local unit and was elected national president in 1893. The *Citizen* described her as a woman of "good old Puritan stock" and claimed, with some exaggeration, that she could "trace her American ancestry back for three hundred years." According to the newspaper, her temperance work brought her into contact with foreigners and alerted her to "the need of a patriotic movement" to guard against "the dangers to our American institutions from indiscriminate immigration." Thanks to Loyal Women like Manchester, the *Citizen* noted, the public was recognizing "the danger threatening our land in consequence of the evils of Romish aggression."[31]

Like many other native-born women's reform groups, the Loyal Women combined education, entertainment, and political action. The Providence branch engaged in activities that ranged from a "grand patriotic lawn-party" and a "red, white and blue supper" to Bible reading and "study of civil government." Carving out a public role under the rubric of patriotism, Manchester traveled around New England and the Midwest to lecture on such topics as "Our Duty as American Citizens." Her 1899 columns in the *Citizen* suggest that her anti-Catholicism reflected less simple bigotry than a complex of political and economic concerns. These included hatred of the machine boss ("crushing freedom" by allowing money to rule politics), resentment of cheap immigrant labor ("those who can subsist upon $10 where it would cost our people $100"), suspicion that the Catholic Church

Edwin McGuinness in 1896, the year he was inaugurated as Providence's first Catholic mayor. The APA and other nativist groups interpreted his election as further evidence that the church was taking over public life. Photograph, courtesy of the Rhode Island Historical Society, RHi X3 7548.

was obstructing the temperance movement ("nine-tenths of the saloons are run by its disciples, and the church gets a big revenue from it"), and discomfort with confession (Catholics "can do any mean thing, knowing that they can receive absolution"). She was by no means exceptional in feeling that Catholic immigrants were a threat to the reforms she believed in and the civil society she cherished.[32]

Nor was Manchester alone in deeming Catholics unsuited for full membership in the nation. Debates over what it meant to be American played out across the country in the immigration-rich and politically tumultuous years of the late nineteenth century. It was a common refrain in Providence, and throughout the United States, that Catholics were "un-American" because they were steeped in an authoritarian tradition and owed their primary loyalty to the pope. Providence Catholics, like their counterparts in cities like Worcester, Massachusetts, responded by proposing alternative Americanisms that accommodated and even celebrated cultural difference. National identity, they argued, was not a static concept rooted in Anglo-Saxon Protestantism but a dynamic idea that should evolve. The nation's vaunted liberties included the right to preserve homeland traditions, they insisted, so that it was anti-Catholics who were un-American.[33]

In Providence, these debates over national identity came to a head during the APA agitation. In addition to boycotting APA-owned businesses and using their St. Patrick's Day parade to show "that Catholicity is alive," Catholics turned APA charges on their heads by insisting nativists were un-American and Catholics the true patriots. In an 1895 speech to the Young Men's Catholic Association, Joseph Osfield Jr. attacked the APA's "unholy, un-American spirit of intolerance" and urged listeners to defend their religion. The APA was "a menace to free government and a blot on the fair escutcheon of the Republic," the *Visitor* agreed. "No word seems more abused at the present day than the term patriotism." As church leaders and APA members tarred one another with the slur "un-American," they revealed the contested and malleable nature of that term.[34]

The APA was part of a wave of anti-Catholicism that gripped the nation in the 1890s as the church expanded. Catholicism already was the largest denomination in the nation and, thanks to a new wave of immigration from southern and eastern Europe, its constituency was growing. So was its infrastructure, as the Third Plenary Council in 1884 had ordered parishes to build parochial schools. At the same time Irish Catholics were gaining political power in cities like New York and Boston, which elected their first Irish mayors in the 1880s, as well as in Providence. Jeremiads such as *Rome in America* (1887) and *Washington in the Lap of Rome* (1888), both written by

Justin D. Fuller, a Boston minister, warned of the church's growing clout. Fuller's warnings gained credibility in some circles when American Catholics asserted their claims on the nation by celebrating the four hundredth anniversary of Columbus's discovery, and when Archbishop Francis Satolli was named apostolic delegate to the United States. In an echo of the 1853 Bedini controversy, the APA founder Henry Bowers speculated the Vatican had sent Satolli to "direct and influence legislation in the country." These concerns about Catholic political influence coincided with the 1893 depression, which sparked complaints that immigrants were stealing jobs and depressing wages.[35]

The nativist surge targeted Jews as well as Catholics. A popular rumor claimed that Jewish financiers were part of a global conspiracy to bankrupt American debtors through rigid adherence to the gold standard. Determined to quash these rumors and be treated as full-fledged Americans after centuries of discrimination in other countries, Providence Jews worked hard to demonstrate their citizenship. Whereas 54 percent of the city's adult men were naturalized in the 1890s, the rate was 67 percent for Jews. Not satisfied with these high numbers, the Hebrew Independent Club organized mass meetings aimed at making every Jew a citizen. Becoming naturalized was not enough, however; it was equally important to act the role. When the Spanish-American War broke out in 1898, two Jewish societies offered bonuses to coreligionists who enlisted. "We are American citizens first, and Jews second," declared community leader James Rose.[36]

Old habits died hard, however, and ethnic and Catholic politics followed two trajectories after 1888 rather than one assimilationist path. Even as immigrants demonstrated more interest in American life, they strove to preserve old world connections. Mutual aid societies urged members to learn English and take out naturalization papers, but also to maintain links to the old country. The Italian Benevolent Society, for example, opened its January 1885 meeting by singing Italian and American "patriotic" songs. A similar dualism was evident during festivals such as St. Jean-Baptiste Day, St. Patrick's Day, and the anniversary of Italian unification. It was a popular strategy for newcomers in Providence, and across the nation, to incorporate American icons into ethno-religious celebrations and old world symbolism into U.S. holidays.[37]

This simultaneous attention to U.S. citizenship and ethnic identity reflected a tension over what it meant to become American. Did assimilation require a rejection of old world identities? In Providence some newcomers sought to resolve the dilemma by distinguishing between a public U.S. citizenship and a private ethnic heritage. Rev. Charles Gaboury, pastor at St.

Charles Borromeo, urged his compatriots to "become American citizens, but to continue to speak French in their families." A more workable compromise was to insist that Americanism and ethnic or religious pride were mutually sustaining. Ethnic Catholics argued that preserving their heritage made them better Americans by enabling them to contribute to the melting pot. Americanism entailed being a voting, English-speaking citizen, but it also meant perpetuating homeland traditions that would strengthen the adopted country. Statements like this were broadcast outward to natives suspicious about expressions of ethnic and Catholic pride, as well as inward to compatriots who feared assimilating meant abandoning their heritage. As J. B. S. Brazeau, president of the fraternal order Union Saint-Jean-Baptiste (USJB), told his compatriots, "The heart of a Canadian is large enough, noble enough to love two countries."[38]

The politicization of the city's Catholic immigrants coincided with an organizational surge among unionists and middle-class reformers, both eager to use the suffrage extension to build a progressive coalition. Union leaders, most of them Irish Catholics or British Protestants, tried to forge an interethnic working-class bloc that would elect friendly representatives and lobby for labor laws. This was, theoretically, possible now that the Bourn Amendment had removed the political distinction between native-born voters and foreign-born nonvoters. "The workers are not ready for an independent political party, and it is doubtful if such a movement would be wise," the Providence labor paper observed in 1893. "But they are ready to throw their ballots against any man who casts his vote against labor measures upon which are pinned the faith and future betterment of those who toil." Workers campaigned for laws to mandate factory inspections (to ensure safe and sanitary working conditions) and restrict child labor. The nine-hour day was another popular cause, especially once the 1893 depression set in. "Less hours for ourselves and less idleness for others," the labor press demanded.[39]

Working-class activists were concerned not only about their treatment in the workplace but also about their voice in municipal affairs. As Providence expanded and officials attended to quotidian matters such as street lighting and trolley routes, city government played a more tangible role in daily life and citizens took more interest in its workings. Providence residents were frustrated to see their control over local affairs weakening as corporations won favors at the expense of the public interest, power shifted from the popularly elected mayor to the city council (chosen by propertied voters only), and the General Assembly took over municipal functions. They realized these last changes represented a strategy to shift power from offices Democrats could elect (thanks to the suffrage extension) to offices Republicans still controlled.[40]

Similar concerns prompted members of the middle class to organize for change. Reformers who had fought for electoral reform now focused on making local government more responsive to its citizens. The city was in shambles after twenty-five years of rule by a Republican machine attuned to corporate interests rather than popular needs. The school system was inadequate, the police force ineffective, the water polluted, and the streets in disrepair. The administration spent too much money without providing adequate services, then raised taxes to compensate for its profligacy. Eager to make urban life more livable, taxpayers, prohibitionists, and clergymen lobbied to expand municipal services and stamp out political corruption. Neighborhood improvement societies agitated for better sewers and more frequent trolley service, some going so far as to advocate municipal ownership of utilities. Business booster groups like the Advance Club called for antibribery laws and repeal of the municipal property rule, hoping to end what President Hiram Howard called "the infamous 'boodle' methods that have so long disgraced our State." Reform groups were especially concerned about the Union Railroad Company, the powerful corporation that affected daily life through its control of trolley routes and ticket prices. Over the course of the decade, resentment at the Union Railroad would unite these civic societies into a coalition with Catholics, immigrants, and unionists.[41]

By the 1890s, then, citizens of all stripes were engaging in electoral politics and community affairs more directly. The franchise extension, despite its limits, seemed to have created the possibility for substantive change. A sense of excitement energized Catholic parishes, ethnic societies, labor unions, and middle-class civic associations behind the goals of urban regeneration and individual rights. This excitement revealed an almost visionary faith in the power of the ballot. The vote held a sacred place in local politics as a critical and hard-won marker of citizenship. Now that all men could vote in state and federal elections, they believed they could make their voices heard despite restrictions on local voting. As the Socialist newspaper *Justice* declared in 1895, "With the ballot in their grasp the workingmen have in their possession a lever with which . . . they can produce greater and more wonderful transformations than was produced by the lamp of Aladdin."[42]

4

"THE LAMP OF ALADDIN"

Immigrants and Politics in the Progressive Era

The supreme act of citizenship is the casting of the ballot. Ballot in hand, the citizen is a sovereign.
        —John Ireland, archbishop of St. Paul, *Visitor*, May 4, 1895

THE POLITICS OF PROTEST

If Providence activists demonstrated remarkable faith in the value of the vote, they were not alone. The local suffrage extension came at a time of nationwide political ferment. Reform movements and third parties exploded in the late nineteenth and early twentieth centuries as workers, farmers, and middle-class progressives sought to reorient government from the rule of money to the needs of the people. Activists joined a variety of organizations—ranging from the Populist and Socialist Parties, to the Knights of Labor and the AFL, to the progressive reform movement—but shared one fundamental conviction: a new elite of "robber barons" was gaining control of the nation and drowning out the voices of ordinary citizens. Seeking to reverse this trend, reformers sought a closer relationship with the state through "direct democracy" measures designed to make politics more accessible and "good government" laws aimed at making elected officials more responsible and responsive. They also tried to curb the power of wealth and protect the rights of workers and consumers through currency reform, antitrust legislation, and workplace and consumer laws. The bitter debates these proposals sparked reflected fundamental disagreements over the nature of citizenship and national identity. Did citizenship entitle one only to basic guarantees of life and property, or to more extensive protections? Did the principle of limited government on which the Constitution rested remain relevant, or did the needs of a modernizing society require a more activist state? Finally, were the Catholic immigrants who filled the growing working class entitled to the same privileges and protections as older Americans?

These were questions that resonated in Providence, whose ruling elite had perfected the art of ignoring popular needs. A small cadre of wealthy industrialists used its economic power and political influence to exploit workers, restrict access to the polls, and defeat calls for good government. Catholic immigrants and ethnics were treated as second-class citizens—unprotected at the workplace, lacking an effective voice in government, and disparaged as "un-American" because of their cultural backgrounds. As chapter 3 demonstrated, the Bourn Amendment, which overturned the restrictions on immigrant voting, was their call to arms. Despite its limits, the new law created thousands of voters and sparked an organizational surge among activists who saw the suffrage extension as the opening wedge for reform. Over the next two-and-a-half decades, ethnic Catholics used their newfound right to vote to demand they be treated with dignity in the workplace and justice in the polity. Acting at various moments in concert with native-born unionists, radicals, and progressives, they employed three strategies in an effort to use the ballot box to address their needs. One tactic involved combining electoral and workplace protest by participating in a streetcar strike and related political campaign. Another (much less popular among Catholics) entailed influencing politics from outside by supporting the city's Socialist movement. A third strategy united Catholics, unionists, and reformers once again behind a crusade to further liberalize the voting laws. In all these ways Catholic immigrants and ethnics used electoral politics to assert their citizenship, insisting they were entitled to participate in public life and enjoy the protection of the state.

"KING CAPITAL'S JUGGERNAUT": THE STREETCAR STRIKE OF 1902

The immediate aftermath of the Bourn Amendment was deeply disappointing to people who believed in the power of the ballot. At the end of the 1890s, reformers had little to show for a series of hard-fought attempts to elect independents and enact progressive laws. Republicans easily maintained control of the legislature, still dominated by small towns, and city government, thanks to the municipal property rule. Voters who mounted insurgencies tended to divide along class, ethnic, or partisan lines, or to elect their candidates only to watch the General Assembly strip those offices of their authority. Successful candidates like Edwin McGuinness found themselves in figurehead positions, so that their elections proved no more than symbolic victories for ethnic, Catholic constituents. Republican legislators blocked attempts to write a new constitution, regulate the workplace, and reduce electoral fraud, and Democrats, plagued by corruption and internal divisions, failed to provide an effective alternative. By 1902, however, there was new unity and determination as unionists, reformers, and Catholic immigrants rallied behind an invigorated Democratic Party and shared frustrations over corporate power and machine corruption. They found their mobilizing issue when the Union Railroad unleashed popular furor by defying an important labor law.[1]

Working-class militancy formed a critical foundation for the 1902 uprising. The end of the 1893 depression had sparked the organizing impulse among workers nationwide, and the Providence labor movement enjoyed heady growth. Between 1894 and 1902, the number of organized workers in the city shot up from twenty-eight hundred to fifteen thousand. The majority were still Irish Catholics and British Protestants, but as newer immigrants found better jobs they too joined unions, although in smaller numbers. Union workers were more united as well as more numerous. The *Journal* noted "the disposition of every labor organization to assist in any way possible the welfare of its fellow organizations." This cohesion was evident in the new Providence Central Federated Union (PCFU). Working-class unity was no small accomplishment in a city where ethno-religious tensions split the workforce and employers did their best to exploit those divisions. Defying these obstacles, organized workers came together to demand union recognition and better conditions and were prepared to strike if refused. "Probably never before, with conditions so prosperous and work so abundant, has there been so intense a spirit of unrest among the wage earners," remarked the state's commissioner of industrial statistics.[2]

Workers were determined to translate their newfound strength into legislative success and electoral power. According to the *State*, a progressive local newspaper, there was nowhere else in the nation "where the wage worker receives less legislative protection for the proper opportunity of securing his wages." It was true, the *Journal* acknowledged, that Rhode Island had only twenty-seven labor laws to Connecticut's forty-six and Massachusetts's ninety, and local unionists sought to redress the imbalance by calling for laws to end convict labor (seen as cheap and unfair competition), outlaw yellow-dog contracts (which required workers to stay out of unions), and institute an eight-hour day (a popular goal at a time when it was common to toil as many as twelve hours a day). Planning to back up legislative demands with electoral pressure, workers formed a Trades Union Economic League with branches across Rhode Island to act as their political arm and coordinate a statewide registration drive. The major parties realized they were witnessing a tidal wave they could not ignore. "Labor in these times 'is a name to conjure by' as the politicians well know, and 'wise in their day and generation,' they seek to put their knowledge to good account," the *Journal* noted.[3]

Organized workers of Irish and British heritage dominated the Economic League but sought to bring other groups into the coalition. They benefited from the fact that newer immigrants were becoming politicized and feeling disaffected with the Republican Party. Many recent arrivals were taking an interest in electoral politics now that they had secured some economic stability and adjusted to their new surroundings. As the *Journal* noted in 1900, the French Canadians "have gone into politics and are there to stay, and have become a political force which must be reckoned with." Some acted on their own initiative, others at the urging of church and community leaders who insisted they prove their Americanism by becoming citizens and voters. "To become a citizen . . . is to acquire the right to vote and by consequence it is to acquire a part of the sovereignty that the people exercise," *Le Jean-Baptiste,* the biweekly French Canadian newspaper, declared in 1902. "To voluntarily refuse this right is to fail at one's duty, is to lack patriotism." It was to lack patriotism not only for the new country (by taking little interest in its public affairs), but also for the old (by refusing to promote the interests of compatriots at the polls). Ethnic leaders were particularly concerned with winning office, and one reason Italian and French Canadian Catholics (as well as Jews) tended to vote Republican was that the party seemed more receptive than its rival to promoting their candidates. Yet by 1902 they had been voting Republican fairly consistently and had few offices to show for it, and many began to question whether another party might serve them better.[4]

As Catholic immigrants and workers cast about for a political vehicle, the Democrats offered an attractive option. Appealing to voters who resented corporate control of politics yet felt socialism went too far, local Democrats reinvented themselves as the party of moderate reform. They appealed to urban workers by endorsing the Economic League's demands, to good government advocates by pledging to reapportion the legislature according to current population statistics, and to ethnic and Catholic voters through a program of cultural pluralism. The party backed up its appealing platform with an intensive outreach that involved launching a massive registration drive, holding nightly meetings working people could attend, and even offering new members baseball tickets. By 1902, reform voters were beginning to coalesce across religious, class, and ethnic lines in the Democratic Party. There they determined to assert their rights as citizens against the Republican machine and its monied allies.[5]

The Union Railroad Company provided an ideal target. In the late nineteenth and early twentieth centuries, citizens across the country launched "car wars" against trolley companies in hope of reclaiming the public domain from corporate influence. The streetcars were an ideal vehicle for the broadly based citizens' alliances needed to undermine business power because they were a site where the rights of workers, consumers, and citizens overlapped. In Providence, the Union Railroad was the corporate behemoth that touched residents' lives most directly. Resentment over its monopoly on trolley service crossed social and party lines, as most people rode the streetcars. Consumers were angry about rising prices and a new emphasis on economy at the expense of passenger convenience and safety. They complained that drivers who were held to tight schedules were driving too fast and causing accidents, and that fewer trips were making for overcrowded cars. "The people are obliged to ride in vehicles which are a disgrace to any civilized community; not only uncomfortable, but absolutely injurious to health and morals," charged Railroad Commissioner Edward Freeman. Consumers' frustrations intersected with streetcar drivers' complaints. The mostly Irish Catholic workforce had enjoyed relatively good relations with the old management, but the new owner was a New York corporation less accessible and accountable to the Providence community. Yet local politicians, beholden to the company's donations, were unwilling to address these issues. The Union Railroad thus represented a larger trend by which corporations were becoming "the masters of the servants of the people," as the manufacturer-reformer Hiram Howard put it. Citizens of all backgrounds were preparing for a showdown with what *Justice* called "King Capital's Juggernaut."[6]

On May 31, 1902, the Union Railroad threw a live match into this volatile mix. One month earlier the legislature had enacted a bill reducing the workday for streetcar employees to ten hours, without a cut in pay. The day before the law was to go into effect, the company announced it considered the law unconstitutional and would reduce the wages of employees who worked only ten hours. The fledgling streetcar union responded by walking out at midnight on June 4, and the community's response was immediate and overwhelming. On the second day of the walkout, more than twenty thou-

By the turn of the twentieth century, streetcar drivers like these, photographed c. 1894, had united with riders in an alliance against the monopolistic Union Railroad Company. Courtesy of the Scott Molloy Collection.

sand residents lined the streets to cheer parading Irish Catholic strikers. A riot broke out as supporters blocked the streetcars, obstructed police wagons, and threw rocks at strikebreakers. The uprising, which involved well-heeled residents as well as working people, was a spontaneous expression of community anger over political corruption and corporate power. Over the next weeks, residents expressed their sympathies with their feet through a boycott that crossed social lines. Parents urged children to harass teachers who rode the trolleys. Merchants refused to sell to scabs. On June 24, French Canadian Catholics attended their annual St. Jean-Baptiste Day festivities wearing "We Walk" badges in support of the overwhelmingly Irish workforce. Their participation was a sign traditional ethnic rivalries were subsiding, at least temporarily, as residents united in their fury over corporate abuse.[7]

Denominational tensions weakened too as the clergy came together to support the workers and what W. A. Gardner, a Methodist minister, called their "industrial rights." The Catholic Church was especially passionate in its support for the Irish strikers. Although Catholics deplored violence, the *Visitor* explained, they recognized that "the right to combine, and by combining to bring a company to its senses, is an unalienable part . . . of the workingman's charter in an industrial world." In the church's eyes, membership in the American and Christian communities entitled workers to rights and subjected employers to obligations. "To defraud laborers of their wages is one of 'the four sins crying to heaven for vengeance,'" the *Visitor* warned.[8]

Despite this unprecedented outpouring of support, workers were no match for the company. A police crackdown, financial constraints (the strikers did not receive strike benefits because they had walked out without permission from their national union), and poor planning undermined the protest. Strikers also split among themselves, with older employees who had higher salaries and long-standing company loyalties reluctant to walk out. Outside the streetcars, Socialists and mainstream unionists feuded rather than joining forces. Thus weakened, the workers could not beat the rich and well-organized Union Railroad. By early July the strike had crumbled, and the company took the protesters back on condition they stay out of the union.[9]

The loss of the strike did not mark the end of the popular upsurge. The defeat only intensified the determination of the city's Catholic, ethnic working class, and its middle-class reform allies, to bring machine and monopoly to their knees. If workers could not defeat corporate power in the workplace, they would attack through the ballot box. The strike, in fact, had clarified links between workplace protest and political action. On the first day of the walkout, 150 strikers marched to Providence City Hall to register. By the time registration closed in late June, records were set in fifteen of the state's thirty-eight municipalities, most of them working-class districts. In September, unionists marched in the largest Labor Day parade in state history bearing signs that demanded better representation in elected office and an end to machine rule. Like the strike itself, these were issues around which the city's diverse reform coalition could rally. The popular uprising thus continued in full force, shifting its focus from the streets to the polls.[10]

As November approached, Democrats led voters into battle against the railroad. The moment had come for citizens to choose "whether the people of the city of Providence are to govern or whether a corporation is going to govern," Democratic Mayor Daniel Granger argued. "We can abolish this government of bosses, corrupters and bribers and have a government of, for and by the people," machinist John T. Cannon agreed in a speech to the Economic League. As in the Dorr War, activists sought legitimacy by invoking the republican principle of popular sovereignty. Members of the clergy, for their part, lent the movement authority grounded in religion. Recognizing a moral imperative in the good government crusade, Episcopalian bishop Thomas March Clark circulated a pastoral letter that encouraged men to do their duty as voters. The *Visitor,* for its part, waxed poetic in its efforts to get out the vote. "In a democracy the suffrage is not merely a right, it is a duty to be fulfilled conscientiously, and at some personal sacrifice," the Catholic newspaper wrote. "When public spirit dies out, the democratic form of government passes into the worst of tyrannies."[11]

Because the property rule crippled working-class power in city elections, reformers focused on the gubernatorial campaign and assembled a team that appealed to voters across ethnic, class, and religious lines. The nominee, Lucius Garvin, who had headed the ERA in the 1880s, was a doctor and former legislator known for his commitment to working-class causes. Born in Knoxville, Tennessee, in 1841 and educated at Amherst College and Harvard Medical School, Garvin came to Rhode Island in 1867 to practice medicine in Lonsdale, a mill village just north of Providence. His practice opened his eyes to the horrific living and working conditions in industrial communities, and he became a passionate advocate for working people. Garvin entered politics in 1883 as a state representative from Cumberland and served sixteen terms in the General Assembly. There he fought for a ten-hour workday, woman suffrage, a constitutional convention (which could undo the inequitable voting laws), and the New York reformer Henry George's "single tax" plan (which would have done away with private land ownership and exploitative landlords). In his speech accepting the Democratic nomination in 1902, Garvin brought together nineteenth-century producerism with twentieth-century progressivism by calling for an alliance between exploited labor and honest capital against monopoly and its political cohorts. His running mate was Adelard Archambault of Woonsocket, nominated in hope of attracting French Canadian and Catholic voters.[12]

Garvin and Archambault proved a winning combination. In a major upset, they defeated antistrike governor Charles Kimball by a margin of almost eight thousand votes. The Democrats had won the governorship for only the sixth time since 1855, thanks to the support of Catholics, workers, immigrants, Prohibitionists, Socialists, and independent Republicans. In capturing the state's highest elected office, the reformers experienced their greatest victory since the Bourn Amendment. "The Brayton machine came pretty near being thrown into the junk heap on Tuesday," the *Journal* observed.[13]

Once in office, however, Garvin was unable to enact an ambitious agenda that included reapportioning the legislature, allowing voters to propose constitutional amendments, and cracking down on electoral fraud. In recent years the General Assembly presciently had robbed the governor of most budgetary and appointive powers for fear the office would fall into reformist hands. This turned the governor into one of the state's "administrative mummies," as Lincoln Steffens put it, who wielded very little power. Republican lawmakers even felt free to humiliate the new governor by walking out for a smoke when he rose to speak. The legislature easily frustrated the chief executive and his supporters by weakening the ten-hour law and granting the Union Railroad a perpetual franchise. "The Democrats didn't do anything but elect a governor who can't do anything but sign notaries' commissions and a lieutenant-governor who can't do anything," "Boss" Brayton remarked with glee. In 1904, the Republicans voted out the upstart governor after two one-year terms and reasserted their grip on the State House. The carefully crafted Bourn Amendment had achieved its goal of extending the franchise without altering the status quo.[14]

At its core, the 1902 uprising was an attempt to reframe the relationship between citizens and the state. Catholic ethnics and Yankee reformers had asserted the supremacy of governed over government and demanded economic protections as well as political access. In addition to rights as voters (participating as equals in democratic elections), they demanded rights as consumers (reasonable prices and adequate services) and workers (fair wages and working conditions). They sought a new conception of citizenship that moved beyond a narrow set of legal guarantees to encompass a broader range of political and economic rights, but the outcome of their uprising suggested the governing system was too biased to allow for reform. To the dismay of the Catholic hierarchy, some responded by seeking change from outside and found a home in the Socialist Party.

"THOU SHALT MAKE THE HIGHEST POSSIBLE USE OF THY VOTE": THE SOCIALIST MOVEMENT

The Socialist Labor Party (SLP) had made a disappointing debut in Providence in the election of 1894, but since then its influence had grown steadily. Its anticapitalist message gained credibility during the 1890s as a depression ravaged working-class communities and mainstream reform movements failed. The radicals also benefited from the surge in working-class militancy, and by the turn of the century a vibrant Socialist Party had overtaken the faction-ridden SLP. In 1906 the new organization reported nine locals statewide, two of them in Providence, with a total of 240 members. Its leaders were Fred Hurst, a native-born merchant of British descent who had started his career as a factory operative; Henry Thomas, a German-born interior decorator; and John Floyd, a cigar maker of unspecified origin. Although last names are an unreliable gauge of ethnicity, it is worth noting that most names that appeared in local newspapers in connection with the party indicated British or German background, with a smattering of Irish and French Canadian (and thus likely Catholic) representation. The city's Italians worked separately through their own Italian Socialist Federation. Although the Socialists' official ranks were small, their influence was not limited to the size of their membership or the number of votes they polled. Robert Grieve, a union printer and reform writer who served as Garvin's private secretary, claimed in a 1906 article that the movement "has had a wide and far-reaching influence, with the result that there is a large amount of latent socialistic sentiment which only needs a suitable occasion and leaders of character and ability to make itself felt." One stronghold was Olneyville, a neighborhood populated by Irish and French Canadian Catholics who stood to benefit from socialism's pro-worker program yet were under enormous clerical pressure to oppose the movement.[15]

Despite some working-class support, local Socialists were not recruiting effectively among organized labor. Several years earlier, the national SLP leader Daniel DeLeon had appeared in Pawtucket and alienated local unions by denouncing them as "a farce and nothing more than a money-making scheme." Attitudes like this had prompted Providence unions to sever their connections with the SLP, and the new Socialist Party was having trouble restoring friendly relations with labor despite overlaps in goals and membership. Local unions neither rejected socialism altogether nor gave up electoral politics for a "pure and simple" trade unionism, but they preferred to work through the Democrats rather than through the left.[16]

Labor's political strategy reflected two pragmatic factors. First, the majority of city workers were Catholics who had been schooled to see socialism as evil and risked the condemnation of priests and coreligionists if they joined the party. Second, voting restrictions and intensive immigration made it difficult for working people to form an effective electoral bloc. As a result they needed to influence politics indirectly by finding advocates within the General Assembly. The Democrats, desperate for the votes of Catholic workers and immigrants, were delighted to form a partnership, and cooperation in the 1902 uprising had cemented the relationship. As a result, the city's labor leaders strengthened their ties with the Democrats at a time when industrial cities such as Brockton, Massachusetts, and Milwaukee were electing Socialist mayors.[17]

Recognizing the difficulty of separating union workers from their Democratic allies, Socialists intensified their appeals to the city's unorganized majority. In so doing they sought to draw working people away from ethnic and religious communities and into a shared "subculture of opposition" that supplemented political loyalties with community ties. The party sponsored balls, banquets, and picnics and appealed to families with special units for women and children. In 1913, a Ladies Auxiliary even held a "Night Before Lent Basket Party and Social Scatter" at Providence Textile Hall. Through activities like these, the party provided members with a social community as well as a political home.[18]

The Socialists were particularly concerned with attracting working-class women. Women wielded considerable influence over family and community life and thus occupied critical positions in blue-collar neighborhoods although they could not vote. The party spoke to them as workers and wives, acknowledging their distinctive problems and priorities. "Women have infinitely more to gain under the Co-operative Commonwealth than men have, because they suffer more under the present system," Margaret Haile noted in her weekly "Talks to Women" column. Haile and her colleagues at the *Labor Advocate* promised female readers socialism would bring them economic independence and political rights, at the same time that they appealed to women more concerned about familial survival than individual freedoms. A 1913 article titled "Why Should a Housewife Be a Socialist?" explained that socialism would reduce prices of household necessities and a woman, thus freed from some economic worries, could be "a brighter, better and kinder wife and mother."[19]

Appeals like this recognized that it was less controversial to appeal to women as caregivers and moral guardians than as political activists. Implying socialism was an avocation rather than a political statement, Haile urged women to spread the word as "missionary work." Encouraging them to see their roles as mothers and Socialists as complementary, her column asked them to train their children in Socialist tenets and songs and support party efforts to limit child labor. Providence women who wished to be Socialists in ways that seemed consistent with traditional gender roles joined Ladies Auxiliaries and handled "the social side of the movement" by organizing fund-raisers and whist drives. Others assumed less conventional roles as speakers, newspaper editors, and traveling lecturers for the Women's Justice Club. The party's approach to women was strategic as well as sexist. By upholding traditional gender roles, the Socialists could argue they were not transforming mothers into activists but simply merging motherhood with activism.[20]

This strategy formed part of a campaign to disprove the popular critique that socialism undermined social stability because it was antifamily, un-American, and un-Christian. According to party members, it was in fact exploitative capitalists who threatened family life and Socialists who fought for "better homes" by demanding shorter hours and limits on child labor. A vote for socialism was a vote for "Home, Family and Children." It also was a vote for America, because with its focus on freedom and opportunity socialism was "the logical conclusion to the Declaration of Independence." Local Socialists took particular care to demonstrate support for the Judeo-Christian traditions so many Rhode Islanders held dear, going to great lengths to illustrate commonality between party tenets and religious beliefs and promote socialism as an alternative site of religious faith and practice. This was a risky strategy that affirmed cherished religious principles yet threatened established places of worship.[21]

Providence Socialists insisted their challenge was to the institutional church rather than to the principles the church purported, but failed, to represent. "The ethics of socialism are identical with the ethics of Christianity," they argued on more than one occasion. "In our society men who preach Christianity are held in high esteem but the men who urge the practice of Christianity are denounced as agitators, mischief makers and cranks," local activist John Francis Smith complained. Claims like this were a defense against the charge that socialism was anti-Christian, as well as a clever manipulation of religious principles. The frequency and passion of such assertions, however, suggest a sincere belief that socialism could implement Christian values in a way the church had failed to.[22]

Providence Socialists had tried to do just that in May 1894 when they opened a "Labor Church" in the Catholic stronghold of Olneyville. Founded by Herbert Casson, a defrocked Methodist minister who had conducted a similar experiment in Lynn, Massachusetts, the "church" was to function as a meeting house in which members learned Socialist principles at a weekly "Sunday school." The Labor Church did more than borrow an institutional structure from places of worship; it also provided an alternative repository for Christian principles. "The Labor Church places itself in the centre of the labor movement, and says: God is here," Casson explained. "The real living religion of our time is to be found in the labor movement." This church's gospel was not Matthew, Mark, Luke, and John, but "the good news of the overthrow of oppression." Members were urged to implement religious principles in industrial life by electing officers who believed in workplace justice. "Thou shalt make the highest possible use of thy vote—regarding it as a most sacred trust," read the church's "Ten Commandments."[23]

The Labor Church enjoyed a short-lived success. "Many fell in with [Casson's] plan," one commentator noted later, "and the organization held a number of meetings." The location of these meetings—Textile Union Hall, Knights of Labor headquarters, and Veteran Fireman's Hall—suggests some support from the mainstream labor movement. Yet the experiment faded from public notice after a year and a half. According to a 1906 retrospective, the church failed once Casson fell out of favor with the city's Socialist leadership because of his moderate politics.[24]

Clerical opposition was no doubt another factor. The Labor Church styled itself as an alternative to the Catholic Church, which was religious home to the vast majority of local workers and whose leaders were the Socialists' staunchest opponents. The antiradical tirades issued by diocesan priests, editors, and lay leaders had several roots. Many Catholics were convinced socialism would undermine social stability and bring the state into family life. They also recognized that antiradicalism was an effective way to prove their own patriotism. Rather than posing a threat to American democracy, they argued, Catholics stood "on the side of law and order and authority against Socialism and Anarchy." Perhaps most important, the Socialist Party was an institutional rival for the limited time and funds of working people. The Labor Church thus served as an early skirmish in a decades-long battle between the Socialist Party and the Catholic Church over which was the true representative of working-class interests and Christian principles.[25]

The church had cause for concern by 1912. By that year the party had grown to eleven branches statewide and become somewhat more diverse in its ethnic makeup—with various branches catering to Jewish, German, English, and Polish members—as well as its gender composition. In addition to a small but committed core of working-class women, the party attracted the support of "a number of bright and gifted women of education and refinement." Over the course of the Progressive Era, these bonds tightened as female activists came to appreciate the Socialists' ardent support for woman suffrage and protective labor laws.[26]

The party's leading light was an Olneyville dentist named James P. Reid. Born into a Catholic family in Providence in 1873, Reid started his career as a bobbin boy in the local mills and was walking picket lines by his teens. He went on to serve as secretary of the National Textile Union, a Providence-based organization with Socialist sympathies, but when the union failed he went to dental college in Philadelphia. Reid returned to practice in Olneyville, the city's activist hotbed, but he saw himself as a Socialist first and a dentist second and was known for undercharging his working-class clients. Reid's principled politics soon earned him a reputation as one of the city's preeminent radicals, and he sought election on the Socialist ticket repeatedly beginning in 1895. When he finally was elected to the General Assembly in 1911, he won the distinction of being the first (and, history would prove, the only) Socialist to hold statewide office in Rhode Island. He appealed to workers in his overwhelmingly Democratic and Catholic district by downplaying his party affiliation and practicing a moderate brand of socialism that put bread-and-butter issues first. "I stand for full votes, but I lay more stress on the demand for full meals," he told a crowd in October. Some contemporaries suggested it was Reid's winning personality, not his Socialist politics, that secured his victory; but his beleaguered party welcomed his election as a sign of great things to come.[27]

As the party celebrated this historic victory, its opponents dug in their heels. Republicans and Democrats combined forces behind one candidate to oppose Reid in Providence's ninth district in 1912 and ran a well-funded campaign with the support of Catholic priests and laypeople. The campaign benefited from two well-publicized incidents that reinforced the impression socialism was a threat to organized religion. On July 7, Italian Catholics at Woonsocket's Church of St. Charles gathered for a solemn ceremony to install their Holy Name Society. Seven Italian Socialists allegedly charged into the church and interrupted the ceremony to "denounce God, churches and religion." The event received extensive coverage in the local press and gave Woonsocket officials an excuse to ban political gatherings in city parks, where Socialists had been holding rallies. Although the party denied involvement, the incident furthered the perception Socialists were antireligious.[28]

Equally inflammatory was an episode that occurred later that summer in the General Assembly. When a bill authorizing funding for a Catholic tubercular sanitarium came up for a vote, Reid was among a minority of lawmakers who opposed funding a religious institution and proposed a state-run facility instead. This stand was principled yet politically unwise. Seizing on Reid's vote as an example of his alleged anti-Catholicism, the *Visitor* ran highly charged articles describing the sanitarium as "Object of James P. Reid's Socialistic Hatred." Reid's boosters explained he was not anti-Catholic but pro-American in that he had upheld the constitutional separation between church and state, yet such claims were drowned out amid a torrent of criticism. Critics like Rev. Thomas F. Cullen of St. Patrick's continued to lash out at their renegade coreligionist, claiming it was impossible to be both a Catholic and a Socialist. "The one lies antithetically against the other," the priest claimed, "and if the church is right, the Socialist is certainly wrong."[29]

In addition to weakening the Socialists through blistering and often un-fair attacks, Catholic leaders adopted a more positive approach that high-lighted their own commitment to working people. Just as Socialists offered an institutional alternative to the church, the church provided an alterna-tive to the party. "True Socialism Practiced by the Church," ran a *Visitor* headline over an article detailing the diocese's extensive efforts to help the poor. In a 1912 speech to an Italian Holy Name Society, Lawrence Grace, a teamster and Catholic labor leader, called the church labor's "most valuable ally."[30]

Facing formidable opposition, the Socialists fought back with a program designed to appeal to Catholic workers as well as reformers and woman suf-fragists. In addition to calling for public ownership of utilities so the city could provide necessities like coal and electricity at reasonable prices, their platform demanded recognition of unions, trolley transfer tickets, safer fac-tories, and most of all a suffrage extension. Despite this attractive platform, labor activists seemed less interested in Reid's campaign than in electing PCFU president Roderick McGarry secretary of state. Even the support of organized labor would have been inadequate to win Reid a second term. Ending his brief but historic moment in the sun, he lost his reelection bid by a vote of 591 to 396. In seeking to explain this crushing defeat, his sup-porters singled out the church's "disgraceful attack" as a decisive factor. "Knowing that there was not one act in Reid's whole record . . . that was not in the interest of the class he represented, they resorted to lies, and, worst of all, used the religious prejudice of the voters as a weapon in their campaign of abuse," charged the *Labor Advocate*. The *Visitor* willingly took credit for the election results with the gleeful proclamation that it was Catholic voters who had defeated Reid.[31]

In truth, Catholic opposition was only one of several reasons socialism fared worse in Providence than in many other industrial communities. In the first decade of the twentieth century, Socialists captured the mayoralty in thirty-three American cities and won two seats in Congress. In Provi-dence the party never won a seat in municipal government, its statewide suc-cesses were limited to Reid's one term, and its presidential vote was below average. In 1912, the peak of Socialist electoral success in this country, pres-idential contender Eugene Debs polled 6 percent of the vote nationwide but less than 3 percent in Rhode Island and just under 4 percent in Providence.[32]

Entrenched party loyalties and a winner-take-all electoral system put third-party candidates at a disadvantage nationwide, but Providence So-cialists faced special obstacles. They had to win over a working class that was not only largely Catholic but also heavily foreign-born and thus likely to be disconnected from electoral politics. They also confronted a municipal property requirement that prevented almost two-thirds of registered voters from casting ballots in most city elections, thus disenfranchising potential Socialists on the municipal level where they might have wielded most influence. Elsewhere American Socialists tended to fare best in city elections, benefiting from the concentration of working-class voters and their ability to elect representatives on the ward level in a way they could not replicate in larger and more expensive contests. In Providence the property rule made even these small victories difficult. "In many places throughout the United States the Socialists have made a greater impression than they have in Rhode Island," observed the reformer Grieve. "Under our system of property qualification they can hardly hope to do anything of that nature here."[33]

Grieve's statement challenged what would become a popular tenet of U.S. political history. According to this theory, Americans failed to develop a viable left in part because most workers could vote and thus felt welcomed into the state.[34] Because the working people of Providence were partially disenfranchised and had good reason to feel hostile toward the state, their city should have been a Socialist hotbed. It was not. The property qualification combined with the influence of the Catholic Church to defuse the potential of socialism in Providence. The city's Catholic workers may have experienced what the historian Richard Oestreicher calls an "untapped reservoir of class sentiment," embracing left-wing alternatives yet unable to demonstrate their support by voting.[35] Without their votes, socialism remained no more than a vocal fringe movement. Reid's demise ended another attempt to redraw the parameters of American citizenship. In arguing for a workers' democracy, he and his allies implicitly had argued the "real" Americans were the Catholic, ethnic working class; but they had failed to surmount the structural obstacles that stood between new Americans and their inclusive vision of national identity.

"AN UNJUST AND UNREASONABLE DISCRIMINATION": PROTESTING THE PROPERTY RULE

While Reid was experiencing his historic victory and defeat, progressives were waging their own struggles. Since the turn of the century the General Assembly grudgingly had responded to their demands by strengthening the factory inspection law, creating a weak system of workers' compensation, placing some limits on child labor (by banning employment of children under sixteen after 8 P.M.), and instituting a fifty-four-hour workweek for women and children. These were only small steps toward workplace justice, and attempts at antitrust legislation and consumer protection were even less successful. Reformers knew that real change, whether of a progressive or Socialist variety, would remain elusive until the biased electoral laws were amended. Sharing this conviction were the overwhelmingly Catholic children of the 1890s immigrants, who were coming of age and encountering voting restrictions for the first time.[36]

These factors came together to generate new interest in electoral reform. The issue had surfaced repeatedly since the enactment of the flawed Bourn Amendment, but by the 1910s Providence progressives had made voting reform their priority. They called for legislative reapportionment, less onerous registration rules, and an end to vote-buying, but the centerpiece of their movement was overturning the property qualification. The repeal campaign—spearheaded by Democrats and supported by ethnic and Catholic leaders, unionists, and Socialists—resonated with calls for good government and appeared to be the precondition for other reforms. As the campaign progressed, it became clear Rhode Islanders remained deeply divided over how to define membership in the nation. Debates over voting revealed larger differences over who was entitled to be a citizen, to which rights citizens were entitled, and which qualities defined good citizenship.

Suffrage reformers believed the property rule was a significant obstacle to social change because it prevented or discouraged so many potential reformers from voting. Adult men could vote freely in state and federal elections, but the property rule prevented about 60 percent of registered voters from casting ballots in municipal contests. This was a crippling exclusion. The city was the level of government at which progressives in other states achieved some of their most notable victories, but in Providence local affairs were tightly insulated from the demands of Catholic immigrants and ethnics and their progressive allies. "In this city, more than one-half of the voting population does not participate in the affairs of the city government," Mayor Joseph Gainer, a Democrat and Catholic, complained in 1913. "What a relic of the dark ages," Haile, the Socialist columnist, remarked with disgust.[37]

Even though the rule applied only to local elections, activists believed it depressed turnout in state and federal contests as well. Because the vote was a "very important test of citizenship," as the *Visitor* put it, any restrictions on the franchise insulted and alienated voters. "I have frequently been asked: 'Why should I register when I will not be allowed to vote as fully as those owning real estate, or those fortunately assessed for personal property?' " Democratic Congressman George F. O'Shaunessy claimed. "Men feel the indignity of the discrimination made against them by virtue of their poverty."

This 1914 cartoon depicts Charles "Boss" Brayton as a puppeteer controlling the state legislature. Anger against Brayton's corrupt Republican machine, which blocked most of the progressive legislation introduced in the General Assembly, convinced many reformers to make another push to liberalize the voting laws. Drawing by Milton Halladay, courtesy of the Rhode Island Historical Society, RHi X3 1617.

O'Shaunessy and his colleagues believed that until workers were recognized as full citizens, with unrestricted access to the ballot, they would not come to the polls. The property restriction was the greatest barrier between the people and their desire for reform.[38]

This was a winning argument although it rested on specious reasoning. The city's workers had demonstrated strong interest in electoral politics since 1888 despite the voting restrictions. Moreover, high immigration and low rates of naturalization probably played as large a role as the property rule in depressing turnout. The beauty of the argument against the property rule was not its tight logic but its broad appeal. The franchise extension would benefit all working people, Catholic and Protestant, ethnic and native-born, and resonated with middle-class women struggling for their own right to vote. It spoke to Socialists, who believed "the ballot box is the only place where the workingman is on an equality with the capitalist," and progressives who wished to expand the reform electorate. Finally, a franchise extension might discourage radical protest by creating a safety valve for discontent. Without this, warned Richard Comstock, a lawyer and Democratic leader, "there is then left no remedy except revolution." With its political ramifications and symbolic import, the suffrage crusade had potential to unite local activists and win votes for the party that spearheaded the effort.[39]

For all these reasons, Providence residents united across cultural and ideological lines to battle the property rule with tireless energy. At least sixty repeal bills were introduced between 1888 and 1928, and one historian claims that the issue arose in the General Assembly almost daily during the Progressive Era.[40] Democrats sponsored most of the repeal bills, hoping a franchise extension would bring them the majorities that had eluded them for so long. Republicans buried these proposals in committee, having no interest in enfranchising people who were likely to vote them out of office.

Suffrage reformers claimed the "almost medieval" property requirement was undemocratic and even illogical. "It cannot for a moment be contended that being taxed for $134 worth of property gives a man the necessary voting qualifications," Providence Democrat Lewis Waterman charged at a 1911 hearing. "The sooner this constitutional provision is repealed the sooner we will have a republican government in fact as well as in name." Senator Addison Munroe, another Providence Democrat, claimed the voting restriction was inconsistent as well as unfair. "If the registry voter is capable of intelligently spending the money of the State, why is he not capable of spending the money of the city?" he asked. "The registry voter has caused no evil by voting for members of the Legislature, neither will he cause evil if he votes for members of the City Council." The property rule, noted the

Labor Advocate, also suggested local workers were inferior to their counterparts in other states. "Why should the citizen of Rhode Island have less right to vote for Alderman and Councilman than the voter of our neighboring States?" asked the Socialist newspaper. "Is the workman of Rhode Island less intelligent than the worker of New York?" Statements like this echoed arguments the Dorrites had made seventy years earlier, and it was no coincidence that state lawmakers staged their first official tribute to Dorr, complete with a monument, in 1912.[41]

The repealers made eloquent arguments but ran up against fierce resistance that rested on political calculation and philosophical conviction. Republican lawmakers believed that the property rule kept them in power by preventing potential Democrats from voting and thus used control of the General Assembly to uphold the law. Although their resistance rested largely on these narrow political motives, they invoked larger justifications. Some Republicans argued that because most taxes were levied on the local level it was fair to limit the municipal vote to taxpayers, and indeed Rhode Island was not the only state to do so. Others invoked the age-old link between property and good citizenship. The Republicans, industrialists, and small-town voters who favored the property rule agreed the vote was a critical marker of citizenship, one to be limited to a better class of citizens who by accumulating property had proved their commitment to the American values of hard work and private ownership. "What good, responsible, upright person couldn't acquire $200 to be taxed?" asked Republican state senator Christopher Champlin. Sharing Champlin's convictions, William P. Sheffield of Newport suggested raising the property qualification from $134 to $500.[42]

As the population of Catholic immigrants grew, many Rhode Islanders became only more convinced that voters should be property owners with a demonstrated stake in the community. According to the state census, the proportion of residents who were first- or second-generation immigrants had risen to almost 69 percent by 1905. That year also marked a shift in the religious balance of power, as the first and only state census to measure religious preference reported that Catholics now comprised just over half the population in Providence and statewide. The property qualification was an effective way to keep the vote from newcomers who might be unfamiliar with American institutions, planning to return to the old country, or intending to use their votes to secure special treatment for churches and parochial schools. When confronted with a petition drive in 1911, the General Assembly agreed to repeal the property rule only if it were replaced with an educational requirement that would prevent many Catholic immigrants from voting. This sentiment was not limited to elites. Even though labor activists were among the most ardent suffrage reformers, a 1914 editorial in *Union Worker Magazine* cautioned against enfranchising immigrants who intended to remigrate. "We may be narrow and bigoted in our belief," the labor periodical admitted, "but we cannot help but feel that unless a voter has a stake in the country he doesn't care much for the country any more than to get what he can out of it."[43]

Union Worker Magazine's comment echoed nationwide concerns about allowing "undesirable" citizens to vote. Providence suffragists were campaigning to loosen their electoral laws at the very moment that the South was enforcing "Jim Crow" laws that prevented African Americans from voting and other states were limiting the suffrage through literacy tests, poll taxes, residency and property requirements, and complex registration rules. Most popular among southerners, rural dwellers, and the middle and upper classes, these laws were defended as attempts to reduce electoral fraud and ensure an educated electorate; yet they also reflected social prejudices and fears about how poor, nonwhite, and foreign-born citizens would vote. Between 1877 and 1926, those states that had allowed aliens to vote upon declaring their intention to naturalize abandoned the practice. Other states required foreign-born citizens to present naturalization papers before registering or voting (as in Rhode Island), or insisted new citizens wait a certain number of days before casting their first ballots. The federal government, for its part, curbed the foreign vote by tightening immigration and naturalization laws, and a proposal to impose a literacy test on prospective immigrants became more popular.[44]

The literacy test movement reflected a nationwide resurgence in nativism. Anti-immigrant and anti-Catholic sentiment had waned in the early years of the twentieth century, thanks to a spirit of optimism generated by the Spanish-American War, the return of prosperity, and the progressives' promise of peaceful social change. But the nativist impulse intensified again after about 1905 as race theories marked "new" immigrants as biologically inferior, natives blamed newcomers for socialism and the prewar depression, and frustrated reformers felt Catholic conservatives were blocking movements for temperance and woman suffrage. In a classic example of bad timing, Providence suffragists sought to extend full voting rights to Catholic, foreign-born workers at the very moment that nativism was rising and voting restrictions were in vogue.[45]

At the same time that Democrats and labor activists were leading the charge against the property rule, women were campaigning for their own right to vote. Among the leaders was Sara MacCormack Algeo, who later wrote a first-hand account of the local woman suffrage movement. Algeo was born in Cohasset, Massachusetts, in 1876 to parents who had emigrated from Scotland and Northern Ireland. She received a bachelor's degree from Boston University, and in 1899 a teaching position at Cranston High School brought her to Rhode Island. She left her job when she married James Walker Algeo in 1907, bowing to the expectation that married women not work as teachers. Even though marriage put an end to Algeo's paid labor, it marked the beginning of her activist career. During her teaching years she had socialized with educated women who sparked her interest in woman suffrage, and now she agreed to organize a College Equal Suffrage League and became active in RIWSA. Having no children, she devoted her time to the suffrage crusade and studying for her master's degree at Brown, which had opened a women's college in 1891. She received her degree in 1911 but chose not to pursue a doctorate, despite the encouragement of her mentor, in order to focus her considerable energies on woman suffrage. Her commitment to reform was evident not only in her tireless campaigning but also in her decision to name her dachshund puppies Suffrage and Prohibition.[46]

By 1912 the Rhode Island campaign reached what Algeo called "fever heat." Since the defeat of 1886 the movement had won some small but notable victories, securing married women the right to own property (in 1893) and enjoy custody of their children (in 1896). But voting rights remained elusive, and in 1912 the suffragists decided to focus their energies on a presidential suffrage bill. Activities continued year-round, concentrating in Providence during the winter and shifting to Newport (along with its well-heeled leaders) in the warmer months. By 1914 suffragists were seizing every stage they could find, speaking in theaters between films and asking clergymen of all denominations to preach about the movement. The clergy, among them Rev. Gaius Glenn Atkins of Algeo's Central Congregational Church, "responded beautifully," she recalled. The cause continued to confront the opposition of "vice" industries, which knew female voters would support temperance and other social hygiene laws, and female antisuffragists, who believed women wielded more influence outside the corrupt world of electoral politics. Yet the movement picked up the endorsement of prominent Democrats like O'Shaunessy and Comstock (both committed to repealing the property rule too) and a number of local newspapers. Even erstwhile opponents like the *Journal*, Algeo claimed, "saw now that women's hour had struck."[47]

In a November 1913 article in the national *Woman's Journal*, Algeo was pleased to report that the local movement was reaching beyond its traditional Yankee base to attract African Americans (the Rhode Island Union of

Colored Women endorsing the cause), Jews and Irish Catholics (the latter wooed by Mary A. D. Brennan, a Brown-educated lawyer, and Sara Fitz, a teacher from New York), and Norwegians and Swedes ("almost universally in sympathy"). Most notable among the latter were Swedish-born Maria Kindberg and Ingeborg Kinstedt of Providence, who drove a "suffrage automobile" from San Francisco to Washington to promote the cause in 1915. Kinstedt, who served as mechanic, challenged female stereotypes by changing the tires twelve times in the course of the journey.[48]

Another source of strength was improved relations with men campaigning against the property requirement. In many cities, Catholic, ethnic, and working-class voters opposed woman suffrage because they believed in traditional gender roles or feared women would vote for hated reforms like prohibition. In Providence the shared sting of disenfranchisement undermined some of these concerns and created a certain commonality between middle-class Yankee women and ethnic working-class men. So did a mutual commitment to workplace legislation. As a result the two movements overcame some (although certainly not all) of the tensions that had divided them earlier and drew closer during the Progressive Era, offering each other hearty endorsements. In June 1902 the Rhode Island Central Labor Union (RICLU) declared its support for woman suffrage, and twelve years later the state Federation of Labor backed a bill allowing women to vote in presidential elections. In so doing they followed the lead of the AFL, which had endorsed woman suffrage.[49]

These cross-class bonds tightened as woman suffragists joined their counterparts in other states in appealing to laboring women on the grounds that they could use their votes to strengthen unions and improve working conditions. Women "have found that men strikers who had votes were very differently treated than girl strikers who had none," Brennan observed in 1913. "We women, and especially we working women, must have the 'vote' to keep themselves [sic] in the industrial world and to help their fellow-working men by being able to refuse to undercut." Some listeners responded to appeals like this. In February 1914, eleven "self-supporting" women visited Republican governor Aram Pothier to ask his support for a pending suffrage bill. According to an account in the *Labor Advocate*, "the Governor dropped his usual suave manner and gesticulated wildly, while proclaiming that Rhode Island women were used better than in any other States in the Union."[50]

Yet even as some woman suffragists built bridges with working people, others distanced themselves. Echoing a rhetoric employed by suffragists nationwide, RIWSA president Elizabeth Upham Yates urged the General Assembly to enfranchise native-born women in order to outweigh immigrant ballots. "One of the great problems of today is the foreign vote," she told lawmakers at a hearing in March 1910. "The way to keep the beam balanced is to give the vote to the American women." Nativist arguments had broad appeal in a state still fearful of unleashing immigrant and Catholic electoral power. According to a *Journal* reporter who covered the hearing, Yates's testimony received "close attention" and hearty applause. Nativism was a bond that linked Yates to the Rhode Island Association Opposed to Woman Suffrage, which claimed more than seventeen hundred members in 1914. At a hearing before the Senate Committee on the Judiciary in February 1914, Mrs. Charles Warren Lippitt spoke for that group when she warned woman suffrage would mean votes for uneducated (and Catholic) immigrants. "I ask you gentlemen to walk . . . over Federal Hill and Atwells Avenue, through Fox Point or to the city dock, and watch the passengers from a Fabre Line steamer, and then ask yourselves if you believe the addition of these 'women citizens' will tend to reform and elevate the electorate," she suggested.[51]

If female leaders on both sides of the suffrage campaign manipulated nativist sentiment, male activists betrayed their sexism. Woman suffragists may have enjoyed the support of many unionists and Socialists, but they had trouble winning over other male politicians. The Democrats finally endorsed woman suffrage in the 1910s, recognizing that women might support their progressive reforms, but their priority remained repealing the property rule for men. As in 1887, the Catholic hierarchy's response was equally disappointing. The *Visitor*'s stance on woman suffrage was more neutral than antagonistic, yet the diocesan newspaper seemed to consider the vote an inherent right of citizenship only so far as men were concerned. The *Visitor* insisted men had the right to an unrestricted franchise, but one editorial argued against woman suffrage on the grounds the vote was "not a natural right . . . not a right that belongs to us merely as citizens." For at least some male suffragists, citizenship stopped at the gender line.[52]

Although the suffrage activists did not display a perfect unity, they did call for reform with increasingly loud voices. "The sentiment against this particular restriction of the suffrage is not weak nor impotent," Democrat Patrick P. Curran warned the General Assembly. "It is not connected to a particular class. It is not restricted to cranks or idealists." By 1913 the movement had grown too strong to ignore, and Republican lawmakers finally pledged to repeal the property rule. Republican support proved short-lived, however. Once the party swept the November elections it killed the repeal bill, confirming the suspicions of activists who had feared that the endorsement was only a ploy to win votes. Republican legislators also quashed a movement to revise the constitution and refused to endorse the presidential suffrage bill for women (a measure they struck down yet again in 1915). The outcome of the latest crusade to democratize local government was profoundly discouraging to reformers. Years of campaigning had produced nothing but a limited veto for the governor (which could be overridden by a three-fifths vote in the Senate), a few weak antibribery laws, and an inadequate reapportionment of the legislature.[53]

FROM ELECTORAL POLITICS TO THE POLITICS OF DESPERATION

A political era that had begun with the excitement of 1888 ended in the demoralization of 1914. Ethnic Catholics and their reformist allies had sought nothing less than to reshape the concept of citizenship. Their campaigns for workplace laws and full access to the vote suggested that citizenship entailed not just "membership of a nation," as the Supreme Court had ruled in response to a woman suffrage case in 1875, but a complex of economic protections and political rights.[54] These demands sent the message that Catholic immigrants and ethnics who comprised the bulk of the working class were real Americans, deserving the same consideration from government as Anglo-Saxon Protestants who dominated the ruling elite.

The failure of these efforts reflected the inadequacies of electoral politics. The lesson of the 1902 uprising, the Socialist movement, and the repeal crusade was that politics had severe limitations as a vehicle for Catholic immigrants and ethnics. The state's governing system was biased against them, thanks to voting restrictions and a legislature dominated by business interests and small-town Yankees. As Algeo lamented, "the legislature is run in such a fashion that it is practically impossible for any measure looking toward the people's interest to get by."[55] These structural obstacles stymied mainstream reformers as well as radicals. Equally problematic was political disunity among the Catholic majority. Although there were moments of cohesion such as the 1902 strike, and points of agreement such as the repeal campaign, for the most part Catholics still split between the two major parties. Finally and perhaps most important, the ballot box had limited use for Catholic immigrants and ethnics disconnected from electoral politics by language, citizenship, and inexperience as well as voting restrictions. This was especially true for the French Canadians and Italians, who had been far less active than the Irish in the political strivings of the previous decades. In the summer of 1914, a violent uprising on Federal Hill suggested that some new Americans had recognized the limits of electoral politics and turned to more desperate means of protest.

After Italian immigrants looted Frank Ventrone's Atwells Avenue store in August 1914 to protest a rise in pasta prices, the windows were boarded up and police patrolled the neighborhood to prevent further unrest. Photograph from the *Providence Evening Bulletin,* courtesy of the Rhode Island Historical Society, RHi X3 8492.

In August 1914, the city's attention shifted from the suffrage campaign to what were literally bread-and-butter issues. Local merchants used the recent outbreak of hostilities in Europe as an excuse to raise prices, anticipating wartime shortages, and resentments ran especially high among Federal Hill Italians angry about the cost of pasta and other essentials. When officials refused to take action, residents took matters into their own hands. Early on the evening of Saturday, August 29, a mob of angry residents vented their frustrations on Frank Ventrone's Atwells Avenue pasta store, smashing windows and helping themselves to the expensive products before moving on to pillage nearby shops. When officers arrived, protesters shouting "Down with the Police!" attacked patrol wagons in anger over years of harassment by the Yankee and Irish force. As violence escalated from hurled stones and flowerpots to bullets, several police officers and demonstrators were injured. Over the next two weeks, three more riots broke out as residents attacked law enforcement officers and looted local businesses in spontaneous outbreaks of frustration. Stones were thrown, windows broken, stores pillaged and gunfire exchanged as police and firefighters battled thousands of women, men, and children on the streets of Federal Hill. As the *Labor Advocate* put it, "Hunger knows no law." The trouble finally subsided on September 14, when neighborhood grocers agreed to reduce prices. The riots had taken a serious toll, injuring dozens of civilians and police officers and costing merchants some twenty thousand dollars in theft and damages. The "Macaroni Riots" were the worst civil disturbance in Providence since the Dorr War.[56]

The Federal Hill melee represented one more skirmish in the ongoing war over what it meant to be American. Although focused on food prices, the riot reflected larger resentments over poverty, political impotence, and the difficulty of preserving old ways in the new country. It was no coincidence that the uprising focused on traditional foodstuffs, which formed a cultural battleground between Catholic immigrants seeking to preserve customs and Protestant social workers promoting "American" ways of life. In calling attention to the price of pasta rather than milk or eggs, rioters pointed to the cultural challenges as well as economic hardships they faced. As an astute reporter for *L'Eco del Rhode Island* put it, they spoke out against "hunger, unemployment and systematic discrimination in America."[57]

Although radical organizers in the IWW and Italian Socialist Federation helped organize the discontent, the riots were spontaneous grassroots demonstrations that attracted broad support within the Italian American community. Arrest records suggest it was not limited to the poorest and most desperate, or to the young and reckless. And unlike other Progressive Era food riots, including a 1910 kosher meat boycott in South Providence, this was not primarily a female affair. Instead the dispossessed came together across social lines in one powerful protest. The Macaroni Riots capped off four years of bitter and often unsuccessful labor agitation, some organized by the IWW, as well as two long and fruitless decades of seeking change through electoral politics. The violent uprising was testimony to ethnic Catholics' inability to resolve their problems through peaceable means, whether their strategy was workplace protest, socialism, or progressive reform. It was a crowd action by people who generally could not or did not vote, whether because of suffrage restrictions or low rates of citizenship. The riot illustrated Catholic immigrants' frustrations over failure to win rights they considered theirs as Americans, as well as enduring ethnic tensions (between Italian rioters and Irish police officers as well as within the Italian community) that made pan-Catholic political action so difficult.[58]

II

THE POTENTIAL OF CATHOLIC ACTIVISM

5

"THE CENTER OF SOCIAL LIFE"

Ethnic Communities and the Catholic Church

We all possess a propensity to gather together in assemblies of one kind or another, and when the Church has organized a society for us, why go elsewhere?

—William Mahar, Providence Holy Name Union,
Visitor, January 12, 1917

THE CHURCH AND THE IMMIGRANTS

In May 1922, the Holy Ghost Council of the KOC organized an eight-day May Festival on Broadway. The *Visitor* announced that the event was to resemble "eight 'Arabian Nights,' eight wonderful evenings of merry-making and joy unexcelled." Activities included nightly open-air dancing as well as games and booths, with different entertainments each evening. The organizers, representing one of the city's largest Italian parishes, brought recreation together with politics by arranging for prominent Catholic office-holders to deliver speeches. With something for everyone, the event was a sure crowd-pleaser. "Not a stone is being left unturned to make the event a success and a source of happiness to all who visit the grounds," the *Visitor* promised.[1]

The Holy Ghost festival is indicative of the central role Catholic parishes played in ethnic communities and politics in the first decades of the twentieth century. The Catholic Church, by virtue of its accessibility and the extraordinary range of services it provided, was the most important institution in the city's ethnic neighborhoods. Many new Americans, finding it difficult to promote their interests through unions or electoral politics, instead turned to parishes as institutions that welcomed and protected them. There they found entertainment and social fellowship through events like the May festival, as well as spiritual solace and material relief. They derived a host of religious and practical benefits by joining the lay organizations that abounded in this era and, as chapter 6 will show, used these groups as political organizing spaces.

Available statistics suggest a significant proportion of Providence Catholics had both a cultural identification and an institutional relationship with the church. In the 1905 state census, 96 percent of Providence residents with an Irish father and 99 percent with an Italian father described themselves as Catholic.[2] In a federal count taken one year later, Catholics made up more than 76 percent of all Providence church members although they comprised just over half the population. Parochial school attendance rates further suggest a relatively strong commitment to Catholic faith and values. Between 1890 and 1919, the proportion of all Providence children age five to fifteen who attended parochial school was consistently about 14 percent (with rates much higher among the Irish and French Canadians than the Italians). Because Catholics constituted about half the population in these years, this figure can be doubled to suggest that close to 30 percent of Catholic children were enrolled in parochial school. This statistic no doubt disappointed priests, who felt every youth should attend a parish school; yet it was fairly impressive at a time when so many Catholics were new immigrants with little money to spare for education.[3]

Neither censuses nor school records measured church attendance rates, but at least one informal survey suggested local Catholics were committed churchgoers. In 1891, the *Journal* polled priests and parishioners in response to the editors' concern that "a spirit of unbelief has developed among the common people." The results suggested that such a fear was unfounded. The survey found that 90 percent of the city's Catholics attended Mass regularly and another 5 percent were absent because of physical disability or work conflicts, leaving just 5 percent unaccounted for. One priest claimed some workers wanted to attend church so badly that they hired replacements to fill their jobs on Sundays. The results of this survey must, of course, be interpreted with great caution. The Catholic Church typically counted all baptized coreligionists as church members, whereas some other denominations determined membership more strictly.[4] It is likely that the survey was biased toward churchgoers, and that some respondents described themselves as regulars even if they attended only on special occasions. Finally, the numbers might have been far lower had the survey been taken twenty years later after the mass influx of Italians.

The diocesan historian Robert W. Hayman suggests that closer to two-thirds of Providence Catholics were regular churchgoers in the early twentieth century, with attendance higher among the Irish and French Canadians than the Italians. If this statistic is accurate, Providence churches fared better than their counterparts in other communities. The historian Jay Dolan estimates that half the nation's Catholics attended Mass regularly in this period and closer to a quarter were active in parish life. Attendance rates may have been higher in Providence because two of the three major Catholic groups placed so much value on churchgoing, and because the large size of the Catholic population lent the church an impressive institutional presence. On the basis of Hayman's estimate and the other statistics, it is safe to infer that a majority of Providence Catholics (and perhaps even a sizable majority) were affiliated with a parish in some way. This makes the church by far the most important arena of interaction in ethnic neighborhoods. Protestant ministers like Harry Kimball noted this with envy, speaking wistfully of the Catholic Church's "hold on the working man."[5]

Parishes prospered in Providence, even among traditionally indifferent groups like the Italians, for four reasons. The first was faith. Many Catholics, even those who arrived as lukewarm believers, looked to religion for solace as they confronted the trials of life in the new world. The second was that even newcomers who had been only occasional churchgoers recognized the American parish as a substitute for village and familial networks that had sustained them at home. Third, ethnic parishes helped to preserve embattled old world identities as immigrants faced pressure to assimilate. Finally, churches served as alternative political vehicles for new Americans who lacked other effective means of self-assertion.[6]

"A BEEHIVE OF ACTIVITY": CHURCH AS COMMUNITY

Across Catholic America, from Boston to Butte, Montana, the parish was the nucleus of neighborhood life.[7] No institution could match it as a source of service and sociability, relief and recreation. This reflected a conscious effort by priests to make parishes much more than places of worship. American Catholicism experienced tremendous growth during the Progressive Era, but it easily could have foundered. Even as a flood of immigrants presented enormous potential for expansion, rival institutions competed for their loyalties and funds. Protestant missions and settlement houses presented conversion as a route to assimilation and upward mobility; left-wing groups like the Socialist Party and IWW seemed to menace church principles; and a secular culture of films and dancehalls threatened Catholic family values with a freer sexuality.[8] To lure coreligionists from these temptations, the church dispensed charity, educated and Americanized its members, and promoted upward mobility. It kept Catholics informed about religious and civic events, sponsored neighborhood celebrations, hosted entertainments, and organized an extensive network of lay societies.

In the decades of mass immigration, when immigrants' needs were great and sources of public assistance few, the church played an indispensable role as social service provider. The diocese operated hospitals, orphanages, and working girls' homes—among them the St. Vincent de Paul Infant Asylum, St. Maria's Home, and House of the Good Shepherd. Individual parishes supplemented these institutions with benefits such as clothing and food baskets. Father Joseph Bourgeois of St. John's in Arctic, a village west of Providence, gave away coal to his poorest French Canadian parishioners. Father Cooney of St. Edward's helped the Irish mill workers in his congregation deal with difficult employers and drunken spouses. St. Bartholomew's and St. Ann's ran day nurseries for their Italian American congregations. The St. Ann's Nursery and Industrial School, founded in 1914, was open from 6 A.M. to 6 P.M. daily to care for the children of working mothers "irrespective of creed or condition of life."[9]

Whereas the neediest Catholics looked to the church for charity, the ambitious took advantage of educational programs that helped them prosper in the new world. More than one-quarter of young Catholics attended parochial schools that provided instruction, encouraged upward mobility, and promoted assimilation as well as knowledge of homeland culture. Other parish resources enhanced participants' skills as workers and homemakers. At the St. Ann's Nursery and Industrial School, run by the Maestre Pie Venerini sisters, young children received instruction in "Froebel's system of work" as well as "numeration" and letter-writing. Older students learned composition, conversation, and dictation along with gender-specific work skills. According to a parish history, girls took classes in cooking, sewing, and embroidery, while boys were trained "along the lines of industrial work." So many local families recognized the value of these courses that by 1918 the school had 183 pupils, sixty-eight paying no tuition. The School of Domestic Arts at St. Mary's, an Irish congregation in Pawtucket, was even more successful. Founded in 1900, the school offered girls and young women free instruction in cooking, dressmaking, and home nursing. The classes proved so popular that the school decided to admit students regardless of faith or nationality, and by 1914 more than four hundred were enrolled.[10]

These French Canadian parochial school students, shown here in an undated photograph, were among many Catholics who used parish resources to achieve upward mobility. Courtesy of the Providence Catholic Diocesan Archives.

Another important skill parishes taught was how to blend into American society. Catholic priests worried that newly arrived coreligionists would patronize Protestant-run institutions like the Immigrant Educational Bureau, which met newcomers at dockside, and Sprague House, a settlement that catered to Italian Americans in Mount Pleasant and Federal Hill. To counter the appeal of these social service providers, priests helped immigrants to become American and middle-class without leaving the parish. According to a 1910 profile in the *Journal*, Father Antonio Bove of St. Ann's felt "the Italians could be best taught the principles of their religion and the duties of good citizenship by educating them according to American methods and American ideas." To this end he gave religious instruction in English, even as his parish's industrial school offered Italian lessons. The industrial school's evening program also instilled "principles of Americanization" so that "the sense of loneliness which the newly arrived foreigner feels, may be forgotten in the promised possession of citizenship." Programs like these made "the Italians and their children good Christians and good Americans," Bove told the *Journal* reporter. "There will be no enemies of society or civilization among them." The Catholic mayor, Joseph Gainer, agreed, commending Bove for making "his people God-fearing, home-loving citizens."[11]

Yet the same priests who promoted assimilation joined laypeople in using, or at least acknowledging, the parish as a repository for ethnic identity. Harkins, who led the diocese from 1886 to 1921, forbade explicitly nationalist expressions such as blessing Italian (or American) flags at church.[12] Yet like his counterparts in other dioceses, he agreed to create national parishes that served specific ethnic groups and whenever possible were run by compatriots. Laypeople eagerly used these national parishes to preserve links to the old world. This trend crossed class and ethnic lines, although it was most pronounced among French Canadians and recent immigrants from all countries.

Catholics wove ethnicity into faith in a variety of ways. French Canadians considered the church the centerpiece of *survivance* and were fiercely determined to speak the native language in their parishes and parochial schools. Saint Jean-Baptiste Day, held every June 24 to celebrate the patron saint of French Canada, symbolized the community's intertwined religious and national origins. At the 1902 celebration the public schools were closed and the streets decorated, and festivities included a Mass and a parade in which church and state officials marched. In its coverage *Le Jean-Baptiste* reinforced this link between civic and sacred with a headline that translates as, "Love for the church and the homeland mingle harmoniously."[13]

Irish Catholics also drew on religion to maintain connections to the old world. They too used their annual celebration, St. Patrick's Day, to express ethnic and religious identity. Yet unlike the French Canadians they did not have to struggle to give their parishes a homeland flavor, for their dominance in the American hierarchy lent the church a distinctly Hibernian tone. Individual parishes reinforced this link by promoting homeland nationalism. Relations between the American church and Irish nationalists could be tense, to be sure, as some groups advocated violent tactics that the Catholic hierarchy could not condone; yet over time there was rapprochement. In the 1880s many Irish American priests endorsed the Irish Land League, an organization devoted to agrarian reform through peaceful tactics, and in Providence St. Edward's sponsored a chapter. By the turn of the century, the city's Irish Catholics regularly debated Home Rule in parish lecture series and collected funds for Irish freedom fighters at church. In 1905, St. Mary's chose St. Patrick's Day as the moment to dedicate its new parish hall. It was natural for Holy Trinity in Central Falls, two-thirds of whose parishioners had Irish-born parents, to use the parish as a vehicle for homeland nationalism.

In March 1920, the congregation raised more money than any other parish in the diocese to support Eamon de Valera's new Irish Republic. Harkins, himself of Irish origin, appears to have sympathized with these efforts. In 1910 Ellen Ryan Jolly of Pawtucket, national chair of the Irish Historical Committee of the Ladies Auxiliary of the AOH, congratulated him on his "recent splendid aid and effective energy" in introducing the "serious study of Irish history" into the diocesan schools.[14]

For the Italians, links between religion and ethnicity tended to manifest themselves outside the parish. Elaborate festivals honoring village patron saints celebrated the homeland and affirmed community solidarity and religious faith. At a typical *festa,* Italian Americans would parade through the streets bearing religious and national icons, stop at church for Mass, then proceed to a picnic and band concert. Demonstrations like these, which the historian Robert Orsi calls "religion in the streets," claimed neighborhood space as sacred space and asserted lay control over expressions of faith.[15] Organized by mutual aid societies and taking place largely outside the church, they often antagonized priests, who resented the threat to their authority and drain on parish finances. But the Italians occasionally imitated the Irish, and pleased their priests, by using the parish itself as a base for activities that connected them to the homeland. In 1909, St. Ann's took up a generous collection for victims of an earthquake that had devastated Messina and Calabria a few months earlier. Ironically it was Bove, the ardent Americanizer, who encouraged parishioners to send money to Italy. For all three ethnic groups, then, the national parish created a bridge between old country and new, enabling immigrants to participate in an American institution without abandoning homeland ties.[16]

Another way in which the church facilitated this transition was by providing information that helped immigrants adjust to their new surroundings. The Sunday *Visitor* was founded in 1875 as the official voice of the diocese. At first the editorship alternated between priests and laypeople, but after 1908 it was filled exclusively by clerics. Many of these priest-editors, among them Rev. J. C. Tennian of St. Mary's in Pawtucket, were drawn from Irish American parishes. Editors worked with a board of directors appointed by the local hierarchy to set newspaper policy, which meant the paper's pronouncements were carefully screened and reflected a distinctively Irish American approach to Catholic and American life. Contents alternated between sacred and secular. The *Visitor* printed local and international Catholic news but also reported on government affairs, offered health and household tips, and took stands on everyday problems such as street repairs and the price of trolley tickets. Run and largely read by Irish Americans, it focused on the news and needs of that community. A number of parishes supplemented the *Visitor* by issuing their own bulletins. Around 1900, Tennian began to publish a small magazine for St. Mary's that carried city as well as parish news. St. Bartholomew's, which served Italian Americans in the Silver Lake neighborhood, started its own bulletin in 1923. *La Campana di Silver Lake* published news of parish events and statistics and created "a bond of unity between pastor and people."[17]

These newsletters encouraged readers not only to attend Mass but also to take advantage of the parish's extensive recreational life. Priests and laypeople recognized that parish socials raised money, cemented loyalty, forged community, and diverted participants from saloons and dancehalls by providing wholesome entertainment. As a result, in any given year the typical ethnic parish sponsored an impressive social calendar of fairs, plays, concerts, bingo games, costume parties, and dances. The annual picnic was much anticipated by Irish congregations, banquets were popular in French Canadian parishes, and patron saint festivals were banner events in Italian neighborhoods. Irish and Italian parishes organized elaborate fairs, offering attractions such as shooting galleries and pie-eating contests and lasting as long as two weeks. According to a history of St. Edward's, "huge crowds turned out for these events." It was easy to see why. "For a dime's admission, one enjoyed a full evening of entertainment and met all one's friends and neighbors." The Italian parish of Holy Ghost exhibited just as much spirit as the Irish St. Edward's, as the aforementioned May festival suggests. During the summers, congregations left Providence for excursions. At the August 1878 outing of the St. Edward's Sunday school, more than eight hundred children and adults boarded thirty-two "party wagons" that transported them to the seaside to the accompaniment of a brass band. They spent the day at the beach enjoying games, boating, baseball, dancing, and dinner. The French Canadian parish of Our Lady of Consolation, in Pawtucket, organized regular boat excursions to St. Ann's shrine in Fall River. Although these outings were billed as "pilgrimages," the parish history notes, "everyone really had a good time." The 'pilgrims' would sing all the way to Fall River, their vocal cords lubricated by beer that the priest would buy wholesale and sell on board.[18]

In addition to attending annual events like the summer outing or church fair, Catholics congregated in parish halls on a weekly and even daily basis. By the Progressive Era churches were building impressive recreational facilities, in part to compete with well-funded Protestant missions and settlements. Even parishes that served working-class populations offered expensive features such as billiard rooms, libraries, reading rooms, gymnasiums,

The St. Ann's baseball team, shown in this undated photograph with Rev. Antonio Bove in the boater hat, was among a plethora of parish organizations laypeople could join. Groups like these encouraged Catholics to socialize with coreligionists and within the church. Courtesy of the Providence Catholic Diocesan Archives.

and bathing facilities. The St. Edward's hall was a good example. Completed in 1917, the facility was open every evening and all day Sunday to parishioners bearing membership cards. It boasted a bowling alley and poolroom, hosted dances and lectures, offered sewing classes, and sponsored weekly basketball games. It was little wonder that, according to the parish historian Rev. Richard Walsh, the hall "soon became a beehive of activity and the center of the social life of the community." Facilities like this also were available in churches serving newer immigrants. St. Bartholomew's (Italian) and Our Lady of Consolation (French Canadian) showed movies on Sundays after Mass. In tune with the nationwide Catholic "decency" campaign, this tradition encouraged parishioners to view clergy-sanctioned films rather than the more risqué alternatives offered at public theaters, as well as ensuring that Catholic boys would meet Catholic girls at the movies. The parents of Edward George St.-Godard, who grew up to be pastor of Our Lady of Consolation, began their courtship when they served as projectionist and pianist at the parish's silent movie showings.[19]

"A RELIGIOUS SOCIETY SUITABLE FOR EVERY PERSON": THE VARIETIES OF LAY ORGANIZATION

Parish halls also provided meeting space for the lay societies that abounded in Providence and across the nation after about 1880. Catholic religiosity intensified in this era as the hierarchy urged women and especially men (traditionally less regular churchgoers) to receive the Eucharist regularly and as a growth in available priests made the sacraments more accessible. These changes fueled a rise in devotionalism—prayers and rituals practiced outside as well as inside church and coordinated by sodalities and confraternities associated with particular saints. The increase in lay organization also formed part of the larger effort to lure immigrants from rival institutions by making the church a community center as well as a place of worship. Moreover, the growth of a Catholic middle class meant that more church members had time and resources to devote to parish life.[20]

"The best evidence of the vigor of any parish is the condition of its societies," the *Providence Tribune* declared in 1914. By this token Providence was a vigorous diocese. In the first decades of the twentieth century, parishioners could join an impressive variety of organizations. Societies generally targeted a particular group (women, men, young adults, or children) and served a specific function: religious (altar guilds and Holy Name societies); moral (temperance groups and Catholic clubs); charitable (women's sewing circles and men's St. Vincent de Paul societies); educational (debating clubs, lecture series, study groups, and literary circles); and recreational (bands, sports teams, drama societies, glee clubs, and scout troops). In 1910 Bove boasted, "In my parish there is a religious society suitable for every person in the congregation." Most of the city's other pastors could have made the same assertion.[21]

A number of societies brought laypeople of all ages into the spiritual heart of the church by engaging them in explicitly religious activities. After first communion children typically joined boys' and girls' sodalities that received the sacraments together once a month. Women who joined the Rosary and Scapular Society repaired vestments and baked communion bread. Those in the Altar Society prepared the church for services and arranged special Masses to commemorate deceased members, thus providing benefits that extended beyond the grave. As Leslie Woodcock Tentler observes, "the promise of a well-attended funeral was an important drawing card for many parish societies in this period." Whereas these groups catered to women, the Holy Name Society rallied men behind a pledge to avoid using the Lord's name in vain. This confraternity encouraged a "spirit of manly piety," reflecting a nationwide effort to promote a "muscular Christianity" that would convince husbands and sons to join wives and sisters at Mass. Church leaders were careful to remind potential members of the benefits they would enjoy. As the *Visitor* noted in 1913, membership "keeps him closer to the Church and as a consequence closer to Almighty God. There is no telling the number of men who have attained their eternal salvation as a direct result of their having affiliated themselves with the Holy Name Society." This pitch was effective, and by 1919 the diocesan Holy Name Union boasted thirty thousand members.[22]

Whereas these groups fostered piety, others promoted religious education. At St. Edward's the Children of Mary and Christian Doctrine societies trained women and men to teach Sunday school, thereby educating both adults and children in the catechism. St. Bartholomew's organized a Children of Ave Maria Club for young people in hope of fostering "many religious habits among them." St. Patrick's was particularly concerned with encouraging piety among boys, less likely than their sisters to become practicing Catholics. Rev. Martin F. Reddy, who led the parish from 1915 to 1948, put a masculine stamp on a traditionally feminine ritual by organizing a Marian procession for boys every May. According to a history of the congregation, "he often boasted that this was the only parish in the diocese where the boys had their own special Sunday to honor Mary . . . and he gloried in the fact that they carried on their ceremonies without feminine assistance."[23]

Some societies pursued a mission that had more to do with Catholic values than religious doctrine. At the Italian parish of St. Bartholomew's the Catholic Club, open to men age sixteen to thirty-five, described itself as "a group of sincere Catholics that will set an example of good to the parish, promote intellectual culture of its members and procure their healthy and moral amusements." The CTAU organized men and boys, mostly Irish Americans, behind a pledge to avoid alcohol. The St. Edward's chapter founded a parish library and sponsored social activities, but its major responsibility was to organize temperance rallies. A parish history describes these late nineteenth-century gatherings in terms reminiscent of Protestant revival meetings: "The building would be packed to overflowing. The large crowd, the roaring organ, and the mass singing of favorite hymns created an atmosphere of unity and commitment."[24]

Literary and political education was the mission of a number of parish societies. By the 1890s, some ten thousand Catholics belonged to more than 250 reading circles across the country, and Providence parishioners embraced the trend. The Brownson Lyceum, which formed in 1857 and operated a downtown meeting room at 193 Westminster Street from 1878 to 1899, enabled Catholic men to attend lectures and participate in discussions and debates. By the time the lyceum closed, eight similar groups were carrying on the same work. One offshoot, the Young Men's Literary Association at St. Edward's, ran a library open after work and all day Sunday—hours that suggested an eagerness to attract working people. The Faber Reading Circle, organized by two young women in Cathedral parish in 1890, met on Sunday afternoons. At each meeting a member presented an essay and the group read from one of Shakespeare's plays.[25]

By the turn of the century, the reading circle was less popular but other educational forums were taking its place. The Irish Americans in St. Michael's Catholic Club, formed in 1906, presented papers at weekly meetings and invited a prominent public figure to speak once a month. At St. Mary's in Pawtucket, the Young Men's Club House included a library with four hundred books and a reading room stocked with magazines and newspapers. In 1912 the Holy Name Society of St. Charles in Woonsocket formed a School for Social Studies to sponsor lectures and encourage debate on "social, industrial and economical" issues. By 1918 the Union of Catholic Parish Clubs was sponsoring a lecture bureau, essay contests, and two debating leagues for its male members. Some Catholics became accomplished public speakers through activities like these. In 1923, a team of Italian Americans from Holy Ghost beat a Boston congregation in a debate over the League of Nations. The *Visitor* proudly attributed the victory to the popularity of the Holy Ghost lyceum, whose weekly lecture series "turns out orators and debaters as a Ford factory does Fords." Although educational forums were most popular in established Irish parishes, enthusiasm clearly crossed ethnic and class lines.[26]

Despite these variations in purpose and membership, lay organizations shared several basic characteristics. One was the expectation that members donate their time on a regular basis. Societies typically met once or twice a month but sometimes as often as weekly. Many assembled after Mass on Sunday, combining religious observance with organizational duties, but just as many gathered on weeknights. The St. Edward's sewing circle, for example, provided a regular social outlet for Irish American women on Friday evenings. Lay society meetings took place inside the church or nearby in the parish hall or parochial school, and agendas varied. In 1907, the *Visitor* described a typical Holy Name meeting as follows: "recitation of the office, instruction on practical topics and benediction of the Most Blessed Sacrament." Other societies had more secular programs, often focused on organizing the socials and fund-raisers for which all were responsible. The tenor of the meeting reflected the size as well as mission of the group. In the 1900s and 1910s lay societies typically reported memberships of one to two hundred, but in 1918 the Holy Name Society of St. Mary's in Olneyville boasted a stunning one thousand members. Subcommittees, by contrast, could be as small as three.[27]

Another commonality among societies was a balance, or tension, between clerical and lay control. Parish governance had grown steadily less democratic since the antebellum period as bishops across the nation asserted authority over Catholic life. Before the Civil War it was common for elected lay trustees to hold title to parish property, administer finances, appoint pastors, and even manage parochial schools. This trend was particularly marked in German parishes, less so among Irish congregations that had a stronger tradition of clerical control. But the power of lay trustees waned over the course of the nineteenth century as the church became more centralized and Irish-controlled, the number of priests increased, clerical opposition to lay governance mounted, and a rise in papal authority sparked a corresponding growth in the power of bishops and priests. This process was not uncontested. In Detroit, for example, lay resistance forced bishops to tolerate elected boards of trustees much longer than they wished to. Foreign-language groups like the Poles and Germans held onto lay control as long as they could, as did parishes with substantial immigrant and working-class populations. For the most part, however, the hierarchical model of church governance prevailed nationwide by the 1920s.[28]

The Diocese of Providence reflected these trends. An 1866 rule made a clear statement about clerical authority by naming the bishop president of the parish corporation. Six years later, another mandate specified that the board also would include the vicar general, the parish priest, and two elected laymen. Records from Holy Ghost from 1890 to 1920 suggest this system offered limited opportunity for lay input. The parish board dealt exclusively with financial issues, and the priest (as treasurer) and bishop (who approved all major transactions) clearly controlled the purse strings. Nonetheless, laypeople wielded some monetary influence because the parish's fiscal health depended on their contributions.[29]

As laypeople's control over church governance declined, their involvement in the social and devotional side of parish life intensified, and here there was room for independence. In encyclicals issued in 1878, 1891, and 1901, Pope Leo XIII declared that the hierarchy should control lay activities. Yet in reality the extent to which clerics supervised lay affairs varied from diocese to diocese and parish to parish, reflecting the personality of the bishop and priest. Whereas authorities in Detroit pursued a policy of "benign neglect," Archbishop William O'Connell of Boston was an empire-builder determined to control lay activities. He replaced many parish orga-nizations with diocesan-wide units he could supervise more easily, required that priests preside over lay events, and even dictated the positions women's societies should take on political issues. In Providence, as in Boston and De-troit, lay societies typically had a priest (appointed by the bishop) as spiri-tual director or treasurer. Records from the turn of the twentieth century show that, in accordance with a decree issued by the Council of Baltimore, these societies had to seek their chaplain's approval before organizing "fairs, picnics, excursions and balls." An 1899 letter from Thomas Leahy of the St. Mary's (Bristol) CTAU promised the bishop that "under no circumstances will dancing be allowed" at its functions, and that "in all matters it is our cus-tom to consult our Pastor and his decision has always been law."[30]

Nonetheless, Harkins ruled with a lighter hand than his contemporary O'Connell. The position of the Providence diocese, as outlined in a 1904 ed-itorial in the *Visitor,* was that laypeople should organize and run their own societies, with regular visits from priests and the "better class of people." It appears to have been largely a formality for lay societies to inform the bishop in writing of their annual programs, major meetings, elections, treasurer's reports, and guest lists for major banquets. Some of these communications were simple announcements while others sought the bishop's approval, but it was extremely rare for him to refuse a request or suggest a change. By the same token, societies regularly invited the diocesan leader to attend their events, but in most cases he gracefully declined. This hands-off approach made sense. During the years of mass immigration, church authorities were overwhelmed by the needs of swelling congregations and could not closely monitor every parish organization. Thus, although there was some clerical supervision and societies cleared important decisions with the priest and bishop, there were opportunities for lay autonomy.[31]

A third and important similarity among lay societies was the nature of their membership. Certain trends emerge from studies of Catholic commu-nities in Providence and other cities. Although men and women organized separately, they joined similar types of societies. This reflected a shift from the nineteenth century, when men tended to join mutual aid and charitable groups while women dominated devotional sodalities. Devotions to partic-ular saints celebrated "feminine" traits such as passivity and mercy, but by the turn of the century the immensely popular Holy Name Society, which fostered "manly" piety, had blurred this distinction. At the same time women were becoming more active in educational and charitable groups. Affected by the turn-of-the-century image of the liberated "New Woman" active outside the home, female Catholics were increasingly likely to see parish societies as means of advancing their education and carving out public roles. Lay organization was most popular among the middle class and, as one study of Boston notes, there was a "hierarchy of clubs" in which some were more exclusive than others. Some organizations required modest annual dues—for example, ten cents for membership in the CTAU and two dollars for the Queen's Daughters—which, though not prohibitive, might have discouraged the poorest parishioners. Nonetheless, membership was by no means a prerogative of the monied, and many clubs united Catholics across economic lines. Membership records from Providence lay societies are too scattered to allow for a statistically significant analysis. Nonetheless, a sample of three organizations—the St. Ann's Society (French Canadian women) in 1904, the St. Mary's Catholic Club (Irish men) in 1911, and the Holy Ghost Council of the KOC (Italian men) in 1922—provides some insights.[32]

The St. Ann's Society seems to have been a fairly typical women's club, providing a social and charitable outlet for parish women who assembled regularly to organize fund-raisers. The four women who served as officers in 1904 were born in French Canada and emigrated between 1856 and 1898. Marie Beaudry, Alexandre Faucher, Georgiania Page, and Esilda Pelletier ranged in age from forty-three to sixty. All were married to Canadian-born men, three of them carpenters (skilled laborers) and one a jeweler (a designation that could mean craftsman or factory operative). Although at least three of the husbands had relatively good blue-collar jobs, none appears in the city tax rolls as a property owner and thus none met the requirements for voting in city elections. Nonetheless, three were citizens and registered voters and the fourth (one of the carpenters) had filed his first naturalization papers. In short, these women formed part of a community of working-class immigrants who were economically stable (but not prosperous) and politically engaged. They had enough leisure time to carve out a space for themselves outside the home, and sufficient commitment to the community to engage in charitable work through their parish club.

The Catholic Club at St. Mary's in Olneyville formed in 1911 in response to Rev. Thomas Grace's desire to "keep the parishioners in touch with one another."[33] The club, aimed at fostering community among parish men, attracted members who were more middle-class and a bit more varied than those of the St. Ann's society. The group was heavily weighted toward professionals and white-collar workers, comprising two merchants, two printers, two doctors, two dentists, one pharmacist, two lawyers, two clerks, two tailors, one weaver, and one construction foreman. Of the fourteen whose citizenship could be determined, two were naturalized immigrants, eleven were the sons of immigrants, and one was the son of natives. Their ethnic origins were almost exclusively Irish, with just one member (Dr. Nicholas Serror) born in French Canada and one (weaver Charles Euart) having an Irish mother but a Scottish father. They ranged in age from twenty-eight to forty-nine, with an average age of thirty-nine. When the 1905 census was taken, about half the members (the younger men) were single, but it is safe to assume that six years later, when the club formed, more had married. Finally, all but four owned enough property to vote in city elections.

The collective portrait that emerges from this 1911 sample is a community dominated by middle-class, second-generation Irish Americans. Overlapping networks of parish, residence, profession, and kinship linked these seventeen men in various ways. Their homes were clustered in a small number of streets surrounding the church, and eleven worked nearby on Westminster Street in the downtown commercial district. The club included three sets of brothers who were in business together. Charles and Joseph Hudson worked in Joseph's tailor shop; James and Thomas Mathews ran a printer's shop; and George and William Troy shared a law practice. St. Mary's had formed in the antebellum period to serve the Irish mill workers of Olneyville, yet its Catholic Club attracted upwardly mobile members of the parish. For these men, the lay society cemented professional connections as well as religious, family, and community bonds.

Strictly speaking, the Holy Ghost Council of the KOC was not a church organization but a fraternal order, organized to provide fellowship and mutual assistance. Yet the KOC had strong links to the church, as evidenced by its decision to organize chapters by parish, and the Holy Ghost unit regularly contributed to parish life by organizing dinners and fund-raisers like the "Arabian nights" festival. In 1922 the group decided to expand its horizons, and those of the parish, by forming a lyceum that would operate a library, sponsor weekly lectures, and organize debates.[34] Occupational distribution and rates of property ownership suggest that the Holy Ghost lyceum, which served a newer ethnic community, was less solidly middle-class than the St. Mary's club. The twenty-seven founding members included four factory workers, one janitor, one mechanic, two printers, three jewelers (two in business for themselves), one grocer, six clerks, one salesman, two draftsmen, one photographer, one pharmacist, one doctor, and three students (one training for the priesthood). Just one was a homeowner and only five others owned enough property to surmount the municipal voting restrictions, a proportion much lower than in the Irish men's club. Of the sixteen who could be located in the census, six were Italian immigrants (half of them naturalized) and ten were the children of Italian immigrants. Single men outnumbered married men, and the average age was twenty-seven. In short, this was an occupationally diverse group of relatively young men who were not yet prosperous but were hoping to be. These twenty-seven Catholics were linked by the bonds of parish and fraternity, and by a desire to advance their education through the debates, lectures, and library their lyceum provided.

Taken together, the portraits of these three societies suggest broader trends in lay organization. Lay societies, like the congregations they served, were ethnically homogeneous but cross-class institutions. By no means was membership limited to the middle class, yet neither did the most marginal members of the congregation join. Instead, these groups brought together professionals with economically stable and upwardly mobile working people. Motives for joining included self-improvement, social fellowship, and community service, as well as commitment to faith and parish. A close look at these groups raises the question of what membership in a lay organization meant for the church, for individual Catholics, and for ethnic communities.

"A PROPENSITY TO GATHER TOGETHER": THE BENEFITS OF LAY ORGANIZATION

From the perspective of the clergy, lay societies were a marvelous way to boost the institutional stability of the parish. Their charitable and social functions created a subculture that discouraged Catholics from looking elsewhere for assistance or enjoyment, as well as for prospective spouses. Lay organizations also promoted Catholic values and channeled parishioners' funds and energies into the church. By raising money, inculcating religious habits, and cementing parishioners' connections to the parish, these societies strengthened the church in invaluable ways.[35]

For laypeople, membership in parish organizations merged sacred and secular and combined individual improvement with community building. Confraternities associated with particular devotions participated in religious rituals that were comforting and even exciting and offered a satisfying blend of formal practices and folk religion. For all groups, ceremonies that took place inside the church emphasized the spiritual aspect of lay organization. The Sodality of the Blessed Virgin Mary welcomed new members through a solemn induction in which the women and girls marched in pairs down the aisle to a reserved section near the altar, whence priests called them by name to the sanctuary rail to receive medals. These ceremonies could be

The St. Ann's band, pictured in 1926 with Bove standing proudly at the center, fostered congregational pride and solidarity. Courtesy of the Providence Catholic Diocesan Archives.

quite large, as in May 1902 when three societies at St. Mary's received 150 new members into their ranks. Once inducted, members took communion as a unit on designated Sundays—entering church together, sitting in the front pews, and receiving the sacraments as a body. Shared rituals like this offered members visibility among the larger congregation (a benefit especially valuable to women not usually recognized outside the home), added a religious dimension to group solidarity, and reminded members that whatever the function of their society its mission was rooted in the church.[36]

This was an important reminder, for it was easy to be distracted by the social side of lay life. The church hierarchy worried about this as early as 1903, using a *Visitor* editorial to remind readers the purpose of lay organization was to foster religious devotion. This warning in no way dampened the social impulse. The Holy Name Society of Holy Ghost held an annual banquet that attracted more than two thousand people in 1928, and the Sodality of Our Blessed Virgin at St. Bartholomew's enjoyed annual summer outings. The Holy Cross Catholic Club assembled for whist parties on Friday evenings; the aforementioned St. Ann's Society organized parish banquets to raise money for charity; and the St. Edward's Ladies Society sponsored bazaars and lawn parties. Although the St. Bartholomew's Catholic Club had a high-minded mission statement about moral and intellectual leadership, a profile in the parish bulletin suggested its activities were mostly recreational—dances, movies, carnivals, and a baseball team. In 1928 the club sought to recruit new members with this inducement: "Not only do you benefit spiritually but you meet many new friends and you have facilities to enjoy yourself."[37]

Whereas some parishioners joined lay organizations to improve their social lives, others signed on for more serious reasons. Membership in a church society provided identity in an impersonal urban environment and created opportunities for social service. Men who belonged to the popular Saint Vincent de Paul Society, a charitable organization that was founded in Paris in 1833 and organized its first Providence chapter twenty years later, raised funds and visited the poor. The local Queen's Daughters, founded in 1908, operated day nurseries, offered millinery and dressmaking classes, ran a music school, and organized sewing guilds to make clothing for poor children. Even societies whose functions were not explicitly charitable raised money that helped build the parish and fund its outreach to the poor.[38]

Lay organization brought together families and communities. Husbands and fathers who devoted time and money to Catholic men's clubs were less likely to patronize saloons. Sons and daughters who participated in parish youth groups had fewer opportunities to frequent dancehalls. Although family members joined separate organizations, they came together at socials and shared a commitment to parish life. And because Catholics typically lived in the vicinity of the church, lay activity reinforced community bonds as well as family ties and congregational cohesion. As Dolan writes, "families were indeed the building blocks of every immigrant community, but the church was the mortar that sought to bind them together."[39]

Lay societies fostered individual improvement as well as strengthening family and community life. Church debating societies and study clubs were opportunities for parishioners, many of whom had left school early to work in jewelry factories or textile mills, to extend their education in less formal ways. In a tradition that extended back to the Catholic confraternities of medieval Europe, church-affiliated fraternal orders like the KOC, Order of Foresters, and USJB acted as Catholic mutual aid societies by helping to pay for funerals or offering life insurance. In Providence, as in nearby Boston, middle-class groups like the Catholic Club facilitated professional contacts. The Providence branch of the Catholic Knights of America described itself as a networking group whose purpose was "to unite fraternally all Catholics of every profession business and occupation."[40]

The diocesan Catholic Club seems to have shared with the Knights a conscious desire to reduce class conflict and instill middle-class values by bringing coreligionists together across social lines. At the club's annual dinner in

1916, its president, Dr. William R. McGuirk, declared its goal was to "unite men" and "abolish much of the envy and many of the petty jealousies arising from a little more prosperity or a little greater success." These examples are indicative of the cross-class nature of parish life. Many parishes united, or sought to unite, compatriots on the basis of shared ethnic identity. Workers who worshipped at St. Francis, for example, rubbed elbows with Joseph Banigan, president of the Woonsocket Rubber Company. Banigan was a hero to his blue-collar coreligionists as the state's first Irish-born millionaire, an ardent Irish nationalist, deep-pocketed Catholic philanthropist, and employer who hired compatriots almost exclusively and treated them exceptionally well—until an 1885 pay cut sparked a bitter walkout. Banigan clearly shared with Protestant industrialists a belief that religion inculcated steady work habits. In 1885, he announced that "regular attendance at some place of public worship, and a proper observance of the Sabbath" would be expected of all employees. "Banigan's commandment," as the edict became known, sparked another walkout and eventually was ignored. As this anecdote suggests, there were limits to the cross-class solidarity religion encouraged. Moreover, congregations serving blue-collar neighborhoods reinforced ties forged at the workplace and union and thus fostered working-class consciousness.[41]

Lay societies filled particularly critical functions for women, regardless of economic position. Although working-class Catholic women played public roles as workers, consumers, and members of neighborhood networks, a parish society was the only formal institution to which most had access in this era. Mutual aid societies tended to limit their membership to men; women could not vote until 1920; and relatively few unions welcomed women into their ranks until the 1930s. Even middle-class women with more time and resources tended to build their clubs and charities around the church. Because religious activity was consistent with women's roles as moral guardians, parishes were places they could be active without violating gender stereotypes or trespassing on male preserves.

There were extensive opportunities to be active. As the historian Paula Kane writes, a Catholic girl "was enveloped from childhood to motherhood by a network of pious institutions."[42] These institutions were female spaces where women could gather, free from work and household responsibilities, and speak, without the oversight of foremen, fathers, or husbands (although sometimes in the presence of priests). Joining a lay society enabled women to influence a religious institution otherwise dominated by male clerics. And even though many women's societies performed domestic duties such as sewing, executing these tasks in the parish hall provided an escape from home. The bonds of friendship formed through these groups represented not only social diversion but also emotional support for women confronting the challenges of life in the new world.

Women and men thus had a host of reasons for joining church societies, and in most cases the spiritual and temporal merged. Charitable and educational societies rested on religious foundations, while religious sodalities served community-building purposes. This melding of sacred and secular was only appropriate. As the most accessible institution in ethnic communities, the parish provided members with a social and spiritual home in an urban setting that otherwise could be alienating and unstructured. This was true not only in Providence but also in other communities. Catholics, writes the historian John McGreevy, "used the parish to define community in a new environment." The parish, as Kane puts it, served "both as a mini-city and as a macro-family."[43] Catholics appreciated these benefits. Certainly strains of anticlericalism remained strong, especially among the Italians. A number of new Americans rejected the church for personal or political reasons, among them a discomfort with its hierarchical structure or antiradical politics, or a belief that converting to Protestantism would facilitate assimilation and upward mobility. But many more welcomed the church as a community center, a trend that was remarkably consistent across lines of class, gender, and ethnicity and over time.

6

"CATHOLICS IN CIVIC LIFE"

Parish Activity and Political Activism

This is their duty toward the Catholic Church, which commands them
to be Catholics not only in private life, but also in civic life.
— George J. Lucas, American Federation of Catholic Societies,
The Importance of Federation, 1903

"A CORPS OF COMMITTED LAYMEN":
THE PARISH AS POLITICAL TRAINING GROUND

At the same time that Catholic parishes were establishing themselves as social centers of ethnic neighborhoods, they also were acting as political training grounds. As chapter 4 demonstrated, many new Americans found neither the union nor the ballot an effective weapon in their struggle for full membership in the nation. It was through community organizations—neighborhood networks, ethnic mutual aid societies, and most of all parishes—that they more successfully organized for change. Catholics active in parish life did more than develop nurturing social networks. They became leaders and organizers, developed informed opinions about current events, learned political processes, and forged alliances. It was only natural for some to become politicians and community activists, using skills and solidarities formed at church to influence life outside the parish. By the Progressive Era, Catholics were beginning to use the institutional and rhetorical resources of religion to raise challenges to employers and civic leaders, fighting for full access to the vote and better treatment at the workplace as well as challenging restrictive ideas about Americanism. Because they represented a majority of the city's population by 1905, it became difficult for politicians to ignore their demands.

The organizational talents developed at church began with the founding of the parish. Unlike their European counterparts, American churches relied on members' contributions in the absence of state subsidies and often were built at lay initiative. Creating a parish required laypeople to act as organizers and fund-raisers, in many cases engaging in what Tentler calls their "first New World experience of large-scale collective action." St. Mary's of Pawtucket, the first Catholic parish in the Providence area, opened in 1829 only after committed laypeople collected twelve hundred dollars. Lay involvement remained critical even when the church became more established. In 1888, Charles E. Gorman, the Providence legislator and suffrage reformer, worked with seven other laymen to raise funds and choose a lot for the new Church of the Blessed Sacrament. Eighteen years later, parishioners at St. Matthew's in Central Falls selected a location for their new church. They did not choose well, as the lot was too sandy to build on, but two hundred men showed up with shovels and toiled until the site was usable. Rev. Antonio Bove of St. Ann's referred to stories like these when he boasted that the city's parishes were not "erected by the gifts of millionaires. They represent the self-sacrifice of the wage earner." These sacrifices generated lasting commitments, as this recollection by John Murphy in the St. Michael's parish history suggests: "I think that when you grow up with a parish, watch the place being dug, get chased by the police for playing in the dug-out cellar, watch the building being put up, you've got to go along with it, you're living it. You see something come from nothing. You've got to have feelings about it." For Catholics like Murphy, parish-building provided an identity around which new communities rallied and a project in which entire families participated.[1]

Once the church was constructed, its survival depended on the energies and skills of the laity. Priests directed spiritual affairs but relied on parishioners to raise funds, teach Sunday school, operate charities, and organize entertainments—in short, to administer the complex structure that made parishes into community centers. At Blessed Sacrament parishioners taught religious education classes, and five years after the parish's founding almost four hundred children were attending the lay-run Sunday school. At St. Edward's, the Christian Doctrine Society administered its own Branch Avenue hall and the Young Men's Literary Association operated a library. The

Catholic Club at Holy Trinity in Central Falls, formed in 1910 for men age eighteen to thirty-five, shouldered enormous responsibilities: organizing lectures, dramas, and dances as well as an annual communion breakfast and moonlight sail; participating in statewide tournaments and debates; publishing a monthly newsletter; raising money for a new club building; and using that facility to show films, host sports competitions, and run classes in gymnastics, language, and domestic science. A St. Edward's history spoke truly when it described societies like these as "leadership-training" groups. Catholics who ran these institutions became organizers and leaders, developing skills they could apply to politics as well as parish life.[2]

Parishes fostered this kind of civic involvement by providing political education. The lyceums, libraries, reading circles, and debating societies discussed in chapter 5 provided extensive information about local and national affairs. Antisocialist speeches had been popular fare at church since the turn of the century. Over the next two decades, in Providence as in Boston, parish-sponsored lectures became steadily more political, focusing less on literature and culture and more on current events such as Irish independence and the League of Nations. In November 1912, U.S. senator James O'Gorman of New York spoke to the St. Charles Holy Name Society in Woonsocket about a federal proposal to subject prospective immigrants to a literacy test. O'Gorman promised to oppose the measure, and the Holy Name Society enthusiastically endorsed his position. The political trend in parish lectures was especially marked in women's clubs, where lecture series once dominated by topics in art and history shifted their focus to women's rights and current events during the 1910s and 1920s. In the latter decade, for example, the citywide Catholic Women's Club heard a lecture on the "International View of the Women's Movement"; the Queen's Daughters learned about "Woman's Civic Duty"; and state representative Isabelle Ahearn O'Neill spoke to the Daughters of Isabella (the women's auxiliary of the KOC) about "Laws Affecting Women in National and State Legislatures." The West Warwick Catholic Women's Club put together a lecture series that touched on such topical issues as "Military Preparedness," "The New Ireland," and "The New World We Now Live In." For women and men, St. Edward's sponsored a series on "political education" featuring state senator Daniel E. Geary and U.S. representative Ambrose Kennedy. Even children received a civic education at church. In the 1930s, boys who joined the new Junior Holy Name Society were instructed in "political science" and "discussion of current events."[3]

Lecture series were most popular among middle-class Irish Americans, but debating and study clubs drew more diverse constituencies. As the membership of the aforementioned Holy Ghost lyceum suggests, activities like this attracted janitors, doctors, and everyone in between. Although not aimed specifically at blue-collar parishioners, they were especially valuable for workers whose formal education had ended early in life. These forums enabled participants to discuss controversial issues such as temperance and socialism and, sometimes to their priests' dismay, to develop their own positions on current events.

The education these groups provided could be substantial. Young men who belonged to the Columbus Union, a "literary and moral improvement" society at Blessed Sacrament, participated in debates every other week. According to the St. Edward's history, in societies like these "a vague knowledge of a given topic was not sufficient. A person had to have a thorough knowledge." In January 1917, for example, the Cathedral and St. Michael's Catholic Clubs met to debate the best solution to intemperance. This was a topic very much in the news, as Congress soon was to consider the Eighteenth Amendment. Participants would have had stacks of newspaper clippings to sort through in preparing to discuss whether voluntary abstinence (the approach Catholics tended to favor) or legal prohibition (increasingly popular among Protestant reformers) was the answer. Parish debating societies thus prompted members to engage with social problems and educate themselves in current events. It was no wonder Richard Walsh, the St. Edward's historian, described one Catholic club as a "corps of committed laymen trained in leadership and public speaking." It was at church that many Catholics developed educated opinions and confidence to air them. Even if priests and parish leaders hoped to use these forums to promote particular agendas, they could not control the opinions developed there.[4]

Active laypeople learned about the political process as well as current events at church. A parish society, like an ethnic mutual aid association, was an exercise in self-government. Societies regulated themselves by writing constitutions and by-laws that ranged from simple to elaborate. The Queen's Daughters' straightforward four-page document spelled out the organization's mission, membership requirements, election rules, and procedures for amending the constitution. At the other end of the spectrum was the national Catholic Daughters of America, which by 1946 had an eighty-page governing document. Implementing by-laws furnished members with skills they could use if they won seats on public commissions. The West Warwick Catholic Women's Club had to learn Roberts' Rules of Order, and the Junior Holy Name Society received instruction in "parliamentary law."[5]

Each organization elected officers annually or as often as every six months. The Christian Doctrine Society of St. Edward's, which chose leaders twice a year, attracted men eager for influence and soon became the most powerful organization in the parish. Some elections were quite large in scale. Men who sought office in the Union of Catholic Parish Clubs in 1917 had to campaign among a membership of four thousand. Lay society elections carried special value for women, barred from voting in lay trustee contests as well as public elections. The *Visitor* was careful to note, however, that when the St. Mary's Immaculate Conception Society chose its officers in 1908, it did so under the supervision of a parish priest. Supervised or otherwise, women eagerly participated in the democratic process. In addition to choosing a slate of general officers, in 1917 the St. Edward's Women's Guild held elections for its "sick" and "entertainment" committees.[6]

As these examples suggest, the political benefits of parish life were particularly useful for women who lacked other vehicles. Through their parish societies they established contacts, developed leadership skills, and seized opportunities for community service. Weekly or monthly meetings, supplemented by all-female retreats and excursions, brought women together on a regular basis and enabled them to discuss problems and devise coping strategies. Raising funds and coordinating mixers taught them to be organizers, while performing in concerts and plays fostered public speaking skills. The St. Edward's Dramatic Club, for example, "provided a corps of competent, confident performers." Among them was Kate Duggan, who performed in "Barney's Courtship" and "Ireland As It Is" on the same evening in 1878. Lecture series, for their part, enabled participants to make presentations as well as hear speeches by prominent citizens. In February 1916, Elizabeth Ballard gave a paper on "Catholic current events" to her associates in the Catholic Girls' Club. Experiences like these fostered confidence and cohesion that encouraged women to be active in community life as well as parish affairs. Lay activity also lent visibility and provided contacts. In June 1920, the Ladies Auxiliary of the AOH organized a grand reception to celebrate the feast of St. Columcille (patron saint of the Irish Republic) and invited the bishop and governor to attend. It was common for middle-class Catholic women to sponsor receptions that church and state officials attended, offering female organizers a rare opportunity to hobnob with civic leaders.[7]

American historians have argued that a "separate spheres" ideology, which gave women control over domestic affairs and placed men in charge of public life, survived well into the twentieth century and created empowering social spaces in which old stock, middle-class women developed a shared consciousness and forged political roles. Using their charitable organizations, they extended women's work as care givers into the neighborhood and staked out a place in public life. In cities like Providence, Boston, and Detroit, churches served a comparable function for Catholics. Parish-based social work provided opportunities for women to come together and play roles in their communities. Even though well-heeled congregants tended to coordinate these activities, working women too could participate. Thus, at the same time that Protestant clubwomen used domestic prerogatives to justify public roles, Catholic women of all classes became active by invoking their duties as homemakers and Catholics. The West Warwick Catholic Women's Club, for example, described its mission as stimulating members "to greater efficiency and usefulness in the solution of present-day religious, civic and social problems." Protestants and Catholics in Providence engaged in similar but separate charities, forming their own settlement houses, as well as coming together in groups like the Rhode Island State Federation of Women's Clubs (RISFWC). Yet they had priorities that reflected distinctive religious and ethnic worldviews. Both were committed to helping the needy, for example, but often in different ways. Protestant clubwomen were likely to argue that birth control and prohibition would improve the lives of working-class families, whereas Catholics tended to oppose the former as violating church teachings and the latter as an unwelcome intrusion by the state into personal life (voluntary abstinence being a superior approach, in their opinion).[8]

The church was of course an imperfect political vehicle for women. Catholicism sent women profoundly mixed messages, praising them as saints and deploring them as sinners. Priests routinely urged women to place family responsibilities before individual needs, so that by the 1920s the city's Catholic women's groups would be lobbying against legalized birth control and the Equal Rights Amendment proposed by the National Woman's Party. On the other hand, the parish provided a rare opportunity to congregate outside the home, acquire political skills, and become active in public life. It also enabled Providence women, like those in Boston, to develop a sense of power rooted in the maternalist ideology of separate spheres.[9]

One such woman was Agnes M. Bacon of Central Falls. Born to Irish immigrants in 1876, Bacon taught grammar school, married a doctor, and became active in the Providence Queen's Daughters. The social work she performed with this group marked the beginning of a public career that straddled the Catholic and non-Catholic worlds. By 1920 Bacon (now widowed) belonged to the Protestant-dominated Rhode Island League of Women Voters (RILWV), as well as sitting on the national board of directors for the National Council of Catholic Women (NCCW) and coordinating its Americanization programs in Rhode Island. She remained active in the NCCW until her death in 1936 at age sixty-one.[10]

Isabelle Ahearn O'Neill's background was very similar to Bacon's, although her career was much more unusual. Born to Irish immigrants in Woonsocket in 1881, O'Neill was the youngest of thirteen children. After studying theater at the Boston College of Drama and Oratory and physical education at Harvard, she returned to Providence to teach parochial school and run her own School of Oratory, Drama and Physical Education. As a young woman she performed in vaudeville and summer stock and such locally produced silent films as "Joe Lincoln's Cape Cod Stories," and her Providence venues ranged from Catholic parish halls to the city Opera House. Enjoying the stage and perhaps inspired by her father, a former councilman, she entered politics and made history in 1922 as the first woman elected to the Rhode Island General Assembly. O'Neill's acting career and divorced status made her a somewhat risqué choice, but her solid Catholic background and maternalist agenda affirmed her respectability. Her Catholic memberships included the Immaculate Conception choir, St. Michael's Rosary and Altar Society, St. Gabriel's Aid Association, and St. Joseph's Hospital Women's League. Like other female politicians of her day, she built her career on "women's" issues such as pensions for widowed mothers, better pay for teachers, and protections for female workers. Not content with the support of her middle-class Irish-American peers, she courted the state's polyglot electorate by delivering speeches in French and Italian. After eight years in the House of Representatives, the popular Smith Hill legislator moved on to the state Senate and served there as deputy Democratic floor leader, the first woman in the nation to hold this position. Another career highlight came in 1924, when she acted as temporary chair of the Democratic National Convention. In 1933 she left the Senate to become legislative agent for the state Narcotic Board she had helped to create. Throughout her career O'Neill was known for her outspoken and principled stands. As one political columnist noted, "She has made it a practice to be heard from regularly and at frequent intervals ever since she was 17 years old." Despite or perhaps because of her unconventional life, O'Neill's coreligionists seized on her as a model of activist Catholic womanhood, frequently inviting her to speak to parish groups on such topics as "Women in Politics."[11]

Although Catholic men had more opportunities for public service outside the parish, the contacts and skills they developed there were no less valuable. Patrick McCarthy was not alone in using church resources to promote his political career. Between the 1890s and 1920s, the Irish American mayor Joseph Gainer, the Italian American judge Antonio Capotosto, and the French Canadian governor Emery San Souci—to name only a few prominent examples—were active in parish life. Aspiring politicians like

Isabelle Ahearn O'Neill, a former vaudevillian and silent film actress, became Providence's first female legislator in 1922. Like many other Catholic politicians, she used religious networks to affirm her respectability and build her constituency. Photograph, courtesy of the *Providence Journal*.

these knew they would encounter public dignitaries at church dedications, priests' funerals, and lay society banquets. They also recognized that being an active Catholic sent a positive message about their values. Aram Pothier, another French Canadian governor, was remembered in his *Visitor* obituary as "a strong supporter of the Church organizations of which he was a member" and a Catholic who "won numerous friends among the clergy." Men like Pothier knew congregations were ready-made constituencies. Because parish lines generally followed geographic boundaries, Catholics who worshipped together usually belonged to the same voting districts. For men of humble origins such as James T. Kennedy, a St. Mary's parishioner who rose from immigrant mill worker to serve as state legislator from 1888 to 1890, the support of fellow Catholics undoubtedly was critical to political success. Like his more famous coreligionists, he benefited from parish connections in building his political career.[12]

Patrick Henry Quinn was among those Catholic men who merged their commitments to parish life and public activism. Born in Warwick, Quinn started his career in the finishing room at Clyde Print Works. In the 1890s he served as District Master Workman of the state Knights of Labor and was active in a short-lived independent political initiative called the Industrial Alliance. He went on to become a lawyer and "man of public importance," chairing the state Democratic Party and running unsuccessfully for governor in 1914. Throughout his busy life he maintained a strong commitment to the church, serving as president of the Rhode Island CTAU and Catholic Club as well as Grand Knight of the KOC. As CTAU president he promoted temperance and Irish Catholic respectability by participating in such public demonstrations as a "monster" temperance rally in Boston in August 1910. This was not the only way in which he used religious contacts to promote a political agenda. In a March 1928 speech to the Queen's Daughters, he urgently encouraged listeners to exercise their newfound right to vote. Women who failed to cast ballots, he told his listeners, did "an injustice, not only to themselves, but also to their children whose interests they could further and protect by taking a hand in the administration of schools and public institutions." Throughout his life Quinn's commitments to church and politics were mutually reinforcing—his faith legitimizing his efforts as labor activist and Democratic politician, and his public influence lending him authority among coreligionists.[13]

By organizing young people as well as adults, the parish started training Catholics for leadership long before they were old enough to be voters or union members. By the time they were adults they were working together to run elections, write constitutions, raise funds, coordinate debates, and organize fairs and picnics—in the process creating alliances that extended beyond the church and into polls and union halls. Catholic lay societies, moreover, were ready-made units that could take on neighborhood problems or engage with city politics, drawing on the righteous indignation and divine sanction religion provided. When the *Visitor* described St. Michael's as "the center of social and political life" in its neighborhood, it could have been referring to any number of Catholic churches. As the personal stories related above suggest, it was most common for Irish Americans to make the transition from parish activity to public activism. But for immigrants and ethnics from other countries too, Catholicism offered an organizational structure and moral authority on which they drew in demanding their rights as Americans. The lay-clerical struggles that periodically disrupted congregations of newer immigrants were, as the historian David Gerber puts it, "breeding grounds for democratic citizenship." In all these ways, parish life encouraged members to engage in life beyond the parish.[14]

"ARE WE NOT ALSO CITIZENS OF THIS COUNTRY?": CATHOLIC POLITICS IN THE PROGRESSIVE ERA

By the Progressive Era, some Providence Catholics (most of them Irish Americans) were consciously using the church as a bridge between private devotion and public activism. Seeking workplace protections, political rights, and recognition as Americans, they began to draw on the resources of religion. This involved using lay societies as organizational vehicles, the diocesan press as a mouthpiece, religious parades as statements, and Catholic doctrine as justification. Their efforts intensified over the following decades, as later chapters will demonstrate, and intersected with a nationwide movement by American Catholics to assert their interests.

Providence's Catholic rights movement began in 1905, when a state census revealed that Catholics now formed a majority in the city as well as the state. According to the latest count, 51.5 percent of the city's 198,635 residents identified as Catholic while 44.5 percent were Protestant and 4 percent Jewish. This finding unleashed a campaign aimed at winning the new majority a proportionate share of power. "We have never received at the hands of the State that consideration which is due to the great number of Catholics," the *Visitor* complained. "There are many things still due to us from the state and these we should insist upon getting." Parishioners scarcely needed to be reminded they faced discrimination in the community (social prejudice), the polity (biased voting restrictions), and the workplace (few protections).[15]

These complaints echoed those of Catholics across the country. As the church's constituency exploded, Catholics grew frustrated that they lacked influence in proportion to their numbers. In Worcester, church leaders responded by promoting what the historian Timothy Meagher calls "militant, pan-ethnic, American Catholicism." This impulse was evident in the national American Federation of Catholic Societies (AFCS), which formed in 1901 to unite coreligionists across ethnic lines and in defense of their interests. At a 1903 gathering in Pennsylvania, Rev. George J. Lucas expressed resentments that his coreligionists shared. "We are some fourteen millions of Catholics, in number one-seventh of the entire population of the United States, yet how small is our influence," he complained. "Why should we stand upon a lower plane than other American citizens?" Bishop James A. McFaul of Trenton, New Jersey, raised the same issue two years later. "Are we not also citizens of this country?" he lamented. "Haven't we the same rights? Because a man is a Catholic, must he be born two or three times in this country before he is an American?"[16]

Church leaders confronted a dilemma in addressing this problem. Political action was necessary, yet was bound to raise red flags in a nation still hypersensitive about Catholic influence. Catholic involvement in public life now extended from urban machines to the highest reaches of federal government, as seen in the appointments of Charles Bonaparte of Maryland as Attorney General in 1906 and Edward Douglass White of Louisiana as Chief Justice in 1910. The 1910s witnessed Protestant-Catholic battles over Sunday closings in New York, parochial school funding in Massachusetts, and making Good Friday a public holiday in Rhode Island. In 1916 Floridians elected as governor the Prohibitionist Sidney Catts, who campaigned on charges that the American Catholic hierarchy was "receiving its orders from Rome" and plotting to destroy "our public schools, the freedom of the press and free speech." When a statue of Columbus was erected near the base of Capitol Hill in 1912, nativists saw further evidence of Catholic influence in public life. Their concerns found voice in a new periodical published in Missouri under the evocative title *The Menace*.[17]

As a result, church leaders in Providence and nationwide were careful to draw the line between partisanship, which they rejected, and political action, which they embraced. Speakers at AFCS annual conventions made it clear they would not endorse candidates or form their own party—actions that could divide members as well as provoke fears about their designs on government—but they would, enthusiastically, lobby on bills that affected the church and its members. This form of politics, declared Bishop Sebastian Messmer of Green Bay, Wisconsin, "becomes the duty of the Catholic layman where it is necessary to defend the rights of the Church." In line with this approach, the *Visitor* encouraged Providence laypeople to assert their rights even as it avoided political endorsements, and Harkins himself took care to avoid any hint of partisanship. In 1906, for example, Robert Goddard, a reformer running for the U.S. Senate, invited the bishop to join his campaign committee. "I never take part in any political campaign nor identify myself publicly with any political party," was the bishop's curt response.[18]

As individuals, however, Harkins's constituents felt no such compunction to distance themselves from the electoral fray. Providence had chosen Edwin McGuinness as its first Catholic mayor in 1895, and now his coreligionists were eager to press on. The mayor, like the governor, was a figurehead position, to be sure, but having a Catholic as titular head of city or state still was an important symbolic victory. In 1906 two Irish Catholics—McCarthy and James H. Higgins (a Holy Name Society member who worshipped at St. Joseph's in Pawtucket)—achieved just such triumphs when they were elected mayor and governor. In a sign that the ethnic Catholic majority was ascending, Higgins became the state's first Catholic governor and McCarthy defeated former governor Charles Warren Lippitt, described in the *Boston Globe* as "a millionaire and a son of the American Revolution." McCarthy was popular among East Side Yankees because he was a "good government" reformer committed to reducing corruption and improving city services, but his memoirs make clear that his Catholic networks were even more critical to his success. In civic addresses he avoided mentioning a Catholic agenda, but when speaking to coreligionists he pointed to a special mission. "Catholic young men form the rank and file of the forces of the Church Militant, in all its work for God and country, conquering all the enemies of both under the banner of the cross," he told the Catholic Young Men's National Meeting in Boston in 1909.[19]

In promoting a Catholic political agenda, McCarthy was preaching to the choir. In 1910, C. Woodbury Gorman, a Providence lawyer, helped found the Rhode Island Federation of Catholic Clubs to promote coreligionists' "spiritual and temporal welfare, especially by organized effort." Gorman clearly believed that in union there was strength, and his efforts to mobilize parish clubs into one cohesive unit reflected the AFCS's concurrent efforts to unite the nation's Catholics. That same year, the Rhode Island KOC formed a committee to promote Catholics' "right to consideration and justice" and defend them whenever they were slandered. One such instance arose that very year, when a Brown University professor declared that Catholics should not teach in the public schools and lay societies countered by campaigning to elect coreligionists to the school committee. In a similar vein, at that year's diocesan Holy Name convention, President James A. Cahill urged members to focus on "promotion and defense of Catholic interests."[20]

In so doing Cahill echoed the pronouncements of Holy Name officers across the Northeast and Midwest, who were coming to see their units as vehicles to combat radicalism and anti-Catholicism. In Detroit, for example, the Holy Name Union mobilized hundreds of men in a successful campaign to persuade businesses to close from noon to three on Good Friday. The Holy Name Society was, as one national leader later put it, "the proper machinery for building up just what we want—a really Catholic Society." This was music to the ears of the AFCS. In the words of Peter E. Dietz, the labor priest who edited the federation's newsletter, "the great social mission of the Catholic American is to make America Catholic." This mission reflected what Paula Kane calls "separatist integration," an attempt by Catholics to seek influence in the larger society without abandoning their special (and in their minds superior) religious identity.[21]

To make America Catholic, however, American Catholics had to be able to vote. It was a major grievance among Providence parishioners, so many of them working-class, that the municipal property qualification affected them disproportionately. For decades, Catholic editors and politicians had protested the property qualification on secular and religious grounds. The vote was, in the *Visitor*'s words, not only a "sacred right" but also a "very important test of citizenship." Any abridgment of this critical right was "an unjust and unreasonable discrimination against every registry voter in the rights guaranteed him as an American citizen." It was exactly the kind of slight the AFCS was encouraging Catholics to resist.[22]

The city's Democrats, Socialists, and unionists also were campaigning against the property rule, but the *Visitor*'s distinctive contribution was to bring God into the debate. The property rule was not only undemocratic but also un-Christian in that it discriminated against Catholics and violated their church's "philosophy of government." Moreover, the restriction prevented them from executing their "sacred duty" to cast ballots, a duty that took on new urgency as the AFCS urged them to use their votes to defend the church. Two Catholic politicians who believed fervently in this "sacred duty" were Gorman and McCarthy, both of whom had been active in the suffrage agitation of the 1880s. Another was James D. Reilly, a Republican state representative from 1912 to 1916 and a founder of the Cathedral Holy Name Society. Reilly was remembered in his obituary for taking "a decided stand in favor of the abolition of the property qualification." Irish Catholic politicians like these—and their coreligionists in the labor movement—continued to spearhead the ethnic suffrage movement, but French Canadian leaders also cared deeply about exercising the right to vote. Father L. Octave Massicotte of St. Charles Borromeo attended the 1902 installation of officers at a French Canadian naturalization club, his presence lending religious sanction to the rite of becoming an active citizen. The 1907 constitution of the Franco-American Foresters, a Catholic mutual aid society, stated that one of its chief goals was to promote naturalization so that members would "be in a position to claim their rights." In all these ways, clerical and lay Catholics threw the authority of their faith behind the suffrage campaign.[23]

The plight of industrial workers was another relevant issue for a church whose congregants were largely working-class, and the *Visitor* waged a vigorous campaign for workers' rights. "To defraud laborers of their wages is one of 'the four sins crying to heaven for vengeance,'" the newspaper warned in 1902. Instead, the *Visitor* urged, employers should apply Christian principles to the industrial world by granting workers higher wages, shorter hours, and a voice in management. During economic downturns, moreover, the state should step in by providing public works jobs and social insurance. Fair treatment of workers, the newspaper argued, would improve society as well as helping the workforce. "Employers have failed to regard their workmen as human beings with rights of citizenship," the *Visitor* charged. "If an employer has the interest of his country at heart and is solicitous for the welfare of his fellow-men upon whom the future glory of the country depends he must also be anxious for the well-being of his workmen who represent the largest and most sturdy class of citizens."[24]

The *Visitor's* blue-collar boosterism resulted from fear that disgruntled workers would turn to socialism, recognition that well-paid workers were more likely to promote Catholic values by forming large families, and commitment to human rights and social justice. These priorities reflected local concerns and church-wide directives, the latter articulated in Pope Leo XIII's *Rerum Novarum* (1891) and Pius XI's *Quadragesimo Anno* (1931). These encyclicals spelled out the church's position on economic justice by condemning socialism and communism on one hand and unbridled capitalism on the other. Inspired by the encyclicals and the growth of the labor movement, and competing with a "trade-union gospel" articulated by socially conscious Protestant ministers in cities like Philadelphia, the American Catholic Church took more interest in workplace reform and adopted a friendlier attitude toward mainstream unions. By the Progressive Era, American priests like Dietz and John Ryan of Minnesota were firm advocates of workers' rights. It was thus consistent with national and international Catholic policy for the *Visitor* to speak out in favor of higher wages and shorter hours, workers' compensation, and curbs on monopoly—and to speak with the authority of religion. As the newspaper put it, the church had "every interest in the laboring man, whose cause belongs to Our Lord and His Church."[25]

Like its counterparts in the AFCS and in other dioceses, the Providence hierarchy discouraged socialism while promoting "responsible" labor organization. A 1902 piece in the *Visitor* instructed unionists to "discourage every tendency to lawlessness, and repress without pity every attempt of the Anarchist or foreign-born agitator to secure an ascendancy among them." Many local clerics preferred a corporatist approach to labor relations, in which employers and workers recognized their mutual interests and worked out disputes through arbitration; yet they were tireless defenders of the "God-given" right to organize and supported walkouts they considered justified. A 1904 *Visitor* editorial summed up the hierarchy's position on workplace conflict: "Without strikes the operatives would never have obtained any betterment of their lot. This does not mean that all strikes are justifiable or bound to be successful." In March 1902, mill owners battling a strike in Olneyville asked clergymen to urge their parishioners to return to work. When Massicotte of St. Charles made an antistrike sermon, his parishioners became "so wrought up over this interference on the part of the clergyman that they left the church," the *Evening Telegram* reported. It was telling that Massicotte was the only priest who agreed to speak out against the strike; others either supported the walkout or remained silent for fear of antagonizing blue-collar worshippers. Lest Massicotte had damaged the church's credentials with working people, later that year the *Visitor* redeemed its reputation by firmly supporting the trolley strike. Throughout this period, moreover, the newspaper reinforced its support for workers by reporting on union news and carrying the union label. This strategy clearly convinced some unionists that the church was an ally. In 1924, for example, the Woonsocket Central Labor Union turned to Bishop Hickey for help in convincing local employers to stop favoring nonunion workers.[26]

Connections between the church and the labor movement were evident at the 1910 Labor Day parade, when marchers doffed their hats as they passed St. Mary's. Afterward some paraders no doubt returned to join their families at the Olneyville parish's annual Labor Day celebration. Open to all Catholics and combining blue-collar pride with family sociability, the festival fostered the larger sense of working-class community missing from most Progressive Era craft unions. Through gestures like this, parishes fostered a broader class consciousness and suggested that the church was a place where working people could come together.[27]

Given the church's friendly stance, and the overwhelmingly Irish American composition of the city's labor movement, many prominent unionists were active Catholics. Some no doubt felt they would increase their stock in the community and the labor movement by being seen at church or belonging to Catholic clubs. It was no coincidence that a number of Rhode Islanders who had been prominent in the Knights of Labor (among them Patrick Quinn and Joseph McGee) also headed Catholic temperance organizations. At a time when labor activists were disparaged as dangerous radicals and Irish Americans as drunken rowdies, membership in a parish temperance society testified to organizers' sobriety and civic-mindedness. Other Catholic unionists such as Lawrence Grace—teamster, state AFL leader, Sacred Heart parishioner, and member of the Holy Name Society and the antisocialist Militia of Christ—truly believed the church was a vehicle for working-class interests. In a 1912 speech to the School for Social Studies at St. Charles, Grace declared all successful labor legislation would "owe its success as much to the prayers as to the activities of men who remain devoted sons of Mother Church."[28]

In addition to benefiting from clerical support, labor activists drew on religious rhetoric in their crusades for economic justice. Religion traditionally has been a "weapon of the weak," a shared language and source of moral authority for people without access to formal means of power. The overwhelmingly Catholic working class of Providence wielded this weapon with finesse. In 1908 union leaders issued a "Ten Commandments for Labor" that included the rule: "Thou shalt not labor more than eight hours for one day's work, nor on the Sabbath nor on any of the holy days." The following year the Socialist *Labor Advocate* published its own "Ten Commandments," among them the admonition "Thou shalt consider the Golden Rule superior to the rule of gold." Even Governor Pothier, a Republican Catholic whose party was not known as a friend of labor, cited the Golden Rule in speaking to a Rhode Island State Federation of Labor (RISFL) convention in Woonsocket in 1913.[29]

Unionists also echoed the *Visitor*'s argument that fair treatment of workers benefited the larger society. In its Progressive Era campaign for higher wages and shorter hours, the city's *Union Worker Magazine* spoke of "the right of the individual not only to exist, but to live by his toil, the sacredness of the capital which the Creator has granted to mankind." In other words, workers who enjoyed decent wages and reasonable hours could live productive Christian lives. Statements like this bolstered the labor movement by combining time-honored Judeo-Christian principles with a new rhetoric of industrial citizenship. In all these ways, Providence Catholics used religion to pursue rights they considered theirs as Americans.[30]

The Irish, as the group most involved in electoral politics and labor activism, dominated these efforts to use church resources to fight for workplace protections and full access to the vote; but newer immigrants joined them in a third and equally important strand of Catholic activism. Immigrants from Italy and French Canada were as committed as the Irish to proving ethnic Catholics "real" Americans deserving the same rights as native-born Protestants. Coreligionists from different countries drew on the resources of religion to articulate a pluralistic vision of national identity that recognized them as full members of the nation. Religious newspapers and pamphlets waged a decades-long campaign to demonstrate compatibility between Catholicism and Americanism. Ethnic organizations and parish societies promoted assimilation as well as preservation of homeland customs. Ethno-religious celebrations (inclusive demonstrations in which Catholics participated regardless of sex, date of arrival, union membership, or political rights) promoted a nuanced Americanism through a complex iconography that melded sacred and secular, old world and new.

On July 16, 1906, Italian Americans took to the streets for the annual feast day of Our Lady of Mount Carmel. After gathering for Mass they paraded through Federal Hill. The streets were lined with spectators brandishing Italian and American flags, as well as pictures of the Virgin Mary clothed in the Italian national colors. Street vendors got into the spirit by adorning pushcarts with patriotic decorations. After the parade, the community assembled for a band concert featuring traditional Italian music. The bandstand was decorated with a large representation of Mary, against the backdrop of an American flag.[31]

This bringing together of old world and new might have seemed incongruous to an outsider who happened upon the scene. In Providence, as in other cities transformed by immigration at the turn of the twentieth century, many native-born Protestants believed newcomers had to shed religious and ethnic traditions to become full-fledged Americans. Those who witnessed the Federal Hill *festa* might have found its melding of American, Italian, and Catholic iconography contradictory. The mixed symbolism seemed natural to the festival goers, however. They considered themselves members of multiple communities and these communities mutually sustaining, so that their Italianness and Catholicism made them better Americans. Through the complex pageantry of their patron saint celebration, they claimed the right to become American even as they remained Italian and Catholic.

Demonstrations like this not only challenged dominant ideas about Americanism but also proclaimed Catholic strength and solidarity. The

In July 1906, Italian Americans marched down Atwells Avenue in the annual celebration of Our Lady of Mount Carmel. The mixed symbolism of their parade, combining U.S. and Italian flags with Catholic banners, suggested it was possible to be American, ethnic, and Catholic at the same time. Silver gelatin print, courtesy of the Rhode Island Historical Society, RHi X3 283.

most powerful statement of this nature was the triennial parade the Providence Holy Name Union began to sponsor in 1910. This massive procession was a rare instance in which coreligionists came together across ethnic and parish lines, and by 1928 it attracted more than 35,000 marchers (dressed to the nines in formal suits and top hats) and 100,000 spectators. The *Visitor* called these demonstrations "Catholic religion in action," and certainly they sent the message that the church was a force to be reckoned with. The Holy Name parades, like smaller religious festivals, demonstrated Catholics' growing solidarity (despite enduring ethnic conflicts) and determination to make their demands heard in the larger community.[32]

In all these ways, during the Progressive Era Catholics began to use the resources of their faith to assert their rights and engage with public life. Religion, of course, was an imperfect political tool. In an age of pronounced divisions between national parishes, churches worked better as vehicles for individual groups than as means of advancing a pan-Catholic agenda. Religion was, moreover, a double-edged sword in the battle for workers' rights. Religious rhetoric could inspire forgiveness as well as protest and serve the mighty as well as the meek. Just as workers invoked the democratic implications of Christianity to justify protests, employers viewed religion as a

Forty thousand priests and laymen marched in the fifth triennial Holy Name parade in 1922, shown here in front of the Cathedral of SS. Peter and Paul. Parades like this demonstrated the growing power and solidarity of the city's Catholic population. Photograph, courtesy of *Providence Journal*.

force for law and order. Clerical support, for its part, lent the labor movement respectability and institutional support, yet imposed a moderating influence, discouraging solutions that were more radical and possibly more effective. And even the support of the church was not enough to push worker-friendly laws through a state legislature dominated by Republicans and their corporate allies. Yet the church's unflagging support for union recognition and friendly labor laws was of enormous benefit, calling attention to blue-collar problems at a time organized labor was weak. And when unionists themselves invoked religious principles, they inspired followers and legitimated struggles.[33]

Another problem with organizing through the parish was the limits on lay autonomy in a hierarchical institution; yet laypeople sometimes asserted themselves in ways of which their priests thoroughly disapproved. To be sure, some or even much parish-based activism represented the laity following clerical orders; yet these activities furnished Catholics with tools they could use in other ways (as chapter 9 will demonstrate). To paraphrase the historian Hugh McLeod, attending a clergy-dominated church was not the same as being dominated by the clergy. Bitter and sometimes spectacular conflicts broke out in Providence's Italian and French Canadian parishes, often over removal of a beloved priest or appointment of an unsatisfactory one. These battles revealed the limits of clerical control and the ability of laypeople to use parish-nurtured political skills to advance their own agendas.[34]

The hierarchical nature of the church, therefore, should not lead historians to dismiss the tremendous value of Catholic parishes as political organizing sites. Parishes provided physical spaces where new Americans developed organizations that strengthened communities and facilitated struggles. Religion offered inspiration and moral authority that strengthened their challenges. And links forged at church reinforced those developed in the neighborhood, workplace, political machine, and union hall. Parish politics offered an alternative for some Catholics, a supplement for others, to labor activism and electoral politics in the first decades of the twentieth century. The church welcomed all Catholics as members and offered them a host of spiritual, social, and material resources with which neither unions nor parties could compete. When structural obstacles prevented Catholics from launching successful strikes or electoral upsets, parish activism provided another means of influencing public life. Catholics used the resources of religion to pursue some of the same goals as progressives and Socialists—workplace justice and political democracy—as well as to advance their interests as a religious community. Rather than distracting new Americans from their crusades for full citizenship, the church provided a vehicle for defending their rights. During the First World War, Catholics would focus less on demanding economic and political prerogatives than on demonstrating their worth as citizens. Wartime activism would center on redefining Americanism in ways that acknowledged ethnic Catholics as members of the nation.

7

"FIGHT LIKE HEROES AND PRAY LIKE SAINTS"

Catholics and the First World War

A great nation may not be of one blood, but must be of one mind.
—Agnes M. Bacon, Providence Queen's Daughters,
Visitor, December 5, 1919

AMERICANISM CONTESTED

Across the nation, the First World War brought debates over national identity into bold relief. German Americans bore the brunt of wartime nativism, yet anti-German sentiment translated into broader suspicion of foreigners. Even as the war created common cause and incorporated new Americans into one national undertaking, it also fueled fears about ethnic difference. The federal Committee on Public Information (CPI) encapsulated this sentiment when it charged, "whoever is homesick for another country is lost for America." Or in the more dramatic words of President Woodrow Wilson, every "hyphenated" American carried a "dagger that he is ready to plunge into the vitals of this Republic." Nativism coincided with a related surge in antiradicalism to create a hostile climate for immigrants and workers across the country. Cincinnati barred aliens from operating pool halls, and Iowa required the speaking of English in schools, church services, and even telephone conversations. Vigilantes in Butte, Montana, murdered Frank Little, a Native American organizer for the IWW, and a mob near St. Louis lynched a young man whose only apparent offense was having been born in Germany.[1]

Although Providence escaped extreme behavior of this nature, its leaders were intensely worried about the civic fitness of the polyglot population. Certainly the city did not face the threats that seemed to menace communities in the Midwest, for its German population was small (just 2 percent of residents were of German birth or parentage) and its political left was weak. Yet Providence was home to an overwhelmingly foreign and, in the minds of natives, insufficiently assimilated population. By 1915, two-thirds of the city's 247,660 residents were of foreign parentage, with the Irish and Italians comprising the two largest groups. In 1910, only 39.5 percent of voting-age immigrant men were citizens, and 8.2 percent of residents age ten and older could not speak English. Assimilationist tendencies varied, to be sure, making a stronger showing among Protestants and English-speakers who fit more easily into Yankee culture, the upwardly mobile, and Jews eager for acceptance after centuries of persecution. Yet even those foreigners who naturalized and learned English often remained committed to old world traditions, especially French Canadians and Poles who believed retaining their language was critical to preserving their faith.[2]

Concerns that immigrants were inadequately Americanized coincided with fears about their political allegiances. More than 17 percent of Providence residents were first- or second-generation immigrants from Ireland, a country whose support for the Allied effort was lukewarm at best because of hostility toward the English. In April 1915, three thousand Irish and German Americans rallied in Providence to demand that the United States remain neutral. Although demonstrations like this were rare, they suggested ethnic Rhode Islanders were beholden to other countries. Many natives blamed ethnic folkways for nourishing rival loyalties and assumed immigrants would not be patriotic Americans until they adopted the language and lifestyle of their new home. Thus in Providence, as across the nation, social homogeneity became a counterpart to political unity.[3]

The wartime obsession with patriotism and assimilation brought new intensity to the decades-old struggle to define Americanism. More than ever before, "old stock" (a term used here to refer to Yankee Protestants) and "new stock" (ethnic Catholics) contended for economic clout and civic influence by arguing about what it meant to be a member of the nation.[4] This debate had two components. The first, the subject of this chapter, was whether Catholic immigrants needed to surrender old world political loyalties, religious practices, and cultural traditions to become American. The second, the topic of chapter 8, was what if any role the state should play in enforcing dominant ideas about national identity. The discussions that ensued revealed how sharply the meanings of Americanism varied for natives and immigrants, for members of different ethnic and religious groups, and for compatriots of different generations or economic positions. But even as Catholics disagreed among themselves over the extent to which they should assimilate and what it meant to do so, they tended to agree they could become American one step at a time, without abandoning older customs and identities.

In these debates religion and ethnicity blurred. Many Rhode Islanders still believed full assimilation required becoming a Protestant as well as a U.S. citizen. To be sure, religious bigotry declined somewhat during the war as national loyalty and political affiliation became greater concerns than religious faith. Yet wartime nativism cast suspicion on Catholics as adherents of a "foreign" church, a perception reinforced by the Vatican's recent decision to exert more control over American church appointments. U.S. policymakers suspected the Vatican's wartime sympathies were with the Central Powers, and Pope Benedict's determination to play a role in the peace negotiations raised familiar concerns about clerical influence over public affairs.[5] Catholics tried to counter fears of this nature by insisting they could be American without abandoning their ethnic and religious heritages. When they argued for the right to preserve traditions, therefore, they were defending religious practices as well as ethnic customs. It was particularly natural for Irish and French Canadian Catholics to draw those links, for they came from cultures in which religious and ethnic identities intermingled.

Wartime debates about national identity brought previously marginalized actors onto center stage. As the focus of local politics shifted from battles over workplace laws and voting restrictions to cultural struggles over assimilation, immigrants gained new visibility as participants in as well as subjects of public debate. This was particularly true in the case of foreign-born women. Americanization campaigns hinged not only on the "male" sphere of citizenship and political allegiance but also on language, religion, and domestic practices, traditions women typically passed on to children. Immigrant women thus served as objects and vehicles of Americanization, while native-born women who attempted to train them were agents in the process. As central players in the wartime Americanization project, women became prominent public actors and used this position to interject ideas about sexual equality into discussions about citizenship and national identity.

In all these ways the war presented an opportunity as well as a challenge for Providence Catholics, most of whom were first-, second- or third-generation immigrants. Pressures to prove themselves patriotic and assimilated were burdensome and at times coercive. Yet once Catholics had demonstrated they were "American," they could campaign more forcefully for rights they should enjoy in this capacity. They also could seek to reshape national identity in ways that recognized the needs and contributions of people who were neither native-born nor Protestant. The war thus represented a pivotal moment in their struggles to achieve what they considered full citizenship.

During the war new Americans demonstrated willingness to become American, within limits. Many worked in harmony with civic leaders to support the war effort. Yet even as they agreed political unity was essential, they differed about whether social conformity—in the form of total assimilation—was a prerequisite. The result was a series of competing efforts to absorb newcomers into American life, as ethnic and religious leaders offered alternatives to assimilation programs sponsored by native-born Protestants. In a parallel war of rhetoric, immigrants rejected "100 Percent Americanism" for a more expansive national identity that coexisted with Catholicism and ethnic pride. More consciously and imaginatively than ever before, they used political speech, public demonstration, and an intricate symbolism to propose an Americanism that left room for old world identities. The institutional resources of the Catholic Church proved especially useful to these efforts.

"AMERICANISM MEANS UNDIVIDED LOYALTY TO THE US OF A"

If Providence residents agreed on one thing during the war, it was that good Americans had to be aggressive patriots. On June 3, 1916, a committee of religious and civic leaders organized a "Preparedness Parade" whose slogan was, " 'Americanism' means undivided loyalty to the US of A." Almost 53,000 residents participated in the six-hour parade, following strict orders that they "march simply as Americans" and bear no banners other than the U.S. and Rhode Island flags. The parade's mission was to demonstrate that "true Americanism . . . reigns supreme in the breasts of Rhode Island's citizens, in spite of the changes wrought by the influx of the foreign-born." The emphasis was on unity across lines of class, gender, and ethnicity, and the *Visitor* was proud to report that "every walk of life" and "every class of workers" were represented. One feature was a human flag comprised of more than fifteen hundred school children. When they joined in song, the *Journal* noted, "they blended their nationalities with their voices, and in their hearts there was but one nation." The parade sent the country's leaders a message about the "unquestioning devotion" of this heavily foreign and Catholic community. It also signaled to locals that the "march of personal desire" was to come to a halt. It was clear to the city's various interest groups that personal goals were to be subordinated to the greater cause of military security. Statements like these set the tone for wartime activism in Providence.[6]

When the United States entered the war ten months later, expectations of

Fifteen hundred school children formed a human flag outside City Hall as part of the June 1916 preparedness parade. Post card, courtesy of the Rhode Island Historical Society, RHi X3 7283.

a firm and visible patriotism intensified in Rhode Island. The General Assembly "earnestly" recommended that all property owners display flags on their premises, and the city council required that every musical entertainment include a rendition of "The Star-Spangled Banner." Feeling that more aggressive patriotism was in order, the RISFWC requested that no people be allowed to appear before a public gathering if they "refuse to lead, sing or play our National songs . . . in the presence of the American flag."[7]

The efforts of civic leaders ranged from hyper-patriotic to downright xenophobic. Education Commissioner Walter Ranger called without success for an investigation of whether Providence parochial schools were feeding their pupils German propaganda, even though very few served German American student bodies. Senate Minority Leader William Troy of Providence, a member of the Democratic Party, which traditionally championed cultural pluralism in Rhode Island, suggested all aliens be registered and anyone who was not totally loyal be "lined up against the wall." Although the latter part of his proposal failed, the General Assembly did require all aliens to register with the authorities and carry their cards with them at all times. Providence may not have witnessed the vigilante violence that plagued other parts of the country, but its natives were not above casting aspersions on their foreign-born neighbors.[8]

Many new Americans, in Providence and nationwide, initially were lukewarm about entering the war because of homeland loyalties and anger against Wilson for recognizing Mexican president Venustiano Carranza, whose government was persecuting Catholic clergymen. As the wartime climate heated up, however, most Providence residents exhibited the loyal support expected of them. These efforts were particularly marked on the part of Catholic editors and lay leaders, eager to disprove the perennial charge that they owed their primary loyalties to the Vatican, and residents of Irish descent, who wished to compensate for their initial opposition to U.S. participation. The city's ethnic and Catholic press used its influence to whip up wartime fervor and demonstrate the loyalty of readers suspect as foreigners and non-Protestants. It was a frequent and accurate refrain that disproportionate numbers of Catholics were serving in the military. Statements like this echoed the pronouncements of the AFCS, whose bulletin ran articles on "American Catholic Preparedness" and claimed that more than half of U.S. Marines were Catholic. The nation's archbishops, for their part, sent Wilson a letter that declared, "We are all true Americans, ready . . . to do whatever is in us to do, for the preservation, the progress, and the triumph of our beloved country."[9]

Church leaders across the nation took this pledge seriously. In April 1917 they formed the National Catholic War Council, a body of clerics and laypeople charged with coordinating church contributions, cooperating with the federal War Department, and serving as a watchdog for Catholic interests. The council's advice to Catholics was to "fight like heroes and pray like saints." It urged every parish to form a war committee, believing that "the parish is the supreme testing place for the length and breadth and depth of Catholic patriotism." Providence congregations rose to the challenge. Catholic clubs and Holy Name societies organized fund-raising drives, and the diocese launched a campaign to enroll one "Victory Girl" or "Victory Boy," or donor, for every parishioner serving in the armed forces. This effort was quite successful although enthusiasm varied markedly among parishes. The French Canadian St. Charles Borromeo enlisted sixty-five of a hoped-for sixty-eight pledges, and the Irish St. Mary's boasted an impressive 232 (surpassing its goal of 161); but the Italians at Holy Ghost did not participate, and those at St. Ann's fell ninety-five pledges short of their goal. This lukewarm response reflected economic privation, political disengagement, and preference for sending money home to Italy.[10]

To encourage individuals to do their part, the war council asked every lay society to fill out a questionnaire about how its members were contributing to the war effort. Surviving responses from Providence suggest that, as with the "victory girl" drive, enthusiasm was strongest among Irish and weakest among Italians. The Providence Catholic Club, a diocesan-wide group dominated by Irish American doctors and lawyers, had an impressive record. Its elite membership raised funds, sat on public commissions, and donated medical expertise. Several—including Dr. Edward F. Carroll and the attorney Edward J. Noons—served as "Four-Minute" speakers, members of a nationwide corps of 75,000 selected by the CPI to whip up war fervor through intensely patriotic speeches. Members of other lay societies served on the Liberty Loan Committee and War Savings Stamp Commission, made their clubhouses available to servicemen, and collected tobacco and rosaries for soldiers. James R. Cannon, a city truant officer and prominent Holy Name Union member, demonstrated particular spirit by founding a "Cannon Club to Shell Berlin from Providence." Lay societies also were eager to document the activities of members serving in the armed forces. Joseph A. Hickey, president of the Cathedral Catholic Club, boasted of the military exploits of fellow member Ernest Berimer, who crept "across no man's land to fix a barbe wired [sic] entanglement, with a pair of Rosary Beads in one hand and the necessary equipment in the other." Anecdotes like this delighted the war council, which appointed a special committee to record Catholic contributions for posterity. In 1921 Michael Williams immortalized these stories in his celebratory *American Catholics in the War*.[11]

Particularly for women, demonstrations of wartime patriotism were an opportunity as well as a burden. Because patriotic works were considered acceptable ways for women to be active outside the home, the war was a chance to engage with public life. While men proved their patriotism through military service, women demonstrated their loyalty in less visible but equally significant ways. The Food Administration relied on the nation's housewives to make its voluntary rationing program work by enduring "wheatless" Mondays and "meatless" Tuesdays, but Catholic women went far beyond these basic contributions. They recognized the opportunity laid out in the war council's 1918 handbook: "The war cannot be fought successfully without the help of the women of the country. There are innumerable tasks which women alone can perform. The opportunities which have arisen for the women in America are among the most wonderful in the history of the world."[12]

Catholic women across the country eagerly availed themselves of these chances. A number went overseas as relief workers after training at the new National Catholic School of Social Service in Washington, D.C. Others served closer to home. New York's League of Catholic Women operated 126 surgical dressing workrooms and worked with public agencies on fund-raising and clothing drives. The city's Catholic Young Women's Patriotic Club formed a clubhouse staffed by eight hundred workers and "equipped for patriotic activities" such as cooking sweets for convalescent soldiers and holding weekly dances for servicemen. The dances offered participants a chance to enjoy the war years, and perhaps engage in sexually permissive behavior, under the rubric of patriotic service. In Providence, laywomen sold liberty bonds, organized fund-raisers, and sponsored "patriotic" entertainments. French Canadian women from five parishes in Pawtucket and Central Falls came together to form a Red Cross auxiliary. Under the direction of Jane Newton (a second-generation Irish immigrant who lived on Providence's East Side), the middle-class Queen's Daughters were particularly active. The club was proud to report to the war council, "No sooner had the call gone forth for help, for soldiers and sailors, than our women, young and old, responded." Many seized on the war as a chance for adventure as well as social service and found that their activities won them unprecedented visibility. One Queen's Daughter went overseas to work as a translator, one was recognized by Treasury Secretary William McAdoo for her contributions to the Liberty Loan drive, and another received a presidential Certificate of Honor for her work as a Four-Minute speaker.[13]

As these examples suggest, the war was a turning point for many American women. Just as native-born Protestants proved their citizenship by working to rouse patriotism and assimilate immigrants, ethnic Catholics used the military crisis to demonstrate their Americanism and integrate themselves into public life. This was evident when the National Ladies Auxiliary of the AOH commissioned a history of its wartime service to create a record of its "patriotic achievements." For Catholic women, the war provided a stage on which they could join with Protestants in acting out their commitment to the nation. Like their husbands, sons, and fathers, they hoped to be remembered as fit citizens once the curtain went down.[14]

Among both women and men, enthusiasm for the war effort varied markedly among ethnic groups. It was middle-class Irish Americans who were most active, as they were most likely to have time and funds to devote to patriotic activities and political contacts to carve out roles for themselves. The French Canadians did their bit, to be sure, no doubt wishing to dismiss lingering concerns that commitment to *survivance* outweighed loyalty to the United States. The USJB issued resolutions affirming support for the war effort and pledging to hang the American flag on its buildings. *Le Jean-Baptiste* filled its pages with blurbs encouraging readers to accept voluntary rations, attend Red Cross fund-raisers and purchase Liberty Bonds. Yet it also urged readers to assist Mother France, and they may have felt torn between putting hard-earned dollars into American relief coffers or sending them across the Atlantic. The Italians no doubt felt a similar conflict. As newer immigrants they had fewer resources to devote, and some took more interest in the progress of the war in Italy than in America's involvement. It was telling that only 18 percent of voting-age Italian men were citizens in 1915, compared with 46.5 percent of the French Canadians and 66.4 percent of the Irish. There was a clear correlation among rates of U.S. citizenship and commitment to the American war effort.[15]

AMERICANIZATION, "OLD STOCK" STYLE

Disappointing rates of naturalization convinced many native-born Protestants it was not enough for foreigners to demonstrate their patriotism through war contributions. To be fully American, they also had to assimilate. Across the country, dominant attitudes toward immigrants had shifted from a nineteenth-century assumption that they would assimilate over time, through a Progressive Era sense that social workers should gently but firmly facilitate the transition, to a wartime conviction that only intensive assimilation would overcome split loyalties and ensure national security. This was evident when the National Americanization Committee altered its slogan from "Many Peoples, But One Nation" to "America First." This change reflected a shift in focus by the citizens' group from providing humanitarian assistance to immigrants to encouraging them to assimilate and become naturalized. Americanization could not be so coercive that its targets became resentful, for national unity was of the essence, but it had to be promoted more aggressively. Assimilation thus became the civilian component of national defense. By encouraging newcomers to learn English and adjust to the expectations of industrial society, Americanization also improved workforce efficiency at a time when smooth production was critical to the Allied effort.[16]

In Providence, the drive for "100 Percent Americanism" was for the most part aggressive without being rigidly intolerant. Civic leaders demanded that immigrants demonstrate commitment to this country by speaking English, adopting middle-class domestic practices, and placing new world loyalties before old world attachments, but they generally tolerated newcomers' holding onto some customs as long as their political allegiances rested firmly with the United States. Although Protestantism was subtly promoted as a component of Americanism, it was not imposed on the overwhelmingly Catholic immigrant population. For the most part the melting pot ideal persisted, as natives acknowledged that immigrants brought traditions which could strengthen the country. In a 1917 speech Morris J. Weisel, secretary of the Rhode Island Immigrant Educational Bureau, spoke of "the American opportunity to blend into the citizenship of the future contributions which the varied races of Europe can contribute." Sentiments like these placed Rhode Islanders in the liberal Americanization camp, as distinguished from the hard-core "100 Percent" Americanizers, and reflected the city's sizable population of immigrants and Catholics and its long history of diversity.[17]

Rather than demanding unilateral sacrifice from immigrants, Providence natives tended to call for mutual exchange between old stock and new. Natives were to extend to foreigners the tools to achieve full citizenship and immigrants, in exchange, would reward the United States with undivided loyalty. Natives, moreover, were to serve as positive examples by living according to national values of freedom and toleration. In October 1916, Dr. Kate Waller Barrett of the U.S. Bureau of Immigration recommended this approach to a gathering of clubwomen at Brown University. "It is for us . . . to cast those things from our lives which we do not want to see in the immigrants," she told her audience. "We must begin by Americanizing ourselves." In Barrett's formulation Americanism connoted state of mind rather than place of birth, and Americanization involved mutual obligation between native- and foreign-born.[18]

On July 4, 1915, Mayor Gainer laid out this bargain. Natives were to abolish the "distinction [that] exists between the native born and the naturalized citizen," while immigrants were to remember that "no matter what country gave you birth, your allegiance is now pledged to the Stars and Stripes, and your fortune, family, and your life itself belongs to the United States of America against any or all of the other nations of the world." Even as Gainer upset traditional hierarchies of citizenship by offering naturalized immigrants equal membership in the body politic, he reinforced those hierarchies by emphasizing the primacy of new world loyalties over old world allegiances. The mayor proffered a welcoming hand to immigrants, but he also raised a finger of warning. American citizenship came with a price.[19]

Moreover, even as the Catholic mayor articulated an egalitarian rhetoric about give and take, most native-born Protestants believed people familiar with the nation's institutions should direct the process of Americanization. This mindset prevailed among the RISFWC, whose members vowed "to make good citizens of the immigrants" and to "teach the immigrant the meaning of real American patriotism." Good citizenship was a lofty but vague ideal, encompassing any variety of meanings that ranged from civic involvement and English language literacy to physical health and community stability. Becoming a citizen was only the first step in becoming an American. As a result, assimilation in Providence was a multifaceted movement that sought to instill middle-class, Protestant standards of civic, linguistic, and personal behavior in a polyglot and largely Catholic population. Uniting these efforts was a shared belief among people of native birth and Protestant faith, and especially those of the female sex, that they were entitled and even obligated to direct the process by which immigrants entered the nation's mainstream.[20]

A series of private and public institutions were to effect this transition. An American Citizenship Campaign Committee chaired by future governor Theodore Francis Green sent representatives into mills and immigrant neighborhoods, issued mass mailings in five languages, sponsored evening classes, and organized mass meetings to encourage immigrants to become citizens. Settlement houses and women's clubs, YMCAs and YWCAs, Protestant churches, and the Immigrant Educational Bureau all promoted naturalization and English language literacy as well as civic education and middle-class domestic practices. These efforts extended from the docks into immigrant neighborhoods and provided facilities that ranged from boarding homes and health clinics to libraries, playgrounds, and gymnasiums. Services like these provided alternatives to "the cheap and dangerous dance hall and the low grade theater," as one settlement worker put it, as well as to union halls, Socialist meetinghouses, and Catholic churches.[21]

The first immigrants arrived at Providence's new State Pier on December 17, 1913. Once the First World War broke out, native-born Protestants stepped up their efforts to meet immigrants like these at the docks and ensure they became suitably assimilated. Photograph, courtesy of the Rhode Island Historical Society, RHi X3 5461.

Whereas facilities like these were aimed at entire families, other institutions targeted young people. Public schools seemed ideal vehicles for the dissemination of American values. "Of all the agencies working to assimilate with the older portions of our population the newcomers, there is none which has a wider opportunity than the public school," Lester Burrell Shippee, a special agent in the state Bureau of Labor, wrote in a report to the General Assembly. Shippee's statement reflected the mood of the times. Nationwide, the Progressive Era had witnessed a spate of educational reforms designed in large part to mold the diverse public into a united citizenry. The Providence school committee echoed a widely held belief when it reported in 1915 that "a democratic form of government can exist only where the people are . . . actuated by similar ideals of freedom and justice." The war intensified the conviction that public schools were sites for promoting patriotic values, forging national unity, and eliminating social differences.[22]

In promoting what it called "intelligent citizenship," the school committee had its work cut out for it. About 14 percent of the city's youngsters were beyond the committee's reach because they attended Catholic schools. Of children enrolled in public schools, more than half lived in homes where a language other than English was spoken. And foreign-born adults—mostly men of Italian, Jewish, Armenian, or Cape Verdean origin—comprised 64 percent of the evening school student body. In its efforts to forge this diverse population into a homogeneous public, the school committee commissioned classes on "English for Coming Citizens" and "Americanization and Citizenship," among other topics. "It is no longer safe to take it for granted that these ideals will be fostered by the home," the committee noted in its 1916 report. We "must work unceasingly to give these children and their parents such ideals of America as will render them devoted citizens." Response to the evening schools was disappointing, however. Annual school committee reports show that attendance plummeted by almost 50 percent between 1914 and 1919, a drop officials attributed to a slowdown in immigration, labor shortage, and remigration of young men (particularly Italians) to serve in homeland armies. Evidently many Providence immigrants had priorities that ranked higher than learning English grammar or reading the Constitution.[23]

It was clear the efforts of schools, settlements, clubs, and charities were insufficient to meet the monumental task of transforming the city's eighty thousand immigrants, most of them Catholics, into "good" Americans. "All agencies together seem woefully inadequate to the task which exists," reported Shippee of the labor bureau. "The task of making a homogeneous whole in which the best elements from all the parts are conserved is a formidable one." Assimilation programs were limited by social and cultural distance between reformers and reformed, and by resistance to an Americanism linked to Anglo-Saxon Protestantism. Although attitudes varied widely among ethnic groups, many immigrants resented the suggestion that they convert, speak English, send children to school, and adopt new domestic practices. "Why should I go to a house-keeping class?" asked Carmela Mastronardi of Federal Hill. "Nobody has to tell me how to keep my house." Some immigrant men, for their part, were enraged when settlement workers urged wives to act independently and take marital disputes to the courts. There were social workers who sought to bridge these barriers by demonstrating respect for ethnic traditions, but these nods to cultural pluralism tended to be superficial and even insulting.[24]

This was evident in February 1918, when the Rhode Island Women's Club held an "inter-racial patriotic session" designed to "develop the American spirit." More than ever, Mrs. Frederick S. Aldrich told the gathering, "should hyphens be eliminated and the citizens of our city become 'all American.'" Becoming American required rejecting foreign allegiances but not abandoning national customs. According to the guest speaker, Weisel of the Immigrant Educational Bureau, "By showing appreciation of what foreigners can bring to us and encouraging them to retain their distinctive handicrafts, Americans will develop in them a new feeling of loyalty to and cooperation with the people of their adopted country." In this vein, foreign-born attendees wore traditional dress, decorated the room with ethnic crafts, and sang homeland songs. The meeting, however, opened with the singing of "America" and closed with "The Star-Spangled Banner," making it clear that ethnic traditions were to be enveloped within an embracing American identity.[25]

This approach troubled many newcomers. Certainly condescension was preferable to the xenophobia witnessed in other parts of the country; yet in equating national tradition with a few quaint songs or handicrafts, the well-bred organizers reduced ethnic culture to a brightly colored vest or colorful ditty. When they assumed immigrants would cast off old world allegiances for the right to sing the "Marseillaise" at ceremonial occasions or dress in traditional garb on Italian feast days, they underestimated the passion that church and homeland continued to inspire. Although some immigrants were eager to be absorbed fully into American society, others felt that assimilation should be only a partial adjustment.

AMERICANIZATION, "NEW STOCK" STYLE

Many of the city's Catholic immigrants and ethnics were willing and even eager to become American, on their own terms. Mutual aid societies, unions, and churches provided alternate routes to assimilation, directed by local leaders rather than Protestant reformers. These self-generated programs proposed a national identity that left much more room for old traditions. Churches in particular sought a balance between encouraging members to assimilate and discouraging them from internalizing American individualism so much they felt free to flout the authority of priest and family, reject Catholicism's communalist mindset, or abandon their faith altogether.[26] The result was a contest between native-born Protestants and ethnic Catholics over ways in which newcomers would enter the nation's mainstream. At the same time, Catholics disagreed among themselves over what it meant to Americanize and the extent to which they should do so. These contests tended to pit middle-class ethnic leaders against newer arrivals of working-class status, or Irish Americans against coreligionists from Italy and French Canada.

The city's immigrants long had used ethnic mutual aid societies as alternatives to Protestant settlement houses and charitable programs. Many immigrants preferred to turn to these institutions, rooted in regional origins, religious affiliations, or occupational ties, for material assistance and social fellowship. This trend was particularly noted among French Canadians, whose commitment to *survivance* fueled sharp suspicion of outsiders and even of fellow Catholics from other countries. Providence mutual aid societies brought together preservation of old world ways with promotion of new world values, but many focused increasingly on the latter during the war years. This tendency was less notable among the Irish, who as northern Europeans fit relatively easily into Anglo-Saxon culture. French Canadian societies, for their part, embraced assimilation uneasily, not wishing to appear disloyal yet worried about weakening their traditions. During the war Club Choquet and Club Franco-Republicain stepped up efforts to promote naturalization, even as other community groups campaigned for bilingual education. Italian mutual aid societies felt the most pressure to Americanize their members, who were marked as outsiders not only because they were the newest ethnic group but also because current racial categories marked them as less "white" than other immigrants.[27]

The middle-class Sons of Italy, which formed a local chapter in 1914 under the slogan "America forever," spearheaded the assimilation drive among local Italians. Its philosophy was, "If the cult of the country of origin is laudable, the cult of the country of adoption constitutes a sacred duty." According to Grand Venerable Luigi Cipolla of Silver Lake, "Our main object is to impress upon the unnaturalized that there are obligations they cannot overlook. They have enjoyed civil liberty, their children have been educated at the expense of the public, they have received liberal wages, and it is their duty to remain here, keep their savings in this country, build homes and assume the responsibilities of American citizenship." Cipolla's statement reflected a conflict within his community over what it meant to be Italian American. Many working-class immigrants rejected his suggestion that they become citizens in gratitude for the benefits they enjoyed in the new country. Among Providence immigrants, only the Greeks and Portuguese were less likely to become citizens. This lack of interest in the formalities of citizenship reflected, among other factors, the fact that nationwide the Italians were more likely to remigrate than most other immigrants.[28]

The emotional pull of the homeland became evident in May 1915. According to the *Providence Evening Telegram*, the city's Italian consulate was "besieged by men anxious to report and be sent home" to serve in the Italian army.[29] This enthusiasm indicated a growth in Italian nationalism, a sentiment initially weak among immigrants who had identified as members of villages or regions rather than a larger nation. Ironically, middle-class compatriots had promoted pan-Italian sentiment before the war in hope of discouraging internal rivalries they considered embarrassing. They had seen becoming Italian as the first step to becoming Italian American, but by the war's onset they had moved on to fuller assimilation while their working-class counterparts continued to celebrate their newfound Italian identity.

Homeland attachments were most immediate for recent immigrants like the Italians, but religious and secular leaders from other ethnic communities tended to agree that their constituents were under-assimilated. As an institution representing a variety of national groups, the Catholic diocese felt a special responsibility to make its members more American. These efforts often involved Irish bishops and lay leaders urging coreligionists from other countries to assimilate. Yet even as they encouraged Catholics to integrate into the national mainstream, they sought to control the process. Hoping to counter the attractions of groups like the YMCA (a Protestant-run institution Catholic leaders mistrusted), the *Visitor* told its readers, "We can and must take care of these Catholic immigrants ourselves."[30]

To this end the diocese operated an impressive network of schools, charitable programs, orphanages, hospitals, working girls' homes, and summer camps. Individual parishes, for their part, provided extensive opportunities for education as well as recreation. Inspired by the successful School of Domestic Arts at St. Mary's and wishing to divert Catholics from Protestant settlements and YWCAs, the Queen's Daughters, Pallottine Sisters, and Franciscan Missionaries of Mary offered homemaking courses of their own. Protestant efforts to promote English language literacy also sparked a rival movement within the Catholic community. In 1918 the Union of Parish Clubs announced it would offer classes for people who could or would not attend evening school, recognizing that parishioners might feel more comfortable learning from coreligionists and in their own neighborhoods. St. Ann's offered instruction in both English and Italian, suggesting that retaining the native language was as important as learning a new one.[31]

Programs sponsored by Catholic parishes and ethnic societies shared the citywide goal of promoting assimilation, but under the aegis of local leadership. Even as they accommodated demands for Americanization, they challenged the assumption that native-born Protestants should direct the process and that assimilation should be "100 Percent." Immigrants who used churches or mutual aid societies as bridges to the new world learned they could be American without abandoning traditional ways, although there were times when commitments to the United States had to come first. In this way, many Catholic immigrants entered national life without leaving their neighbor-

The International Institute at the Providence YWCA, shown here in 1929, was one of many Protestant-run organizations that provided services for immigrants. To counter the "pulling power" of groups like this, Catholics formed their own outreach networks that encouraged newcomers to adjust to American life without leaving the church. Silver gelatin print, courtesy of the Rhode Island Historical Society, RHi X3 8584.

hoods or parishes. Community institutions thus co-opted the Americanization drive to promote a more expansive concept of national identity.

"GOD AND COUNTRY, FAITH AND FLAG": TOWARD AN INCLUSIVE AMERICANISM

Efforts to forge a more inclusive Americanism worked hand-in-hand with a campaign to demonstrate that old and new world identities could co-exist. Catholics in particular saw the war as an opportunity to integrate their religion into the life of the nation. Diocesan priests and editors sought to prove that Catholicism and Americanism were compatible, while the laity engaged in an elaborate pageantry to show that old world traditions were consistent with new world identities. In these ways, ethnic Catholics at once challenged nativism and used the war to reshape ideas about Americanism.

Concerned that wartime nativism would foster anti-Catholic sentiment, diocesan leaders (like their counterparts across the nation) launched a public relations campaign to demonstrate commonalities between Catholicism and Americanism. The overarching theme was that their coreligionists had played a formative role in the discovery of the new world and the founding of the American nation. "Our Catholic American Title Deeds date back to the Norse explorers of the twelfth century," claimed a pamphlet circulated in Providence in 1917. This leaflet echoed an eloquent speech that Martin H. Glynn, former governor of New York, delivered at a Memorial Day demonstration in Washington, D.C., that same year: "Catholic patriotism ploughs the Atlantic with Columbus and with Balboa it looks upon the Pacific from the peak of Darien. With Leif Ericson it skirts the shores of Vineland and with Sebastian Cabot sees the snows of Labrador. . . . With Father Mare it finds our mines of turquoise and with Father Hennepin locates our mines of coal; with a Franciscan it finds the salt springs of Onondaga, and with the Jesuits discovers the oil wells of Lake Erie, the copper of Lake Superior and the lead of Illinois." Since the days of discovery, Catholics argued, they had promoted familial and civic stability in a variety of ways. The *Visitor* was fond of pointing out that diocesan institutions improved social welfare and reduced the tax burden by relieving the city of the care of some of its poor and the education of a sizable minority of its youngsters. Rather than being separatist or subversive, the *Visitor* claimed, parochial schools were "nurseries of the purest patriotism." Individual Catholics, for their part, were superior Americans because their religion encouraged industry, social service, and respect for authority. "Good Catholicism is inclusive of good citizenship," the *Visitor* argued. "And usually the better Catholic one is the better citizen he makes."[32]

In insisting on the salutary influence of their values and institutions, Catholics made a larger point: rather than being un-American or undemocratic, their religion reinforced the U.S. government. In fact, Gainer claimed, the laws of the church ensured the prosperity and stability of the state. "No man need be afraid that the Catholic Church will ever ask him to do anything not for the good of the community," the Catholic chief executive told the St. Edward's Holy Name Society in January 1917. "If a man will only obey the Church, he cannot go wrong." Gainer's words echoed those articulated by Catholic priests and politicians across the nation during the war, and the *Visitor* offered his sentiment a ringing endorsement. "No institution on earth has stood more unflinchingly for obedience to authority than the Catholic Church. It is the very breath of her life," the newspaper declared. "Obedience to God in a Catholic way does not necessarily interfere with obedience to government." Statements like these transformed Catholic respect for authority, often cited as proof of a slavish devotion antithetical to American individualism, into an asset at a time when government was demanding unquestioning obedience of its citizens.[33]

Efforts to forge links between Catholicism and Americanism represented both a nod and a challenge to prevailing ideas about national identity. Catholics simultaneously obliged the nation's leaders with the patriotism expected during the war and contested an Americanism rooted in Protestant culture by demonstrating their contributions to the nation's past and present. Their challenge was to carve out a place for themselves in public life without awakening long-standing concerns about an unholy union between church and state. When Rev. James Craig (of St. Sebastian's on the tony East Side) recited a prayer at Gainer's 1917 inaugural, the *Visitor* noted, "Neither City nor State is going to suffer from the fact that a Catholic clergyman invoked a divine blessing upon their activities for the coming year." Craig's appearance suggested a marked change since 1895, when Bishop Harkins had refused to participate in the inauguration of the city's first Catholic mayor. Even during the hypercharged atmosphere of the war, Rhode Islanders seemed more willing to acknowledge that Catholics could engage in politics without upsetting the traditional separation between church and state. This is only one example of the avenues through which the war offered ethnic Catholics a chance to reshape Americanism in a way that recognized them as members of the national community.[34]

Rank-and-file Catholics joined church leaders in demonstrating the harmony between old world and new. During the war they tried harder than ever to incorporate American icons into expressions of religious faith and ethnic identity. The February 22, 1918, edition of *Le Jean-Baptiste,* for example, printed both the "Star-Spangled Banner" and the "Marseillaise" on its editorial page. On the parish level, lay societies played the national anthem at meetings and used gatherings to affirm "devotion to church and loyalty to nation." Notre Dame du Sacre-Coeur held a demonstration to recognize 310 parishioners serving in the military, and a parade to honor French Canadian soldiers from Pawtucket began with a High Mass at Saint Jean-Baptiste. In June 1916, the St. Michael's Holy Name Society held a "preparedness card party" whose four hundred attendees received as favors tiny submarines equipped with candy torpedoes. The gathering ended in a dance during which red, white, and blue streamers were thrown over participants in an attempt to envelop them in American tradition.[35]

Rev. Antonio Bove of St. Ann's was particularly eager to merge ethnicity, Catholicism, and Americanism. At a July 4, 1917, celebration sponsored by the Sons of the American Revolution, he declared, "Patriotism is derived not from accident of birth . . . but from those principles on which national life is based." In 1918 his parish's lawn festival featured a game called "Get the Kaiser" and screened a film titled *The Unbeliever*, described in a parish leaflet as a "Religious and Patriotic Super Feature of Romance and Action." Two weeks after the armistice, St. Ann's organized a parade and High Mass to commemorate the victory. As the *Providence News* described the procession, "In the shadow of the American and Italian flags were Miss Jennie Di Lucca as Liberty, and Miss Amilea Caldarone as Italia." The parade culminated at the church, where Bove gave a "patriotic" sermon in which he reminded listeners that to be a good Catholic was to be a good citizen. A parish history written a few years after the war remarked upon Bove's efforts to merge American patriotism with Catholic piety and Italian pride. "During the war Father Bove was second to none in exemplifying civic pride, civic duty, civic responsibility. He urged his people to love America's cause and ever appreciate their constitutional rights," the parish historians claimed. Yet "the Monsignor's love for America does not detract from his love for his native Italy."[36]

Efforts to integrate Catholicism and Americanism continued well after hostilities ceased. In March 1919, the city's Irish Americans added an interesting twist to their St. Patrick's Day parade. The procession, in which eight thousand marchers proclaimed ethnic pride and demanded self-determination for Ireland, finished on the State House lawn where two thousand children assembled in the shape of an American flag. This symbolic act literally incorporated the city's Irish Catholics into the body politic. At a time when natives were demanding "100 Percent Americanism," the paraders proposed an alternative conception that made room for old world identities.[37]

Much more than transparent declarations of loyalty, demonstrations like these were acts of resistance against the assumption that Catholics and immigrants were second-class citizens. Moreover, they were inclusive actions that incorporated men, women, and children into public movements for their rights. These statements were directed inward as well as outward, reassuring new Americans who feared that assimilation endangered their traditions as well as natives who felt threatened by old world culture. Street spectacle thus provided a stage on which Catholics asserted their citizenship and challenged the dominant narrative of Americanism as native-born and Protestant. In addition to cementing links to the old country, these celebrations carved out space in the new world. Religious rituals and ethnic parades formed part of a larger wartime strategy in which the new stock staked a claim on Americanism at a time when it was critically important to do so. By assisting in the war effort, demonstrating eagerness to assimilate on their own terms, outlining their contributions to social order, and illustrating the harmony between old world and new, they proved they were American and redefined what that meant. In so doing they hoped to gain control of the language of Americanism and use that language to win their rights. Like African American activists and native-born woman suffragists in other parts of the country, Providence Catholics hoped to turn wartime contributions into peacetime access to politics and the state.[38]

8

"THE FORCE OF COMPULSION"

Americanism and the Wartime State

Our republic can be made safe, efficient and enduring only by the development, through the right kind of education, of a citizenship physically and intellectually sound and embued with the spirit and ideals of true Americanism.

—National League of Women Voters,
Bulletin of the Committee on American Citizenship, May 1920

"THE WAR FOR DEMOCRACY": NEW AMERICANS DEMAND THEIR RIGHTS

Ironically, the war eroded many of the rights the city's Catholic immigrants had hoped to secure. Although they made some progress in using rhetoric and pageantry to prove their patriotism and propose a national identity that incorporated their traditions, they were largely unsuccessful in using the power of the state to defend their rights and promote their vision of Americanism. When struggles between old stock and new moved from the streets of the city to the halls of the legislature, ethnic Catholics lost out. During the war, most Americans looked to the state less as protector of individual rights than enforcer of national unity. They channeled the crusading impulse that had informed imperialism and progressivism into a new drive to achieve "100 Percent Americanism" through the coercive powers of government. Well-born natives, some of whom had resisted progressive re-form as a threat to limited government, now used the state to ensure na-tional loyalty and cultural conformity. And the same new Americans who called on government to guarantee economic protections and political rights resisted the extension of state control into personal life, selectively co-opting their rivals' former argument that big government was un-American.

The result was a series of contests informed by these competing and curiously reversed definitions of Americanism. Old and new stock Rhode Islanders fought over local efforts to promote assimilation through the schools and a national movement to regulate behavior through prohibition. Two relics of Progressive Era activism were ongoing campaigns to overturn suffrage restrictions and improve working conditions. After the war ended, a local Red Scare raised new concerns about immigrant radicals and rein-forced the drive for forceful assimilation. These divisive cultural issues split erstwhile allies, as native-born Protestant reformers advocated measures to which ethnic Catholics objected strenuously. At the same time, cultural pol-itics gave new visibility to native-born women as reformers and immigrant women as objects of reform.

Public schools figured prominently in wartime discussions of American-ism and the uses of state power. Always viewed as assimilationist vehicles, the nation's schools now became virtual arms of the War Department. In addition to offering classes in English and citizenship in accordance with the U.S. Bureau of Education's "War Americanization Plan," public schools across the country implemented government-approved "war study courses" that encouraged patriotism and presented the conflict from an Allied per-spective. Providence schools, like those in other communities, stopped teaching German and eliminated books "objectionable for their pro-Ger-man character." The city's Catholic leaders could not resist these programs without incurring charges of disloyalty, but they raised their voices against one measure they found particularly offensive.[1]

In 1917 the RISFWC spearheaded a successful movement to teach child-care in the Pawtucket schools. This measure reflected wartime concerns about physical well-being, as well as widespread perceptions that the best way to improve immigrant lifestyles was to target children and their largely female caretakers. To Catholics, however, this example of state paternalism violated parental prerogatives, undermined the tradition of hands-off gov-ernment, and (although directed at public schools) sparked fears about reg-ulation of parochial institutions. Fourteen Pawtucket priests, led by the Irish church of St. Mary's, signed a petition objecting to the program on these grounds. The *Visitor* for its part complained, "The State has of late become so solicitous for the welfare of its members that it has assumed the role of father and mother." The infant hygiene controversy pitted well-educated advocates of "scientific" childrearing against ethnic, Catholic traditionalists. The latter resented this effort to indoctrinate children with newfangled practices and promote an Americanism rooted in middle-class, Protestant values. The implementation of the program was a victory for Rhode Islanders who believed in the old stock approach to Americanization.[2]

At the same time that infant hygiene classes sought to assimilate young women, military training targeted their brothers. Since the Progressive Era, patricians had touted universal military training as a way to defuse social conflict by providing a shared experience for young men from different backgrounds, and their arguments gained new resonance once war broke out. In May 1915, the Providence school committee ruled unanimously to require military training for high school boys, despite opposition from unionists and Socialists who called the measure coercive and woman suffragists who presumably objected on pacifist grounds. The following year, the controversial program expanded to include drill classes for women and girls. One local school even initiated a "Junior Police" program to "enlist the best boys of each class on the side of the teachers and in the interest of authority and good order." Promoted as "a laboratory for training in citizenship," the program no doubt sought to discourage the radical politics immigrants were thought to espouse.[3]

If schools sought to assimilate young people, prohibition aimed at reforming their parents. Temperance was a complicated issue in Providence, where sentiments did not divide neatly along class or ethnic lines. Although Catholics, immigrants, and workers generally resented curbs on drinking as curtailments of individual liberties, many Irish Americans had joined the crusade in the nineteenth century as a marker of respectability and, as the *Labor Advocate* put it, a means of "knocking out the profits of the liquor traffic." The CTAU offered a compromise in the form of abstinence "by persuasion, example and precept," in the *Visitor*'s phrase, rather than by law. The temperance crusade also resonated with calls for urban regeneration and good government, and during the Progressive Era city voters repeatedly agreed to regulate the corrupt liquor industry by licensing saloons.[4]

During the war, rising concerns about the health of soldiers and civilians, anxieties about the behavior of workers and immigrants, and a desire to punish German brewers strengthened the temperance crusade nationwide. Yet at the same time the movement was losing the support of Catholics, troubled by the shift from voluntary abstinence to legalized prohibition, and Irish Americans, many of whom had achieved upward mobility and no longer needed to prove respectability by endorsing temperance. Cardinal James Gibbons of Baltimore went so far as to call the proposed Eighteenth Amendment a "national catastrophe." As a result, when Congress sent the amendment to the states it encountered stiff resistance in Catholic communities like Providence. Although many wives undoubtedly favored prohibition, recognizing that drinking took an emotional and financial toll on their families, their opinions were drowned out by the louder voices of men who argued that drinking was an issue best left to local regulation or individual discipline. The city's Catholic leaders were especially vocal, arguing the measure would undermine religious freedom—by making it difficult to secure communion wine, a usage ultimately exempted—and limited government. Prohibition, the *Visitor* noted, was based on "the wrong assumption that the State is the supreme authority on every matter under the sun, and that legislation is the panacea for every evil that frail human flesh is heir to." Sentiments like these were so pervasive that Rhode Island refused to ratify the Eighteenth Amendment, the only state other than Connecticut to withhold its approval. Local lawmakers even went so far as to petition, unsuccessfully, to be excused from implementing the measure, and it took them until 1922 to enact a state enforcement bill.[5]

According to the AFCS, prohibition and the infant hygiene program were typical of the dangers that menaced Catholics across the nation during and after the war. A December 1918 article in the federation's bulletin pointed with alarm to proposals in other states to inspect convents and tax church institutions. "It would seem . . . that Catholics are going to be deprived of their elemental rights as citizens of this great and liberty-loving republic," the article concluded. "No matter where we turn . . . we find efforts made to burden and oppress the Catholic Church and its members in the practice of their religion."[6] At the same time, a new federal requirement that prospective immigrants pass a literacy test threatened plans for Catholic family reunification and undermined America's long-standing (if already compromised) reputation as an open door. Collectively, these measures affirmed a new Americanism that subordinated individual liberties to cultural conformity. Catholics tried to tar these uses of state power as violations of national tradition. Throwing back the language of Americanism at the Americanizers, they insisted that extending state power into personal life undermined First Amendment freedoms and subverted the tradition of small government. For elites who made the law and influenced public opinion, however, individualism and states' rights were to be subordinated to a new concept of national identity that emphasized unity and federal control.

Although the city's ethnic, Catholic majority resented state intrusions into their personal lives, they nonetheless invoked the power of the state as they struggled to improve their positions as voters and workers. In the battle for political rights, woman suffrage and the property qualification intersected once again. Rhode Island women, like their counterparts across the nation, threw themselves into the war effort and hoped to be rewarded with the franchise. After finally winning the right to vote in presidential elections in 1917, they pressed on and joined national leaders in arguing for full suffrage as "an important war measure." As the state suffrage association claimed, this would ensure that "the war for democracy for which we are gladly and willingly giving our very best may not be fought in vain but that a real and true democracy may be established throughout the world—which can never be accomplished without the extension of the franchise to women." This logic was persuasive. On January 6, 1920, Rhode Island became the twenty-third state to ratify the Nineteenth Amendment.[7]

The city's workingmen had hoped to ride the coattails of the Nineteenth Amendment by enacting a companion law to repeal the property rule. The two suffrage camps had grown closer during the war. In 1916, seven hundred unionists, ministers, professionals, and public officials formed a Men's League to support woman suffrage. The following year Agnes M. Jenks, president of the local woman suffrage association, boasted that her work was "receiving strong backing from men of all classes and parties." The daughter of immigrants from England and French Canada, Jenks was married to a silversmith with an Irish-born mother. Her husband made a good enough living to set up his family in an apartment on the elegant East Side, just blocks from Brown University, but they did not own their home. As an upwardly mobile second-generation immigrant with a multinational heritage, Jenks was well positioned to forge alliances across class and ethnic lines. Suffragists like Jenks demonstrated support for repealing the property rule, a concern of the working-class women to whom they hoped to appeal. In a particularly strong statement, Sara Algeo lambasted the requirement as "a remnant of the dark ages if ever there was one." In 1915 the state's three woman suffrage organizations merged into the Rhode Island Equal Suffrage Association, the name of the new group indicating opposition to all franchise restrictions.[8]

Democrats did their best to foster connections between woman suffrage and the property qualification that disadvantaged their ethnic, Catholic constituents. When the General Assembly met to consider the Nineteenth Amendment, they tried to add a clause exempting women from the property rule in hope this would make it easier to overturn the requirement for men later. Not surprisingly, Republicans agreed to ratify the measure only if the property restriction applied to women too. The Republican majority carried the day, and Rhode Island women were enfranchised under the condition that only property owners would vote in city elections. This was a rule that affected women disproportionately because they were less likely than men to own property in their own names.[9]

The city's Catholic, ethnic majority responded to the Nineteenth Amendment with mixed feelings. Woman suffrage theoretically doubled their electorate; yet voting was a right far more likely to be exercised by educated natives than by immigrant and working women who faced barriers of citizenship, language, and illiteracy. Forty-one percent of the city's voting-age women were immigrants in 1920, and of this group half were not citizens and 19 percent could not write in any language. Moreover, until the federal Cable Act was passed in 1922, American-born women who married foreigners lost their citizenship and thus their right to vote. Finally, the property rule barred a significant proportion of Providence women from full access to the ballot on the basis of class position. In 1922, only 32 percent of registered women (and 45.7 percent of registered men) owned enough property to vote in city elections. Thus, even though the franchise no longer followed lines of gender, it retained a sharp class bias. Working people, many of them Catholic and foreign-born, who had contributed to the war as soldiers and civilians saw retention of the property rule as a slap in the face.[10]

Workers were somewhat more successful in securing rights as industrial citizens during the war. Nationwide, the conflict presented labor with new restrictions and opportunities. Although strikers risked being censured as selfish subversives, the importance of industrial production to the Allied effort gave labor leverage in the workplace and a voice in Washington. The National War Labor Board (NWLB) provided some protection for the rights to organize and bargain collectively. The crusade to "make the world safe for democracy," moreover, legitimated the quest for industrial rights, and working people across the nation manipulated the language of Americanism in their struggles. In 1917 the nation's workers launched a strike wave of unprecedented proportions, and during the war AFL membership virtually doubled, with gains especially noted in war-related industries like metals and electrics.[11]

Joining their counterparts across the country, Rhode Island's largely Catholic working class seized on the war as an opportunity to bolster its position at the workplace. Some 214 strikes broke out in the state between 1916 and 1919, with 1916 by far the most strike-bound year. Most strikes took place in textile mills, but rubber workers, streetcar employees, and machinists also staged confrontations. Of the walkouts whose results were recorded in the

On April 18, 1917, Governor R. Livingston Beekman signed a law allowing Rhode Island women to vote in presidential elections. Male suffragists were disappointed that neither this act nor the Nineteenth Amendment overturned the property qualification that put the overwhelmingly Catholic working class at a disadvantage. Silver gelatin print, courtesy of the Rhode Island Historical Society, RHi X3 1880.

labor commissioner's wartime reports, 41 percent resulted in some improvement in wages or working conditions. Among the most notable victories was securing a forty-eight hour week in many local mills. This new militancy translated into significant growth for organized labor. Statewide, the number of union workers increased almost 57 percent between 1916 and 1919. By the latter year nearly 14 percent of the state's wage earners were organized and over 20 percent of Providence workers belonged to unions, the highest proportion to date.[12]

Confident in labor's wartime leverage, United Textile Workers (UTW) president John Golden warned New England mill owners in May 1918 that loomfixers would strike unless they received a 15 percent raise. Employers, already having granted several raises in hope of retaining their wartime workforces, offered a compromise the union found unacceptable. On July 1, loomfixers across New England went on strike. A federal negotiator settled the conflicts in Massachusetts and New Hampshire by convincing employers there to raise wages by the desired 15 percent, but Rhode Island mill owners refused to compromise. "What the War Labor Board should do, and do that very promptly, is to pick out the ringleaders in the strike and send them to Camp Devens where the rigid training and the prospect of early shipment to France would give them a new viewpoint," argued the trade paper *Fibre and Fabric*.[13]

Management's intransigence prompted workers to dig in their heels. Inspired by the idealistic rhetoric of the war years, operatives from French Canada, Poland, and Portugal joined older immigrants in the walkout, fostering new unity in an industry traditionally divided along lines of skill and ethnicity. By early August the UTW estimated that more than eight thousand workers (including several thousand immigrants) were striking at twenty-eight mills across the state. Each side fought the other with the weapon of Americanism. While War Department officials called the strikers unpatriotic, a UTW official claimed they were using "the only means at their command to obtain a wage sufficient to enable them to live as self-respecting citizens and examples of . . . Americanism."[14]

Even as rhetoric like this inspired mill workers and created unprecedented unity, the strike worried Golden of the UTW. Never enthusiastic about organizing unskilled workers and now fearing that a mass influx of operatives would create institutional chaos, he convinced the strikers to return to work in August on the understanding that the NWLB would engineer an acceptable compromise. By the fall of 1918, however, the federal board was losing its potency as employers saw the war drawing to an end. Recognizing their advantage, Rhode Island mill owners headed off the

NWLB hearing and fired strike leaders without federal retribution. By January 1919, the strike was lost and most of the union's wartime gains were reversed. The loomfixers did not win their pay raise, and most unskilled workers (many of them Catholic immigrants and ethnics) remained outside the textile union. Local mill operatives had lost the moment of possibility the war had presented. Once hostilities ceased in Europe, workers in Rhode Island and across the nation watched their wartime advantages dissipate. The labor shortage ended as production fell and returning soldiers looked for jobs; and with the war over the government lacked the leverage and, many Americans felt, the right to intervene in industrial relations.[15]

New Americans in Providence had proved little more successful in using the state to promote economic and political rights than in preventing it from infringing on cultural freedoms. Woman suffrage was a tremendous step forward, but one intended to reward middle-class Yankees who had supported the war and were far more likely to vote than were Catholic, ethnic women of the working class. Retention of the property rule was a major disappointment for working people, and advances at the workplace proved largely short-lived although wartime experiences did lay the groundwork for labor's gains in the 1930s. The war had validated the belief that the state should enforce social unity but undermined the conviction that it should protect its neediest citizens and give them a political voice. Americanism had been construed in a way that placed the powers of the state more firmly than ever behind the interests of the old stock. This tendency only intensified in the hypercharged atmosphere of the postwar Red Scare.

"BOLSHEVISM OF THE REDDEST HUE": THE RHODE ISLAND RED SCARE

On April 6, 1919, the Russian celebrity Catherine Breshkovsky appeared before a large audience at Providence's Opera House. Breshkovsky, known as "Little Grandmother of the Revolution," had participated in the democratic upheaval of March 1917, only to leave Russia in disgust after the Bolshevik uprising in November. By 1919 she was bringing her anticommunist message to eager audiences across the United States and had come to Providence at the invitation of Protestant women's clubs. Shortly after she began her speech, some fifty men and women, mostly self-identified Bolsheviks of Russian origin, interrupted the lecture with "revolutionary shouts and songs." The disturbance turned into a battle of the lungs, as demonstrators sang "The Red Flag" and other members of the audience tried to drown them out with "The Battle Hymn of the Republic." Providence police officers escorted the protesters out of the theater but declined to imprison them. "There was nothing as serious as to call for arrests," Walter A. Presbey of the police board commented. The *Providence Evening Bulletin* disagreed, claiming the Opera House disturbance had represented "Bolshevism of the reddest hue, the type that is running rampant over Europe to-day."[16]

Subsequent investigations convinced lawmakers something serious was indeed going on. A reporter for the *Providence News* discovered that "Russian reds have rooms in Palace Casino where they meet nightly." Equally alarming was the ease with which radicals had pulled the wool over the eyes of a hapless police surveillance team. Officers had been attending their meetings and were present on the night they planned the Opera House disturbance but, forced to rely on members to interpret, were unaware of the scheme. "There was nothing to which a single objection could be taken," remarked a red-faced Lieutenant Frank Carney. These revelations seemed to disprove the police board's claim that the Opera House protesters were "simply a few foreigners who got together for the occasion."[17]

Eager to compensate for its initial nonchalance, the city threw the book at these Rhode Island reds. At Mayor Gainer's recommendation, the city council voted unanimously to request a state law punishing any antigovernment statement with a hefty penalty. In the eyes of city lawmakers, the punishment fit the crime. "By the most flagrant abuse of the constitutional right of free speech [the Bolsheviks] are endeavoring to create throughout our country riot and confusion and to force a disintegration of our institutions," Gainer charged, forgetting he too was abusing that First Amendment right. The city council hailed Gainer's position, and a Republican councilman, Edward E. Austin, called for more drastic measures. "Shoot them! Hang them!" he cried. Although state lawmakers failed to enact either man's proposal, the council's position revealed deep-seated fears that the immigrant city of Providence was a breeding ground for radicalism.[18]

The Opera House incident was the most colorful moment in Providence's postwar Red Scare. Across the nation, strikes and bombings ignited a spate of antiradical repression that drew on deeper concerns about the spread of international communism, loyalties of the immigrant population, growth in labor radicalism, and economic and emotional dislocations that followed the war. Immigrant radicals provided a new enemy against which the nation could unite. "The battle to make the country safe is not yet won," the National Security League, a patriotic society, announced in 1918. "The enemy but wears a different guise."[19]

Providence, home to a small radical movement and large immigrant population, joined in the hysteria. Even before the Breshkovsky confrontation, the city council had forbidden the public display of any statement "opposed to organized government or . . . derogatory to morals." Revelations that followed the Opera House disturbance prompted further crackdowns. In June 1919, U.S. Attorney General Harvey A. Baker reported that authorities were "drawing tighter the cordon about the ring of anarchists, Bolsheviks and alien agitators in the State" and were prepared to pounce. "There are some harmless black snakes coiled up in their corners and hissing," he remarked, "but the first time a real poisonous reptile sticks up its head to bite we will be ready to land on it and grind it into the dirt." Six months later, federal agents corralled twenty-two alleged Communists in conjunction with the nationwide Palmer Raids. James P. Reid, the Socialist dentist and former legislator, escaped arrest, but his home and office were raided along with a Communist boarding house and other suspected radical hot spots. Italian anarchists watched helplessly as authorities suppressed their newspaper, *Cronoca Sovversiva,* and jailed its editor and subscribers. Federal Hill's Karl Marx Club disbanded, its Dean Street headquarters becoming home to the Sons of Italy. With the local IWW chapter already crushed during the war, these efforts ensured the demise of the city's small left. They also spoke to the triumph of a repressive and nativist Americanism that tolerated no challenge to the status quo.[20]

"QUICK AMERICANIZATION IS THE SOLUTION"

The Red Scare intensified the contest between native-born Protestants and foreign-born Catholics over the meanings of Americanism, and the determination of the former to assimilate the latter through a combination of voluntarism and state power. Before the armistice, a sense of common cause had restrained nativism, and fear of alienating immigrants from the war effort had softened the "100 Percent Americanism" drive. With the war won and antiradical hysteria in high gear, Americanization now proceeded more coercively. Although forceful assimilation was preferable to deportation, it still struck immigrants as un-American and a misuse of government authority. It also came as something of a surprise. Like woman suffragists and African American activists across the country, new Americans were confident they had demonstrated their patriotism and would be rewarded with full admission to the body politic. "The war has proved the loyalty and the patriotism of foreign-born Americans," *Le Jean-Baptiste* proclaimed with pride. The "brilliant record" of immigrant soldiers, agreed the *Providence Jewish Chronicle,* showed that newcomers were "worthy of the privileges and responsibilities of American citizenship." A pastoral letter issued by the nation's Catholic bishops and archbishops in September 1919 repeated this theme: "The traditional patriotism of our Catholic people has been amply demonstrated in the day of their country's trial. And we look with pride upon the record which proves, as no mere protestation could prove, the devotion of American Catholics to the cause of American freedom." Now that new Americans had demonstrated their commitment to the nation, it was time for the nation to award them with a full complement of rights. Echoing a rhetoric employed by reformers across the country, the city's Catholics looked to the postwar period as a moment of possibility for positive social change. The war had subordinated struggles for justice to the cause of military victory, but its conclusion would provide new opportunities for economic and political equality.[21]

Many of the city's natives had different priorities as they navigated the tumultuous postwar years. If new Americans believed the war had demonstrated their patriotism, the old stock felt the conflict had exposed the dangers of a large and unassimilated foreign-born population. Compounding their fears were local events like the 1918 loomfixers' strike as well as the nationwide turbulence of 1919. Like their counterparts across the country, many native-born Protestants concluded there were Communist conspiracies in the works and blamed them on immigrant radicals. Whereas German bullets had not posed a direct threat during the war because no fighting took place on U.S. soil, the domestic unrest of 1919 suggested a more immediate menace.

Although it was unlikely that new Americans loyal to the Catholic Church would embrace communism in significant numbers, they seemed threatening in other ways. One concern was the growth in international allegiances among the ethnic population. Irish nationalism and Zionism surged nationwide in the postwar period, buoyed by Wilson's determination to incorporate the principle of self-determination into the Treaty of Versailles. In Providence, congregations such as St. Mary's raised funds for Irish freedom fighters and sponsored an unprecedented spate of lectures on homeland history; the *Visitor*'s editorial pages were filled with letters advocating Irish independence; and the Holy Name Union issued resolutions demanding Home Rule. A March 1920 rally for Irish independence attracted so many listeners (including William Hickey, the new bishop) to the Majestic Theater that thousands were forced to stand outside, straining to hear the speakers' inspiring rhetoric from the street on a cold late winter day. Acting on a similar impulse, Providence Jews convinced the General Assembly to pass a resolution supporting creation of a homeland in Palestine. Actions like these reinforced the impression that immigrants still straddled two worlds rather

Providence residents celebrated the Allied victory in Exchange Place in 1919. Catholics and immigrants were optimistic about the postwar era, assuming they had proved their patriotism and would be treated as full Americans in reward. Silver gelatin print by John R. Hess, courtesy of the Rhode Island Historical Society, RHi X3 307.

than standing firmly within the United States. National leaders including Wilson complained that the competing demands of "hyphens" were undermining support for the peace treaty.[22]

Compounding fears about immigrants' patriotism were anxieties about their mental and physical well-being. Wartime examinations of the nation's soldiers had revealed alarmingly high rates of illiteracy and poor health. Although these problems crossed ethnic lines, they were thought to be worse in immigrant households where education levels tended to be lower and foreign domestic practices (rather than dire poverty) were blamed for poor health. "The great war revealed serious dangers to our national life arising from illiteracy, an unAmericanized and unassimilated foreign population, and a failure properly to conserve the physical well being of all citizens," a National League of Women Voters publication declared in May 1920.[23]

The entry of women into the electorate underlined the need for civic education. There was a widespread perception that many of these new electors were unprepared to vote responsibly. Rhode Island suffragists sought to educate immigrant women by holding civics classes and citizenship meetings around the state. Many of these classes took place in churches, perhaps in recognition that immigrants would feel more comfortable in familiar institutions. A Women's Independence Day added a sense of festivity to the act of registering and impressed upon women "the close relationship between patriotism and voting. No good American neglects his ballot." These efforts intersected nicely with the postwar Americanization drive and sought to dispel anxieties about female votes.[24]

This confluence of concerns about immigrants' civic and physical fitness intensified the assimilation drive. Providence reformers, particularly well-to-do women, seized on the crusade with enthusiasm. The RISFWC headed an effort that crossed religious lines, involving middle-class clubs like the Queen's Daughters and the Council of Jewish Women. Uniting these groups was a conviction that "club women of today have a great duty to perform . . . a great problem to solve and quick Americanization is the solution," as Rhode Islander Etta V. Leighton of the National Security League told RISFWC members in November 1919. "We must insist that he who comes to America must be loyal to America." Hoping to improve its immigrant outreach, the RISFWC sponsored Americanization meetings and sought out assimilated role models to hold up to the rest of the community. In January 1920, the Council of Jewish Women invited Sadie Wunsch, a young immigrant, to speak to members about the "limitations" of her homeland and the extraordinary advantages she enjoyed in the United States. "To the Jew, America has been a Paradise," she told her enthusiastic audience. "I love every star in the flag, every blood red stripe for it has given to me a home, a friendship and a future."[25]

As during the war, reformers invoked the power of the state in their efforts to produce a city of nicely assimilated Sadie Wunsches. A citywide campaign run by employers, unionists, school officials, and civic leaders ranged from benign (having merchants post signs that urged consumers to become citizens) to coercive (asking employers to furnish evening schools with names and addresses of workers who would benefit from "personal invitations"). In 1919, the General Assembly enacted an Americanization bill that mandated evening school (public or private) for immigrants age sixteen through twenty who could not read, write, or speak English. Anyone who refused would pay a one-dollar fine for each unexcused absence, up to twenty dollars per year, and repeat offenders would be confined to an institution until they reached the age of twenty-one. In enacting these strict measures Rhode Island joined twenty-nine other states that promoted Americanization through night classes (compulsory in some states) but did not go so far as the fifteen states that ordered private and public elementary schools to conduct all classes in English.[26]

In Providence these measures produced results that were noteworthy but not stellar. Federal census reports indicate that between 1910 and 1920, the percentage of residents age ten and older who could not write in any language fell from 7.8 percent to 5.9 percent. The proportion of those who could not speak English fell more markedly, from 8.2 to 3.9 percent. Americanization programs were only partially responsible, as a wartime drop in immigration had reduced the proportion of residents who were foreign-born from 34 percent to 25.5 percent in the decade after 1910.[27]

The RISFWC, for one, was eager for better results. The federation worried that night schools, whose students were overwhelmingly adult and male, were failing to reach a significant number of foreigners. To be sure, rates of literacy and English-speaking were lower among women. In 1920, 4.7 percent of females age ten and older could not speak English, as opposed to 2.9 percent of males. Among people of voting age, 8.3 percent of women and 6.6 percent of men could not write in any language. Clubwomen hoping to redress this imbalance launched a campaign to send public school teachers into immigrant households, where they would teach English and civics as well as "American standards in the home." Even though the Providence school committee refused to implement the measure, it agreed that "either more persuasive inducement or the force of compulsion" was needed.[28]

Providence Catholics resisted "the force of compulsion" by fighting radicalism and promoting assimilation on their own terms. They embraced the antiradical drive, seeing leftists as mortal enemies and anticommunism as a way to prove their American credentials; but they resisted measures that enabled Protestant reformers or state authorities to interfere with church autonomy and individual rights. As during the war, they sought to prove their Americanism through their own institutions and according to their own beliefs, and to seize on the political climate as an opportunity to advance their interests. Benefiting from the fact that Americans now feared "foreign" ideologies more than "foreign" religions, the Catholic diocese presented itself as a bulwark against bolshevism. The *Visitor* filled its pages with antiradical tirades and patriotic statements, and Hickey issued a ringing denunciation of communism at the 1919 Holy Name parade. Laypeople articulated similar sentiments. In a 1919 address, Francis I. McCanna reminded fellow members of the KOC that "Americanism is synonymous with law and order." It was vital for prominent Catholics like McCanna to demonstrate that parishes and lay societies were partners in the project of postwar stability, not separatist institutions that distracted members from national life. These efforts mirrored those of other ethnic and religious leaders to fend off the Red Scare by proving their fervent commitment to the United States.[29]

It was equally critical for new Americans to support the postwar assimilation drive, but in their own ways. In June 1919, an Americanization conference at City Hall brought together public officials and old stock reformers with Catholic and ethnic community leaders. In attendance were Luigi Cipolla of the Sons of Italy and Rev. Antonio Bove of St. Ann's, as well as Msgr. Peter Blessing (former editor of the *Visitor*), labor unionists, and representatives of French Canadian, Armenian, Polish, Portuguese, and Syrian organizations. Their presence broadcast commitment to Americanization as well as desire that Anglo-Saxon Protestants not control the process.[30]

On a national level, Catholic War Council activities mirrored this approach. A series of speeches, pamphlets, and press releases issued in 1919 revealed a determination to use church resources to promote a tolerant and Catholic variant of Americanization. The council called for a gentle program that encouraged newcomers to retain their language, culture, and religion even as it urged them to learn English and civics. It also suggested an individualized approach that recognized ethnic differences and used assimilated immigrants as agents in the process. "All immigrants are not to be classified together and treated alike," the council argued. "Foreign-born citizens will play an important part in developing the idea of American citizenship among the immigrants of their own races."[31]

In addition to promoting a pluralistic approach to Americanization, Catholic spokesmen sought to soften the drive by infusing it with democratic ideals the Red Scare was threatening. As the war council noted in February 1919, opportunity, fair play, equal rights, and "the hatred of oppression" were among the national values immigrants should learn. Economic opportunity and industrial democracy were equally central to the council's vision. In a May 1919 speech Rev. John O'Grady, secretary of the council's Reconstruction Committee, suggested that some immigrants had refused to assimilate because "it was difficult for them to appreciate the ideals of a country which permitted its great employers to work them for unreasonably long hours, for insufficient wages, and under conditions prejudicial to their health and welfare." To redress this situation, O'Grady explained, the war council was promoting "industrial justice and a more equitable distribution of wealth" as components of its postwar program. The AFCS agreed with this logic. "If we are serious and really wish to make our foreign-born, real Americans let us throw aside much of our sham, our economic and our social sham and make America what the foreigner thought it was before he came into our midst," its spring 1919 bulletin declared. "Let us give the foreign-born an American standard of living and we will at once solve 90 per cent of our problems."[32]

As these local and national examples suggest, when Catholics affirmed their commitment to patriotism and assimilation they were not simply capitulating to the postwar obsession with unity and order. Their defensive hyper-patriotism in the Red Scare years was in part survival strategy, in part clever tactic. By participating in assimilation campaigns, new Americans influenced the ways in which they entered the national mainstream. By demonstrating their patriotism, they won the right to challenge abuses perpetrated in the name of Americanism. The *Visitor* repeatedly deplored the efforts of "bogus patriots" to use the flag to justify discriminatory or "reactionary" measures. Similarly, the *Rhode Island Jewish Review* took care to reprint a statement, issued by a national conference of rabbis, that "our first loyalty is to . . . Americanism, which means freedom of the individual, the establishment of justice and the emphasis, above all racial distinctions, of our common humanity." This carefully worded statement at once affirmed Jewish patriotism and challenged a Red Scare Americanism that violated First Amendment rights and discriminated against foreigners. Even at the peak of postwar repression, the city's newcomers refused to accept a version of national identity that violated their most cherished rights.[33]

AMERICANISM REFRAMED

The war and its aftermath thus intensified debates over definitions of citizenship and Americanism. In the eyes of most old stock Rhode Islanders,

Americanism meant naturalizing, voting, learning English, and pledging loyalty to the United States. For many it went further to include a lifestyle rooted in middle-class, Protestant values and practices. During the war, this Americanism also entailed supporting a strong central government that would impose these standards on a diverse population. The Catholic immigrants of Providence accepted some elements of this project, rejected others, and added a few of their own. Many acknowledged the importance of becoming voting, English-speaking citizens but refused to relinquish traditional lifestyles, religious rituals, and homeland attachments. They agreed to adopt the political formalities of their newfound citizenship without surrendering the cultural trappings of the old world. Others rejected even these political attachments, but this did not mean they refused to engage with public life. For many Providence immigrants, being an American was less about being a participant in the polity than being an active member of a parish, union, or neighborhood. Their Americanism was less about unquestioned loyalty to a nation than about respect for a code of values and set of rights.

In the war over Americanism and the uses of state power, the city's elites triumphed in the short term. Their insistence on patriotism and unity placed new Americans on the defensive and undermined struggles for economic and political justice. The language of citizenship changed, as immigrants continued to demand their rights but devoted equal attention to defending their civic fitness. Reform politics were transformed as well, as public attention shifted from progressive legislation to assimilation campaigns. The process of nation-building is inherently coercive, as Gary Gerstle argues, and indeed the wartime drive for national unity forced many new Americans to assimilate more than they wished to.[34]

Nonetheless, the war years were not a total retreat for Catholic immigrants and ethnics. Assertions of patriotism and good citizenship, at first glance a defensive strategy, had potential to be subversive. Even though they had little choice about whether they would become American, they insisted on redefining what this meant. In refusing to surrender their traditions, they rejected a restrictive and static national identity for a complex and dynamic model that brought together old world and new. At the same time, Catholic women entered public life more visibly as patriotic contributors and (in 1920) as voters. After the war Catholics, female and male, learned to manipulate their newfound status as Americans to their advantage. Having demonstrated their commitment to the nation, they argued they were entitled to certain benefits. Indoctrinated about the duty of civic involvement, they became politically active in defense of their rights. Newly fluent in the language of Americanism, they used this rhetoric to demand justice. Once liberated from their wartime constraints, they would insist on an Americanism that respected cultural prerogatives as well as economic rights, and they would defend this vision from the assaults of employers and civic leaders. In the 1920s struggles between old stock and new would hinge on the language of Americanism once again, but this time new Americans would manipulate the rhetoric more successfully.[35]

III

THE FLOWERING OF CATHOLIC POLITICS

9

"THE CHURCH'S SHOCK TROOPS"

Catholics in the Postwar World

Local organizations must realize that as isolated units they can do little or nothing. It is only as a great, united body that they can influence public thought and public action.

—National Council of Catholic Women,
News Sheet, December 1926

TROUBLE ON FEDERAL HILL

On a warm Sunday in July 1920, Providence police officers received an unexpected summons to the Church of the Holy Ghost on Federal Hill. One hundred Italian women were trying to forcibly remove their priest, and it took a posse of armed officers to stop them. "The people absolutely want to remove Father Belliotti," observed the local newspaper *Il Corriere*, "and they are intent on doing so at whatever cost and by whatever means." The reporter was right. Over the next months the police regularly were called in to keep the peace at Holy Ghost, as parishioners assembled for demonstrations aimed at ousting Rev. Domenico Belliotti and the Scalabrini Fathers who ran the parish. At an August assembly, the appearance of one priest "unloosed such an uproar of screams and protests that it had the actual character of a riot," *Il Corriere* reported. "No more Scalabrini!" the crowd yelled. "Either you get out or we will drive you out with force!" When Bishop Harkins removed Belliotti only to replace him with another Scalabrini priest (Rev. Angelo Strazzoni), some protesters concluded that force was the only solution. On the morning of Sunday, November 7, police officers arrested four women and three men who had interrupted a service by shouting for the priest's removal and demanding the keys to the church.[1]

This dramatic series of events was the culmination of a fifteen-year battle between the Scalabrini, a northern Italian order, and the southern Italian laypeople of Holy Ghost. For years parishioners had complained the priests were materialistic snobs rather than humble servants of God. "No one would think that they are Priests," the Holy Name Society grumbled. "Their demeanor, their clothes . . . their well-combed and perfumed hair, their manner of living . . . the levity with which they speak of their ministry and of articles of religious belief, everything in them gives unmistakable signs that their faith is lukewarm, if not entirely gone." Particularly galling was Belliotti's habit of wintering in the South to improve his poor health, leaving his assistants to tend the flock in cold, gray Providence.[2]

Worse still, parishioners charged, the Scalabrini were dismissive of patron saints and feast days. In July 1906, one year after he assumed leadership of the congregation, Belliotti had raised the parish's collective dander by tangling with the Madonna of Mount Carmel *festa*, one of the most popular celebrations on the community's religious calendar. On the day in question the organizers arrived at Holy Ghost one hour late to find the priest understandably annoyed and their reserved seats filled by other parishioners. As Silvestro Del Deo and Angelo Mendillo of the Maria Del Carmine Society charged in a heated petition to Harkins, "The reverend father . . . became irritated and cursed Her name and also the day that he donned the priestly garments. . . . He replied . . . that we did not control him and that if we said another word, he would not let us enter the church and that furthermore he saw no difference between the Blessed Virgin and St. Rocco or any other saint." Such words were anathema to a people for whom patron saint worship played an important role in both religious practice and ethnic identity. The 1906 affair was one in a series of conflicts that rocked Holy Ghost and other Italian parishes during the first decades of the twentieth century.[3]

These long-simmering tensions exploded in the summer of 1920. Harkins's decision to reassign Father Vincenzo Vicari, a popular assistant priest not affiliated with the Scalabrini, to another parish unleashed a flood of impassioned letters to the bishop and even the Vatican. The Holy Name president, Daniele Ionata (an Italian-born weaver), and his fellow members demanded the return of Vicari, whom they credited with "rescuing from this religious sloth thousands of Italians" through his "real Catholic spirit" and his sympathy for the poor. Belliotti, by contrast, conducted himself "as the manager of a business establishment instead of a pastor," charged a letter

The Federal Hill parish of Holy Ghost, shown here in an undated photograph, was the site of a popular uprising in 1920. Lithograph, courtesy of the Rhode Island Historical Society, RHi X3 7471.

signed by Irene De Battista and four other parish women. "He is never willing to raise his hand or do anything whatsoever unless he is compensated." Moreover, the women complained, he claimed "there is no one above him in this diocese and he can do whatever he pleases without being accountable to anyone."[4]

The Vicari controversy posed a major problem for the spiritual lives of the Holy Ghost Catholics and the institutional health of the diocese. Parishioners pleaded with the bishop to help them at what they termed a "terrible" moment. "We have been minimized, insulted, beaten, arrested, denounced to the civil authority as a flock of primitives and criminals," charged one petition. "And after so much, after such a disgrace to our name, to our dignity . . . we are told to be compelled to return to our executioners." This seemed intolerable, and many threatened to leave the parish if Vicari did not return. "The church will close with no one attending anymore," one Catholic warned the bishop. "God is present at other churches, and also at home," noted Enrico Bellifante, a laborer and active parishioner. Bellifante's statement sent diocesan officials a message disturbing on two counts. Disgruntled Italians might take advantage of the Protestant missions that peppered their neighborhood, but they were just as likely to practice their faith in a "domus"-centered religion that recognized homes as valid sites of worship.[5]

Given the size of the anti-Scalabrini movement, both threats were cause for concern. Although community spokesmen dismissed the uprising as the work of a discontented fringe, at least eighteen hundred individuals and eighteen church societies signed petitions demanding the Scalabrini's ouster and Vicari's return. A movement of this magnitude threatened the viability of Rhode Island's flagship Italian parish. Hickey, who had assumed leadership of the diocese only recently, did not wish to sacrifice the advances his predecessors had made among the Italians. He refused to bring back Vicari, whom some suspected of fomenting the uprising, but he finally found an acceptable leader who brought peace to the troubled parish. According to one parish retrospective, Rev. Flaminio Parenti restored order because of his charismatic personality, his inspired leadership, and the increase within the congregation of second-generation immigrants less committed to popular forms of worship and less divided by the regional rivalries that had split their parents' generation. Anecdotal evidence from parishioners suggests it was Parenti's steely determination and firm control that brought the parish back in line. As Linda Perrotta, who attended Holy Ghost as a child, recalled, "He ruled the roost." In addition to naming this more effective pastor, Hickey created a new Federal Hill parish, devoted to the same Madonna of Mount Carmel whose feast day had touched off the trouble fifteen years earlier.[6]

To understand the rebellion at Holy Ghost, one must begin with the rebels themselves. A systematic study of a sample of petition signers suggests the petitioners were a relatively stable group.[7] A majority were married, more than one-third owned homes or small businesses, and their average age was thirty-nine. This was not a community of young and rootless transients, yet by no means was it a prosperous group. In fact, theirs was a distinctly working-class uprising. Of those people whose occupations could be identified, forty-two—almost half the sample—were common laborers. Eight held factory jobs of indeterminate skill level; three were building trades workers; five were in service industries (holding jobs such as waiter or chauffeur); sixteen owned or worked in small businesses like groceries or barber shops; nine held office jobs such as clerk or insurance agent; two were students; and nine were widows or housewives. Given the working-class character of the rebellion, it is not surprising that economic issues played a role. When the parishioners complained about the priests' expensive habits and winters in Florida, they expressed class tensions that divided the congregation and the larger community.

This also was an uprising of new Americans. Of those petitioners whose nativity and citizenship could be determined, sixty were Italian immigrants and the other two were the children of Italians. Although the newcomers had been in the country an average of seventeen years, only one-third had become citizens. As a result, disagreements over assimilation and ethnicity informed the Holy Ghost affair. The conflict between the Scalabrini and their congregation reflected regional tensions that typically split ethnic communities between older immigrants and priests from northern Italy and newer arrivals from the south (although Belliotti himself, unlike most of the Scalabrini, was Sicilian). The dispute over the Madonna of Mount Carmel festival was typical of the conflicts that inflamed ethnic parishes when priests discouraged an old world, popular religion in favor of an Americanized or institutional form of worship. Although it is important not to overstate the extent to which new immigrants clung to an unchanging folk religion, it is true that tensions of this nature contributed to the troubles at Holy Ghost.[8]

Conflicts like this pitted recent arrivals against community leaders as well as priests. Speaking for their middle-class readers, *L'Eco del Rhode Island* denounced the rebellion as "unwisely indecent and ludicrous," and *Il Corriere* feared it would "dishonor us in the eyes of the Americans." During the war, prominent Italians had worked hard to portray their compatriots as well behaved and assimilated. The Holy Ghost uprising undermined these efforts and pointed to internal disagreements over what it meant to be American. Community leaders associated assimilation with orderly behavior and upward mobility, but protesters may have felt they were acting in distinctly American ways by rebelling against injustice. Indeed, their recent experiences as soldiers or civilian contributors to the war no doubt encouraged them to think of themselves as Americans with a duty to defend national traditions and a right to make their voices heard. Clearly the war had not produced a consensus within ethnic Providence about the imperative of assimilating or what it meant to be American. Internal negotiations over these delicate questions would continue well into the 1920s.[9]

Gender too played an important role in the uprising, and here a disclaimer about the sample is in order. The women and men of the parish collected petitions separately and in fact the women amassed almost twice as many signatures, yet the petition that survives in full is the men's. Moreover, although 14 percent of the names on the full petition appear to be female, the sample is skewed toward men because they are easier to find in public records. As a result only nine of the ninety-six petitioners discussed here were women, but this should not obscure the central role they played as demonstrators, petitioners, and letter-writers. The rebellion offered a rare opportunity to voice frustrations with an institution where they formed the bulk of the faithful but worshipped under the direction of male clerics, as well as to protest discrimination in the larger community. Yet this was by no means a single-sex protest. In fact, the passionate involvement of parish men challenges the assumption that Italian religiosity was primarily a female affair.

Finally, this was an uprising by people who lacked other institutionalized means of self-assertion. Only ten petitioners in the sample had jobs likely to be unionized. At least thirty-nine were aliens and thus nonvoters—and that does not include the thirty-six whose citizenship could not be determined. Even if all had been citizens, only thirty-seven (just over one-third of the sample) owned enough property to vote in city elections. In short, many people in this community lacked access to vehicles such as the union and the ballot. They turned instead to the church to express resentments over gender inequities, economic oppression, and mounting pressures to assimilate.

The troubles at Holy Ghost were symptomatic of larger tensions within the city's Catholic community at the dawn of the "new era." During the war, ethnic and religious leaders had sought to unite constituents behind the war effort and depict them simply as "Americans" (even as they complicated the meaning of that term). Yet just as divisions between natives and immigrants exploded once the hostilities ceased, tensions within ethnic communities reemerged. The uprising at Holy Ghost illustrated how deeply regional rivalries, gender tensions, class conflicts, styles of worship, and debates about Americanism continued to fracture Providence's Catholic majority. These problems fostered divisions within ethnic parishes, as well as pitting congregations of newer immigrants against the Irish American hierarchy.

Yet even as the Holy Ghost affair pointed to internal divisions, it suggested Catholic parishes had enormous potential as political vehicles in the postwar era. Conflicts like the one at Holy Ghost testified to the contested vitality of the church. The parish remained critically important to many immigrants and ethnics, despite widespread fears about the effects of secularization and Protestant-led Americanization campaigns. And as the movement at Holy Ghost demonstrated, parishioners who had cut their political teeth as members of lay societies could mobilize into effective pressure groups. The challenge facing clerical and lay leaders was to direct these skills and energies outward, away from internal squabbles and into well-organized movements. Catholics had spent the war years demonstrating their civic fitness. Now it was time to demand their civil rights. If they could unite and channel their energies in coherent directions, their church would become a formidable player in city affairs and its members could use that power to assert their interests.

"A NEW ORDER OUT OF CHAOS": THE CATHOLIC MISSION IN POSTWAR AMERICA

This agenda dovetailed nicely with that of America's leading Catholics after the war. Forging a united and aggressive Catholic citizenship was a priority for church leaders, in Providence and across the nation, in the postwar era. During the 1920s the hierarchy, with lay support, engaged in a three-pronged strategy to enhance the influence of the church and its faithful. First, Catholic leaders launched a public relations campaign to demonstrate that their religion should play a central role in the postwar world. Second, they promoted interethnic unity by forming lay organizations that brought people together across parish boundaries and social lines. Finally, they conducted a civics campaign that urged men and especially women to be active in politics and community affairs. Spearheading these efforts was the National Catholic Welfare Conference (NCWC), formed in 1919 to succeed the war council as the agency coordinating Catholic social work and political activism. The agency began as the National Catholic Welfare Council, but in 1923 it changed its name from "council" to "conference" to clarify its status as a voluntary body without power to legislate church policy. Supervised by an administrative board of ten bishops and archbishops, the NCWC oversaw departments of immigration, motion pictures, social action, education, press, legal affairs, lay activities (including the national committees of men and women) and, in subsequent decades, youth and Catholic Action study. Its organization reflected a new confidence and determination on the part of the church.[10]

Nationwide, the 1920s marked the beginning of what historians have called the confident or triumphal phase of American Catholicism. Having proved during the war that Catholicism was fundamentally American, church leaders now sought to make America more Catholic. As Jay Dolan writes, their efforts were "not aimed at the adaptation of religion to culture, but at the conversion of culture to religion." Catholics saw the postwar years as a period of flux in which they could carve out influence for their church, not only through a "bricks-and-mortar" physical expansion but also by defending their rights and promoting their values. They justified this strategy by arguing they had special civic obligations, invoking a concept of citizenship that merged their responsibilities as Catholics and Americans.[11]

The end of the war, and the widespread disillusionment that followed the disappointing Treaty of Versailles, created a spiritual vacuum into which the church hoped to move. No sooner had hostilities ceased than American Catholics mobilized to seize the opportunity they saw before them. "There is a distinct Catholic viewpoint to the work of Reconstruction," claimed the war council's 1918 handbook. "Now more than at any other time in the history of the Church," Michael J. Slattery of the council wrote to a colleague, "is it necessary to express Catholic principles in social action which can reach the great world so sorely needing the light of the truth." A March 1920 pamphlet issued by the war council agreed, arguing the end of the war proved that "materialist and rationalist philosophies" were "morally and spiritually bankrupt." There was "a real hunger of the soul for spiritual truth," and the church should "assist in creating a new order out of chaos." In February 1920, the nation's highest-ranking Catholic clerics issued a pastoral letter that articulated a program along these lines. As the war had demonstrated, efforts to "regulate human affairs without any reference to God" had failed miserably. Religion, they insisted, "must be the foundation not only of the individual, but the corner stone of the nation." At a time when Americans longed for what the Republican presidential candidate Warren Harding called a "return to normalcy," Catholics believed that their faith offered a clear guide.[12]

Providence's Catholic leaders agreed with this logic. Clerics and laypeople argued their religion provided a moral compass for a dislocated nation because it was synonymous with Americanism and good citizenship. "Your chief object under God and the salvation of your souls is the preservation of Catholic, American principles; or, put it the other way—American, Catholic principles," Hickey told an assembly of Providence women in April 1924. Statements like these echoed wartime pronouncements and suggested a special civic obligation. "Catholics have more to give America," Mayor Gainer told the St. Margaret's Holy Name Society. "They possess a sure guide, the Church, that possessing all that make for good citizenship they can do more for the preservation of American ideals and fundamental rights than any other body of citizens."[13]

Fair treatment at the workplace was chief among these rights, and Catholics (inside and outside Providence) felt they had a special role to play in the tumultuous world of labor relations. "Re-Christianizing industry" was a particular goal for church leaders as they navigated the postwar years. Many of them worried that as veterans returned to civilian life there would be an unemployment crisis, labor unrest, and left-wing agitation, a concern borne out by the national strike wave of 1919. Hoping to avert further problems of this nature, the war council and NCWC called for a program of federal activism that anticipated the New Deal: instituting social insurance and a minimum wage; recognizing unions and their right to collective bargaining; and hiring unemployed workers on public works projects. But the solution did not lie with government alone; employers too had an obligation to treat workers with justice and dignity. As Boston's Archbishop O'Connell wrote in a 1921 pastoral letter, "St. Peter was a fisherman, St. Paul was a tentmaker. . . . Let [employers] remember that before God . . . all men are equal. . . . Let them have regard for the dignity of the workman." Some American employers were acknowledging this responsibility (and seeking to reduce turnover and improve productivity) by introducing "welfare capitalist" measures like health insurance and paid vacations, but O'Connell voiced a popular Catholic perspective when he argued that material benefits were not enough. "Religious ideals," he wrote, "alone will bring lasting peace in industrial relations." Words like these resonated in Providence, where the southward flight of the textile mills weakened the workers' position and sparked a major strike in 1922.[14]

Catholic pronouncements on the labor problem revealed that the church's postwar agenda had two sides. Even as leaders invoked the concepts of duty and sacrifice, they urged coreligionists to aggressively defend their rights—as workers, as immigrants or ethnics, and as members of a religious community. "With no design or thought of forming a political party, but with the single purpose of serving God and country, Catholic laymen must organize to protect their rights as American citizens," Archbishop Michael

S. Curley of Baltimore told a gathering of Providence men in March 1922. In Curley's clever formulation, when his coreligionists defended their interests they served God and country rather than working for personal gain, because individual rights were what made this nation great. Any violation of those rights required a vigilant resistance, the *Visitor* agreed. "The Church never attempts to dictate the politics of any man," the newspaper stated in 1924. "But when a law is proposed which invades her own proper sphere she wants her children to have an intelligent knowledge of it and assume a militant attitude towards it." The council could have been referring to any number of recent federal laws—the Eighteenth Amendment, the Johnson-Reed Act restricting immigration, or various proposals to extend federal control over education—that Catholics saw as violations of individual rights, familial prerogatives, and religious values. The concept of an aggressive and Catholicized citizenship resonated in Providence, where Catholics still lacked a proportionate share of economic power and political clout. If they were to become players in the postwar world, they would have to transform their diverse and divided ranks into a cohesive and politically engaged force. Bitter conflicts like the one at Holy Ghost were to be averted, and united action would be the order of the day.[15]

"A SPLENDID SPIRIT OF COOPERATION": FORGING CATHOLIC UNITY

The persistence of parish boundaries posed a formidable problem for church leaders. Ethnic tensions that divided Providence Catholics were typical of the fissures that fractured dioceses across the country. The Holy Ghost uprising had been a civil war that pitted one part of a congregation against another, but other conflicts set national parishes against the Irish American hierarchy. These conflicts raged with special intensity in the French Canadian community. Disagreements between laypeople and church authorities arose when parishioners with a tradition of lay autonomy confronted a hierarchy that insisted on centralized control, or when congregations demanded to be ministered to by compatriots, operate bilingual parochial schools, or engage in folk practices like the veneration of patron saints. These demands presented dilemmas for diocesan administrators, torn between accommodating the wishes of the laity and encouraging an Americanized form of worship accessible to all Catholics and acceptable to outsiders.

In Providence this stance put Irish American bishops at odds with French Canadian parishioners, who considered churches central to *survivance*. Like the Polish Catholics who filled the churches of the Midwest, New England's French Canadians believed religion was "above all a heritage," as *Le Jean-Baptiste* put it. They fused faith, language, and customs into a seamless whole and felt it was impossible to disentangle the three, and as a result they demanded priests who were compatriots and promoted the French language in parishes and parochial schools. Many agreed with a sentiment voiced at the USJB's 1906 convention: "Take away our language and you take away our religion." Moreover, like the Poles, the French Canadians were used to a democratic, localized system and disliked the centralized structure of the American church.[16]

Tensions did not dissipate as the French Canadians settled into life in the United States. Even as they grew more likely to naturalize and vote, they remained fiercely opposed to real or perceived attempts to Americanize their church. In fact, becoming American made some only more determined to assert rights they felt they had earned. "We are citizens of this country and have proved more than once that we were among the most loyal," noted a speaker at the 1906 convention. "But loyalty does not mean that we must be cowards; that we must surrender our rights." At the same time, several highly publicized slights after the turn of the century—including repeated failures to name French Canadian bishops to head New England dioceses—intensified the conviction the church was dangerously assimilationist. A group of Catholic journalists in Woonsocket, the "Quebec of New England," resolved to launch a vigorous resistance whenever they felt their rights were violated. In this climate incidents that seemed insignificant to outsiders, such as Harkins's decision to speak in English when dedicating a parish in nearby Fall River in 1906, could ignite controversy. When the bishop tried to install a Belgian order at St. Ann's in Woonsocket in 1914, parishioners conducted a pew rent strike and formed a vigilance committee to prevent the Marist Fathers from entering the rectory. Harkins finally brought in a new priest and moved the Marists to another parish, but the incident still rankled in the minds of the "ultranationalists." The war only inflamed these ethnic tensions. The crusade to protect mother France from German tanks reinforced the French Canadians' homeland pride, at the same time that the drive for "100 Percent Americanism" made them more sensitive about cultural autonomy. Once the war ended and the parameters of political debate widened, they felt free to resist assimilation without appearing disloyal.[17]

Troubles in the French Canadian and Italian parishes presented an administrative headache and public relations debacle for diocesan leaders, and they sought to undermine interethnic struggles by encouraging coreligionists to unite behind a shared identity as American Catholics. This was not a new goal. Since the turn of the century, Harkins had sought to undermine ethnic and parish divisions by urging laypeople to join diocesan-wide organizations that would foster broader Catholic consciousness. One was the Union of Parish Clubs, formed in 1911 as the Catholic Athletic League. The union sought to foster "a spirit of co-operation amongst the Catholic men and boys in the furtherance of Catholic ideals and duties." A tempting recreational lineup that included sports tournaments, pool and cribbage games, debates, lectures, and social mixers attracted about four thousand members by 1917, but the majority came from Irish American parishes and most officers had Irish names. This was typical of organizations that crossed parish lines. Citywide women's and men's clubs attracted middle-class Irish Americans, but most working people remained committed to individual parish societies. Many were recent immigrants to whom parish-based ethnic identities remained more salient and middle-class clubs seemed unfamiliar. French Canadians of all classes, moreover, viewed pan-ethnic organizations as a threat to *survivance*. It was for this reason they had refused to join the AFCS or attend its annual conventions. According to an August 1916 report in the *Providence Tribune,* community leaders explained that despite their shared faith with Catholics from other countries, "their human aspirations, their hopes, their material interests are entirely different if not antagonistic." French Canadian leaders urged compatriots to join the USJB instead.[18]

After the war, Providence church leaders resolved to heal internal rifts by promoting diocesan organizations more aggressively. These efforts coincided with a parallel drive to create a nationwide community of American Catholics. "Parochial, diocesan and provincial limits must be forgotten in the face of the greater tasks which burden our collective religious resources," the war council declared in 1918. In laying out its postwar program at a conference the following year, the body's General Committee on Catholic Affairs spoke again of "the need of a common direction and of a center of activity. . . . We are all bound together, diocese to diocese, and soul to soul." Although the war council faded out of existence, its drive for Catholic cohesion did not. The new NCWC was equally eager to promote "Unity Among All Catholics," as one of its pamphlets was titled, but also to assure member organizations that affiliating with the national federation would not undermine local autonomy. It was the particular goal of the National Council of Catholic Men (NCCM) and the NCCW, two of the conference's subgroups, to promote lay unity across parish, diocesan, and ethnic lines. The NCCM hoped, in the words of a speaker at its 1926 conference, to be "a swift athlete in the cause of Christ's Church—an air squadron flying to meet any emergency." But cohesion was the prerequisite to effective action.[19]

Providence's Catholic leaders did their best to promote these efforts, and laypeople responded with enthusiasm. According to Michael Slattery, now national director of the NCCM, Providence was the first city to organize a diocesan council and thus "an inspiration to all of our field workers." Evincing a "splendid spirit of cooperation," almost every parish in the diocese (including the disruptive Holy Ghost) had formed a chapter by April 1923. Irish Americans at St. Mary's were so enthusiastic that an organizational meeting attracted an "overflow" crowd. Joseph M. Tally of Providence, a businessman who sold prayer books and religious articles as well as serving as a notary public and running a travel agency, headed the NCCM's local chapter and later served as vice president of its national executive committee. A parallel effort to promote the NCCW brought representatives of fifty parishes to a meeting at the Narragansett Hotel, presided over by Jane Newton of the Queen's Daughters, in August 1922. The following year the Catholic Young Men's National Union, whose goals included "furtherance of practical Catholic unity," held its annual convention in Providence.[20]

The genius of these national groups was that they enabled Catholics to both preserve and transcend ethnically based parish boundaries. The fundamental organizing unit was the parish council, but units came together from time to time as part of a broader organization. Many of the nation's Catholics responded to this approach. The NCCW filled its newsletters with reports of crowded organizational meetings in cities including Baltimore, New York, Chicago, Milwaukee, and Boston. Yet in Providence and elsewhere, enthusiasm remained strongest among Irish Americans. They recognized that nationalizing the American Catholic community would make for effective political action, enhance the stature of the church, and concentrate control under an overwhelmingly Irish American bishopric. This no doubt alienated other ethnic groups. So too, perhaps, did a suspicion that Catholic leaders were promoting their own "100 Percent Americanism" by demanding pan-ethnic unity within an "American" Catholic Church.[21]

The corollary to forging cohesion within the Catholic community was projecting an image of strength to outsiders. The Diocese of Providence, still smarting from the public relations disaster at Holy Ghost, was particularly concerned with proving Italian Americans were committed Catholics. The *Visitor* proudly reported on the smashing success of missions among the Italians in the early 1920s, some of which claimed standing-room-only crowds. At the same time, diocesan-wide demonstrations suggested "staunch Catholicity" was not limited to the Italians. A 1923 drive to raise one million dollars for parochial high schools surpassed its goal within several weeks, despite the New England textile slump. The triennial Holy Name

Parade, for its part, typically attracted well over 100,000 Catholics in a powerful statement of religious unity.[22]

Perhaps the most poignant illustration of Catholic power came in July 1922, when Hickey returned from his first official visit to the Vatican to the equivalent of a religious ticker tape parade. State officials and private citizens lined the streets of Cranston, just south of Providence, to greet their popular spiritual leader. "Never in the history of Rhode Island has one seen a reception as grand and as pleasing," crowed *Le Jean-Baptiste*. Demonstrations like these sent the message the church and its members were a force to be taken seriously.[23]

"SO MANY WILLING HANDS ARE IDLE": MOBILIZING CATHOLIC WOMEN AND MEN

To reorient Catholics from ethnic rivalries and toward a shared religious identity was only the first step in enhancing the influence of their church. The next task, in Providence and nationwide, was to transform the faithful into an educated and engaged electorate. In September 1919 the war council's Committee on Catholic Affairs voiced a widespread concern when it declared, "So many willing hands are idle, so many silent tongues could preach Catholicism persuasively." Determined to mobilize these hands and tongues, American church leaders launched a drive to encourage civic involvement. A war council campaign urged immigrants to naturalize and vote, taught them English and civics, and promoted what it called active citizenship. The *Visitor* agreed it was "a religious duty to do one's part in maintaining the Government." The NCWC circulated a "Fundamentals of Citizenship" in fourteen languages and implemented a civics course in Catholic elementary schools.[24]

From the perspective of the NCWC, study clubs offered a particularly effective way to prepare the laity to engage with public affairs. "In a country like ours where public opinion can play the deciding role in the settlement of most questions, it is of fundamental importance for every American to be well and correctly informed on all questions of public moment," the welfare conference noted. Study clubs were to be small and engaged groups that assembled people of diverse occupations and interests once a week to discuss any number of topics outlined in NCWC study guides. These ranged from "Christian art" to "labor problems" to "current legislation." A priest or layperson with some knowledge of the subject at hand facilitated discussions, but the focus was on self-education. Although the NCWC issued study outlines and published a detailed guide titled "How to Conduct a Study

Club," it offered a fair amount of latitude. The "how to" guide encouraged participants to discuss as well as listen, urged leaders to tolerate differences of opinion, and suggested that clubs assemble in members' homes as well as parish facilities. The council clearly intended its study outlines as no more than starting points for inquiry, for it urged club members to supplement these guides with their own research. The laity seems to have responded warmly to this approach. The NCCW had received more than 250 requests for outlines from forty-one states by 1924, and New York's Paulist Radio Station (WLWL) broadcast a popular "Study Club Hour."[25]

The women's council was especially enthusiastic, recognizing the study club as an invaluable means of political education and action for its members. The NCCW, in fact, urged participants to do more than simply read and deliberate. "Turn your study clubs into investigating committees to learn a subject and then to report back . . . with conclusions," its October 1929 newsletter suggested. "Make them Catholic Action Committees." These "action committees" would "train leaders for the community," creating a cadre of laypeople who would "fight gallantly in the defense of Catholic rights." Cleveland's *Catholic Bulletin,* employing similarly martial imagery, described the clubs as "the church's shock troops."[26]

Providence Catholics embraced this campaign to inform and mobilize the laity. This had been a goal of the city's religious and lay leaders for two decades, and the educational forums that abounded in the Progressive Era had been popular in a variety of national parishes. Now priests and laity seized with enthusiasm on the national civic education drive. The *Visitor* ran new columns that kept readers up to date on the doings of Congress and state legislatures. The Union of Holy Name Societies organized a lecture bureau, and individual parishes continued to sponsor study groups and debating clubs. The Daughters of Isabella, for example, had a twenty-five-member study club that met on the third Friday evening of each month to discuss various institutions engaged in social work. Anna Fennessy, a Providence Catholic, was invited to speak at an NCCW convention in St. Paul about her success in promoting study clubs among women in her diocese.[27]

In Providence and across the nation, the civic education campaign took particular aim at women. The war had constituted a watershed for women, many of whom had assumed "men's" jobs or engaged in relief work that took them beyond their parishes and neighborhoods and in some cases outside the country. At the same time, Americanization programs embraced cultural projects in which they served as both agents and targets. These activities prompted many women to think of themselves as public servants with obligations that extended beyond the home. With the enactment of the

Nineteenth Amendment in 1920, they also became recognized members of the polity.

The American church never had taken an official position on woman suffrage, although its attitudes had been overwhelmingly negative. In Providence the hierarchy's stance, as voiced through the *Visitor*, had been less hostile than ambivalent. This no doubt reflected the loose coalition between woman suffragists and ethnic, Catholic opponents of the property qualification. After 1920, church spokespeople, in Providence and across the country, adjusted to the new law by declaring women were duty-bound to vote, albeit under the direction of clergy and male relatives. In fact, many clerics and lay leaders saw woman suffrage as a grand opportunity. The Nineteenth Amendment doubled the number of potential Catholic voters, infusing the polity with electors who could create a formidable lobby for church-friendly policies. Hoping to capitalize on this political sea change, the national women's council sought to build nothing less than a "great army of Catholic women." They "must recognize their responsibility in what is a real contest between the forces for good and the forces for evil in our land," its newsletter declared. "By united and enlightened effort Catholic women can now do wonderful things for God, Home and Country." The *Visitor* agreed wholeheartedly. Catholic women presented an electoral counterweight to the "radical suffragists" whose agenda, the Providence paper charged, ranged "from race suicide to teaching young school children to forget how to blush." They also could provide a bulwark against bolshevism, whose philosophy of big government presumably offended Catholic mothers who did not wish the state to intrude into family life.[28]

Finally, women craving public roles could channel their energies into church-based Americanization programs. It was in this era, writes the historian Charles Morris, that the church's "immigrant-processing machinery approached the efficiency of legend." The NCCW was an important part of this machine. The women's council railed against the Johnson-Reed Act (which discriminated against newer immigrants from southern and eastern Europe, many of them Catholic) and continued the wartime policy of providing a Catholic approach to Americanization. Operating under the slogan "a Catholic friend for every Catholic newcomer," the council urged chapters to teach immigrants English, help them naturalize, and get them to church. In some parishes, prominent laypeople personally tutored immigrants and sponsored their citizenship applications. The NCCW sought not only to control the process by which Catholic immigrants Americanized but also to promote a kinder, gentler approach to assimilation. It argued immigrants had "the right to be different, the right to a free self-expression."[29]

Agnes Bacon headed the NCCW's national Committee on Americanization and Naturalization in addition to serving as its Americanization director in Rhode Island. Her work was designed to draw newcomers into parish
life and provide an alternative to the outreach of the largely Protestant
RILWV. That organization ran a "Free Non-Partisan Citizenship School for
Women," as well as offering a mentorship program in which a native-born
woman spent a year tutoring an immigrant about "the real spiritual meaning of American citizenship." The Protestant and Catholic women agreed
that Americanizing involved becoming a citizen, voter, and English-speaker;
where they differed was on whether it also entailed becoming Protestant. By
sending out a cadre of its own female social workers, the Catholic Church
helped to ensure that immigrants became American without leaving the
parish. In all these ways, Catholic women represented a powerful vehicle for
the church.[30]

The problem was getting them to the polls. Women had the misfortune
to secure the franchise just as shifts in political culture were discouraging
citizens from voting. Some "progressive" reforms, ostensibly designed to
make government more accessible, had in fact shifted control from elected
officers to professional bureaucrats less accountable to the public. In the late
nineteenth and early twentieth centuries, moreover, states north and south
created poll taxes and registration requirements to keep immigrant, working-class, and black voters from the polls. Finally, the partisan, street-based
politics of the nineteenth century had given way to professional campaigns
run by a distant party apparatus and to a one-party system in which Republicans controlled the North and West and Democrats the South. As a result, turnout in presidential elections in the 1920s fell to just over half the
electorate, from an average of almost 80 percent in the late nineteenth century. As the pacifist and feminist Suzanne La Follette put it, women had won
the suffrage "at the very period when political rights are worth less than they
have been at any time since the eighteenth century."[31]

Moreover, female voters confronted a special set of problems that did not
disappear when the Nineteenth Amendment became law. Woman suffrage
had received legal sanction, but women still faced structural obstacles and
social proscriptions that discouraged independent activism. Those who
wished to form voting blocs faced a dilemma: alone they lacked the clout to
win concessions from male office-holders, but within male-dominated parties they had trouble advancing their agendas. Now that women had the vote
they lacked a unifying issue around which to rally, and even with such a
cause they would have faced a two-party system hostile to independent challenges. In Providence, female voters also confronted a municipal property

requirement that affected them disproportionately. For all these reasons, many American women eschewed the vote in favor of the voluntarist strategies of the pre-suffrage era.[32]

Electoral statistics in Providence bore out the perception that many women were not voting. Only 45 percent of the women qualified to vote, as opposed to 48 percent of men, registered in the elections of 1920, 1922, and 1924. Participation probably was even weaker among Catholic women, who were likely to confront obstacles of language, citizenship, demanding schedules (a problem for overburdened housewives as well as women who worked for wages), and the property rule. Catholics no doubt comprised the majority of the sixteen thousand voting-age women who were not citizens in Providence. If these women were to constitute a new army of political warriors, they would have to be guided to the polls.[33]

In Providence and nationwide, the result was a civic education campaign aimed specifically at Catholic women. The NCCW urged members to "form classes for the study of civic problems." If domestic responsibilities prevented a woman from joining a study club, she should establish "a citizenship school for herself." Marshaling the power of religion behind its "Get-Out-The-Vote" campaign, the council urged women to go "to the polls in defense of the principles sacred to Christian civilization." Providence leaders broadcast a similar message. Hickey urged every woman in his diocese to join a study club, and Gainer encouraged them "to take a vital interest in and make a constant study of the problems confronting city government." As the city's leading Catholic politician, Gainer was committed to educating the women of his church about their new responsibilities as voters. "Be proud of having attained citizenship. No greater favor or honor can be conferred upon you," he told the Queen's Daughters in 1922. "Prove yourself proud moreover by never failing your obligation to citizenship, namely, to register each year. Any man or woman too apathetic to do this, should not be regarded as citizens." The imperative of voting was a constant refrain among religious and lay leaders, who told women this was a "religious obligation," a familial duty, and an "obligation to citizenship." In these efforts the Providence diocese had the backing of no lesser authority than the Vatican, which in 1920 proclaimed that it was Catholic women's duty to exercise their newfound right to vote.[34]

The challenge was to encourage women to be politically active without provoking behavior considered untoward. To this end Providence church leaders, like their counterparts in Boston, articulated a version of "domestic feminism" that urged women to extend their roles as homemakers and Catholics into community service. The Providence hierarchy endorsed the

NCCW position that women must "act as one" on legislation "affecting the welfare of women and children, and the dignity of marriage and parenthood." It was to protect family and church that Catholic women in Providence and across the nation were told to campaign for widows' pensions, higher wages, shorter working hours, and censorship of sexually provocative films, and to oppose legalized birth control and the Equal Rights Amendment. Some of these positions placed economic expediency before the traditional Catholic priority of keeping the state out of the home. The *Visitor* joined local laypeople in endorsing Isabelle Ahearn O'Neill's mothers' aid bill, suggesting that its benefits to destitute families outweighed the dangers of government presence in private life. It was for similar reasons the NCWC endorsed the federal Sheppard-Towner Act, which provided health care for poor women and infants.[35]

In encouraging women to take positions on these initiatives, Catholic leaders invited them to assume unconventional roles as activists in order to preserve traditional gender roles and family structures. To do so, Hickey told a mass meeting of Providence women, was not really to engage in politics but simply to protect institutions that made America great. Echoing rhetoric suffragists had used in their efforts to win the vote, Hickey and his colleagues repeatedly urged women to vote on the grounds they would restore order and morality to political life. Adding a Catholic twist to this logic, they argued that women would do the country a particular service by promoting their religious values. It was this added priority that distinguished the legislative program of Catholic women from the otherwise similar agenda of the RILWV.[36]

Priests and prominent laypeople hoped that in pursuing this variant of domestic feminism, women would become activists without rejecting gender stereotypes or reordering family priorities. To reinforce this point, they urged women to become politically active without abandoning "the standards of Catholic womanhood in manners as well as in morality." As George Hurley, a Providence lawyer, said in an address to the Queen's Daughters, "the ideals of womanly womanhood need not be discarded when women enter politics." In a speech to the St. Sebastian's Women's Guild, O'Neill urged women in the same breath to lobby for a mothers' aid bill and "be careful and modest in your style of dress." Moreover, the *Visitor* advised, women should not take their jobs too seriously by pursuing careers or joining trade unions. These cautionary messages reflected the endurance of gender stereotypes but also defused fears that women who became politically active would neglect their families.[37]

It is difficult to determine whether Providence's Catholic women followed prescriptions of this nature, but it is clear many were eager to launch themselves into public life. Elizabeth T. Doyle, president of the women's auxiliary of the AOH, worked with fellow suffragists to get women to the polls, and the Tabernacle Society at Sacred Heart in East Providence conducted voter registration drives. Citywide Catholic women's councils organized legislative committees and worked with state officials on issues such as mothers' pensions that affected maternal and child welfare. The local chapter of the NCCW served as "a watchtower on legislative and civic matters," the *Visitor* observed in 1933, calling on "its large membership to voice their protests or approval of a measure." Among those who responded were Sarah T. Bartley of the Catholic Women's Club and Newton of the Queen's Daughters, who wrote letters protesting the proposed Smith-Towner Act that would have increased federal control over education by placing authority over public and private schools under a new cabinet position. The Providence County Ladies Auxiliary to the AOH passed a resolution urging Rhode Island congressmen to repeal the Johnson-Reed Act, which the women described as an "injustice to all liberty loving people," and support Irish independence. Bacon of the NCCW helped galvanize a protest against the Cooper bill, which would have extended federal aid to rural health programs and thus raised red flags about state intervention in private life. Parish and citywide clubs campaigned against birth control (as did their counterparts in Detroit) and the Equal Rights Amendment. In 1935, fifteen women's groups complied with the bishop's request that they write their congressmen to protest the Pierce Amendment, which would have allowed contraceptive information to be sent through the mail. The Daughters of Isabella, for their part, proudly reported "we have been particularly watchful of legislation introduced in Congress and in our State Legislature, and when necessary have protested the passage of laws which aim at our religion—very innocent in guise, but often anti-Catholic." Other local women organized Americanization programs and engaged in charitable work. At the peak of the busy Christmas season in 1921, more than two thousand women gathered at the Victory Theater to hear Hickey and Agnes G. Regan, executive secretary of the NCCW, describe how they might contribute to social welfare. The assembly poignantly demonstrated women's eagerness to support their church and expand the parameters of their lives.[38]

This was true not only in Providence but across the nation. The successful and energetic NCCW eclipsed its male counterpart. The women's council ran a School of Social Service and a placement bureau for social workers, operated settlement houses, published information on relevant legislation, and was in regular contact with government agencies. The NCCM undertook just two major initiatives, providing secular publications with articles about Catholicism and broadcasting a weekly radio (and later television) show called "The Catholic Hour." Laywomen in Providence and other communities clearly recognized that becoming activists under the aegis of Catholic womanhood was a clever way to stake out roles otherwise denied them. In joining a political crusade promoted by clerical and lay leaders, they did more than obey orders. They sought to make public life more reflective of female needs and values as well as more Catholic. They also took advantage of the chance to engage in nontraditional activities such as issuing resolutions to lawmakers, corresponding with members of Congress, attending the NCCW's Washington, D.C., service school, and traveling to national conferences. When the women's council urged its members to be "leaders, not followers," it captured the hunger of Catholic women to forge public roles. The *Visitor* spoke truly in 1920 when it noted "the increasing power and responsibility of Catholic womanhood."[39]

Even though Catholic men had more opportunities to be political outside the church, they too seized on church organizations as a way to influence public life. The Holy Name Union cooperated with Hickey in his "holy crusade to preserve the Christian morality," part of a nationwide Catholic campaign against "indecent" films and literature. The USJB joined women's groups in protesting the Smith-Towner bill, and the NCCM lobbied for a measure that would help immigrants without proof of legal entrance to naturalize. Other lay activists focused their energies on getting out the vote. In 1924, Tally of the NCCM launched a naturalization and voter registration drive in local parishes. Four years later, he circulated a letter to female religious orders reminding members they needed to register by June 30. "May we respectfully remind you that the Nuns of your Community should attend to this important duty at once," he wrote.[40]

Enthusiasm for public service divided along class and ethnic lines, however. In Providence, citywide Catholic clubs continued to attract a constituency that was largely Irish American and middle-class. Members of the NCCW's local board of directors, for example, consistently had last names that were almost exclusively Irish or British. As in Boston, women and men who engaged in lobbying, voter registration, and social work fit a similar social profile. These Catholics had the education and leisure to pursue public careers. They advocated issues, such as limits on child labor and birth control, that probably appealed to foreign-born and working-class coreligionists as Catholics but presented them with economic dilemmas as members of struggling households. Class divisions like those that had emerged during the Holy Ghost affair continued to rankle, splitting parishes internally and preventing working-class parishes from uniting with well-heeled congregations in diocesan-wide political actions. For all these reasons working-class Catholics were less touched by the church's civic education campaign. It would take a series of threats from outside to unite coreligionists across lines of class, gender, and ethnicity and into a more cohesive and engaged electorate.[41]

10

"THE RELIGIOUS ISSUE IN POLITICS"

Catholics and Protestants in the 1920s

We are inclined to be optimistic over the presence of the religious issue in politics. The continual crying of wolf is bound to react upon the professional alarmists.

— *Visitor,* October 5, 1928

PROTESTANTS MOBILIZE

As ethnic Catholics amassed their "shock troops," native-born Protestants responded with alarm. Nativism and anti-Catholicism surged across the nation in the early 1920s. The isolationism that gripped America after the disappointing Treaty of Versailles translated for some into a mistrust of all things foreign, and postwar developments seemed to provide real cause for concern. A rise in immigration (after a wartime lull) enlarged the foreign-born population; a postwar depression sparked familiar charges that newcomers were taxing the economy; and an outbreak of prohibition-fueled lawlessness was blamed on ethnic gang leaders like Chicago's Al Capone. Equally perturbing was the finding, documented by the 1920 census, that for the first time more Americans lived in cities than on farms or in small towns. Farmers and villagers (who tended to be native-born, Anglo-Saxon, and Protestant) were dismayed to see the nation's power shifting to its multiethnic urban centers. The cities were the source of the hedonistic consumer culture and freer sexuality that threatened an older morality. And the Catholics who tended to live there were more numerous—they would comprise almost 20 percent of the U.S. population by 1930—and assertive than ever. This assertiveness was evident in national organizations such as the NCWC and public demonstrations like the Twenty-Eighth International Eucharistic Congress, a weeklong celebration that brought a million Catholics to Chicago in 1926. Many older Americans felt these changes threatened the foundations of their lives and resolved to regenerate American society by restoring it to its small-town, Anglo-Saxon, Protestant roots. The result was a series of culture wars between old stock and new over issues like prohibition and immigration restriction.[1]

In Providence, the Protestant counterattack had the unexpected consequence of mobilizing and, to a degree, uniting the Catholic population. During the 1920s Catholics confronted a series of assaults that targeted, or seemed to target, them on the basis of faith. Most notable were a law limiting parochial school autonomy and the rise of a local Ku Klux Klan. As they mobilized to defend their rights as Americans and Catholics, they rallied for the first time across ethnic lines and around a shared religious identity. These threats from outside moved them in a way the pleas of priests and community leaders had not. Cracks remained in the alliance, as revealed by a bitter internal controversy over parochial school funding. But by the end of the decade this religious community was beginning to form an electoral coalition that would transform political culture and ideas about citizenship in Rhode Island. This trend first manifested itself in Catholic support for presidential candidate Alfred E. Smith in 1928.

"A MONOLINGUAL NATION?": MOBILIZING AGAINST THE PECK ACT

On April 19, the last day of the 1922 legislative session, Republican lawmakers pushed through a bill limiting bilingual instruction in parochial schools. This law, known as the Peck Act, opened one of the most controversial chapters in Rhode Island legislative history. Language long had been a cultural battleground in the state, with most skirmishes involving the French Canadians. Their passionate commitment to *survivance* prompted a fierce determination to educate children in bilingual parochial schools, which created tensions with public school authorities as well as Irish American bishops. As early as 1883, the state Board of Education had noted with concern the immigrants' attachment to their native tongue. "The danger to civilization today is not from without, but from within," its annual report declared. "The heterogeneous masses must be made homogeneous." The result was a state law that required all private school instruction to be in English, but the law was ignored widely. Most nineteenth-century Americans saw little need to promote assimilation, assuming that inevitably immigrants would be absorbed into the melting pot. Over time many French Canadians seemed to do just that as they remigrated less frequently, became citizens, avoided labor unrest, and achieved economic stability. Speaking French did not seem to prevent them from becoming American. By 1907, Carroll Wright, who had issued a blistering indictment of the French Canadians as Massachusetts labor commissioner in 1881, noted with pleasure that "no other nationality has developed as rapidly and in as satisfactory a manner."[2]

During and after the war, however, many natives abandoned the melting pot ideal for more aggressive Americanization. Revelations of widespread inability to speak English aroused concerns that the immigrant was "an easy prey for the treasonable agitators who talk in his own tongue," the *New York Times* wrote in 1919. Pronouncements like these rang true in Rhode Island, which in 1920 had a higher proportion of first- and second-generation immigrants than any other state. "Disorders in the cities of New England have been caused principally by aliens who do not speak the language of this country and who in consequence do not understand the spirit of American institutions," the *Journal* agreed. "The language question has been neglected too long." English language illiteracy, traditionally viewed as an obstacle to assimilation, now loomed as a threat to national security. State lawmakers responded with the aforementioned 1919 Americanization law, which mandated evening school instruction for young adults.[3]

Postwar labor militancy deepened concerns about immigrant radicalism. Determined to reverse labor's wartime gains, local mill owners insisted laborers return to working fifty-four hours a week for wages reduced by as much as 20 percent. When workers resisted, employers threatened to move south, where wages were lower and labor laws even weaker. Despite this threat, in January 1922 the state's mill operatives joined textile workers along the East Coast in the industry's longest strike to date. Rhode Island strikers returned to work at the end of the summer under a disappointing compromise. Yet the strength of their protest, uniting workers across lines of sex and ethnicity and attracting the support of Catholic priests and Democratic politicians, had alarmed industrialists and their allies in the General Assembly. Republican lawmakers saw this labor militancy as proof the ethnic workforce had to be Americanized more forcefully. They responded with the Peck Act.[4]

The 1922 law mandated that private schools teach the same curriculum as public schools and teach it in English. Only subjects not taught in the public schools could be conducted in other languages. Although the measure ostensibly left room for bilingual instruction, state administrators could expand the mandatory curriculum until there was no time left for extra classes in foreign languages. The law also transferred supervision of private schools from local committees, generally responsive to the community's dominant ethnic group, to the state Board of Education. The Peck Act echoed similar efforts in other states. Oregon enacted a law, later declared unconstitutional, that virtually required students to attend public schools. In Michigan it took a campaign by the Detroit Diocesan Union of Holy Name Societies to defeat a proposal to close every private grammar school in the state.[5]

No sooner did the Rhode Island bill become law than parishioners mobilized, determined to protect their rights as Catholics and Americans. Because parochial schools were integral components of parishes, a threat to their autonomy was a threat to religious freedom. Limits on bilingual instruction also undermined cultural preservation and the right to free speech, and the law subverted limited government by extending state control over education. The Peck Act seemed a blatant attempt to undermine Catholics' growing influence, and it was as Catholics that they challenged it. The anti-Peck movement fostered a measure of the unity church leaders had been seeking, bringing coreligionists together across lines of ethnicity and sex. Even though the law was most offensive to the French Canadians, it menaced the religious freedom valued by Catholics from other countries. It also dealt with religion and education, considered part of the female sphere, and targeted schools run by nuns. This made the law an issue on which women could take stands without violating gender stereotypes.

As debate over the Peck Act heated up, each side invoked the authority of Americanism to plead its case. The controversy highlighted disagreements over three fundamental aspects of Americanism. Did it require a rejection of ethnic tradition? Must it remain synonymous with small government? And would its promise of religious freedom become a reality? Adhering to "100 Percent Americanism," old stock supporters claimed that the law was essential to national unity. Without Peck, they argued, Rhode Island would remain a modern-day Tower of Babel. "Within fifteen minutes from [Providence] you can pass from America into a foreign land," complained Charles Carroll, state deputy director of vocational education. "From the multiplicity of tongues has sprung all the curses of the human race, because of it no man in Europe lives without fear of his neighbor, because of it millions of men in the last ten years have lost their lives." Carroll's implication was that the melting pot model had failed and more forceful measures were in order. In fact, the militancy of the anti-Peck movement convinced the bill's supporters of the need for complete and coercive Americanization. "They not only do not fear the hyphen," charged Robert Cloutman Dexter, author of a study of local immigrants. "They glory in it, and are using every effort to preserve it." Speaking for a coalition of patriotic leagues and women's clubs, the RILWV lambasted Peck opponents as "subversive of our ideals of American citizenship."[6]

Peck's Catholic opponents responded by arguing for a pluralistic Americanism that left room for ethnic tradition. Echoing their wartime rhetoric, they insisted that bilingualism did not detract from patriotism or civic mindedness. They backed up this claim by encouraging compatriots to naturalize and vote even as they continued to speak the native tongue. "It is impossible to allow that our common love of our country could be endangered by the language we speak in our families," charged the Woonsocket paper *La Tribune*. "Where is there a monolingual nation? Where is the great empire in which all the subjects speak nothing but the same idiom?"[7]

The French Canadians were not alone in making arguments of this nature. Even though they spearheaded the opposition, they had the support of some Italian American laypeople and Irish American clerics. At the dedication of Holy Ghost's parish school in 1923, Judge Antonio Capotosto, a pillar of Providence's Italian community, echoed French Canadian rhetoric about the harmony between Americanism, Catholicism, and ethnic pride. "The best way to combat and overcome the many 'isms,' that are destroying . . . our faith and our country, is a good Christian education," he told his audience. In no way, he added, did foreign language instruction in parochial schools produce divided loyalties. "I teach [my children] Italian not because I want them to show any allegiance to Italy, but because I do not want them to forget the home of their forefathers," he noted. "It's America first, and it's America last!" Yet in between, he implied, was room for old world traditions to coexist with new world ways. Even Hickey, leader of an Irish American church hierarchy many French Canadians found insensitive to their cultural priorities, actively opposed the bill. For Hickey, the threat to church autonomy outweighed the hope that all Catholics would assimilate into an "American" church. The Peck Act also may have reminded him of English colonists' attempts to impose their language on the Gaelic-speaking Ireland of his ancestors.[8]

If the Peck Act reflected the postwar trend toward 100 Percent Americanism, it also represented a related propensity to achieve this through a growth in centralized power. From the perspective of native-born Americanizers like members of the RISFWC, the nation's schools were performing vital work by assimilating young people, and thus it made sense to concentrate their supervision. This was the reasoning behind the proposed Smith-Towner Act, which aroused heated opposition from organizations like the NCCW because it would have allowed federal regulation of parochial as well as public schools. In Providence, Catholic priests and laypeople issued resolutions and organized protest rallies at which they lambasted this measure as a threat to familial prerogatives, local autonomy, and religious freedom. The USJB, for example, denounced the bill as "undemocratic," "socialistic," and "against the spirit of our Constitution."[9]

With the passage of the Peck Act in 1922, the debate over centralized power moved from Congress to the Providence State House. Opponents called the bill an "un-American" violation of the tradition of small government. Governor Emery San Souci, a French Canadian and a Republican, agreed. "It is the duty of every good citizen to resist this dangerous tendency in order to keep this country true to the splendid principles laid down by its great founders," he declared. *Le Jean-Baptiste* was careful to note its readers did not oppose the teaching of English; it was centralized authority they mistrusted. Invoking the bogey of bolshevism, Democratic representative Edouard Belhumeur of Woonsocket even suggested the Peck Act smacked of the "administrative despotism" practiced in Soviet Russia.[10]

Even as Catholics invoked the tradition of small government to argue against the unpopular law, their major concern was its impact on religious freedom. Not surprisingly, Peck provoked an immediate reaction from the Catholic hierarchy. The day after the law was enacted, French Canadian priests denounced it from their pulpits. Hickey met with San Souci and recommended that the governor veto the bill, then called French Canadian priests and lawmakers to a conference at which he explained in French that he opposed the measure as a threat to the church. "I have studied the French language, I love it well and I am convinced that language is a powerful force for the conservation of faith," he told his audience. The speech enabled Hickey to rally opposition to a bill that impinged on church autonomy, as well as to score points with French Canadians who suspected that outsiders like himself did not recognize the role of language in *survivance*. In going on record against Peck, Hickey seized an opportunity to unite Catholics in defense of religious freedom.[11]

The Democrats, for their part, knew resisting the Peck Act would help them attract Catholic voters. The bill was the brainchild of the Republicans, who clearly felt it would attract more native voters than it would alienate ethnics. The measure placed San Souci in a terrible dilemma, trapped between Republican loyalties and ethnic bonds and certain a choice either way would imperil his career. After agonizing over his response, the ironically named chief executive (whose name loosely translates as "without worry") finally vetoed the bill, only to watch the state Supreme Court overturn his veto on the grounds he had waited too long. San Souci had come down on the side of his compatriots and coreligionists, but his hesitation had been fatal. Catholics, already angry about his calling out the National Guard during the textile strike earlier that year, now had a cultural grievance with him. The Democrats, by contrast, had opposed the Peck Act as steadfastly as they had supported the strike, recognizing an opportunity to drive a wedge between the Republicans and their ethnic supporters.[12]

Resentment over the Peck Act combined with anger about the failed strike to reconfigure local politics. In the November elections a number of Italian and French Canadian voters joined Irish coreligionists in voting Democratic. Thanks to their support the minority party enjoyed its first gubernatorial victory in fifteen years, won almost every other statewide office, and significantly increased its share of General Assembly seats. The House was split evenly between the major parties; and although the Democrats fell just short of securing control in the Senate, their newly elected lieutenant governor, Felix Toupin, would preside over that body. The election was to prove the first step in a gradual but decisive political realignment.[13]

The Peck controversy, however, did not end with the Democratic triumph. Despite its gains the party remained unable to move its anti-Peck initiatives through the Senate, and it was not until 1925 that lawmakers overturned the unpopular law. A slowdown in immigration, following the federal restrictions of 1921 and 1924, reduced anxieties about assimilation. Concluding that the threat was ebbing, local school authorities went so far as to suggest that the city stop wasting its money teaching immigrants English in free night schools. Ethnic Catholics had won the Peck war, yet their victory had as much to do with migration patterns as with their own resistance. The Peck controversy had brought them together in defense of religious freedom, but it would take more to forge them into a truly cohesive and effective political force.[14]

"KATHOLICS, KOONS AND KIKES": CHALLENGING THE KU KLUX KLAN

That catalyst came in the hooded form of the Ku Klux Klan. Founded in the aftermath of the Civil War, outlawed by Congress in 1871, and reborn on Stone Mountain, Georgia, in 1915, the Klan grew into a bona-fide mass movement in the 1920s. The organization captured the distorted desire of small-town Americans to turn back the clock to a time they saw as simpler and better—a pre-modern era when women wore long skirts and did not vote, African Americans were enslaved, and the nation's ethnic composition was largely northern and western European. The Klan also created a community for people disoriented at a time of rapid social and demographic change. Like nativist secret societies popular in the nineteenth-century North, it orchestrated elaborate rituals that brought excitement to small, isolated communities. Yet despite its roots in an earlier era it was a product of the 1920s—promoted by a clever advertising team and appealing to the consumerist and entrepreneurial spirit of the decade with heavily marketed paraphernalia such as white robes and hoods.[15]

The modern Klan was known for its adaptability. It skillfully tapped into local prejudices, targeting African Americans in the South, bootleggers in the Midwest and Catholics, Jews, and foreigners in the Northeast. The Klan's links to militant Protestantism (in membership and rhetoric) rendered it particularly suspicious of Catholics. Klan spokesmen invoked old fears about Catholic political power, warning of a "hierarchical Church, which, like an octopus, has stretched its tentacles into the very vitals of the body politic of the nation." They even made the odd claim that "Jesus was a Protestant."[16]

In Rhode Island the Klan coalesced in 1923 around a hatred for Catholics and immigrants. Far from a fringe group of uneducated yokels, the organization included state legislators, town officials, police officers, manufacturers, clergymen, dentists, and members of the American Legion and National Guard. A study of Klan membership found that unskilled workers comprised only a minority, perhaps because the annual dues of fifteen dollars equaled more than one week's factory wages. The organization fared well in small towns as well as in the Providence metropolitan area, where its leaders lived.[17]

The local Klan assembled frequently, burning crosses and holding initiation rallies as well as gathering for weddings and dinner dances. Members went so far as to circulate propaganda in the Providence public schools under the guise of a current events curriculum, until authorities found out and put a stop to the practice. More successful was a series of lectures by Helen Jackson, a prostitute and modern-day Maria Monk who regaled her audiences with false but lurid stories about her former life as a nun. The Klan acquired a popular following through events like these, but official response was swift and condemnatory. Both major parties denounced the group, although Republicans were said to have done so reluctantly. The *Journal*, for its part, lambasted the organization as "un-American in the highest degree, and particularly hostile to the historic spirit of Rhode Island."[18]

Despite this opposition, Klan activity intensified as the 1924 elections approached. Facing a threat from the left in the form of Robert La Follette's national Progressive Party, and disturbed by the militancy of the Catholic anti-Peck movement, the Klan sprang into action to defend the mythical America of an older era. Members sent Peck opponents warnings to "leave the state and stay out of it," were suspected of setting a fire at a black school in North Scituate, and allegedly branded crosses on the skin of a French Canadian reporter who intruded on a Woonsocket rally. "I saw them actually burn a cross at the entrance of Roger Williams Park," recalled David Kolodoff, a Jewish radical who was eight years old in 1924. "I got so scared, I didn't leave the house." June, the last month to register to vote in the fall elections, witnessed an outburst of mass meetings and initiations. Most notable was a tri-state gathering in Foster at which eight thousand people assembled to hear Alabama senator Tom Heflin rage against "katholics, koons and kikes."[19]

Following on the heels of the Peck controversy, the Klan's attacks convinced Catholics that their religious freedom, cultural prerogatives, and even personal safety were in peril. They responded with a counteroffensive that urged coreligionists to rally behind a shared religious identity. When Klan supporters circulated anti-Catholic broadsides in Providence, the *Visitor* denounced the pamphlets as the work of Satan. "No one but the prince of lies could gather so many and so diabolical an assortment of calumnies," its editors charged. Throughout the spring of 1924, the *Visitor* filled its pages with articles urging Catholics to vote against enemies of religious liberty. At a mass meeting organized by the NCCW in April, Hickey urged listeners to cast ballots so that "the citizenship of America may be preserved, and that patriotism in its true sense . . . may be preserved." Lay Catholics responded with enthusiasm. Joseph Tally, the local NCCM leader, stepped up his efforts to naturalize and register every Catholic parishioner. When the Women's Tabernacle Society at Sacred Heart in East Providence held a meeting on voter registration work, more than one hundred parishioners showed up to get out the Catholic vote.[20]

The Democrats, for their part, recognized another opportunity to make inroads among Catholics and joined in the agitation. Mayor Gainer, a Catholic and Democrat, won Hickey's congratulations when he took a stand against Klan efforts to circulate propaganda in the public schools. His party's organ, the *Providence News*, launched an anti-Klan crusade and wasted no opportunity to make the not unsubstantiated claim that the group enjoyed close ties to the Republican Party. Although that party spurned open ties to the Klan, the Klan was clear about where its political sympathies lay. On Oc-

The Rhode Island Ku Klux Klan rallied in Georgiaville in 1927. The popularity of the Klan and its influence within the local Republican Party united Catholics across ethnic lines in defense of religious freedom. Photograph, courtesy of the *Providence Journal*.

tober 26, three thousand members gathered in Greenville to "pledge allegiance to the Republican ticket."[21]

The Klan overcame this vigorous opposition and held its own in the November elections. Frustrating the Democrats' hopes of riding an anti-Klan wave to victory, Rhode Islanders elected a number of Klan-endorsed candidates and gave the Republicans their largest statewide victory ever. Presidential politics had worked to the advantage of the party, which rode the coattails of Calvin Coolidge, a New Englander renowned for crushing the 1919 Boston police strike while governor of Massachusetts. The Democrats had to rally behind a lackluster corporate lawyer named John Davis, poorly equipped to stem the hemorrhage of votes to the charismatic La Follette. Moreover, local Republicans mended fences with some French Canadian and Catholic voters by nominating Aram Pothier, who pledged to amend the Peck Act if returned to the governor's mansion.[22]

Another decisive factor in the election was what would go down in local history as the "stink bomb" affair. The Democrats remained committed to reworking the state's outdated constitution to benefit themselves and the urban working class by repealing the property requirement and reapportioning the legislature. In January 1924, state senator Robert Quinn had introduced a bill calling for a referendum on a constitutional convention, only to watch the proposal languish in Republican committee. Quinn and his fellow Democrats knew the Senate would kill the proposal but were determined to bring it to a vote to expose their rivals' stubborn opposition to electoral reform.[23]

Taking advantage of the fact that their own Felix Toupin presided over the Senate, the Democrats initiated a memorable filibuster designed to force the referendum bill to a vote. By late spring the filibuster was in its sixth month and tempers were running high. On June 19, a thug allegedly hired by the Republicans set off a bromine gas bomb in the Senate chamber. By the time Toupin restored order the Republicans had taken refuge in a hotel just across the Massachusetts border. Beyond the jurisdiction of Rhode Island, they remained there all summer and vowed not to return until constitutional government was restored. The Democrats' strategy had backfired badly, forcing a six-month legislative impasse and making the state a national laughing stock. In January, reelected Republican senators returned to Providence and restored business as usual. Despite the Democrats' energetic championing of Catholics' cultural pluralism, religious freedom, and working-class rights, they lost the momentum they had acquired in 1922. They also failed to stop the Klan in its tracks.[24]

The Klan's moment proved brief, however. In the General Assembly, Klan-endorsed legislators lobbied without success for measures to prevent miscegenation, prohibit membership in societies with foreign leadership, and annul nuptial contracts by which non-Catholic spouses agreed to send children to parochial schools. Although some Republicans enjoyed ties to the Klan, party leaders knew they had gone too far with the Peck Act and could not afford to further alienate ethnic and Catholic voters. Once elected, Klan lawmakers, like the Know-Nothings before them, were unable to translate their agenda into law.[25]

The Klan ran into further trouble in March 1928, following a disturbing revelation that it had infiltrated three companies of a state militia unit. Eager to shake off perceptions that the group was an arm of the Republican Party, the General Assembly launched an investigation. It did not have to dig deep to discredit the Klan's local leadership. State Dragon John W. Perry, supposedly a wounded war hero and scion of one of the state's oldest families, turned out to be a former altar boy of black and Portuguese descent (a discovery that dismayed supporters who had admired him as a model of Anglo-Saxon Protestantism). He had resigned from a Connecticut police department after being caught in a tryst with a married woman while on duty, and his alleged war wound was the result of a failed suicide attempt. Bad publicity like this soon combined with the distractions of the Great Depression to prompt the Klan's rapid demise in Rhode Island, and similar tales played out across the nation. In state after state, support dwindled as Klan officials failed to achieve results, internal squabbling undermined unity, and personal scandals compromised claims of moral superiority.[26]

In Rhode Island, the Klan had forced into bold relief tensions between Protestants and Catholics and debates over the meanings of Americanism. With its coercive promotion of values identified as Protestant, native-born, and small-town, the vigilante group represented an extreme version of the prejudices that informed the Peck Act, the Eighteenth Amendment, and immigration restriction laws. Even though many local Yankees agreed with some of the Klan's fundamental premises, they opposed its tactics and were forced to condemn the group on those grounds. Organs like the *Journal,* rarely a champion of cultural pluralism, denounced the Klan as un-American. "Hundred-per-cent Americans must set their faces resolutely against the craven practices, false logic and wicked prejudices of the uncourageous society that draws its sustenance from ignorance, illiberality and a fundamental disregard of the true doctrines of Americanism," the newspaper railed.[27] Thus, even as the Klan exposed the ugly nativism and religious bigotry that continued to infect Rhode Island, it discredited these impulses through its extremism. Moreover, it inspired new Americans to defend themselves by uniting, at least temporarily, behind a shared identity as Catholics. The Klan's attempt to impose an old and restrictive national identity unwittingly legitimated a newer and more expansive model that acknowledged Catholics as Americans and inspired them to defend their rights.

DIVISION AND UNITY: THE SENTINELLE AFFAIR

Even as the Klan and Peck controversies encouraged a degree of the unity and mobilization church leaders were striving for, they ignited one final and conclusive schism within the Catholic community. Hypersensitive about cultural prerogatives in the wake of these attacks, a group of French Canadians became embroiled in a heated conflict with diocesan administrators who seemed to be threatening *survivance.* In 1923, Hickey launched the aforementioned drive to raise one million dollars for an ambitious high school building program and authorized congregations that did not meet quotas to draw the difference from parish treasuries. The campaign set off warning bells for Woonsocket ultranationalists, who had resolved to be more militant about cultural preservation in the wake of the Peck Act. They worried the fund drive would divert money from individual churches and place parochial schools under the control of Irish American officials, making it more difficult to keep the French language alive at bilingual parish schools. They were particularly disturbed about the opening of a multiethnic diocesan high school in Woonsocket. Even though Mount St. Charles Academy provided bilingual instruction, it admitted young people who were not of French Canadian heritage.[28]

The Woonsocket ultranationalists galvanized into action, calling themselves "Sentinelles" to signify their need to be on the watch for threats to *survivance*. Leading the resistance, Elphege Daignault, a journalist and lawyer, petitioned the Vatican to stop the fund drive on the grounds it would place an unfair tax on parishioners and endanger existing parochial schools. The Sentinelles focused on the legality of the fund drive, challenging the bishop's right to assess parish funds for diocesan-wide programs, but their real mission was to secure parish autonomy and subvert the centralized structure of the American Catholic Church.[29]

In the course of their multiyear campaign the Sentinelles appealed to authorities civil and religious, published a newspaper, and conducted pew rent strikes and parish boycotts. The controversy degenerated into name-calling—Hickey was a "Judas" and the Sentinelles were "Satanic Bolsheviks"—and even physical violence. In early 1928, when Pope Pius XI excommunicated Daignault and fifty-five followers who had brought a civil suit against Hickey, the Sentinelles realized they had gone too far. They successfully sought absolution, returned to the church, and allowed their movement to die. In the meantime, the diocesan fund-raiser that had set off the affair surpassed its one-million-dollar goal.[30]

Sentinellism drew its power from a combination of cultural and economic frustrations the Peck Act and textile strike had sharpened. The movement enabled workers to express economic grievances even though it was spearheaded by middle-class professionals. It was no coincidence that mass rallies regularly were held at two working-class parishes that lay in the shadow of the Manville Jenckes textile mills, site of a bitter and failed 1927 walkout. Like Manville Jenckes, a large Yankee-owned corporation, the diocesan fund drive raised the menace of outside forces encroaching on community life. By linking the threats of Yankee employers and Irish church administrators, the Sentinelle movement offered a focus for working people under a barrage of economic and cultural assaults.[31]

At the same time that Sentinellism provided a rallying point for workers against outsiders, it exposed deep fault lines within the French Canadian community. The affair followed a decades-long debate between militancy and moderation in the quest for *survivance*. This debate pitted a small band of ultranationalists against a larger group of moderates increasingly uncomfortable with their rivals' eagerness to stage confrontations with civic and religious leaders. The French Canadians remained firmly committed to preservation of their culture, but most agreed that in attacking the church the Sentinelles had gone too far.[32]

The Sentinelle affair forced French Canadians to confront whether they should subordinate ethnic loyalties to a broader unity as American Catholics. Daignault's followers suggested national affiliation should take precedence over religious affinity if the two conflicted, at the very time diocesan leaders were cultivating Catholic unity at the expense of ethnic particularism. "It is not the blood in one's veins that makes the Catholic, but it is belief in a doctrine and submission," Hickey insisted. "We are Catholics for salvation, but French Canadians only by accident of birth," agreed anti-Sentinellist J. Albert Foisy. These sentiments were popular. Although Sentinelle rallies attracted thousands of supporters, a majority of French Canadians (as well as coreligionists from other countries) condemned the agitation. The extremity of the Sentinelles' methods prompted compatriots to choose Catholic unity over nationalist rivalries. In this way, even as the ugly battle divided the community and diverted energies from parish building, it ultimately strengthened the movement for Catholic cohesion. This growing unity manifested itself in the election of 1928.[33]

THE "BROWN DERBY" CAMPAIGN: RALLYING BEHIND AL SMITH

When Governor Smith of New York launched his presidential campaign in 1928, Providence Catholics were well positioned to rally behind their coreligionist. The Klan and the Peck Act had convinced them to band together to protect religious freedom, and the Sentinelle affair had exposed the dangers of letting that unity dissipate. At the same time, the 1927 execution of Italian-born Nicola Sacco and Bartolomeo Vanzetti (convicted of murdering two men during an armed robbery in Brockton, Massachusetts, in 1920), offered further evidence of prejudice against a non-Protestant immigrant population. Across the nation, Sacco and Vanzetti became a cause célèbre among radicals, intellectuals, and Italian Americans who felt the anarchists had been convicted because of ethnicity and politics rather than convincingly documented guilt. In Providence new Americans recognized in the case a nativist undercurrent that threatened all of them, and they worried the arrests would garner support for more draconian Americanization programs and immigration laws. The local movement to reverse the convictions made unlikely allies among Italian Fascists and radicals, American Socialists, the PCFU, and the Catholic Church. Even the stridently antiradical *Visitor* called for a new trial and warned against convicting the men because of their politics. Rank-and-file Italians, for their part, drew on religion to protest the convictions.[34]

In August 1927, the Virgin Mary made a surprise appearance in Providence. For days her image mysteriously hovered on the wall of a Federal Hill building. Streets were filled and businesses disrupted as crowds assembled to regard the phenomenon. When the Narragansett Electric Company removed the bulb from a nearby street lamp, the image disappeared; but thousands of believers continued to assemble nonetheless. The *Journal* finally sent a reporter to Federal Hill to get to the bottom of the mystery. Several onlookers told him Mary had appeared in Providence because God was unhappy about the impending execution of Sacco and Vanzetti. The "Miracle on Federal Hill," as the incident became known, was a powerful example of the way in which religion informed protest. Even as relatively few Italians participated in diocesan-wide activist groups like the NCCM, some turned to religion to make grassroots political statements.[35]

Coming on the heels of the executions, the anti-Catholic agitation that surrounded Smith's campaign nationwide reinforced the sense that prejudice remained rampant and freedom of worship was endangered. In cities like Providence and Worcester, the election exposed enduring religious rivalries and aroused the Catholic electorate. The election thus brought to a head the struggle between two versions of Americanism—one rooted in middle-class, Protestant culture and the other demanding a place for Catholicism in the nation's life—that had been raging with particular intensity since the First World War. It also presented Catholics with an opportunity to implement political skills developed at church, draw on the civic education the NCWC was promoting, and demonstrate the degree of unity forged over the previous decade. The Smith campaign inspired coreligionists to launch the cohesive and effective political effort their religious and lay leaders had been urging since the end of the war.

Smith held enormous appeal in Providence. As the Catholic son of an Irish-born mother, he understood the fears and frustrations his coreligionists felt over the Peck Act and the Klan. Raised on the streets of New York City, amidst the smells of the Fulton Fish Market, he spoke the language of urban workers. Finally, "Alcohol Al," a vocal opponent of prohibition, was tremendously popular in a state that had rejected the Eighteenth Amendment. When Smith made a campaign stop in Providence, one supporter attended the rally bearing a placard that read, "Remember November 6—BEER!"[36]

Smith had the good fortune to run at a time when Rhode Island Republicans were losing the allegiance of Catholic, ethnic, and working-class voters. With the exception of its victory in 1924, the party had suffered a series of setbacks over the course of the decade. A prolonged and early depression (a result of the textile industry's southern flight) undermined Republicans' long-standing claim to be the party of prosperity, and resentments lingered over their support for the mill owners during the 1922 textile strike. Hoping to capitalize on these economic tensions, the Democrats issued a platform that denounced "the hypocritical attitude of the Republican Party in trying to make the people of Rhode Island feel that there is unbounded prosperity when so many of them are without employment."[37] Worse still, Republicans had demonstrated little respect for the cultural prerogatives of the ethnic, Catholic majority. It was they who had advocated the Peck Act and enjoyed ties to the Klan, and whose national leaders supported prohibition and immigration restriction. These divisive issues drove a wedge between the party and its constituency of Italian and French Canadian Catholics.

Even without these problems, the Republicans would have had trouble stemming the hemorrhage of Catholic votes to Smith. The Democratic contender had potential to accomplish three goals dear to Providence's religious and lay leaders: defuse religious prejudice; unite voters on the basis of religious affinity; and legitimate the church as a player in public life. Clearly delighted about his candidacy for these reasons, diocesan priests and editors had to steel themselves to navigate his campaign with caution. Smith's nomination reawakened long-standing concerns about union between church and state, and to support him on the grounds of faith would fuel fears that the Vatican had designs on the U.S. government. At the 1928 Holy Name parade, Hickey spoke to these concerns in a carefully worded speech that insisted the church was nonpartisan and uninterested in political power.[38] The *Visitor*, for its part, ran a series of editorials suggesting voters should neither support Smith because he was Catholic nor oppose him for that reason.

Smith's personal appeal and ability to connect with local issues made 1928 an exceptionally lively campaign year in Providence. Labor activists and Catholic leaders worked to get out the vote, even as the latter studiously avoided an endorsement. So many Democrats wished to attend their national convention that party leaders gave each representative half a vote in order to double the size of the delegation. Excitement extended beyond the ranks of seasoned activists. The *Visitor* predicted women would play a critical role in the election, and indeed registration rates rose significantly among female voters in Providence. More than 51 percent of all voting-age women registered in 1928, as compared with an average of 37.2 percent for the years 1920 through 1926. Of women actually qualified to vote, 61.2 percent registered in 1928. Attacks on Smith's religion clearly spoke to women, who comprised the majority of regular churchgoers, and in mobilizing against these attacks they could argue they were defending their faith rather than engaging in politics. This is undoubtedly why Tally of the NCCM made a special effort to get nuns to the polls that year.[39]

Grassroots excitement was visible on October 25, when a visit from Smith transformed Providence into a massive street festival. "Fire engines screeched, band instruments blared, torpedoes tossed by youngsters exploded, tickertape floated in a sinuous maze . . . automobile horns blasted, shrill whistles and locomotives screamed, confetti and shredded newspapers descended in blinding drifts, and an airplane marked with words of welcome swooped an aerial salute," the *Journal* observed. When police tried to remove a flag display on the grounds this was permitted only on national holidays, the Democratic mayor, James Dunne (who had replaced Gainer as the city's chief executive in 1926), stopped them by insisting that Smith's visit was an event of national import.[40]

As Dunne had suggested, the 1928 election was a historic one. More than 64 percent of qualified voters cast ballots, the highest number since the Cleveland-Harrison contest of 1892, an era when turnout rates were much higher. Smith was only the fourth Democratic presidential candidate ever to carry Rhode Island. Although the margin of his statewide victory was slender—51 percent to Hoover's 49—his was a major accomplishment. Predictably he fared best in urban areas, capturing 58 percent of the vote in Providence and well over two-thirds in some of the city's Catholic and Jewish districts.[41]

Local Democrats happily rode Smith's coattails. Even as Republicans carried the statewide elections, the minority party significantly improved its position in the General Assembly. In Providence Democrats achieved their most notable victory to date, securing all citywide offices, winning a strong majority on the city council, and coming just short of an even split on the board of aldermen. That board was the upper chamber; but if just one Republican broke ranks to create a tie, Dunne could break the tie in the interest of his constituency of Catholics, immigrants, and working people. Although Smith lost the national election, in Providence his supporters won a symbolic and strategic triumph.[42]

Smith's campaign marked the start of a political realignment that would reshape American politics during the New Deal by bringing Catholics, immigrants, Jews, and African Americans into the Democratic Party. In Providence this shift had been developing throughout the 1920s, and thus the 1928 election was a culmination as well as a starting point. With Smith's assistance, the local Democrats cemented a new partnership with many Italian and French Canadian Catholics as well as the much smaller populations of blacks and Jews. Although middle-class ethnic newspapers like *L'Eco* and *Le Jean-Baptiste* remained staunchly Republican, echoing traditional arguments about the full dinner pail, working people came together across ethnic lines to conclude that their interests lay with the Democrats. This shift reflected far more than the appeal of a popular presidential contender. It resulted from a decade of highly charged cultural politics in which many Catholics fled a Republican Party whose policies were increasingly nativist for the pluralistic Democrats.[43]

The 1928 election marked the coming of age of Catholic immigrants and ethnics, in both a literal and a political sense. In Providence as in other communities, second-generation immigrants were turning twenty-one and entering the electorate in far greater numbers than their foreign-born parents had. Intensifying their political engagement was the civic education campaign that urged Catholics to be informed and active voters. Their sense of civic obligation intensified as they confronted attacks that seemed to target them on the basis of faith. Moreover, these were attacks that focused on the familial and cultural prerogatives of which women typically took charge. As coreligionists came together across lines of sex, ethnicity, and generation to fend off these assaults, they began to cohere around a shared identity as Catholics and Democrats. Many Catholics, particularly French Canadians, still clung to particularistic ethno-religious traditions and remained sensitive to threats to these customs, but they were proving themselves capable of rallying as Catholics when the occasion demanded.

If the 1928 election demonstrated the power Catholics could wield when they cooperated, it also affirmed their ideas about Americanism. The culture wars of the 1920s represented the latest skirmish in an ongoing battle to define national identity. As during the war, Yankees insisted that to be American was to be a U.S. citizen, an English-speaker, and a Protestant, and in some cases they turned to the state to enforce this conviction. New stock Rhode Islanders countered that being American meant enjoying religious freedom and cultural expression, and they proved better able to protect these prerogatives than they had during the war. The Peck Act was overturned, the Klan died out, and the Catholic presidential contender carried the local elections.

These debates over Americanism were in some ways a replay of wartime discussions, yet their focus had shifted somewhat from ethnicity to religion. These categories were closely linked, of course, but it was notable that local nativists now seemed more concerned with the Catholicity than the nativity of new Americans. This reflected the fact that, with the exception of a brief postwar resurgence, immigration had decreased because of the war and federal quotas. Now the "other" was less likely to be foreign born but just as likely to be non-Protestant and more likely to be politically active. As a result, debates over Americanism became increasingly focused on religious affiliation, and religious freedom became a more critical component of Catholics' citizenship than ever before. This focus on cultural prerogatives did not eclipse the other rights Catholics considered theirs as Americans. In fact, at the same time that they fought for the social right of religious freedom they were waging another battle for the political right to vote. The culture wars of the 1920s took place alongside a legislative struggle over the property qualification which also culminated in the election of 1928.

11

"THIS VERY IMPORTANT TEST OF CITIZENSHIP"

Suffrage Reform and Its Aftermath

The leaders in Rhode Island do not believe in democracy. . . . They pre-
fer the rule of a Kaiser-boss to the rule of the people.

—James Dealey, *Political Situations in Rhode Island*

and Suggested Constitutional Changes, 1928

"GIVE BACK TO THE PEOPLE THEIR GOVERNMENT":
REPEALING THE PROPERTY RULE

The Catholic mobilization of the 1920s combined with other factors to renew interest in electoral reform. Catholics who came to the polls
to fight for their church grew more aware than ever that municipal voting
restrictions were undermining their political power. Their calls to repeal
the hated property rule were echoed by female and ethnic voters, entering
the electorate and experiencing voting restrictions for the first time, and
workers seeking political solutions to economic problems. This popular
groundswell merged with growing determination by reformers to modern-
ize state government and Democrats to repeal electoral laws that disadvantaged them. By the end of the decade repeal sentiment was so strong
Republican lawmakers could ignore it no longer, despite pressure from
small-town and corporate supporters to retain the status quo. As this happened, the potential for an empowered and effective Catholic electorate
grew.

The property qualification cast as wide a net in the 1920s as it had at the turn of the century. Since 1902, when the *Providence Journal Almanac* began to report annual voting statistics, a fairly consistent 60 percent of registered voters in Providence had failed to meet the requirement. This meant almost two-thirds of the electorate had no say in municipal elections other than in the choice of four executive officers who held little power. As the 1920s roared for other Rhode Islanders, a significant proportion of the city's working class still found it difficult to accumulate even $134 in real or personal property. Immigration restrictions had reduced the influx of poor newcomers, to be sure, yet the textile decline curtailed opportunities for upward mobility. And even though the city's new female voters could hold title to property (independently or jointly with male relatives), they were less likely than their husbands and sons to do so. For women and men without sufficient assets, the property qualification was a symbolic as well as practical barrier to voting, for it labeled them second-class citizens. So did the biased registration rules. Unpropertied voters still had to re-register for every election; those born in other countries had to present citizenship papers every time they registered; and the enrollment period ended on June 30, long before the November elections. Because of these restrictions, reformers charged, many citizens failed to vote even in the state and federal elections where the property rule did not apply.[1]

In the wake of the Nineteenth Amendment, women were feeling the sting of the voting restriction for the first time. Between 1922 and 1928 an average of 34 percent of registered women voters, as opposed to 48 percent of registered men, had enough property to vote in city elections. Catholic women in particular resented this political disability at a time when they were under enormous pressure from church leaders to demonstrate their civic and religious fitness by voting. Old stock women, for their part, worried the restriction was preventing female laborers from joining a women's voting bloc. Now that the Nineteenth Amendment was law, former suffragists could focus their energies on remaining electoral limits. The property qualification has been "considered somewhat of a joke both within and without the State," Sara Algeo wrote in 1925. "It looks now as though the time is near when this unseemly anachronism may be consigned to the dump of useless and antiquated laws where it properly belongs." Sharing her sentiment, the RILWV formed an important part of the repeal coalition. The league denounced the property rule as a "blot on the escutcheon of our State" and circulated a special newsletter urging members to support the repeal campaign. If the organization had any class-based misgivings about ending the property rule, it subordinated them to the goal of getting out the female vote.[2]

Politicization of the ethnic electorate created additional pressure for reform. During the war new Americans had begun to think of themselves as real Americans, deserving to be treated as such. Like African Americans, those ethnics who served in the armed forces found it galling to return from a crusade to "make the world safe for democracy" to second-class citizenship. Being banned from city elections was an obnoxious marker of their subordinate position, and the insult rankled as they became more active in politics. Immigration restrictions were reducing the influx of nonvoters and fostering among ethnics a greater attachment to America now that it no longer was easy to commute between old world and new; because each sending nation now had annual quotas, immigrants who left the United States might not be able to reenter. The resulting sense of permanence fueled a rise in naturalization rates among most groups and fostered interest in American politics. At the same time second-generation immigrants (many of them Italian) were coming of age, entering the electorate, and lobbying against discriminatory legislation. Even those who attained middle-class status, and full access to the franchise, smarted at the electoral insult their working-class compatriots had to bear. Thus, although Irish Americans continued to dominate the ethnic suffrage movement, other groups were taking more interest than ever in the voting rules.[3]

The vast majority of ethnic voters were Catholics, undergoing their own politicization as members of a religious community. The culture wars of the 1920s made them more sensitive to violations of rights and more determined to redress these injustices. One was the property rule, which undermined efforts to lobby for church-friendly laws and fend off assaults such as the Peck Act and the Ku Klux Klan. It also violated their beliefs about citizenship. Many Catholics felt American citizenship encompassed a variety of rights that should be awarded equally to all members of the nation. To hold and exercise the vote, claimed the *Visitor,* was a particularly "important test of citizenship." For Catholic voters, therefore, the property rule was both a political obstacle and a barrier to full Americanism.[4]

In December 1922, the *Visitor* captured the sentiments of many laypeople in a fervent denunciation of the property rule. A strongly worded editorial scored the "absurd and unjust" rule for violating the democratic principles of Christianity and discriminating against workers and Catholics. The property requirement led to "the separation of the electorate into classes," the newspaper argued. "It gives dignity to the man of money and in the giving deprives the workers of a lot of self-respect." Combining interdenominational rivalry with democratic rhetoric, the *Visitor* opined that such distinctions were an outgrowth of the Protestant Reformation. This logic was somewhat shaky. A Protestant constituency of Republican lawmakers and small-town voters supported the property rule, to be sure; yet the repeal movement also had the support of Protestant good government reformers. Nonetheless, rhetoric like this helped rally Catholics against a restriction that affected them particularly.[5]

Labor activists agreed with Catholic leaders that the vote was a critical right. In fact, political strategies became more important than ever for the overwhelmingly Catholic working class at a time when unions were exceptionally weak. The disappointing 1922 textile strike and the mills' southern flight only reinforced workers' sense of powerlessness. Working people also were frustrated about the city's refusal to spend money on public services such as sanitation and their own inability to influence these decisions through the vote. Full access to the polls would give them a valuable tool in their quest for improved standards of living as well as more abstract goals of social justice. In 1924, Thomas McMahon, a Rhode Islander who headed the UTW, issued a ringing endorsement of the repeal campaign: "I am in the fight to give back to the people their government."[6]

The 1920s suffrage movement, like its predecessors, united Catholics and working people with Protestants and middle-class reformers. Most notable among the last group was a Brown University political scientist, James Quayle Dealey, a long-time good government advocate. In 1928 Dealey issued *Political Situations in Rhode Island*, a colorful diatribe against the state's administrative structure and electoral oddities. Dealey blasted Providence city government as bloated, inefficient, and hamstrung by subservience to the General Assembly. Rhode Island's Senate, he went on, was the only one that still gave each municipality one vote regardless of population, making it "the most undemocratic and most unrepublican" state senate in the nation. It was "like a man's appendix, which once had utility and justification, but now exists only to add to surgeons' fees." Worse still, the Assembly was governed by bosses who, "like the old man of the sea on Sindbad's neck, dictate at pleasure legislation, finances, taxation and state policy, leaving to voters merely the passive function of casting 'me too' votes." Sharp as these tirades were, Dealey reserved special venom for the property rule, "a situation almost unique in the *civilized* world." The state of the state was a profound embarrassment to reformers like Dealey. "We stand before the country as a sort of museum of antiquities, a collection of 'has beens,'" he complained. Dealey was correct in singling out the local voting restrictions as "almost unique." As of 1920 six states still mandated that only taxpayers vote on referendums involving expenditures, and four limited elections for the school board (an entity with a large budget) to taxpayers and parents; but Rhode Island's rules were the most draconian.[7]

Responding to pressure that crossed religious, class, and ethnic lines, the Democrats (who never had abandoned their campaign against the property rule) intensified their efforts. Lawmakers flooded the state legislature with repeal bills as well as proposals to relax registration rules. Although their primary goal was to make it easier for supporters to vote, their arguments rested on higher principles. John J. McGrane, a former Democratic state senator, denounced "the iniquitous unAmerican theory that places property above honesty, wealth above intelligence, and a tax receipt above an honorable discharge from the Army or Navy." His colleagues invoked the Revolutionary concept of popular sovereignty, echoing Dorr's claim that people had the right to create a government of their choosing. If the reformers were refused, they threatened, registry voters would "swarm from all over the State to the State House and in their thousands terrify the plutocrats by another bloodless revolution like that of Thomas W. Dorr."[8]

It was Democrats who spearheaded the repeal movement, yet by the late 1920s the campaign was bipartisan. Some Republicans bowed to expediency, realizing continued opposition would further alienate the ethnic and working-class voters they were struggling to hold onto. Others supported the movement out of democratic conviction or a sense that times had changed. The original intent of the requirement, noted the former Republican state senator Sidney Clifford, was to ensure that a "more intelligent or responsible class of voters" would control municipal finances. No longer, however, was property worth $134 "a guarantee that the voter is either a responsible or a substantial citizen." Moreover, he added, the role of city government had expanded far beyond financial planning, and it was unfair to deny residents a voice in matters that affected their lives even if they did not pay taxes.[9]

The local movement for a suffrage extension mirrored national trends. Many states still had laws that made it difficult for immigrants, paupers, and especially African Americans to vote, yet there was some sympathy for electoral reform after 1920. This reflected in small part a more democratic political ideology, in large part the fact that there were fewer reasons for limiting access to the ballot. Reduced immigration calmed fears about foreign-born political influence, and declining turnout suggested Americans were less interested in voting and did not have to be kept from the polls. The growing influence of paid lobbyists and private interest groups, and the growth of nonelected commissions, meant individual voters had less effect on policies and the officers who created them. Finally, the Nineteenth Amendment's failure to produce an effective women's bloc indicated that additional suffrage extensions would make little difference. For all these reasons, Americans began to reconsider the need to restrict white voters' access to the polls. Between the end of the First World War and the onset of the Second, several northern and southern states repealed their poll taxes, California and Oregon overturned bans on Chinese voting, and Pennsylvania eliminated its taxpaying requirement.[10]

Reflecting these national trends and responding to local pressure, in 1927 the General Assembly made history by agreeing to put a repeal bill before voters the following November. The amendment would allow urban residents full access to the ballot, regardless of economic position, provided they had lived in Rhode Island two years and in their municipality six months. To the relief of suffrage activists, the bill did not include a proposal by senator James F. Sherman of Portsmouth to replace the property requirement with a three-dollar poll tax. The suffrage extension was part of a larger program of constitutional reform. Two other proposals would enable voters to register every two years rather than annually (in keeping with the state's biennial election system) and reapportion the Senate to give Providence three more representatives. This last measure included a built-in safeguard that limited any municipality's representation to six so that the growing cities never would outvote the towns. This, explained the Republican Clifford, would allow "the more conservative element of the state to exercise a salutary check upon their more impulsive city friends."[11]

When Rhode Islanders came to the polls in November, they voted for democracy with a powerful voice. The combination of the Smith campaign and suffrage referendum sparked the highest turnout in Providence since 1892, and electors overwhelmingly approved the voting changes. The repeal proposal won 85 percent of the vote in a statewide referendum in which registry voters could participate, and the biennial registration and Senate reapportionment measures easily passed as well. In every case, most of the "no" votes came from the small towns. In Providence and other cities, the groundswell of Catholics coming out to vote for Smith and his vision of cultural pluralism made for strong majorities in favor of democratic change.[12]

Despite some grumbling from small-town electors, most Rhode Islanders welcomed this political modernization. The suffrage extension affected an estimated one hundred thousand urban voters, of whom sixty thousand lived in Providence. A disproportionate number were ethnic Catholics who had been mobilizing over the course of the decade. The amendment brought Rhode Island's government into the twentieth century. The property rule, "against which there has been a determined and continuous agitation for years is a relic of the days when Rhode Island was an English colony," observed the *Providence Evening Bulletin*. "There could be no better way for this State to mark the beginning of the second century of the existing system of popular government," the *Journal* agreed. Almost one hundred years after Luther and Dorr began their quest for democracy, universal suffrage seemed to be the law in Rhode Island.[13]

It was evident to keen observers, however, that subtle restrictions remained in place. To assuage lingering concerns that voters without property would carelessly dispense taxpayers' dollars, the 1928 law created municipal budget commissions as checks on irresponsible spending. The commissioners were to be elected by all voters but would remove fiscal decision-making from the larger electorate. Equally notable was the fact that residents of some towns, as opposed to cities, still had to own property worth $134 to vote on financial questions. The 1928 act authorized towns to dismantle this rule but did not require that they do so. No doubt voters there feared that as cities grew overcrowded and mass transportation improved, ethnic urbanites would seep into the suburbs; or perhaps they clung to the conviction that only taxpayers were responsible voters. Retaining this final property restriction would ensure that newcomers who failed to prove their competence by accumulating taxable assets would not influence local politics. Finally, voters in both towns and cities (like their counterparts in many other states) continued to confront registration rules that made it difficult to vote. A few years later the *Visitor* would complain that thanks to these rules the state still had "three classes of voters, the real, the personal and the registry."[14]

Nonetheless, ethnic Catholics had achieved a critical victory. By no means had they been alone in promoting reform, but their support formed a critical component of the repeal coalition. Now they were positioned better than ever to achieve citizenship in the way they understood the term. Thanks to the demise of the voting restrictions, they could consider themselves full political citizens even if the registration system remained biased against them. They already had defended their social right to religious freedom by fending off the Peck Act and the Klan and by giving Smith a local victory in 1928. Now they resolved to use their new electoral clout to secure the category of rights that still eluded them: the economic right to protections at the workplace.

THE BLOODLESS REVOLUTION: TRANSFORMING STATE POLITICS

Like the 1888 Bourn Amendment, the 1928 suffrage extension sparked a sense of possibility among Catholic, ethnic workers and their political allies. Citizens rushed to take advantage of the more liberal franchise. They looked first to the major parties as a vehicle of change, but when this proved disappointing they embraced a variety of third-party alternatives. Communism, fascism, and a labor party each promised to win discontented voters rights they considered theirs as Americans. It was only when faced with these threats that the Democrats reshaped themselves as a legitimate party of reform, as they had at the turn of the century. In a marked contrast to the earlier period, however, this time the party was able to deliver on its promises.

In Providence, turnout and registration rates after 1928 reflected a new faith in electoral politics. According to the annual *Providence Journal Almanac*, the average turnout in mayoral, gubernatorial, and presidential elections rose from 52 percent of people qualified to vote (by virtue of sex and citizenship) in the 1920s to 66 percent in the 1930s. Registration rates increased more dramatically, from 59 to 78 percent of qualified voters. The changes were even more impressive than the numbers suggest, for the proportion of people who qualified to vote had grown considerably because of woman suffrage, repeal of the property rule, a slowdown in immigration, and a rise in naturalization.

This new political engagement reflected national trends as well as local reforms. Across the United States, more people voted after 1928 because of immigration restrictions (which, as in Rhode Island, encouraged naturalization and active citizenship), entry into the electorate of second-generation immigrants, the crisis of the Great Depression (which brought previously inactive voters to the polls), the mobilizing efforts of the new CIO, the Smith campaign, and the appeal of Franklin D. Roosevelt (a blueblood with a remarkable ability to connect with rank-and-file citizens). As U.S. senator John Pastore later reminisced, "He was the quintessential president. He looked like a president, he talked like a president, he acted like a president. . . . He gave hope to the people of the country; he came up with a solution to the Depression." It was notable, however, that during the 1930s, presidential turnout rates in Providence were higher than national averages and in some years significantly higher. This was a trend that started in 1920 but became far more marked after 1928. The citizens of Providence had won greater access to the vote and were determined to flex their new electoral muscles.[15]

Local Democrats and their Catholic, ethnic, and working-class supporters sought to capitalize on the electoral surge and earned steady but slow progress for their efforts. Over the next years the party assumed control of Providence government and all statewide offices and secured a first-time majority in the House. Yet the Senate (still apportioned in favor of Republican small towns) remained elusive, and Democratic bills continued to meet with defeat there. In 1934 the party came frustratingly close to reversing its disadvantage, falling just two seats short of a majority in the upper chamber. This near-victory proved more than the eager Democrats could handle, and they moved swiftly and somewhat unscrupulously to make the election theirs.[16]

In a well-orchestrated coup, party leaders opened the 1935 session by announcing that two state Senate elections (in the rural towns of Portsmouth and South Kingston) had been contested and a bipartisan committee would recount the votes. Before Republican lawmakers knew what was happening, the committee declared Democratic victories in both contests and swung the Senate in that party's favor. Now in control of the General Assembly, the Democrats sprang into action with a massive political reorganization. Within a few hours, they gained control of all three branches of state government for the first time in state history.[17]

The "Bloodless Revolution," as the upset became known, seemed to some Rhode Islanders a fitting conclusion to the democratic agitation Dorr and Luther had initiated one century earlier. In fact, Governor Theodore Francis Green invited this comparison in a cleverly worded radio address that invoked "the spiritual presence of the Patron Saint of the Democratic Party in Rhode Island, Thomas Wilson Dorr." It was Dorr's "indomitable advocacy of the rights of the people" that inspired the party to such bold and unconventional action, the governor explained. As in 1842, when the government failed to respond to the will of the people, the people took matters into their own hands. The Bloodless Revolution took less than twenty-four hours but altered state politics for decades to come.[18]

That transformation did not result automatically, however. To the dismay of many voters, the Bloodless Revolution produced a shift in leadership but not substance. Upon taking office, Democrats forgot their decades-old promises to Catholics, ethnics, workers, and reformers and instead engaged in a mad scramble for the perks their rivals had monopolized for so long. Petty squabbles over power and patronage obscured the party's traditional platform of workplace protections and constitutional change. It seemed the Democrats' demands for "good government" had really been calls for a system that would give them more latitude as minority party. Once in power, they benefited from rules that allowed the majority to dominate patronage and legislation. Moreover, now that they controlled the perks, they hoped to secure voter loyalty without going to the trouble of enacting progressive laws.[19] Catholics, immigrants, and workers had hoped the new leadership would translate their vision of Americanism into law. This vision called for political democracy, in which all citizens' voices counted equally, and industrial democracy, in which laborers' demands were heard at the workplace. But the Democratic Party, heady with its newfound power, demonstrated little interest in securing for its constituents the rights they considered their American birthright.

Disappointment with the outcome of the Bloodless Revolution in Providence coincided with discontent over the slow progress of the New Deal nationwide. Across the country, Roosevelt's failure to bring a quick end to the Depression or challenge the economic inequities that had helped bring it on prompted many Americans to seek alternatives to the two-party system. National Communist Party membership rose from about eighteen thousand to sixty-five thousand in the 1930s, and thousands of jobless workers joined Communist-led Unemployed Councils. Millions of other people searching for answers found them in Rev. Charles Coughlin's National Union for Social Justice (quite popular in Catholic Providence), senator Huey Long's Share Our Wealth movement, or Dr. Francis Townsend's old age pension clubs. In Providence, disaffection with the Roosevelt administration combined with disappointment over the failures of local leadership to create a powerful current of discontent.[20]

The Depression hit Providence hard. The city economy still relied heavily on textiles (already in decline because of southern competition) and jewelry (a luxury few consumers could afford during the economic crisis). Marked declines in these flagship industries caused unemployment to soar to 32 percent (or about 35,000 workers) in 1932. Outside Providence, more than 50 percent of workers in the textile-dependent Blackstone River Valley lost their jobs. Extensive relief efforts by public officials and private charities cushioned the blow, but suffering still was prolonged and intense. In Providence as in other communities, the economic crisis produced a crisis in public confidence and sparked a flirtation with third parties.[21]

The anticapitalist critique and innovative organizing of the Communist Party held some appeal. In 1930 James P. Reid, the radical dentist, helped form an Unemployed Council that staged marches on the State House to demand public works jobs and old age pensions. Reid, who had switched his allegiance from socialism to communism by this time, also formed a Right-to-Live Club to lobby for unemployment relief and organize public works employees. In 1933 the club garnered unfavorable publicity when it led one thousand of those workers in a strike over a rumored wage cut. An investigation by the *Visitor* revealed that the president of this largely Catholic group was James Conroy, a Communist and lapsed member of the church. Although Conroy and his fellow organizers denied they were using the club to promote "red doctrines," the membership voted to purge them nonetheless.[22] With the exception of these sporadic organizing efforts, communism made little headway in Depression-era Providence. Leftists who had expected the suffrage extension to bring more sympathetic voters to the polls were disappointed. Providence radicals confronted an implacably hostile Catholic Church, a government willing to co-opt protest by providing unemployment relief, and a working-class electorate that invested its hopes in the rising Democratic Party.

It was the right that appealed to a larger and more vocal minority of residents eager to use their votes to achieve change. Fascism had been building slowly in Providence since Benito Mussolini came to power in Italy in 1922, but it gained momentum in the 1930s. The suffrage extension inspired Italian Americans, who resolved to form a "militant uncompromising" voting bloc and secure a share of elected offices proportionate to their status as the city's largest immigrant group. Frustrations mounted as their political fortunes advanced only slowly and the Depression continued in full force. As many Italian voters lost faith in American democracy, they looked to fascism as an attractive alternative. They saw Mussolini as a model for the strong leader needed to pull the United States out of its economic crisis, and his crusade to strengthen Italy as a parallel to their own quest to "overcome barriers of discrimination," as the *Italian Echo* put it, and acquire political power. The diocese's Italian American priests, for their part, recognized that fascism could unite congregations, promote family stability, and encourage obedience to authority. In 1929 Mussolini had resolved his tensions with the Catholic Church by recognizing the Vatican as a sovereign state and declaring Catholicism his nation's official religion. After that point his foreign ministry developed close ties with Italian American priests, recognizing parishes as institutions that could discourage radicalism and foster national pride among the country's far-flung sons and daughters.[23]

The movement had broad appeal in Providence. Fascists infiltrated the Sons of Italy, the city's largest and most respected Italian society, and formed Benito and Rachele Mussolini societies. Seeking to appeal to the younger generation, they organized special schools to promote cultural pride and arranged for students to take inexpensive trips to the homeland. In April 1936, hundreds of local women made a poignant gesture of support by donating their gold wedding bands to help Italy "in her gallant war to end barbarism and slavery" in Ethiopia. In exchange they received steel rings, a recognition of their contribution and tangible connection to the movement. For partisans like these, to be Italian was to be Fascist. Fascism, declared the *Echo*, is "irrevocably and completely stamped on the soul of the Italian people."[24]

The popularity of fascism created complications for an ethnic group whose leaders were eager to assimilate and cement their positions in national life. Fascism seemed to represent the antithesis of American individualism and small government. Local Italians tried to surmount this problem by insisting fascism and Americanism were in fact compatible. The Benito Mussolini Society of Federal Hill declared that its goals were "to preserve the traditions of the mother country but also notably to serve the American nation." Local partisans backed up statements like these with symbolic efforts, as when students at the Dante Alighieri School closed their end-of-year assembly by singing the "Star Spangled Banner."[25]

Not all Italians found these messages convincing. Fascism inspired firm devotion but equally passionate hatred. A small cadre of leftists who had survived the Red Scare reemerged to organize anti-Fascist groups like the Risorgimento and Mateotti clubs, the latter named after a Socialist senator assassinated by Fascists in Italy in 1924. In this they had the support of erstwhile rivals in the mainstream labor movement, which made its opposition to fascism clear. In 1930 the *Journal* observed, "While it is possible for Democrats and Republicans to fraternize . . . without friction, it would be provoking a civil war on a miniature scale to bring together a Fascist and an Anti-Fascist."[26]

Fascism created particular tensions between Italians and the Democratic Party, which was trying to cement its interethnic, Catholic voting coalition. Italian voters had been moving into the party since the 1920s, wooed by its support for workers' rights and cultural pluralism, yet remained concerned it was insensitive to the aspirations of their homeland. Wilson had helped to craft the Treaty of Versailles, which offered Italy few rewards, and Roosevelt condemned the Ethiopian invasion by forbidding Americans to sail on Italian ships. Local Democrats seemed scarcely more sympathetic. When Green attended an anti-Fascist meeting in 1935, an *Echo* headline warned, "Anti-Fascist Means Anti-Italian, Governor Green." Some voters saw this slight as part of a larger pattern of anti-Italian behavior, demonstrated by Democrats' refusal to place a statue of the nineteenth-century nationalist Giuseppe Garibaldi on city grounds or make Columbus Day a state holiday. The *Echo* printed bitter invectives that charged the party with corruption, bigotry, and, ironically, dictatorship.[27]

Democrats responded swiftly, seeking to mollify local Fascists before they drew compatriots into a rival bloc. Green commissioned a State House tablet to recognize Giovanni da Verrazzano's 1524 discovery of Narragansett Bay and included an "Italian Day" in the state's tercentenary celebration. In addition to recognizing Italian contributions to the state's past, Democrats looked to the future by promoting Italians within the party structure. This was a relatively painless maneuver for the party now that it enjoyed a lock-hold on patronage and had enough perks to divide among ethnic groups. Careful concessions of this nature placated the most vocal Fascist critics.[28]

John Pastore was the most prominent of this new generation of Italian American Democrats. A second-generation immigrant raised in poverty on Federal Hill after his father (a successful tailor) died, Pastore helped support his family by working on a jewelry press while attending Classical High School. Unable to afford Brown University, he attended law school in the evenings (in the days before a college degree was a prerequisite) while working as a clerk during the days. Pastore passed the state bar examination in 1932 on his first try, only to begin his career at the peak of the Depression. The bright young lawyer had trouble finding paid work and entered politics in part because he needed the money; state representatives made five dollars a day when the legislature was in session. Pastore's entry into public life reflected the ongoing importance of Catholic parishes as political networking sites. One Sunday morning in the fall of 1933, shortly after marching in a rally to support FDR's National Recovery Act, he waited outside St. Bartholomew's for Tommy Testa, the Italian American Democratic boss of Silver Lake. "Mr. Testa," he said, "I'd like to go into politics." One year later, the young Democrat was elected to represent Providence's eleventh district in the state legislature.[29]

Benefiting from his own considerable talents and from pressure on the Democrats to promote Italian Americans, he moved to the district attorney's office in 1937, was elected lieutenant governor in 1944, and one year later, at age thirty-eight, found himself governor when J. Howard McGrath resigned to accept a position in the Truman administration. After serving a second term as governor, Pastore entered the U.S. Senate in 1950, where he worked for civil rights laws and nuclear test bans until stepping down in 1976. His crowning moment came when he delivered the keynote address at the Democratic National Convention in August 1964. Pastore was the first Italian American to serve as governor or U.S. senator in any state, and his meteoric career symbolized a breakthrough for his compatriots (and coreligionists) in Rhode Island and across the nation.[30]

It took more than political appointments, however, for the Democrats to win over organized labor, whose discontent posed a far greater problem. For decades labor activists had been working with Democrats to overturn the property rule, and they expected the party's ascent to usher in a labor-friendly regime. Relations became strained in September 1934, when Green called out the National Guard to quell rioting by workers participating in a national textile strike. When the Bloodless Revolution failed to generate a

John O. Pastore was one of the most notable ethnic, Catholic politicians to advance in the wake of Rhode Island's Bloodless Revolution. Silver gelatin print, courtesy of the Rhode Island Historical Society, RHi X2 4123.

revolution in labor law the following year, unionists began to doubt whether the Democrats were any more labor-friendly than their predecessors. These doubts coincided with new militancy among organized labor, spurred by the pro-union provisions of the National Recovery Act. As unions sprang up in jewelry factories, restaurants, and theaters, labor leaders realized they could translate workplace solidarity into independent political action.[31]

At its convention in April 1935, the RISFL began serious discussions about forming a third party. "Candidates kowtow to Labor and then give us the ha! ha! after election. They play us for a lot of 'suckers,'" one delegate complained. "We will not be able to accomplish anything constructive in the way of legislation until we form a political party of our own," agreed a speaker from the UTW, a union representing a heavily female industry where third-party sentiment was strong. The RISFL president, William Connelly, was careful to note that his objections were to local Democrats rather than the national party. By 1935, the latter had demonstrated its commitment to working people through the path-breaking Wagner and Social Security acts, which recognized unions and provided unemployment and old age insurance. "Labor will go down the line with the President," Connelly told his members, "but it should not support those traitors in the Democratic Party" of Rhode Island.[32]

That October, male and female delegates representing a cross-section of ethnic groups went on record in favor of a labor party. This was to be an "anti-capitalist, anti-fascist" labor party that would stand "for the rights and needs of all working people and against fascism and war." Although led by unionists, it would be open to "farmers, Negro organizations, poor middle classes, and all workers' political organizations." Its platform would call for more generous unemployment insurance, more jobs for the unemployed, and wages that ensured "an American standard of living." If the rank and file voted to support the leadership's position at a March convention, delegates resolved, they would form a third party.[33]

Democrats, stung into action, responded with an impressive spate of labor legislation. New laws placed stricter limits on child labor, instituted a minimum wage and forty-eight hour week for women and children, expanded workers' compensation, and limited the use of injunctions (court-issued bans on picketing) in labor disputes. Seeking to assure labor it would be a partner in the new regime, the Democrats placed a few prominent unionists in state offices. Workers were especially pleased when the party chose the UTW's Thomas McMahon as labor commissioner. Catholic workers also welcomed the appointment of Edmund W. Flynn, a coreligionist, as chief justice of the state Supreme Court. Local reformers joined workers in noting these developments with glee. "We are receiving compliments from every side about the accomplishments of the Rhode Island legislature," boasted Alice Hunt, president of the Rhode Island Consumers' League. The progress was "nothing short of amazing," agreed Herbert Parsons of the Massachusetts Child Council. "Rhode Island seems to have gone to the top in progress in regard to . . . labor legislation." Although Democrats failed to match their labor record with badly needed constitutional reforms to make state government more efficient and less corrupt, they did enough to secure their reputation as the people's party.[34]

The Democrats successfully co-opted the third-party impulse through these concessions. Their Catholic, ethnic supporters had shown signs of jumping ship in favor of a labor party, fascism, and, in much smaller numbers, even communism, but their belated gestures won back much of this needed constituency. When voters came to the polls in November 1936, they expressed overwhelming confidence in the state's new leaders. In an election that witnessed records in registration and turnout, Democrats swept the city and state contests to win their greatest victory yet. These results, of course, reflected broader trends. Nationwide, presidential turnout reached its highest level in twenty years and Democrats rode to victory on the strength of their Second New Deal.[35] These national factors gave local Democrats an edge, but alone they did not explain the party's unprecedented victory. Taking a page out of Roosevelt's book, Rhode Island Democrats had weakened third-party agitation through worker-friendly laws and undermined ethnic tensions with symbolic gestures and political appointments. After 1936, discussion of a labor party virtually disappeared and Italian Americans became a critical part of the Democratic coalition. After the Second World War, the return of prosperity and the onset of the Cold War gave the party little to fear from a marginalized left.

With the exception of a few temporary setbacks, the 1936 election instituted a period of Democratic hegemony that lasted until 1956 on the state level and into the 1970s in Providence. The local Democrats, like their national counterparts, benefited from the support of an interethnic, interracial "New Deal" coalition. Taking advantage of their tight control of government, they held onto these voters through patronage jobs, political nominations, and progressive labor laws even as they faltered on constitutional reform and anticorruption initiatives. The new Democratic machine now controlled Rhode Island as tightly as its Republican predecessor had.[36]

There was, however, a major difference in the composition and priorities of the new ruling coalition. Until 1936 the state was governed by a Republican machine beholden to wealthy industrialists and small-town Yankees. After this point Rhode Island was under the leadership of a Democratic Party that, despite close ties to business, worked closely with Catholic, ethnic, and labor leaders. Another realignment that began in 1956 established for the first time a competitive two-party system in which both parties catered to the needs of Catholics, immigrants, and unionists.[37] Money still wielded tremendous influence and older immigrants continued to lord it over the new, but gone was the oligarchy of the pre-1936 era. Rhode Island was by no means a paragon of good government, but it did become a democracy in that it responded to the needs of its majority.

With the Democrats' 1936 victory, Catholics came of age politically. The suffrage extension recognized them as full members of the nation, and the Bloodless Revolution enthroned a Democratic Party that recognized their parishes and unions as partners in public life. From 1936 onward, they enjoyed a degree of political influence previously denied them. They used that influence to secure their vision of an America in which rank-and-file citizens had a voice and enjoyed a variety of social, economic, and legal rights.

CONCLUSION

In 1842, Catholic immigrants in Providence began a century-long struggle to integrate themselves into the nation's public life. Challenging an Americanism grounded in Anglo-Saxon Protestantism, they argued for a pluralistic model that incorporated their ethnic and religious traditions. Rejecting the notion that citizenship entailed little more than "membership of a nation," as the Supreme Court had argued in 1875, they demanded religious freedom, economic protections, and political access. By 1935 these new Americans had made considerable headway, securing the political right to vote, the economic right to state-mandated protections at the workplace, and the social right to cultural expression and religious freedom. Of course the battle was not over, for important exceptions remained. Biased registration rules still curtailed the right to vote. Labor laws and powerful new unions failed to protect most workers who did not toil in factories, a group that was largely female and foreign-born. Nonetheless, it was undeniable that Catholic immigrants and ethnics had improved their positions in economic and public life. Most fundamentally, they had broadened the parameters of national identity by forcing many old stock Protestants to accept them as Americans.

This transformation evolved through a series of economic, demographic, and political turning points. The first was the development, by the turn of the twentieth century, of a Catholic middle class comprised largely of Irish Americans with the time, skills, and contacts to advocate for themselves. The second was the 1905 report that Catholics comprised a majority of the Providence population. This announcement emboldened them to advance their interests more aggressively, knowing it would be difficult for the Yankee political elite to ignore the needs of a clear and vocal majority. Next came the First World War, in which Catholics' military and civilian contributions demonstrated their commitment to the United States and gave them the right to argue for a more inclusive national identity. Having proved they were American, after the war they joined coreligionists across the nation in seeking to make America more Catholic. This well-organized movement defended the rights of the laity as well as the priorities of the hierarchy. The next milestone was the Johnson-Reed Act of 1924. Although a number of laypeople rightly condemned the law as discriminatory, they reaped political benefits in that the measure inspired newcomers (many of them Catholic) to become citizens and voters and to assimilate and move into the middle class. In the process they transformed themselves from threatening outsiders into upwardly mobile Americans who appeared to have internalized a "Protestant" work ethic. It no longer seemed incongruous to Yankees to think of Catholic immigrants and ethnics as Americans who deserved full benefits of citizenship. The final turning point came in 1928 when voters repealed the property qualification for city elections. This amendment combined with nationwide shifts in public culture after 1928 to incorporate ethnic Catholics more fully into American politics.

Throughout these struggles, religion provided a critical tool. As this book has demonstrated, over time Providence Catholics became skilled at using religion to enter and influence public life. In an era when so many lacked access to unions and electoral politics, they learned to be political through their parishes. Laypeople drew on education and skills honed at church to argue for rights in the larger community, turned their lay societies into activist vehicles that lobbied legislators and got out the vote, used parish networks to forge public careers, and invoked religious rhetoric to justify demands.

To be sure, there were serious limits to becoming political through an institution that was hierarchical and often inconsistent. By the 1910s church leaders were urging the laity to take responsibility for advancing a Catholic agenda, yet they sought to dictate that agenda. Women in particular received mixed signals, encouraged to be activists but also to observe traditional gender roles, to promote some laws that could improve their lives (mothers' pensions and protective labor laws) but to oppose others (most notably, legalized birth control). More generally, clerics tended to be conservative on social issues like film censorship and women's rights, yet progressive on economic matters such as workplace laws and social insurance. And this economic progressivism had its limits. Priests promoted mainstream unions and moderate labor laws that would humanize capitalism, but they railed against left-wing unions and parties whose agendas were more transformative.

This last issue has led many social historians to dismiss the Catholic Church as a negative influence in ethnic and working-class communities. Priests and bishops did indeed discourage Catholics from joining radical institutions that would have fought hard for them and might have produced noteworthy results. Nonetheless, to dismiss the church as antiradical and apolitical is to miss the mark on two counts. First, in choosing church membership over radical politics, Catholics often made reasoned and practical choices. Simply put, parishes offered a plethora of spiritual, material, and organizational resources with which radical movements could not begin to compete. This was especially true in Providence, where a particularly undemocratic electoral system gave third parties very little room to maneuver. Catholics who threw in their lot with the church rather than the Socialist or Communist Party practiced the art of the possible. Second, in dismissing church membership as apolitical, historians subscribe to a narrow definition of politics. If politics is defined at its most basic as engaging in organized actions to affect one's community and improve one's life, then being a Catholic could be an intensely political experience. Parishes were training grounds where members learned to make demands of employers and civic leaders and, more fundamentally, to challenge restrictive ideas about Americanism.

By the mid-1930s, the terrain was changing as unions and electoral politics became far more accessible to immigrants and ethnics. In Providence, this shift did not diminish the role of the church as community center and organizing site. Parishes continued to function as spiritual guides, social gathering places, relief providers, and alternative political spaces during the Depression, even as parishioners found it easier to join unions and cast ballots. Relief was available from state and federal agencies, yet lingering distrust of outsiders and the stigma of going "on the dole" prompted many Catholics to turn inward for assistance.[1] In Providence they found it in diocesan social service agencies, a church building program that created jobs for the unemployed, and a host of parish-based charities coordinated largely by women. They frequented parish halls more than ever in search of inexpensive recreation and fellowship, so that Catholic social life boomed as the economy went bust. Parishioners also joined church study clubs and attended Catholic industrial conferences, seizing on these forums as opportunities to understand the economic crisis and discuss solutions. These institutions were particularly important to women and newer immigrants, many of whom remained disconnected from unions and politics. The *Visi-*

tor, for its part, continued to serve as a mouthpiece for workers' interests, joining with its readers to call for social insurance and union protections long before Congress signed off on the Social Security and Wagner acts. Finally, Catholics looked to the church for the spiritual solace they needed more than ever. The local popularity of the new cult of St. Jude, patron saint of hopeless causes, attested to the need for divine intercession at a time of crisis. In all these ways, the church remained relevant to ethnic communities and politics even after other institutions became more welcoming.[2]

To place a microscope over Catholic parishes in Providence is to glimpse larger trends in late nineteenth- and early twentieth-century American political and social history. Providence was distinctive in the unusually large size of its Catholic and immigrant populations and the exceptionally undemocratic nature of its politics. Its difference was one of degree and not kind, however. Rather than being an exception, it was a place where broad trends played out in bold relief. I hope that this study of Providence inspires further attention to the critical roles churches played in ethnic politics and communities a century ago, and still play today. In an age when democracy had severe limits, parishes served as alternative organizing sites where members mobilized for change. Catholic churches thus formed part of an ethnic political landscape that also included unions, machines, fraternal orders, and mutual aid societies. To overlook the political dimensions of parish culture is to miss an important part of the story of how immigrants entered and influenced public life. It was through their parishes that many new Americans proved they were Americans.

ABBREVIATIONS USED IN THE NOTES

CMSNY	Center for Migration Studies of New York
CUA	Catholic University of America Archives
HG	Holy Ghost Papers
HNS	Holy Name Society Papers
MWC	Men's and Women's Committee Papers
NCCM	National Council of Catholic Men Papers
NCCW	National Council of Catholic Women Papers
NCWC	National Catholic Welfare Conference Papers
PCDA	Providence Catholic Diocesan Archives
PCFU	Providence Central Federated Union Papers
RC	Reconstruction Committee Papers
RIHS	Rhode Island Historical Society
RILWV	Rhode Island League of Women Voters Papers
RISA	Rhode Island State Archives
RISFWC	Rhode Island State Federation of Women's Club Papers
USJB	Union Saint-Jean-Baptiste Papers
WC	National Catholic War Council Papers

NOTES

INTRODUCTION

1. Mary Josephine Bannon, ed., *Autobiographic Memoirs of Hon. Patrick J. McCarthy* (Providence: Providence Visitor Press, 1927), 1–2, 5–6, 9–16, 28–32, 278–80, 286.

2. Ibid., 32–33, 35, 193, 280; and *Providence Journal*, 14 December 1888.

3. Bannon, *Autobiographic Memoirs*, 43–45, 279–81, 286–87.

4. Ibid., 45, 255, 282.

5. Bureau of Industrial Statistics, *Census of the Foreign-Born Population of Rhode Island, Bulletin 1: Part 1 of the Annual Report for 1907* (Providence: E. L. Freeman, 1907), 1081; Bureau of Industrial Statistics, *Church Statistics and Religious Preference, Bulletin 2: Part 1 of the Annual Report for 1907* (Providence: E. L. Freeman, 1907), 274; and John S. Gilkeson Jr., *Middle-Class Providence, 1820–1940* (Princeton: Princeton University Press, 1986), 7.

6. Robert A. Orsi, *The Madonna of 115th Street: Faith and Community in Italian Harlem, 1880–1950* (New Haven: Yale University Press, 1985), xv.

7. Jürgen Habermas, "The Public Sphere," *New German Critique* 1 (1974): 50.

8. Teresa Anne Murphy, *Ten Hours' Labor: Religion, Reform, and Gender in Early New England* (Ithaca: Cornell University Press, 1992); Jama Lazerow, *Religion and the Working Class in Antebellum America* (Washington, D.C.: Smithsonian Institution Press, 1995); William R. Sutton, *Journeymen for Jesus: Evangelical Artisans Confront Capitalism in Jacksonian Baltimore* (University Park: Pennsylvania State University Press, 1998); and Mark S. Schantz, *Piety in Providence: Class Dimensions of Religious Experience in Antebellum Rhode Island* (Ithaca: Cornell University Press, 2000).

9. Mel Piehl, *Breaking Bread: The Catholic Worker and the Origin of Catholic Radicalism in America* (Philadelphia: Temple University Press, 1982); David M. Emmons, *The Butte Irish: Class and Ethnicity in an American Mining Town, 1875–1925* (Urbana: University of Illinois Press, 1989); Ken Fones-Wolf, *Trade Union Gospel: Christianity and Labor in Industrial Philadelphia, 1865–1915* (Philadelphia: Temple University Press, 1989); Gary Gerstle, *Working-Class Americanism: The Politics of Labor in a Textile City, 1914–1960* (New York: Cambridge University Press, 1989); and Mary Lethert Wingerd, *Claiming the City: Politics, Faith, and the Power of Place in St. Paul* (Ithaca: Cornell University Press, 2001).

10. David G. Dalin, ed., *American Jews and the Separationist Faith: The New Debate on Religion in Public Life* (Washington, D.C.: Ethics and Public Policy Center, 1992); Jon Gjerde, *The Minds of the West: Ethnocultural Evolution in the Rural Middle West, 1830–1917* (Chapel Hill: University of North Carolina Press, 1997); Thomas A. Tweed, *Our Lady of the Exile: Diasporic Religion at a Cuban Catholic Shrine in Miami* (New York: Oxford University Press, 1997); Timothy J. Meagher, *Inventing Irish America: Generation, Class, and Ethnic Identity in a New England City, 1880–1928* (Notre Dame: University of Notre Dame Press, 2001); Jonathan D. Sarna and David G. Dalin, eds., *Religion and State in the American Jewish Experience* (Notre Dame: University of Notre Dame Press, 1997); and the Hispanic Churches in American Public Life project (http://www.hcapl.org).

11. Michael Kazin, *Barons of Labor: The San Francisco Building Trades and Union Power in the Progressive Era* (Urbana: University of Illinois Press, 1987), 282; J. T. Salter, *Boss Rule: Portraits in City Politics* (New York: McGraw-Hill, 1935), 18; and John M. Allswang, *Bosses, Ma-*

chines, and Urban Voters, 2d ed. (Baltimore: Johns Hopkins University Press, 1986), chaps. 2 and 3.

12. M. Craig Brown and Charles N. Halaby, "Machine Politics in America, 1870–1945," *Journal of Interdisciplinary History* 17 (1987): 587–612; Steven P. Erie, *Rainbow's End: Irish-Americans and the Dilemmas of Urban Machine Politics, 1840–1985* (Berkeley: University of California Press, 1988); Terrence J. McDonald, *The Parameters of Urban Fiscal Policy: Socio-economic Change and Political Culture in San Francisco, 1860–1906* (Berkeley: University of California Press, 1986); Reed Ueda, "Naturalization and Citizenship," in *Harvard Encyclopedia of American Ethnic Groups*, ed. Stephan Thernstrom, Ann Orlov, and Oscar Handlin (Cambridge: Harvard University Press, Belknap Press, 1980), 747; and Mark Wyman, *Round Trip to America: The Immigrants Return to Europe, 1880–1930* (Ithaca: Cornell University Press, 1993), 9–10.

13. Alexander Keyssar, *The Right to Vote: The Contested History of Democracy in the United States* (New York: Basic Books, 2000), chap. 5; Frances Fox Piven and Richard A. Cloward, *Why Americans Don't Vote*, 2d ed. (New York: Pantheon, 1989), chaps. 3–4; James J. Connolly, *The Triumph of Ethnic Progressivism: Urban Political Culture in Boston, 1900–1925* (Cambridge: Harvard University Press, 1998), chap. 4; and Michael E. McGerr, *The Decline of Popular Politics: The American North, 1865–1928* (New York: Oxford University Press, 1986).

14. Emmons, *Butte Irish*, 103–21; and Judith E. Smith, *Family Connections: A History of Italian and Jewish Immigrant Lives in Providence, Rhode Island, 1900–1940* (Albany: State University of New York Press, 1985), chap. 4.

15. Smith, *Family Connections*, 127–28; Paula Baker, "The Domestication of Politics: Women and American Political Society, 1780–1920," *American Historical Review* 89 (1984): 620–47; Nancy A. Hewitt, "In Pursuit of Power: The Political Economy of Women's Activism in Twentieth-Century Tampa," in *Visible Women: New Essays on American Activism*, ed. Nancy A. Hewitt and Suzanne Lebsock (Urbana: University of Illinois Press, 1993); Ardis Cameron, *Radicals of the Worst Sort: Laboring Women in Lawrence, Massachusetts, 1860–1912* (Urbana: University of Illinois Press, 1993); and Paula Hyman, "Immigrant Women and Consumer Protest: The New York City Kosher Meat Boycott of 1902," *American Jewish History* 70(1980): 93.

16. Leslie Woodcock Tentler, "Present at the Creation: Working-Class Catholics in the United States," in *American Exceptionalism? U.S. Working-Class Formation in an International Context*, ed. Rick Halpern and Jonathan Morris (New York: St. Martin's Press, 1997), 40.

CHAPTER 1. THE DORR REBELLION OF 1842

1. Marvin E. Gettleman, *The Dorr Rebellion: A Study in American Radicalism: 1833–1849* (New York: Random House, 1973), 101–2; and Patrick T. Conley, *Democracy in Decline: Rhode Island's Constitutional Development, 1776–1841* (Providence: Rhode Island Historical Society, 1977), 328–29.

2. Conley, *Democracy in Decline*, 315, 328.

3. Peter J. Coleman, *The Transformation of Rhode Island, 1790–1860* (Providence: Brown University Press, 1963), 220, 254, 270; Conley, *Democracy in Decline*, 48, 274; James Quayle Dealey, "Government," in *A Modern City: Providence, Rhode Island, and Its Activities*, ed. William Kirk (Chicago: University of Chicago Press, 1909), 142; Chilton Williamson, *American Suffrage: From Property to Democracy, 1760–1860* (Princeton: Princeton University Press, 1960), 243–45; William G. McLoughlin, *Rhode Island: A History* (New York: W. W. Norton, 1986), 128; Mark S. Schantz, *Piety in Providence: Class Dimensions of Religious Experience in Antebellum Rhode Island* (Ithaca: Cornell University Press, 2000), 99; and Superintendent of the Census, *Report upon the Census of Rhode Island, 1865* (Providence: Providence Press Co., 1867), lv.

4. Conley, *Democracy in Decline*, 218; Carl Gersuny, "A Biographical Note on Seth Luther,"

in *Peaceably If We Can, Forcibly If We Must! Writings by and about Seth Luther*, ed. Scott Molloy, Carl Gersuny, and Robert Macieski (Providence: Rhode Island Labor History Society, 1998), 76, 78; Louis Hartz, "Seth Luther: The Story of a Working-Class Rebel," in *Peaceably If We Can*, 53–57; and Carl Gersuny, "Seth Luther," in *American National Biography*, ed. John A. Garraty and Mark C. Carnes (New York: Oxford University Press, 1999), 14: 151.

5. Hartz, "Seth Luther," 57–58, 65; Gettleman, *Dorr Rebellion*, 19; McLoughlin, *Rhode Island*, 129; and Jacob Frieze, *Concise History of the Efforts to Obtain an Extension of Suffrage in Rhode Island; From the Year 1811 to 1842* (Providence: Benjamin F. Moore, 1842), 22–23.

6. Coleman, *Transformation of Rhode Island*, 263, 268; Conley, *Democracy in Decline*, 237, 269; Williamson, *American Suffrage*, 243; Alexander Keyssar, *The Right to Vote: The Contested History of Democracy in the United States* (New York: Basic Books, 2000), table A.2; and Seth Luther, "An Address on the Right of Free Suffrage," in *Peaceably If We Can*, 12, 15–16.

7. Luther, "Free Suffrage," 9; Coleman, *Transformation of Rhode Island*, 268; and Seth Luther, "An Address Delivered Before the Mechanics and Working-Men of the City of Brooklyn on the Celebration of the Sixtieth Anniversary of American Independence," in *Peaceably If We Can*, 47.

8. Schantz, *Piety in Providence*, 88–90, 107, 188, 191, 200 (Tillinghast quotation); Gersuny, "Biographical Note," 77; Robert Macieski, " 'Ye Cannot Serve God and Mammon': Seth Luther's Working-Class Morality," in *Peaceably If We Can*, 89–95; Carl Gersuny, "Young Luther in Debt," *Rhode Island History* 56 (1998): 52; and Seth Luther, "An Address on the Origins and Progress of Avarice," in *Peaceably If We Can*, 29.

9. Schantz, *Piety in Providence*, 110; Frieze, *Concise History*, 21; Macieski, "Ye Cannot Serve," 101; and Gettleman, *Dorr Rebellion*, 10, 21.

10. Gettleman, *Dorr Rebellion*, 12–17, 32–33; Conley, *Democracy in Decline*, 280–81; McLoughlin, *Rhode Island*, 130; and Charles Hoffman and Tess Hoffman, *Brotherly Love: Murder and the Politics of Prejudice in Nineteenth-Century Rhode Island* (Amherst: University of Massachusetts Press, 1993), 13.

11. Gettleman, *Dorr Rebellion*, 22, 24–29; and McLoughlin, *Rhode Island*, 129–30.

12. Coleman, *Transformation of Rhode Island*, 272; Conley, *Democracy in Decline*, 296–97, 302; Schantz, *Piety in Providence*, 200–201; *Journal*, 9 June 1912; Joyce M. Botelho, *Right and Might: The Dorr Rebellion and the Struggle for Equal Rights* (Providence: Rhode Island Historical Society, 1992), 29 ("American citizen" quotation); and Gettleman, *Dorr Rebellion*, 39.

13. McLoughlin, *Rhode Island*, 130; Conley, *Democracy in Decline*, 295, 322, 360; Frieze, *Concise History*, 29; Robert W. Hayman, *Catholicism in Rhode Island and the Diocese of Providence, 1780–1886* (Providence: Diocese of Providence, 1982), 39–40, 46; *Providence Directory. 1841* (Providence: H. H. Brown, 1841), 62; Duff to Dorr, Providence, 11 November 1841, Duff to Dorr, Fall River, 2 March 1842, Duff to O'Connell, Providence, 17 September 1844, and Duff to Dorr, San Francisco, 11 December 1852, Dorr Papers, John Hay Library, Brown University.

14. Conley, *Democracy in Decline*, 295, 309; Russell J. DeSimone and Daniel C. Schofield, eds., *The Broadsides of the Dorr Rebellion* (Providence: Rhode Island Supreme Court Historical Society, 1992), 29; Schantz, *Piety in Providence*, 107, 198, 200, 206–7; and Frieze, *Concise History*, 39. In his sixth chapter, Schantz interprets the Dorr Rebellion as a conflict between "bourgeois" and "plebeian" religious cultures.

15. McLoughlin, *Rhode Island*, 130; DeSimone and Schofield, eds., *Broadsides*, 29; General Assembly, *Constitution of the State of Rhode Island and Providence Plantations* (Providence: Knowles and Vose, 1842); *Proposed Constitution of the State of Rhode Island and Providence Plantatations as Finally Adopted by the People's Convention*, Rhode Island State Archives (hereafter cited as RISA); Williamson, *American Suffrage*, 252; and Coleman, *Transformation of Rhode Island*, 278.

16. Conley, *Democracy in Decline*, 311; Gettleman, *Dorr Rebellion*, 46 ("Greek temple" quotation); and Williamson, *American Suffrage*, 252 ("genteel" quotation).

17. J. Stanley Lemons and Michael A. McKenna, "Re-enfranchisement of Rhode Island Negroes," *Rhode Island History* 30 (1971): 3; Conley, *Democracy in Decline*, 311–12; Schantz, *Piety in Providence*, 99; Keyssar, *Right to Vote*, table A.5; and *Proceedings of the Rhode Island Constitutional Convention, 1841–1842, Memorial of Colored Citizens*, RISA.

18. Gettleman, *Dorr Rebellion*, 52, 78; Conley, *Democracy in Decline*, 315, 323; and Williamson, *American Suffrage*, 253.

19. Frieze, *Concise History*, 58–59; Conley, *Democracy in Decline*, 317, 319; McLoughlin, *Rhode Island*, 133; Williamson, *American Suffrage*, 254–55; and Gettleman, *Dorr Rebellion*, 90–91, 93.

20. Gettleman, *Dorr Rebellion*, 118, 120–22; Hartz, "Seth Luther," 59; Conley, *Democracy in Decline*, 339; Schantz, *Piety in Providence*, 203; and Frieze, *Concise History*, 91.

21. Conley, *Democracy in Decline*, 341, 343–44, 347–48.

22. Frieze, *Concise History*, 99; Conley, *Democracy in Decline*, 349–51; Hartz, "Seth Luther," 60 (Luther quotation); and Gettleman, *Dorr Rebellion*, 123.

23. Hayman, *Catholicism, 1780–1886*, 46; Potter to Francis, 1 May 1842, Henry A. L. Brown Papers, Rhode Island Historical Society (hereafter cited as RIHS); Francis to Potter, 3 May 1842, Elisha R. Potter Jr. Papers, RIHS; and *150th Anniversary. Cathedral Parish of SS. Peter and Paul. 1837–1987* (Providence: Cogens, 1987).

24. Conley, *Democracy in Decline*, 341–42 (White quotation); Gettleman, *Dorr Rebellion*, 168; and Schantz, *Piety in Providence*, 207–8, 210–11.

25. Gettleman, *Dorr Rebellion*, 145; Conley, *Democracy in Decline*, 372; and Chilton Williamson, "Rhode Island Suffrage since the Dorr War," *New England Quarterly* 28 (1955): 37.

26. *Proposed Constitution of the State of Rhode Island and Providence Plantations* (Providence: Knowles and Vose, 1842); Keyssar, *Right to Vote*, 59–65; Coleman, *Transformation of Rhode Island*, 244; and Gettleman, *Dorr Rebellion*, 130 (Potter quotation).

27. *Proposed Constitution*; Keyssar, *Right to Vote*, 30–31, 65–66; *Proposed [People's] Constitution;* and Williamson, *American Suffrage*, 259.

28. Conley, *Democracy in Decline*, 374, 377; and Coleman, *Transformation of Rhode Island*, 285.

29. Williamson, *American Suffrage*, 258; Gettleman, *Dorr Rebellion*, 160–62, 165; DeSimone and Schofield, eds., *Broadsides*, 64; Hoffman and Hoffman, *Brotherly Love*, 81; Botelho, *Right and Might*, 65–67, 85; Conley, *Democracy in Decline*, 368, 371; Gersuny, "A Biographical Note," 81–86 (Luther quotation); and Carl Gersuny, "In Remembrance of Seth Luther," in *A History of Rhode Island Working People*, ed. Paul Buhle, Scott Molloy, and Gail Sansbury (Providence: Regine, 1983), 6.

30. Keyssar, *Right to Vote*, 29, 33, 66.

31. Ibid., 5–6; Williamson, *American Suffrage*, 5, 11–19; and Robert J. Dinkin, "The Suffrage," in *Encyclopedia of the North American Colonies*, ed. Jacob Ernest Cooke (New York: Charles Scribner's Sons, 1993), 1: 364–65.

32. Williamson, *American Suffrage*, 47, 76–78; and Keyssar, *Right to Vote*, 7, 20, 29, 33, 54–65, tables A.1 and A.5–A.7.

33. Keyssar, *Right to Vote*, 33–43.

34. Ibid., 44–49.

35. McLoughlin, *Rhode Island*, 63, 115–26; Keyssar, *Right to Vote*, table A.8; Coleman, *Transformation of Rhode Island*, 82–83, 159–60, 221, 223; and Superintendent of the Census, *Census of Rhode Island, 1865*, lv.

36. Ray Allen Billington, *The Protestant Crusade 1800–1860: A Study of the Origins of American Nativism* (New York: Rinehart, 1938), 132; Gettleman, *Dorr Rebellion*, 8–9, 45; Francis W. Goddard, *The Political and Miscellaneous Writings of William G. Goddard* (Providence: Sidney S. Rider and Brother, 1870), 58–59, 68, 89–90; and Conley, *Democracy in Decline*, 230, 232, 277, 321.

37. Goddard, *Political and Miscellaneous Writings*, 151; Conley, *Democracy in Decline*, 255 (Dorr quotation); and General Assembly, *Report of the Committee on the Action of the General Assembly, on the Subject of the Constitution* (March 1842), RISA.

38. Conley, *Democracy in Decline*, 274, 322 (*Journal* quotation); Coleman, *Transformation of Rhode Island*, 220; and Dale T. Knobel, *"America for the Americans": The Nativist Movement in the United States* (New York: Twayne, 1996), 108.

39. Williamson, *American Suffrage*, 255; Conley, *Democracy in Decline*, 322 (*Journal* quotation); and "Native American Citizens! Read and Take Warning!" (1842), Broadside File, RIHS.

40. Conley, *Democracy in Decline*, 276, 322; Joshua Rathbun, Tiverton, to Dorr, 25 March 1842, Dorr Papers; and Keyssar, *Right to Vote*, 67–70.

41. Billington, *Protestant Crusade*, 1–2, 7–16, 18; McLoughlin, *Rhode Island*, 6–10; David H. Bennett, *The Party of Fear: The American Far Right from Nativism to the Militia Movement*, 2d ed. (New York: Vintage, 1995), 19; and Conley, *Democracy in Decline*, 323.

42. Jay P. Dolan, *The American Catholic Experience: A History from Colonial Times to the Present* (Notre Dame: University of Notre Dame Press, 1992), 97, 101; Billington, *Protestant Crusade*, 21–22; and Conley, *Democracy in Decline*, 71.

43. Dolan, *American Catholic Experience*, 103, 105–18.

44. Knobel, *"America for the Americans,"* 43; Charles R. Morris, *American Catholic: The Saints and Sinners Who Built America's Most Powerful Church* (New York: Vintage, 1997), 64–65; and Bennett, *Party of Fear*, 68–75.

45. Knobel, *"America for the Americans,"* 2, 42, 49, 52–53, 123; Billington, *Protestant Crusade*, 42–43, 199; Bennett, *Party of Fear*, 76–77, 83–84; and Morris, *American Catholic*, 73–75.

46. Billington, *Protestant Crusade*, 67–76, 89, 99–100; and Bennett, *Party of Fear*, 41–47.

47. Morris, *American Catholic*, 60–62; Billington, *Protestant Crusade*, 220–34, 300–303; and Hayman, *Catholicism, 1780–1886*, 77–78. See Hoffman and Hoffman, *Brotherly Love*, for more on the Gordon case.

48. Bennett, *Party of Fear*, 55; and Billington, *Protestant Crusade*, 325–29.

49. Billington, *Protestant Crusade*, 386–88, 407; Superintendent of the Census, *Census of Rhode Island, 1865*, lvi; Hayman, *Catholicism, 1780–1886*, 123, 136–40; Larry Anthony Rand, "The Know-Nothing Party in Rhode Island: Religious Bigotry and Political Success," *Rhode Island History* 23 (1964): 109–14; McLoughlin, *Rhode Island*, 141–42; and General Assembly, *Acts and Resolves of the General Assembly, May 1856* (Providence: A. Crawford Greene and Brother, 1856), 29.

50. Knobel, *"America for the Americans,"* 143–44, 149; Bennett, *Party of Fear*, 125, 127, 131, 134; and Billington, *Protestant Crusade*, 423–30. See also Tyler Anbinder, *Nativism and Slavery: The Northern Know Nothings and the Politics of the 1850s* (New York: Oxford University Press, 1992).

51. Conley, *Democracy in Decline*, 360, 369; DeSimone and Schofield, eds., *Broadsides*, 77; Schantz, *Piety in Providence*, 263; and Duff to Dorr, 11 December 1852.

CHAPTER 2. IMMIGRATION IN THE NINETEENTH CENTURY

1. Superintendent of the Census, *Rhode Island State Census, 1885* (Providence: E. L. Freeman, 1887), 239; and Robert W. Hayman, *Catholicism in Rhode Island and the Diocese of Providence, 1780–1886* (Providence: Diocese of Providence, 1982), 300.

2. Superintendent of the Census, *State Census, 1885*, 215, 225, 245; Patrick J. Blessing, "Irish," in *Harvard Encyclopedia of American Ethnic Groups*, ed. Stephan Thernstrom, Ann Orlov, and Oscar Handlin (Cambridge: Harvard University Press, Belknap Press, 1980), 530–31; Kerby A. Miller, *Emigrants and Exiles: Ireland and the Irish Exodus to North America* (New York: Oxford University Press, 1985), 58, 102–21, 193, 195, 201, 204, 252–61, 297; and Hasia R. Diner, *Erin's Daughters in America: Irish Immigrant Women in the Nineteenth Century* (Baltimore: Johns Hopkins University Press, 1983), 6.

3. Blessing, "Irish," 530; Patrick T. Conley, *The Irish in Rhode Island: A Historical Appreciation* (Providence: Rhode Island Heritage Commission and Rhode Island Publications Society, 1986), 10; Miller, *Emigrants and Exiles*, 267; and Hayman, *Catholicism, 1780–1886*, 118.

4. *Journal*, 17 January 1887; and Miller, *Emigrants and Exiles*, 269–70, 296, 326, 342.

5. Patrick T. Conley, *The Irish in Rhode Island: A Historical Appreciation* (Princeton: Rhode Island Heritage Commission and Rhode Island Publications Society, 1986), 10–11, 18–19; Diner, *Erin's Daughters*, 74, 94; Hayman, *Catholicism, 1780–1886*, 32, 82, 300; and Blessing, "Irish," 531–32.

6. Miller, *Emigrants and Exiles*, 61, 67, 436–37; Blessing, "Irish," 535; David A. Gerber, *The Making of an American Pluralism: Buffalo, New York, 1825–1860* (Urbana: University of Illinois Press, 1989), 333–35; Mark Wyman, *Round Trip to America: The Immigrants Return to Europe, 1880–1930* (Ithaca: Cornell University Press, 1993), 10; Superintendent of the Census, *State Census, 1885*, 149, 356–57; Michael E. McGerr, *The Decline of Popular Politics: The American North, 1865–1928* (New York: Oxford University Press, 1986), chap. 2; and Mary Josephine Bannon, ed., *Autobiographic Memoirs of Hon. Patrick J. McCarthy* (Providence: Providence Visitor Press, 1927), 45.

7. Conley, *Irish in Rhode Island*, 15–16; and *Providence Visitor*, 16 February 1917.

8. Miller, *Emigrants and Exiles*, 312, 369, 512.

9. Hayman, *Catholicism, 1780–1886*, 39; Conley, *Irish in Rhode Island*, 19–20; and Eric Foner, "Class, Ethnicity, and Radicalism in the Gilded Age: The Land League and Irish-America," *Marxist Perspectives* 1 (1978): 23.

10. Jay P. Dolan, *The Immigrant Church: New York's Irish and German Catholics, 1815–1865* (Notre Dame: University of Notre Dame Press, 1975), 45, 56–57; Miller, *Emigrants and Exiles*, 22, 73–74, 82–83, 98, 126–27, 327, 331, 420, 464; Emmet Larkin, "The Devotional Revolution in Ireland, 1850–75," *American Historical Review* 77 (1972): 636; and Harold J. Abramson, "Ethnic Diversity within Catholicism: A Comparative Analysis of Contemporary and Historical Religion," *Journal of Social History* 4 (1971): 366–67.

11. Dolan, *Immigrant Church*, 51, 56–58; Miller, *Emigrants and Exiles*, 331; Hayman, *Catholicism, 1780–1886*, 22–49; *150th Anniversary. Cathedral Parish of SS. Peter and Paul. 1837–1987* (Providence: Cogens, 1987); Mark S. Schantz, *Piety in Providence: Class Dimensions of Religious Experience in Antebellum Rhode Island* (Ithaca: Cornell University Press, 2000), 168; and *Saint Patrick Church. Providence, Rhode Island. 150 Years. 1841–1991* (n.p., n.d.).

12. Miller, *Emigrants and Exiles*, 332, 526; Schantz, *Piety in Providence*, 260–61; *The Consecration of SS. Peter and Paul's Cathedral. Sunday, June 30th, 1889* (Providence: Corporation of SS. Peter and Paul, 1889), 39, 43; Conley, *Irish in Rhode Island*, 15; Richard A. Walsh, *The Centennial History of Saint Edward Church, Providence, Rhode Island, 1874–1974* (n.p., n.d.), 79; and D'Arcy to Harkins, Providence, 28 April 1893, St. Michael's Papers, Providence Catholic Diocesan Archives (hereafter cited as PCDA).

13. Hayman, *Catholicism, 1780–1886*, 59–61; Thomas V. Cassidy, *Saint Mary Church of Pawtucket, Rhode Island: A Sesquicentennial Story, 1829–1979* (n.p., n.d.), 69; *Saint Patrick Church*, 3–4; Walsh, *St. Edward Church*, 56–57; and Miller, *Emigrants and Exiles*, 526.

14. Elliott Robert Barkin, "French Canadians," in *Harvard Encyclopedia*, 388, 390–93; Gerard J. Brault, *The French-Canadian Heritage in New England* (Hanover, N.H.: University Press of New England, 1986), 52, 54–56; and Albert K. Aubin, ed., *The French in Rhode Island: A Brief History* (Providence: Rhode Island Heritage Commission and Rhode Island Publications Society, 1988), 11, 13.

15. Aubin, *French in Rhode Island*, 5–6, 13–14, 20; Brault, *French-Canadian Heritage*, 59, 61; *Journal*, 14 October 1888; and Barkin, "French Canadians," 393–94.

16. Brault, *French-Canadian Heritage*, 62–63, 67–68; *Journal*, 14 October 1888, 2, 3 January 1895; Barkin, "French Canadians," 394; Gary Gerstle, *Working-Class Americanism: The Politics of Labor in a Textile City, 1914–1960* (New York: Cambridge University Press, 1989), 40; and

Mary H. Blewett, *Constant Turmoil: The Politics of Industrial Life in Nineteenth-Century New England* (Amherst: University of Massachusetts Press, 2000), 202, 226, 297.

17. *Journal*, 14 October 1888; Brault, *French-Canadian Heritage*, 7, 65–66, 82; and Richard S. Sorrell, "Sentinelle Affair (1924–1929)—Religion and Militant Survivance in Woonsocket, Rhode Island," *Rhode Island History* 36 (1977): 70.

18. Aubin, *French in Rhode Island*, 13; Gerstle, *Working-Class Americanism*, 26; Superintendent of the Census, *State Census, 1885*, 356–57; and *Providence Evening Telegram*, 27 December 1903.

19. Jon Gjerde, *The Minds of the West: Ethnocultural Evolution in the Rural Middle West, 1830–1917* (Chapel Hill: University of North Carolina Press, 1997), 229; Blewett, *Constant Turmoil*, 201; *Journal*, 14 October 1888, 23 December 1900; and Aubin, *French in Rhode Island*, 6, 21. See Gjerde's chap. 8 for a discussion of immigrants in the Midwest who entered politics to defend ethnic group interests and in so doing came together across ethnic lines.

20. Barkin, "French Canadians," 390; Abramson, "Ethnic Diversity," 368–70; Aubin, *French in Rhode Island*, 13; and Brault, *French-Canadian Heritage*, 9, 16–29. Falardeau is quoted in Abramson, 369.

21. Barkin, "French Canadians," 370–71; and Aubin, *French in Rhode Island*, 17–19 ("church meant home" quotation).

22. Brault, *French-Canadian Heritage*, 9, 66, 68–73, 75; Aubin, *French in Rhode Island*, 15; and Hayman, *Catholicism, 1780–1886*, 182–83, 231, 233, 264–80.

23. Carmela E. Santoro, *The Italians in Rhode Island: The Age of Exploration to the Present, 1524–1989* (Providence: Rhode Island Heritage Commission and Rhode Island Publications Society, 1990), 1; Judith E. Smith, *Family Connections: A History of Italian and Jewish Immigrant Lives in Providence, Rhode Island, 1900–1940* (Albany: State University of New York Press, 1985), 24, 26, 28; Commissioner of Labor, *Report of Commissioner of Labor Made to the General Assembly for the Years 1916–1917–1918–1919* (Providence: E. L. Freeman, 1921), 271, 274; Virginia Yans-McLaughlin, *Family and Community: Italian Immigrants in Buffalo, 1880–1930* (Urbana: University of Illinois Press, 1982), 26–33, 158–59; and Humbert S. Nelli, "Italians," in *Harvard Encyclopedia*, 547.

24. Santoro, *Italians in Rhode Island*, 3, 7; Yans-McLaughlin, *Family and Community*, 26–28, 38–44; *Journal*, 21 May 1887, 7 October 1888, 20 February 1893; Smith, *Family Connections*, 35, 41, 153; and Ruth S. Morgenthau, *Pride without Prejudice: The Life of John O. Pastore* (Providence: Rhode Island Historical Society, 1989), 11–12.

25. Smith, *Family Connections*, 47–61; *Journal*, 19 February 1893; Nelli, "Italians," 554; and Yans-McLaughlin, *Family and Community*, 47–48, 178, 196.

26. *Journal*, 26 June 1892, 19, 20 February 1893.

27. Santoro, *Italians in Rhode Island*, 6; Smith, *Family Connections*, 153; Commissioner of Labor, *Report*, 224; Yans-McLaughlin, *Family and Community*, 48–49, 178; Wyman, *Round-Trip to America*, 11; Superintendent of the Census, *Rhode Island State Census, 1895* (Providence: E. L. Freeman, 1898), 630–31; and Superintendent of the Census, *Report of the Superintendent of the Census for the Year 1925: Presented to the General Assembly by Peck Barrington, 1926*, table 6, RISA.

28. Santoro, *Italians in Rhode Island*, 38; Yans-McLaughlin, *Family and Community*, 110, 131; *Journal*, 21 May 1887; Paul Buhle, "Italian-American Radicals and Labor in Rhode Island, 1905–1930," *Radical History Review* 17 (spring 1978): 126, 128–31; Nelli, "Italians," 552; and Morgenthau, *Pride without Prejudice*, 15, 43, 56.

29. Santoro, *Italians in Rhode Island*, 26–27; Yans-McLaughlin, *Family and Community*, 130; and Smith, *Family Connections*, 127–28, 132–33, 142–43, 152, 155–56, 162. For a discussion of immigrant women's neighborhood networks, see Ardis Cameron, *Radicals of the Worst Sort: Laboring Women in Lawrence, Massachusetts, 1860–1912* (Urbana: University of Illinois Press, 1993).

30. Abramson, "Ethnic Diversity," 372–76; and Rudolph J. Vecoli, "Prelates and Peasants:

Italian Immigrants and the Catholic Church," *Journal of Social History* 2 (1969): 222–23, 228–29, 233.

31. Vecoli, "Prelates and Peasants," 230, 233–35, 247–48 (*America* quotation), 262–63; *Journal*, 21 May, 30 August 1887, 7 October 1888; Santoro, *Italians in Rhode Island*, 14; and Robert W. Hayman, *Catholicism in Rhode Island and the Diocese of Providence, 1886–1921* (Providence: Diocese of Providence, 1995), 209–10.

32. Vecoli, "Prelates and Peasants," 230–31, 235–42, 266; *History of the Holy Ghost Parish, Providence, Rhode Island* (Providence: Service Plus Press, 1966); and Harkins Diary (2 April 1910, 20 September 1913, 5 July 1917), Harkins Papers, PCDA.

33. John F. Sullivan and Vincenzo F. Kienberger, *Storia della Parrocchia di S. Anna, Providence, R.I. In Occasione del Giubileo d'Argente Sacerdotale del Parroco, 1900–1925* (n.p., n.d.), 5, 9, 12; and Hayman, *Catholicism, 1886–1921*, 184–85.

34. Robert A. Orsi, *The Madonna of 115th Street: Faith and Community in Italian Harlem, 1880–1950* (New Haven: Yale University Press, 1985), chap. 7; and Vecoli, "Prelates and Peasants," 258.

35. *Visitor*, 29 July 1889; *Holy Ghost*; *Journal*, 17 August 1890; and Hayman, *Catholicism, 1886–1921*, 182.

36. Peter J. Coleman, *The Transformation of Rhode Island, 1790–1860* (Providence: Brown University Press, 1963), 220; Superintendent of the Census, *State Census, 1885*, 215, 225, 239, 356–57; Commissioner of Labor, *Report*, 274; and Hayman, *Catholicism, 1780–1886*, 300.

37. Smith, *Family Connections*, 9–10; John S. Gilkeson Jr., *Middle-Class Providence, 1820–1940* (Princeton: Princeton University Press, 1986), 59, 137; John Hutchins Cady, *The Civic and Architectural Development of Providence* (Providence: The Book Shop, 1957), 150, 156, 159; and Scott Molloy, *Trolley Wars: Streetcar Workers on the Line* (Washington, D.C.: Smithsonian Institution Press, 1996), 47–48, 51–52, 88.

38. Gilkeson, *Middle-Class Providence*, 141–42, 150.

39. Smith, *Family Connections*, 10; and Cady, *Civic and Architectural Development*, 149–50, 153, 155, 167, 171–75.

40. Smith, *Family Connections*, 11, 16; Santoro, *Italians in Rhode Island*, 7–8; Gilkeson, *Middle-Class Providence*, 138, 263; and Cady, *Civic and Architectural Development*, 161–62.

41. Gilkeson, *Middle-Class Providence*, 220–22, 226, 228–36; Cady, *Civic and Architectural Development*, 147, 161; and Molloy, *Trolley Wars*, 81.

CHAPTER 3. CORRUPTION AND PROTEST IN THE GILDED AGE

1. Superintendent of the Census, *Rhode Island State Census, 1885* (Providence: E. L. Freeman, 1887), 149, 349.

2. *Journal*, 14 December 1888; and David Roediger, *The Wages of Whiteness: Race and the Making of the American Working Class* (New York: Verso, 1991).

3. *Journal*, 14 December 1888; *Providence Morning Star*, 4 October 1876; and Robert W. Hayman, *Catholicism in Rhode Island and the Diocese of Providence, 1780–1886* (Providence: Diocese of Providence, 1982), 157.

4. *Star*, 11 December 1874; *Providence Evening Bulletin*, 1 August 1877; Patrick T. Conley, *The Irish in Rhode Island: A Historical Appreciation* (Providence: Rhode Island Heritage Commission and Rhode Island Publications Society, 1986), 16; U.S. Senate, Select Committee, *Massachusetts and Rhode Island. Discrimination against Foreign-Born Citizens*, 4, RIHS; and *Telegram*, 16 November 1887.

5. Scott Molloy, *Trolley Wars: Streetcar Workers on the Line* (Washington, D.C.: Smithsonian Institution Press, 1996), 118; John S. Gilkeson Jr., *Middle-Class Providence, 1820–1940* (Princeton: Princeton University Press, 1986), 181; and Lincoln Steffens, "Rhode Island: A State for Sale," *McClure's*, February 1905, 337.

6. Molloy, *Trolley Wars*, 66–67; and Robert Power, "Rhode Island Republican Politics in the Gilded Age: The G.O.P. Machine of Anthony, Aldrich, and Brayton" (B.A. thesis, Brown University, 1972), 55.

7. John D. Buenker, "The Politics of Resistance: The Rural-Based Yankee Republican Machines of Connecticut and Rhode Island," *New England Quarterly* 47 (1974): 229–30; and Elmer E. Cornwell Jr., "Party Absorption of Ethnic Groups: The Case of Providence, Rhode Island," *Social Forces* 38 (1960): 207–8.

8. Ellen Hartwell, "Political Extremism and the Quest for Absolutes in Rhode Island, 1900–1935" (B.A. thesis, Brown University, 1972), 2; Chilton Williamson, "Rhode Island Suffrage since the Dorr War," *New England Quarterly* 28 (1955): 41–42; and Buenker, "Politics of Resistance," 230.

9. William G. McLoughlin, *Rhode Island: A History* (New York: W. W. Norton, 1986), 155; and U.S. Senate, *Massachusetts and Rhode Island*, 2–6.

10. Gilkeson, *Middle-Class Providence*, 60–61, 182–83; and McLoughlin, *Rhode Island*, 159.

11. Paul Buhle, "The Knights of Labor," in *A History of Rhode Island Working People*, ed. Paul Buhle, Scott Molloy, and Gail Sansbury (Providence: Regine, 1983), 21–23; Gilkeson, *Middle-Class Providence*, 105–13; and Molloy, *Trolley Wars*, 40.

12. Sara M. Algeo, *The Story of a Sub-Pioneer* (Providence: Snow and Farnham, 1925), 75, 82, 89; Elizabeth Cooke Stevens, "From Generation to Generation: The Mother and Daughter Activism of Elizabeth Buffum Chace and Lillie Chace Wyman" (Ph.D. diss., Brown University, 1993), 162, 165–67; and McLoughlin, *Rhode Island*, 160.

13. Elizabeth Cady Stanton, Susan B. Anthony, and Matilda Joslyn Gage, *History of Woman Suffrage* (Salem, N.H.: Ayer, 1985; rpt., Indianapolis: Hollenbeck Press, 1902), 4: 909–11 (page citations are to the reprint edition); Stevens, "From Generation to Generation," 289–90, 293–94; and Algeo, *Story of a Sub-Pioneer*, 82.

14. Stevens, "From Generation to Generation," 249–51, 290–91; Williamson, *American Suffrage*, 279; *Star*, 23 November 1885; and *Visitor*, 11 April 1887.

15. Hayman, *Catholicism, 1780–1886*, 301; Williamson, "Rhode Island Suffrage," 41; *Star*, 1 April 1882; *Journal*, 7 December 1888; and *Visitor*, 16 February 1917.

16. Hayman, *Catholicism, 1780–1886*, 293–96, 301–2; and Henry Bowen Anthony, "Limited Suffrage in Rhode Island," *North American Review* 324 (1883): 116, 118.

17. Dale T. Knobel, *"America for the Americans": The Nativist Movement in the United States* (New York: Twayne, 1996), 158–67, 169–76, 180–81, 184, 186.

18. Hayman, *Catholicism, 1780–1886*, 303; and Mary Nelson, "The Influence of Immigration on Rhode Island Politics, 1865–1910" (Ph.D. diss., Harvard University, 1954), 3–5.

19. *Journal*, 17 November, 14 December 1888; and Superintendent of the Census, *State Census, 1885*, 349.

20. General Assembly, *Acts and Resolves of the General Assembly of the State of Rhode Island and Providence Plantations, March 1887* (Providence: E. L. Freeman, 1887), 296; *Providence Journal Almanac, 1889* (Providence: Providence Journal Co., 1889), 33; Williamson, "Rhode Island Suffrage," 43; Hartwell, "Political Extremism," 2–3; and Nelson, "Influence of Immigration," 182 n. 15.

21. Alexander Keyssar, *The Right to Vote: The Contested History of Democracy in the United States* (New York: Basic Books, 2000), 120–23, 133.

22. Superintendent of the Census, *State Census, 1885*, 149, and Superintendent of the Census, *Rhode Island State Census, 1895* (Providence: E. L. Freeman, 1898), 618–19, 630–31; *Providence Journal Almanac, 1889*, 35; *Providence Journal Almanac, 1893* (Providence: Providence Journal, 1893), 39; and *Providence Journal Almanac, 1897* (Providence: Providence Journal, 1897), 36. Foreign-born men comprised 39 percent of the population of voting-age men in 1885 but 43 percent in 1895.

23. Superintendent of the Census, *State Census, 1885*, 149, 356–57, *State Census, 1895*, 630–31; and *Journal*, 23 March 1896.

24. Mary H. Blewett, *Constant Turmoil: The Politics of Industrial Life in Nineteenth-Century New England* (Amherst: University of Massachusetts Press, 2000), 297–99; and *Journal*, 5, 27 October 1881, 8 December 1890, 2 March 1892, 26 July 1895.

25. *Journal*, 21 November 1890, 5 May 1892, 23 September 1896.

26. *Visitor*, 19 May 1894; and John Ireland, *American Citizenship. An Address, Delivered Before the Union League Club, in Auditorium Hall, Chicago, Ill., February 22nd, 1895* (Buffalo: Catholic Truth Society, 1895), 3, 10.

27. For a discussion of late nineteenth-century ethnic conflicts over temperance and woman suffrage in the Midwest, see Jon Gjerde, *The Minds of the West: Ethnocultural Evolution in the Rural Middle West, 1830–1917* (Chapel Hill: University of North Carolina Press, 1997), chap. 10.

28. David H. Bennett, *The Party of Fear: The American Far Right from Nativism to the Militia Movement*, 2d ed. (New York: Vintage, 1995), 171, 173–74; and John Higham, *Strangers in the Land: Patterns of American Nativism, 1860–1925*, 2d ed. (New York: Atheneum, 1963), 62–63, 80–86.

29. *Journal*, 25 November 1893, 23 March, 30 October 1894; Power, "Republican Politics," 157; *Woonsocket Patriot*, 4 April 1890; and *Boston American Citizen*, 20 March, 27 April, 25 May, 8 June, 9 November 1895, 28 March, 18 April 1896.

30. Conley, *Irish in Rhode Island*, 16; *Visitor*, 23, 30 November 1895; Molloy, *Trolley Wars*, 93; Harkins Diary, 2, 29 December 1895, Harkins Papers, PCDA; and *Citizen*, 7 December 1895.

31. *Citizen*, 5, 12 December 1896.

32. Ibid., 8 February, 9, 30 May, 5 September 1896, 19, 26 August, 21 October, 4 November 1899.

33. Timothy J. Meagher, *Inventing Irish America: Generation, Class, and Ethnic Identity in a New England City, 1880–1928* (Notre Dame: University of Notre Dame Press, 2001), 200; and Gjerde, *Minds of the West*, 61, 63.

34. *Journal*, 25 November 1893, 15 January 1894, 9 April 1895; and *Visitor*, 28 September 1895, 18 January 1896.

35. Knobel, *"America for the Americans,"* 196, 198; Jay P. Dolan, *The American Catholic Experience: A History from Colonial Times to the Present* (Notre Dame: University of Notre Dame Press, 1992), 271–72; and Bennett, *Party of Fear*, 171–72.

36. Higham, *Strangers in the Land*, 92–94; Patrick Janson, "Organized Impulses of Resistance and Assimilation within the Providence Jewish Community, 1880–1921," *Rhode Island Jewish Historical Notes* 9 (1984): 143; and *Journal*, 31 December 1891, 8 March, 16 May 1898.

37. *Journal*, 10 January 1885.

38. Ibid., 25 June 1885; and *Le Jean-Baptiste*, 25 June 1902.

39. *Providence Justice*, 9, 23 September, 18 November 1893; and *Journal*, 23 March 1894.

40. Gilkeson, *Middle-Class Providence*, 183–84.

41. Nelson, "Influence of Immigration," 157–58, 229; and Gilkeson, *Middle-Class Providence*, 183–90.

42. *Justice*, 21 September 1895.

CHAPTER 4. IMMIGRANTS AND POLITICS IN THE PROGRESSIVE ERA

1. For more on failed attempts at reform in the 1890s, see Evelyn Sterne, "All Americans: The Politics of Citizenship in Providence, 1840 to 1940" (Ph.D. diss., Duke University, 1999), chap. 2.

2. John S. Gilkeson Jr., *Middle-Class Providence, 1820–1940* (Princeton: Princeton University Press, 1986), 128; Scott Molloy, *Trolley Wars: Streetcar Workers on the Line* (Washington, D.C.: Smithsonian Institution Press, 1996), 125; and *Journal*, 25 May 1902.

3. Ellen Hartwell, "Political Extremism and the Quest for Absolutes in Rhode Island, 1900–

1935" (B.A. thesis, Brown University, 1972), 43; *Journal,* 4 May, 1 June, 22 December 1902; and Molloy, *Trolley Wars,* 125–26.

4. *Journal,* 23 December 1900; and *Le Jean-Baptiste,* 13 June 1902.

5. *Journal,* 10, 16 October 1901, 5, 12, 25 May, 1 June 1902; and Molloy, *Trolley Wars,* 126.

6. Molloy, *Trolley Wars,* 67–77, 98–109, 140, 175–77; and *Justice,* 2 September 1895.

7. Molloy, *Trolley Wars,* 112, 132, 135, 137, 147–49.

8. Ibid., 151; *Journal,* 20 October 1902; and *Visitor* 7, 21 June 1902.

9. Molloy, *Trolley Wars,* 137–39, 153–57.

10. Ibid., 159, 162.

11. *Journal,* 1 November 1901, 12, 23 May 1902; and *Visitor,* 11 January 1902.

12. Carl Gersuny, "Uphill Battle: Lucius F. C. Garvin's Crusade for Political Reform," *Rhode Island History* 39 (1980): 57–59, 61–62; and Molloy, *Trolley Wars,* 164, 168.

13. Molloy, *Trolley Wars,* 166, 168–69 (*Journal* quotation); Mary Nelson, "The Influence of Immigration on Rhode Island Politics, 1865–1910" (Ph.D. diss., Harvard University, 1954), 317–27; and Lincoln Steffens, "Rhode Island: A State for Sale," *McClure's,* February 1905, 352.

14. Gersuny, "Uphill Battle," 64–65; Steffens, "Rhode Island," 345, 348–49; and Molloy, *Trolley Wars,* 169–70.

15. Paul Buhle, "Socialist Labor Party," in *Encyclopedia of the American Left,* ed. Mari Jo Buhle, Paul Buhle, and Dan Georgakas (New York: Garland, 1990; rpt., Urbana: University of Illinois Press, 1992), 714 (page citations are to the reprint edition); Robert Grieve, "Growth and Present Status of Socialism in Rhode Island: Twelve Years of Party Politics and Its Results," *Journal,* 22 April 1906; Paul Buhle, "Italian-American Radicals and Labor in Rhode Island, 1905–1930," *Radical History Review* 17 (spring 1978): 125; Gilkeson, *Middle-Class Providence,* 122–23, 200; and Richard Padden Clark, "The Struggle, Victory and Defeat of James P. Reid: A Socialist in Rhode Island, 1893–1912" (M.A. thesis, Rhode Island College, 1975), 5. For a discussion of early socialism in Providence, see Clark, "James P. Reid," chap. 1, and Sterne, "All Americans," 88–92.

16. *Journal,* 19 March 1903.

17. Richard Judd, "Municipal Socialism," in *Encyclopedia of the American Left,* 493.

18. *Providence Labor Advocate,* 2 February, 19 October 1913. The concept of a "subculture of opposition" comes from Richard Oestreicher, *Solidarity and Fragmentation: Working People and Class Consciousness in Detroit, 1875–1900* (Urbana: University of Illinois Press, 1986).

19. *Justice,* 29 September, 6 October 1894; and *Labor Advocate,* 12 October 1913.

20. *Justice,* 22 September, 17 November 1894, 27 April, 15 June 1895; *Labor Advocate,* 24 November 1912, 28 December 1913, 5 April 1914; and *Journal,* 24 October 1896.

21. *Justice,* 1 September, 3 November 1894, 2 November 1895.

22. Ibid., 10 October 1894, 30 March 1895.

23. *Journal,* 7, 14 May 1894; and *Justice,* 30 June 1894, 14 September 1895.

24. Grieve, "Socialism in Rhode Island."

25. Hugh McLeod, *Piety and Poverty: Working-Class Religion in Berlin, London, and New York, 1870–1914* (New York: Holmes & Meier, 1996), 145; and *Visitor,* 2 June 1911.

26. *Labor Advocate,* 8 September 1912; and Grieve, "Socialism in Rhode Island."

27. Clark, "James P. Reid," 4, 13, 46, 51, 55–56, 87, 97; and Paul Buhle, "Labor Personalities: James P. Reid," in *A History of Rhode Island Working People,* ed. Paul Buhle, Scott Molloy, and Gail Sansbury (Providence: Regine, 1983), 44.

28. *Labor Advocate,* 13 October 1912; *Journal,* 8, 29 July 1912; and *Cold Spring News,* 18 August 1912.

29. *Labor Advocate,* 29 September, 10 November 1912; *Visitor,* 1 November 1912; and Clark, "James P. Reid," 87.

30. *Visitor,* 19 May 1911; and *Woonsocket Evening Call,* 16 November 1912.

31. *Labor Advocate,* 31 August, 8, 22, 29 September, 13, 20 October, 10 November 1912; *New*

England Labor Digest, October 1912, 5; Providence Journal Almanac, 1913 (Providence: Providence Journal Co., 1913), 56; and Visitor, 8 November 1912.

32. Providence Journal Almanac, 1913, 46. A survey of election results in the Providence Journal Almanac between 1887 (its first issue) and 1940 reveals that Providence Socialists never won a citywide office or a seat on the city council. Whether the party captured any lesser office such as a seat on the school committee is unknown, as the Almanac does not specify the affiliation of candidates in those races.

33. Grieve, "Socialism in Rhode Island."

34. Alan Dawley, Class and Community: The Industrial Revolution in Lynn (Cambridge: Harvard University Press, 1976), 70; and Ira Katznelson, City Trenches: Urban Politics and the Patterning of Class in the United States (Chicago: University of Chicago Press, 1981), 64.

35. Richard Oestreicher, "Urban Working-Class Political Behavior and Theories of American Electoral Politics, 1870–1940," Journal of American History 74 (1988): 1276.

36. Visitor, 19 December 1913; and John D. Buenker, "Urban Liberalism in Rhode Island, 1909–1919," Rhode Island History 30 (1971): 45–46.

37. Visitor, 10 January 1913; and Justice, 17 November 1894.

38. Visitor, 29 October 1926; and Journal, 9 March 1911.

39. Justice, 23 March 1895; Gilkeson, Middle-Class Providence, 200–201; Sara M. Algeo, The Story of a Sub-Pioneer (Providence: Snow and Farnham, 1925), 237; and Journal, 9 March 1911.

40. John D. Buenker, "The Politics of Resistance: The Rural-Based Yankee Republican Machines of Connecticut and Rhode Island," New England Quarterly 47 (1974): 223. My estimate of sixty repeal bills is based on evidence from newspaper accounts, secondary sources, and legislative records at RISA.

41. Journal, 9 March 1911, 9 June 1912; and Labor Advocate, 22 September 1912.

42. Alexander Keyssar, The Right to Vote: The Contested History of Democracy in the United States (New York: Basic Books, 2000), 133, 167–68; Buenker, "Urban Liberalism," 39; Labor Advocate, 29 March 1914; and William P. Sheffield, The Qualifications and Duties of an Elector: The Method of Altering a Constitution and of Representation in Legislative Assembly (Newport: Ward, 1907), 5.

43. Bureau of Industrial Statistics, Census of the Foreign-Born Population of Rhode Island, Bulletin 1: Part 1 of the Annual Report for 1907 (Providence: E. L. Freeman, 1907), 1081; Buenker, "Urban Liberalism," 39; and Union Worker Magazine, March 1914, 6.

44. Keyssar, Right to Vote, 120–23, 128–29, 136–46, 168–69, table A.12.

45. David H. Bennett, The Party of Fear: The American Far Right from Nativism to the Militia Movement, 2d ed. (New York: Vintage, 1995), 179–80; and John Higham, Strangers in the Land: Patterns of American Nativism, 1860–1925, 2d ed. (New York: Atheneum, 1963), chaps. 5–7.

46. Algeo, Story of a Sub-Pioneer, 14, 26, 34, 37, 39, 47, 51, 92, 112–13, 119, 250–51.

47. William G. McLoughlin, Rhode Island: A History (New York: W. W. Norton, 1986), 160; and Algeo, Story of a Sub-Pioneer, 104–5, 123, 128–29, 147, 152, 182–83, 190–91, 235–37.

48. Algeo, Story of a Sub-Pioneer, 143, 152, 162, 164, 276–79.

49. John D. Buenker, "The Urban Political Machine and Woman Suffrage: A Study in Political Adaptability," Historian 33 (1971): 265–66; Journal, 21 October 1898, 15 March 1911; Labor Advocate, 29 March 1914; and Algeo, Story of a Sub-Pioneer, 95, 188–89.

50. Labor Advocate, 26 October 1913, 22 February 1914.

51. Journal, 3 March 1910; and Algeo, Story of a Sub-Pioneer, 181–84.

52. General Assembly, "Resolutions Introduced in the House" (15 March 1912, 12 March 1913), and "Resolutions Introduced in the Senate" (29 January 1915), Rhode Island State Library; Buenker, "Urban Liberalism," 40; and Visitor, 26 November 1904, 30 October 1914.

53. Journal, 9 March 1911; Labor Advocate, 29 March, 10, 17 October 1914; Buenker, "Urban Liberalism," 43; Algeo, Story of a Sub-Pioneer, 242; Hartwell, "Political Extremism," 58–59; and Buenker, "Politics of Resistance," 216.

54. *Minor v. Happersett*, 88 U.S. 627 (1875).

55. Algeo, *Story of a Sub-Pioneer*, 209.

56. Joseph W. Sullivan, *Marxists, Militants, and Macaroni: The I.W.W. in Providence's Little Italy* (Kingston: Rhode Island Labor History Society, 2000), 29, 51, 53–58, 61–62, 70, 79, 87; Buhle, "Italian-American Radicals," 138; and Joseph W. Sullivan, " 'Every Shot a Cannon Ball': The IWW and Urban Disorders in Providence, 1912–1914," *Rhode Island History* 54 (1996): 62.

57. J. Ellyn des Jardins, "Federal Hill House: Its Place in Providence and the Settlement Movement," *Rhode Island History* 54 (1996): 107; Elizabeth Ewen, *Immigrant Women in the Land of Dollars: Life and Culture on the Lower East Side, 1890–1925* (New York: Monthly Review Press, 1985), 176; and Buhle, "Italian-American Radicals," 137.

58. Sullivan, *Marxists, Militants, and Macaroni*, 30–50, 52–53, 82–84.

CHAPTER 5. ETHNIC COMMUNITIES AND THE CATHOLIC CHURCH

1. *Visitor*, 12 May 1922.

2. Bureau of Industrial Statistics, *Church Statistics and Religious Preference, Bulletin 2: Part 1 of the Annual Report for 1907* (Providence: E. L. Freeman, 1907), 274–75. Because the 1905 census does not distinguish between French and British Canadians, it is impossible to determine what proportion of French Canadians identified as Catholic; but it is likely this number would have been close to 100 percent.

3. Bureau of the Census, *Religious Bodies: 1906. Part I* (Washington, D.C.: GPO, 1910), 480, 482; School Committee, *Report of the School Committee for the Year 1918–1919* (Providence: Providence Press, 1919), 71; and Joel Perlmann, *Ethnic Differences: Schooling and Social Structure among the Irish, Italians, Jews, and Blacks in an American City, 1880–1935* (New York: Cambridge University Press, 1988), 68–69.

4. *Journal*, 20 December 1891; Bureau of the Census, *Religious Bodies: 1906*, 24; idem, *Religious Bodies: 1926. Part I* (Washington, D.C.: GPO, 1930), 16; and idem, *Religious Bodies: 1936. Part I* (Washington, D.C.: GPO, 1941), 20. Certain Protestant denominations limited membership to people who made a conscious decision to become baptized and join a congregation. Rabbis initially counted as members only heads of families (usually men), but beginning in 1926 they included "all persons of the Jewish faith living in communities in which local congregations are situated." To achieve some consistency in its numbers, the federal religious census (taken in 1890 and then decennially beginning in 1906) limited its counts to people age nine (the typical age of a Catholic first communion) and older and, later, thirteen and older.

5. Robert Hayman, telephone conversation with author, 27 January 1998; Jay P. Dolan, *The American Catholic Experience: A History from Colonial Times to the Present* (Notre Dame: University of Notre Dame Press, 1992), 207; and Minutes (22 October 1920), Rhode Island Council of United Church Women Papers, RIHS.

6. Historians have debated whether immigrants simply replicated their places of worship or adapted them to serve their needs in the new world. For the former position see Oscar Handlin, *The Uprooted: The Epic Story of the Great Migrations That Made the American People* (Boston: Little, Brown, 1952), chap. 5. For the latter see John Bodnar, *The Transplanted: A History of Immigrants in Urban America* (Bloomington: Indiana University Press, 1985), chap. 5.

7. Dolan, *American Catholic Experience*, 204, 207–8; David M. Emmons, *The Butte Irish: Class and Ethnicity in an American Mining Town, 1875–1925* (Urbana: University of Illinois Press, 1989), 97; and John T. McGreevy, *Parish Boundaries: The Catholic Encounter with Race in the Twentieth-Century Urban North* (Chicago: University of Chicago Press, 1996), 13.

8. For more on religious conversion as a means of Americanization and upward mobility, see Kristen Petersen Farmelant, "Trophies of Grace: Religious Conversion and Americanization in Boston's Immigrant Communities, 1890–1940" (Ph.D. diss., Brown University, 2001), chap. 5.

9. *Le Jean-Baptiste,* 23 January 1903; Richard A. Walsh, *The Centennial History of Saint Edward Church, Providence, Rhode Island, 1874–1974* (n.p., n.d.), 54; *50th Anniversary, 1907–1957. Golden Jubilee. St. Bartholomew's Parish. Providence, Rhode Island* (n.p., n.d.); *Visitor,* 22 May 1935; and John F. Sullivan and Vincenzo F. Kienberger, *Storia della Parrocchia di S. Anna, Providence, R.I. In Occasione del Giubileo d'Argente Sacerdotale del Parroco, 1900–1925* (n.p., n.d.), 18.

10. Jay P. Dolan, *The Immigrant Church: New York's Irish and German Catholics, 1815–1865* (Notre Dame: University of Notre Dame Press, 1975), 118–19; Leslie Woodcock Tentler, *Seasons of Grace: A History of the Catholic Archdiocese of Detroit* (Detroit: Wayne State University Press, 1990), 239, 245; Sullivan and Kienberger, *Storia della Parrocchia,* 18; "Report of St. Ann's Day Nursery and Industrial School, 1918," St. Ann's Papers, PCDA; Robert W. Hayman, *Catholicism in Rhode Island and the Diocese of Providence, 1886–1921* (Providence: Diocese of Providence, 1995), 507–8; and John H. McKenna, *The Centenary Story of Old St. Mary's, Pawtucket, R.I., 1829–1929* (Providence: Providence Visitor Press, 1929), 46.

11. J. Ellyn des Jardins, "Federal Hill House: Its Place in Providence and the Settlement Movement," *Rhode Island History* 54 (1996): 102–4; Paula Kane, *Separatism and Subculture: Boston Catholicism, 1900–1920* (Chapel Hill: University of North Carolina Press, 1994), 56; *Journal,* 11 September, 30 October 1910; and Sullivan and Kienberger, *Storia della Parrocchia,* 17–18 (Gainer quotation), 28.

12. Hayman, *Catholicism, 1886–1921,* 214.

13. *Le Jean-Baptiste,* 25 June 1902.

14. Walsh, *Saint Edward Church,* 55–56; *Visitor,* 25 February 1905; John P. McGuire, *History of Holy Trinity Parish. Central Falls, Rhode Island* (privately printed, 1939), 46–47; and Jolly to Harkins, Pawtucket, 12 April 1910, Ancient Order of Hibernians Papers, PCDA.

15. Robert A. Orsi, *The Madonna of 115th Street: Faith and Community in Italian Harlem, 1880–1950* (New Haven: Yale University Press, 1985), xiii; and McGreevy, *Parish Boundaries,* 22.

16. *Bulletin,* 2 January 1909; and Dolan, *Immigrant Church,* 162.

17. Thomas F. Cullen, *The Catholic Church in Rhode Island* (North Providence: The Franciscan Missionaries of Mary, 1936), 452–56; McKenna, *Old St. Mary's,* 45–46; and Stephen Almagno, *The Days of Our Years. Saint Bartholomew's Parish, Providence, Rhode Island, 1907–1969* (n.p., n.d.), 21.

18. Walsh, *Saint Edward Church,* 44, 63; and *Our Lady of Consolation Parish, Pawtucket, Rhode Island* (South Hackensack, N.J.: Custombook, 1975), 9.

19. Walsh, *Saint Edward Church,* 134–49; *La Campana di Silver Lake,* June 1928, St. Bartholomew's Papers, Center for Migration Studies of New York (hereafter cited as CMSNY); and *Our Lady of Consolation,* 9.

20. Dolan, *American Catholic Experience,* 205, 211–20; and Tentler, *Seasons of Grace,* 169–70, 174–82, 228.

21. *Providence Tribune,* 29 November 1914; and *Journal,* 30 October 1910.

22. Tentler, *Seasons of Grace,* 168, 186, 200–11; Walsh, *Saint Edward Church,* 40, 130; *Visitor,* 7 January 1909, 17 January 1913, 19 September 1919; Dolan, *American Catholic Experience,* 232; and Kane, *Separatism and Subculture,* 79, 80–82.

23. Walsh, *Saint Edward Church,* 50; *La Campana,* 19 January 1936; and *St. Patrick's Parish, 1841–1973. A Brief History* (Providence: Service Plus Press, 1973).

24. *La Campana,* June 1927; and Walsh, *Saint Edward Church,* 41–42. For more on the CTAU, see John F. Quinn, "Father Mathew's Disciples: American Catholic Support for Temperance, 1840–1920," *Church History* 65 (1996): 624–40.

25. Dolan, *American Catholic Experience,* 256; Hayman, *Catholicism, 1886–1921,* 606–7; and Walsh, *Saint Edward Church,* 52–53.

26. Hayman, *Catholicism, 1886–1921,* 608–10, 703; *Call,* 4 November 1912; and *Visitor,* 14 June, 27 September 1918, 11 May 1923.

27. Walsh, *Saint Edward Church*, 94; *Visitor*, 26 January 1907; and St. Mary's Card (26 December 1918), "Holy Name Society, Pennsylvania-Wisconsin," Men's and Women's Committee, Committee on Special War Activities (hereafter cited as MWC Papers), National Catholic War Council Papers (hereafter cited as WC Papers), Catholic University of America (hereafter cited as CUA).

28. Dolan, *American Catholic Experience*, 110–11, 165–94; Dolan, *Immigrant Church*, 48–50, 164; and Tentler, *Seasons of Grace*, 58, 72–74, 128–29, 152, 219–24, 425–26.

29. Dolan, *American Catholic Experience*, 179; Thomas V. Cassidy, *Saint Mary Church of Pawtucket, Rhode Island: A Sesquicentennial Story, 1829–1979* (n.p., n.d.), 47; "Minutes of the Holy Ghost Corporation," Holy Ghost Parish File, CMSNY; and Leslie Woodcock Tentler, "On the Margins: The State of American Catholic History," *American Quarterly* 45 (1993): 109.

30. Dolan, *American Catholic Experience*, 194; Kane, *Separatism and Subculture*, 206; Tentler, *Seasons of Grace*, 228, 391; McGreevy, *Parish Boundaries*, 15; Edward H. Divine and Thomas Quinn to Harkins, Providence, 19 May 1899, and Thomas Leahy to Harkins, Bristol, 8 July 1899, Catholic Total Abstinence Union Papers, PCDA.

31. *Visitor*, 23 January 1904. These observations about lay autonomy are drawn from correspondence in the following organizational and parish files at PCDA: Knights of Columbus, National Council of Catholic Women, Our Lady of Lourdes, Providence Catholic Women's Club, St. Michael's, Union of Catholic Parish Clubs, and West Warwick Catholic Women's Club.

32. Dolan, *American Catholic Experience*, 233, 324, 328–29; Tentler, *Seasons of Grace*, 64–65, 179, 213–18; Kane, *Separatism and Subculture*, 96; *Constitution, By-Laws and Rules of Order of the Catholic Total Abstinence Union of the Diocese of Providence* (Providence: C. W. Littell, 1886), 11–12; and *Constitution of the Queen's Daughters*, 1, Queen's Daughters Papers, PCDA. Names of the members of these societies appeared in *Le Jean-Baptiste*, 8 January 1904, and *Visitor*, 17 March 1911 and 28 April 1922. Information about these individuals in the following paragraphs comes from city directories and tax lists and the 1920 federal census (all at RIHS) and the 1905 state census (at RISA).

33. *Visitor*, 17 March 1911.

34. Ibid., 28 April, 19 May 1922, 11 May 1923.

35. Kane, *Separatism and Subculture*, 101. The concept of a Catholic "subculture" comes from Kane.

36. Dolan, *American Catholic Experience*, 234, 238–39; unidentified newspaper article, Holy Ghost Parish File; and *Visitor*, 31 May 1902.

37. *Visitor*, 28 March 1903; *Providence News*, 2 April 1928; *La Campana*, June 1927, June 1928, 5 August, 25 November 1934; *Le Jean-Baptiste*, 27 November 1903; and Walsh, *Saint Edward Church*, 116–17. The format for *La Campana* citations varies because the parish bulletin alternated between a monthly and a weekly format.

38. Dolan, *American Catholic Experience*, 214; *One Hundred Years: St. Michael's Parish, 1859–1959* (n.p., 1959); Cullen, *Catholic Church*, 443–44, 446; Walsh, *Saint Edward Church*, 43; *The Queen's Daughters. Twenty-Fifth Anniversary* (n.p., 1933), Queen's Daughters Papers, PCDA; and *Visitor*, 12 February 1915.

39. McGreevy, *Parish Boundaries*, 13, 19–21; and Dolan, *American Catholic Experience*, 204.

40. *Visitor*, 17 April 1897, 14 May 1915; Catholic Order of Foresters 948 card, "Catholic Order of Foresters, Pennsylvania-South Dakota," MWC; Joanna J. Melodia to Bishop William Hickey, Providence, 9 January 1932, Holy Ghost Papers, PCDA (hereafter cited as HG Papers); Kane, *Separatism and Subculture*, 96–97; and Providence Branch 53, Knights of America Card, "Catholic Knights of America: Oregon-Tennessee," MWC.

41. Kane, *Separatism and Subculture*, 97; *Visitor*, 3 March 1916; and Scott Molloy, "No Philanthropy at the Point of Production: A Knight of St. Gregory against the Knights of Labor in the New England Rubber Industry, 1885," *Labor History* 44 (May 2003): 205–6, 230–31.

42. Kane, *Separatism and Subculture*, 201–2.

43. McGreevy, *Parish Boundaries*, 28; and Kane, *Separatism and Subculture*, 112.

CHAPTER 6. PARISH ACTIVITY AND POLITICAL ACTIVISM

1. Leslie Woodcock Tentler, "Present at the Creation: Working-Class Catholics in the United States," in *American Exceptionalism? U.S. Working-Class Formation in an International Context*, ed. Rick Halpern and Jonathan Morris (New York: St. Martin's Press, 1997), 138; Robert W. Hayman, *Catholicism in Rhode Island and the Diocese of Providence, 1780–1886* (Providence: Diocese of Providence, 1982), 22; *The Church of the Blessed Sacrament in Providence, Rhode Island, Celebrates Its First One Hundred Years, 1888–1988* (n.p., n.d.), 23; *St. Matthew's Church, Central Falls, Rhode Island, 1906–1981* (South Hackensack, N.J.: Custombook, 1981), 4–5; *Journal*, 30 October 1910; and *Saint Michael's Parish, 1859–1984: One Hundred Twenty-Five Years* (n.p., n.d.).

2. *Blessed Sacrament*, 28–29; Richard A. Walsh, *The Centennial History of Saint Edward Church, Providence, Rhode Island, 1874–1974* (n.p., n.d.), 53, 99; and John P. McGuire, *History of Holy Trinity Parish, Central Falls, Rhode Island* (privately printed, 1939), 36–40.

3. Paula Kane, *Separatism and Subculture: Boston Catholicism, 1900–1920* (Chapel Hill: University of North Carolina Press, 1994), 216; *Call*, 4 November 1912; *Visitor*, 4 November 1921, 9 March 1923, 2 March 1928; C. Loretta Nolan to Bishop Hickey, West Warwick, undated, West Warwick Catholic Women's Club Papers, PCDA; Walsh, *Saint Edward Church*, 138; and Michael L. Coffey to Hickey, 19 September 1930, Holy Name Society Papers, PCDA (hereafter cited as HNS Papers).

4. *Blessed Sacrament*, 29; Walsh, *Saint Edward Church*, 52, 98; and *Visitor*, 26 January 1917.

5. *Constitution of the Queen's Daughters*, Queen's Daughters Papers, PCDA; *Constitution, Laws and Rules of the Catholic Daughters of America, Adopted April 2, 1904, with Amendments to and Including the Year 1946* (n.p., n.d.), Catholic Daughters of America Papers, PCDA; *Constitution and By-Laws of the Catholic Women's Club of West Warwick* (n.p., n.d.), 8, West Warwick Catholic Women's Club Papers; and Coffey to Hickey.

6. Walsh, *Saint Edward Church*, 49–50; *Visitor*, 19 December 1908, 19 October, 16 November 1917; and Jay P. Dolan, *The American Catholic Experience: A History from Colonial Times to the Present* (Notre Dame: University of Notre Dame Press, 1992), 233.

7. Walsh, *Saint Edward Church*, 53; and *Visitor*, 18 February 1916, 4 June 1920.

8. Paula Baker, "The Domestication of Politics: Women and American Political Society, 1780–1920," *American Historical Review* 89 (1984): 630–32; Kane, *Separatism and Subculture*, 202–5, 218, 249; Leslie Woodcock Tentler, *Seasons of Grace: A History of the Catholic Archdiocese of Detroit* (Detroit: Wayne State University Press, 1990), 76–79, 226–27; and *Constitution and By-Laws*, 3.

9. Kane, *Separatism and Subculture*, 203.

10. *Journal*, 17 December 1936; *Visitor*, 5 December 1919, 30 October 1925; *News Sheet to Organizations*, January 1927, National Council of Catholic Women Papers (hereafter cited as NCCW Papers, CUA), National Catholic Welfare Conference Papers (hereafter cited as NCWC Papers), CUA; and *Telegram*, 8 February 1920.

11. Mary Carey McAvoy, "Isabelle Ahearn O'Neill: Little Rhody's Lone Theodora," *Woman's Voice* 26 (March 1931): 12, 31; Katherine Gregg, "Isabelle Ahearn O'Neill: A Starring Role at the State House," in *Women in Rhode Island History* (Providence: Providence Journal Co., 1994), 16; "Autobiography" and "Scrapbook, 1897–1918," Isabelle Ahearn O'Neill Papers, RIHS; and *Visitor*, 9 March 1923.

12. *Visitor*, 25 July 1913, 5 February 1928.

13. Thomas Williams Bicknell, *The History of the State of Rhode Island and Providence Plantations* (New York: American Historical Society, 1920), 4:36; *Journal*, 29 January, 19 February

1894; Evelyn Sterne, "All Americans: The Politics of Citizenship in Providence, 1840–1940" (Ph.D. diss., Duke University, 1999), 90–91; Scott Molloy, *Trolley Wars: Streetcar Workers on the Line* (Washington, D.C.: Smithsonian Institution Press, 1996), 167; and *Visitor*, 5 August 1910, 2 March 1928.

14. *Visitor*, 28 April 1977; and David A. Gerber, *The Making of an American Pluralism: Buffalo, New York, 1825–1860* (Urbana: University of Illinois Press, 1989), 323–24.

15. Bureau of Industrial Statistics, *Church Statistics and Religious Preference, Bulletin 2: Part 1 of the Annual Report for 1907* (Providence: E. L. Freeman, 1907), 274; and *Visitor*, 15 September 1906, 27 April 1907.

16. Timothy J. Meagher, *Inventing Irish America: Generation, Class, and Ethnic Identity in a New England City, 1880–1928* (Notre Dame: University of Notre Dame Press, 2001), 269; *The AFCS: Brief Statement of Its Aims and Purposes* (Kaukauna, Wis.: Sun Print, n.d.), George J. Lucas, *The Importance of Federation* (n.p., n.d.), and *Proceedings of the Executive Board Sessions of the AFCS* (Cincinnati: Jos. Berning, 1905), 26, AFCS Papers, University of Notre Dame Archives.

17. James Hennesey, *American Catholics: A History of the Roman Catholic Community in the United States* (New York: Oxford University Press, 1981), 207; Dale T. Knobel, *"America for the Americans": The Nativist Movement in the United States* (New York: Twayne, 1996), 239–41; and Tentler, *Seasons of Grace*, 272.

18. *Proceedings* (1905), 23–24; Lucas, *Importance of Federation; Proceedings of the Fourth National Convention of the AFCS* (Cincinnati: Jos. Berning, 1904), 55; *Brief Statement; Proceedings of the Second National Convention of the AFCS* (Cincinnati: Jos. Berning, 1902), 14; and Sam Bullock to Harkins, Providence, 6 August 1906, Goddard Campaign Committee Papers, PCDA.

19. Robert W. Hayman, *Catholicism in Rhode Island and the Diocese of Providence, 1886–1921* (Providence: Diocese of Providence, 1995), 667; *Journal*, 17 September 1927; and Mary Josephine Bannon, ed., *Autobiographic Memoirs of Hon. Patrick J. McCarthy* (Providence: Providence Visitor Press, 1927), 112, 191–93.

20. Gorman to Harkins, Providence, 11 March 1910, Rhode Island Federation of Catholic Clubs Papers, PCDA; and *Visitor*, 13 May, 1 July, 23 September 1910.

21. Tentler, *Seasons of Grace*, 209–11; *Digest of the Minutes of the First Annual Convention of the Archdiocesan and Diocesan Spiritual Directors of the Holy Name Society of the United States and Canada* (n.p., 1929), 4, HNS Papers; Sandra Yokum Mize, "Dietz, Peter E.," in *The Encyclopedia of American Catholic History*, ed. Michael Glazier and Thomas J. Shelley (Collegeville, Minn.: Liturgical Press, 1997), 434–35; *Bulletin of the AFCS*, March 1915, 1; and Kane, *Separatism and Subculture*, 3. The AFCS's priorities included stamping out socialism and promoting mainstream unionism, enacting pro-worker legislation, defeating the proposed literacy test for immigrants, strengthening divorce laws, censoring "indecent" literature and movies, obtaining public funds for parochial schools, and securing priests' rights to administer sacraments in public institutions such as prisons.

22. *Visitor*, 30 October 1914, 13 October 1916, 29 October 1926.

23. Ibid., 10 October 1908, 25 April, 8 December 1922; *Le Jean-Baptiste*, 10 January 1902; and *Constitution et Lois Generales des Forestiers Franco-Americains* (n.p., n.d.), 5–6, Franco-American Foresters Papers, PCDA.

24. *Visitor*, 21 June 1902, 17 December 1904.

25. Charles R. Morris, *American Catholic: The Saints and Sinners Who Built America's Most Powerful Church* (New York: Vintage, 1997), 150–51; Ken Fones-Wolf, *Trade Union Gospel: Christianity and Labor in Industrial Philadelphia, 1865–1915* (Philadelphia: Temple University Press, 1989); Dolan, *American Catholic Experience*, 329–40, 342–43; and *Visitor*, 8 November 1902.

26. Visitor, 5 July 1902, 13 February 1904, 9 September 1910, 27 April 1934; *Journal*, 24 March

1902; *Telegram,* 24 March 1902; Eugene Benoit and Charles A. Winsor to Hickey, Woonsocket, 2 October 1924, Woonsocket Central Labor Union Papers, PCDA.

27. *Visitor,* 2, 9 September 1910.

28. Scott Molloy, "No Philanthropy at the Point of Production: A Knight of St. Gregory against the Knights of Labor in the New England Rubber Industry, 1885," Labor History 44 (May 2003): 209; *Journal,* 29 October 1937; Mel Piehl, *Breaking Bread: The Catholic Worker and the Origin of Catholic Radicalism in America* (Philadelphia: Temple University Press, 1982), 36; Hayman, *Catholicism, 1886–1921,* 703; and *Call,* 16 November 1912.

29. James Scott, *Weapons of the Weak: Everyday Forms of Peasant Resistance* (New Haven: Yale University Press, 1985); *Union Worker Magazine,* June 1908, 6; *Labor Advocate,* 15 January 1913; and *Visitor,* 19 December 1913.

30. *Union Worker Magazine,* March 1913, 10.

31. *Bulletin,* 16 July 1906; and *Journal,* 17 July 1906.

32. *Visitor,* 23 September 1910, 3 October 1913, 28 September 1928; and *Le Jean-Baptiste,* 28 September 1928.

33. For discussions of ways in which religion both strengthened and weakened labor activism, see Fones-Wolf, *Trade Union Gospel;* Jama Lazerow, *Religion and the Working Class in Antebellum America* (Washington, D.C.: Smithsonian Institution Press, 1995); Teresa Anne Murphy, *Ten Hours' Labor: Religion, Reform, and Gender in Early New England* (Ithaca: Cornell University Press, 1992); and Mark S. Schantz, *Piety in Providence: Class Dimensions of Religious Experience in Antebellum Rhode Island* (Ithaca: Cornell University Press, 2000).

34. Hugh McLeod, *Religion and the Working Class in Nineteenth-Century Britain* (London: Macmillan, 1984), 53.

CHAPTER 7. CATHOLICS AND THE FIRST WORLD WAR

1. John Higham, *Strangers in the Land: Patterns of American Nativism, 1860–1925,* 2d ed. (New York: Atheneum, 1963), 215, 217, 248; David H. Bennett, *The Party of Fear: The American Far Right from Nativism to the Militia Movement,* 2d ed. (New York: Vintage, 1995), 183; Dale T. Knobel, *"America for the Americans": The Nativist Movement in the United States* (New York: Twayne, 1996), 246–47; and David M. Kennedy, *Over Here: The First World War and American Society* (New York: Oxford University Press, 1980), 68, 73.

2. Commissioner of Labor, *Report of Commissioner of Labor Made to the General Assembly for the Years 1916–1917–1918–1919* (Providence: E. L. Freeman, 1921), 267–69, 272–73; Bureau of the Census, *Thirteenth Census of the United States Taken in the Year 1910: Abstract* (Washington, D.C.: GPO, 1913), 486; and Bureau of the Census, *Thirteenth Census of the United States Taken in the Year 1910: Volume I. Population* (Washington, D.C.: GPO, 1913), 1283.

3. Commissioner of Labor, *Report,* 268–69; and *Le Jean-Baptiste,* 9 April 1915.

4. One could argue that older immigrants like the Irish had become "old stock" by the First World War, but for the purposes of distinguishing the city's ethnic Catholic majority from its Anglo-Saxon Protestant minority, the term "new stock" will be used here to refer to Irish, French Canadian, and Italian Catholics as well as Jews and other newer ethnic groups.

5. Higham, *Strangers in the Land,* 218; Bennett, *Party of Fear,* 184–85; Gerald P. Fogarty, *The Vatican and the American Hierarchy from 1870 to 1965* (Wilmington, Del.: Michael Glazier, 1985), 195–207; and James Hennesey, *American Catholics: A History of the Roman Catholic Community in the United States* (New York: Oxford University Press, 1981), 227–28.

6. *Visitor,* 2 June 1916; and *Journal,* 4 June 1916.

7. Secretary of State, *Acts and Resolves Passed by the General Assembly of the State of Rhode Island and Providence Plantations, at the January Session,* A.D. 1917 (Providence: E. L. Freeman, 1917), 379; Common Council, *Resolutions and Orders of the Common Council of the City of Providence. January, 1916, to January, 1917* (Providence: Providence Printing, 1917), 303; and "An-

nual Report, 1917–18," Minutes, Executive Board and General Federation Meetings, Rhode Island State Federation of Women's Clubs Papers, RIHS (hereafter cited as RISFWC Papers).

8. Donna Thomas, "The *Providence Visitor* and Nativist Issues, 1916–1924," *Rhode Island History* 38 (1979): 55; John D. Buenker, "Urban Liberalism in Rhode Island, 1909–1919," *Rhode Island History* 30 (1971): 50; and General Assembly, *Acts and Resolves of the General Assembly, May 1856* (Providence: A. Crawford Greene and Brother, 1856), 101–2.

9. Hennesey, *American Catholics*, 222–24, 26; *Bulletin of the AFCS*, May 1917, 1, and January 1918, 1; and *Handbook of the National Catholic War Council* (Washington, D.C.: National Catholic War Council, 1918), 7–8.

10. *Handbook*, 9–12, 42–43; Hennesey, *American Catholics*, 226; Michael Williams, *American Catholics in the War: The National Catholic War Council, 1917–1921* (New York: Macmillan, 1921), 219, 228; and *Visitor*, 13 December 1918.

11. William H. Canfield to Michael J. Slattery, Providence, 18 September 1918, "Catholic Young Men's National Union: RI-Wisconsin," MWC Papers; Kennedy, *Over Here*, 61; James R. Cannon (26 August 1925), Biography Cards, Private Collection, Robert W. Hayman, Providence; St. Mary's Card (26 December 1918), "Holy Name Society: Pennsylvania-Wisconsin," and Joseph A. Hickey to Slattery, Providence, 15 October 1918, "Casa Maria—Catholic Ladies Literary Association," MWC Papers; and *Handbook*, 25.

12. *Handbook*, 14.

13. Hennesey, *American Catholics*, 228; "Report of the League of Catholic Women" (19 April 1917 to 1 September 1918), 1–3, Burke-Muldoon Papers, WC Papers (hereafter cited as Burke-Muldoon Papers); "Yearly Report: Catholic Young Women's Patriotic Club of the National Catholic War Council," 7–8, Burke-Muldoon Papers; *Visitor*, 17 May 1918; *Le Jean-Baptiste*, 27 July 1917; and "Report of the War Activities of the Queen's Daughters of Providence, RI" (3 May 1921), "Queen's Daughters—Missouri-Texas, 1921," MWC Papers.

14. *Visitor*, 6 September 1918.

15. *Le Jean-Baptiste*, 25 April 1917; and Commissioner of Labor, *Report*, 280.

16. Higham, *Strangers in the Land*, 234–45, 250.

17. Unidentified newspaper article (c. January 1917), General Activities Scrapbooks, RISFWC Papers.

18. Unidentified newspaper article (c. October 1916), General Activities Scrapbooks, RISFWC Papers.

19. *Telegram*, 4 July 1915.

20. *Journal*, 27 September 1914; and *Tribune*, 3 February 1916.

21. "Supplemental and Final Report," American Citizenship Campaign Committee Papers, RIHS; Commissioner of Labor, *Report*, 234–37; J. Ellyn des Jardins, "Federal Hill House: Its Place in Providence and the Settlement Movement," *Rhode Island History* 54 (1996): 101–6; John S. Gilkeson Jr., *Middle-Class Providence, 1820–1940* (Princeton: Princeton University Press, 1986), 247–56; and Minutes (23 November 1918), RISFWC Papers.

22. Commissioner of Labor, *Report*, 240; and School Committee, *Report of the School Committee for the Year 1914–1915* (Providence: Providence Press, 1915), 64.

23. School Committee, *Report of the School Committee for the Year 1915–1916* (Providence: Providence Press, 1916), 44, 47–48, 51; School Committee, *Report, 1914–1915*, 60–61; School Committee, *Report of the School Committee for the Year 1916–1917* (Providence: Providence Press, 1917), 89; and School Committee, *Report of the School Committee for the Year 1918–1919 (Providence: Providence Press, 1919)*, 20–21.

24. Commissioner of Labor, *Report*, 241, 271; and des Jardins, "Federal Hill House," 107–13.

25. *Bulletin*, 16 February 1918.

26. Jon Gjerde, *The Minds of the West: Ethnocultural Evolution in the Rural Middle West, 1830–1917* (Chapel Hill: University of North Carolina Press, 1997), 54, 66–67, 69.

27. Judith E. Smith, *Family Connections: A History of Italian and Jewish Immigrant Lives in*

Providence, Rhode Island, 1900–1940 (Albany: State University of New York Press, 1985), 132, 140; *Le Jean-Baptiste*, 4 December 1914, 28 February 1916; and *Visitor*, 29 September 1916.

28. Smith, *Family Connections*, 162; *Journal*, 8 December 1918, 21 December 1919; Commissioner of Labor, *Report*, 280; and Mark Wyman, *Round Trip to America: The Immigrants Return to Europe, 1880–1930* (Ithaca: Cornell University Press, 1993), 11.

29. *Telegram*, 24 May 1915.

30. *Visitor*, 26 February 1916.

31. Robert W. Hayman, *Catholicism in Rhode Island and the Diocese of Providence, 1886–1921* (Providence: Diocese of Providence, 1995), 507–8; and *Visitor*, 14 June 1918.

32. *Visitor*, 12 January, 20 July 1917, 2 August 1918; and Martin H. Glynn, *Catholic Patriotism in the United States* (1917), Pamphlet Collection, Rare Books and Special Collections, CUA.

33. *Visitor*, 12 January 1917.

34. Ibid., 23 December 1915, 5 January 1917.

35. *Le Jean-Baptiste*, 21 September 1917, 22 February, 6 July 1918; and *Visitor*, 16 June 1916, 20 April 1917.

36. *Journal*, 5 July 1917, 24 November 1918; "Annual Lawn Festival" Flyer (1918), St. Ann's Scrapbook, St. Rocco and St. Ann Churches, 1903–1970, CMSNY; *Bulletin*, 25 November 1918; and John F. Sullivan and Vincenzo F. Kienberger, *Storia della Parrocchia di S. Anna, Providence, R.I. In Occasione del Giubileo d'Argente Sacerdotale del Parroco, 1900–1925* (n.p., n.d.), 24.

37. *Visitor*, 18 March 1919.

38. Gary Gerstle, *Working-Class Americanism: The Politics of Labor in a Textile City, 1914–1960* (New York: Cambridge University Press, 1989), 9.

CHAPTER 8. AMERICANISM AND THE WARTIME STATE

1. David M. Kennedy, *Over Here: The First World War and American Society* (New York: Oxford University Press, 1980), 55, 65; and School Committee, *Report of the School Committee for the Year 1917–1918* (Providence: Providence Press, 1918), 13, 15.

2. *Visitor*, 19 January 1917; unidentified newspaper article (c. January 1917), General Activities Scrapbooks, RISFWC Papers; *Bulletin*, 9 February 1917; and School Committee, *Report of the School Committee for the Year 1916–1917* (Providence: Providence Press, 1917), 12–13.

3. Kennedy, *Over Here*, 145–46; School Committee, *Report of the School Committee for the Year 1914–1915* (Providence: Providence Press, 1915), 11–13; *Labor Advocate*, 29 May, 26 June, 10 July, 11 September 1915; and School Committee, *Report, 1916–1917*, 13, 44–45. See also Michael Pearlman, *To Make Democracy Safe for America: Patricians and Preparedness in the Progressive Era* (Urbana: University of Illinois Press, 1984).

4. *Labor Advocate*, 21 December 1913; *Visitor*, 12 August 1910. The annual *Providence Journal Almanac* records repeated votes in favor of a local license law.

5. John F. Quinn, "Father Mathew's Disciples: American Catholic Support for Temperance, 1840–1920," *Church History* 65 (1996): 640; James Hennesey, *American Catholics: A History of the Roman Catholic Community in the United States* (New York: Oxford University Press, 1981), 231–32; *Visitor*, 25 January, 15 March 1918; John D. Buenker, "Urban Liberalism in Rhode Island, 1909–1919," *Rhode Island History* 30 (1971): 50; *Le Jean-Baptiste*, 18 June 1920; and Donna Thomas, "The *Providence Visitor* and Nativist Issues, 1916–1924," *Rhode Island History* 38 (1979): 57.

6. *Bulletin of the AFCS*, November-December 1918, 3.

7. *Journal*, 18 April 1917; *Tribune*, 26 May 1918; *Bulletin*, 7 January 1920; and unidentified newspaper article (c. January 1920), General Activities Scrapbooks, RISFWC Papers.

8. *Journal*, 18 April 1917, 24 February 1918, 20 July 1919; and *Tribune*, 15 June, 20 July 1919. Information on Jenks comes from the 1920 census.

9. Buenker, "Urban Liberalism," 41–42.

10. Bureau of the Census, *Fourteenth Census of the United States Taken in the Year 1920: Volume III. Population* (Washington, D.C.: GPO, 1922), 916; and *Providence Journal Almanac, 1923* (Providence: Providence Journal Co., 1923), 161.

11. Joseph A. McCartin, *Labor's Great War: The Struggle for Industrial Democracy and the Origins of Modern American Labor Relations, 1912–1921* (Chapel Hill: University of North Carolina Press, 1997), chaps. 1 and 3, 104–18; Gary Gerstle, *Working-Class Americanism: The Politics of Labor in a Textile City, 1914–1960* (New York: Cambridge University Press, 1989), 45; and Joe McCartin, "The Textile Workers' 'Great War': The Rhode Island Loomfixers' Strike of 1918 and the Failure of Wartime Labor Organizing," in *Working in the Blackstone River Valley: Exploring the Heritage of Industrialization,* ed. Douglas M. Reynolds and Marjory Myers (Woonsocket: Rhode Island Labor History Society, 1991), 123, 128–29, 134–35.

12. Commissioner of Labor, *Report of Commissioner of Labor Made to the General Assembly for the Years 1916–1917–1918–1919* (Providence: E. L. Freeman, 1921), 49, 51, 125–205; Paul Buhle, "Italian-American Radicals and Labor in Rhode Island, 1905–1930," *Radical History Review* 17 (spring 1978): 139; and Norma LaSalle Daoust, "The Perils of Providence: Rhode Island's Capital City during the Depression and New Deal" (Ph.D. diss., University of Connecticut, 1982), 63–65. The Labor Commissioner's annual reports do not offer numbers on strike and union membership for 1914 and 1915.

13. McCartin, "Textile Workers' 'Great War,' " 128, 130–33.

14. Ibid., 135–37.

15. Ibid., 138–39; and Kennedy, *Over Here,* 271. For more on labor's postwar losses see McCartin, *Labor's Great War,* chap. 7.

16. *Bulletin,* 7 April 1919; and unidentified newspaper article (c. April 1919), General Activities Scrapbooks, RISFWC Papers.

17. *News,* 8 April 1919.

18. *Bulletin,* 8 April 1919.

19. John Higham, *Strangers in the Land: Patterns of American Nativism, 1860–1925,* 2d ed. (New York: Atheneum, 1963), 255–56. See also see Robert K. Murray, *Red Scare: A Study in National Hysteria, 1919–1920* (Minneapolis: University of Minnesota Press, 1955), and M. J. Heale, *American Anticommunism: Combating the Enemy Within, 1830–1970* (Baltimore: Johns Hopkins University Press, 1990).

20. Common Council, *Resolutions and Orders of the Common Council of the City of Providence: January, 1917, to January, 1918* (Providence: Providence Printing Co., 1918), 342; *Journal,* 7 September, 7 October 1917, 6 June 1919, 3, 4, 30 January 1920; Buhle, "Italian-American Radicals," 142; and Joseph W. Sullivan, *Marxists, Militants and Macaroni: The I.W.W. in Providence's Little Italy* (Kingston: Rhode Island Labor History Society, 2000), 96.

21. Higham, *Strangers in the Land,* 224, 250, 255; *Le Jean-Baptiste,* 19 September 1919; *Providence Jewish Chronicle,* 14 March 1919; and *Pastoral Letter of the Archbishops and Bishops of the United States Assembled in Conference at the Catholic University of America, September 1919* (Washington, D.C.: National Catholic War Council, 1920), 34.

22. *Visitor,* 28 March, 10 October 1919, 5 March 1920; *Jewish Chronicle,* 28 March 1919; and Dale T. Knobel, *"America for the Americans": The Nativist Movement in the United States* (New York: Twayne, 1996), 255.

23. *Bulletin of the Committee on American Citizenship,* May 1920, 1, Publications, Record Books and Scrapbooks, Rhode Island League of Women Voters Papers, RIHS (hereafter cited as RILWV Papers).

24. *Journal,* 24 February 1918, 26 October 1920; Sara M. Algeo, *The Story of a Sub-Pioneer* (Providence: Snow and Farnham, 1925), 251; and *Tribune,* 5 June 1919.

25. *Visitor,* 5 December 1919; Minutes (8 November 1919; 15 January, 21 January 1920), RISFWC Papers; and *Journal,* 17 January 1919.

26. School Committee, *Report of the School Committee for the Year 1919–1920* (Providence:

Providence Press, 1920), 26–27; General Assembly, *Acts and Resolves Passed by the General Assembly of the State of Rhode Island and Providence Plantations, at the January Session,* A.D. 1919 (Pawtucket: Pawtucket Linotyping, 1919), 212–14; Sara Errington, " 'The Language Question': Nativism, Politics, and Ethnicity in Rhode Island," in *New England's Disharmony: The Consequences of the Industrial Revolution,* ed. Douglas M. Reynolds and Katheryn Viens (Kingston: Rhode Island Labor History Society, 1993), 97–98; and Higham, *Strangers in the Land,* 260.

27. Bureau of the Census, *1910 Census: Abstract,* 586; idem, *1910 Census,* 1: 1283; idem, *1920 Census,* 3: 916; and idem, *Fourteenth Census of the United States Taken in the Year 1920: Volume II. Population* (Washington, D.C.: GPO, 1922), 1201.

28. Bureau of the Census, *1920 Census,* 2: 351, 1201; idem, *1920 Census,* 3: 916; *Bulletin,* 10 June 1921; *Journal,* 30 May 1921; and School Committee, *Report, 1919–1920,* 27.

29. David H. Bennett, *The Party of Fear: The American Far Right from Nativism to the Militia Movement,* 2d ed. (New York: Vintage, 1995), 194, 197; *Journal,* 6 October 1919; and *Visitor,* 17 January 1919.

30. *Tribune,* 5 June 1919.

31. "Untitled Publicity Document," Americanization File, Reconstruction Committee, Council on Special War Activities, WC Papers (hereafter cited as RC Papers).

32. "Program" (4 February 1919) and "Address by Dr. O'Grady at Americanization Conference" (12–15 May 1919), 1, 4, Americanization File; and *Bulletin of the AFCS,* March-April 1919, 2.

33. *Visitor,* 16 July, 20 November 1920; and *Rhode Island Jewish Review,* 16 July 1920.

34. Gary Gerstle, "Liberty, Coercion, and the Making of Americans," *Journal of American History* 84 (1997): 556–58.

35. Gerstle, *Working-Class Americanism,* 8–9.

CHAPTER 9. CATHOLICS IN THE POSTWAR WORLD

1. *Il Corriere del Rhode Island,* 17 July, 14 August 1920 (translated by Robert W. Hayman); Robert W. Hayman, *Catholicism in Rhode Island and the Diocese of Providence, 1886–1921* (Providence: Diocese of Providence, 1995), 211; and *Journal,* 14 October, 8 November 1920.

2. Holy Name Society of Holy Ghost to Donato Sbarretti, Providence, 19 September 1921 (trans. Hayman), HG Papers; and Hayman, *Catholicism, 1886–1921,* 210.

3. *The Parish of the Holy Ghost, Providence, Rhode Island, 1889–1989: 100th Anniversary* (Tappan, N.Y.: Custombook, 1989), 19; Hayman, *Catholicism, 1886–1921,* 210; and Societa di Mutuo Soccorso Maria S.S. Del Carmine to Harkins, Providence, 23 September 1906, HG Papers.

4. Hayman, *Catholicism, 1886–1921,* 190; Holy Name Society to Sbarretti; and Irene De Battista et al. to Hickey, Providence, c. June 1920, HG Papers.

5. Enrico Bellifante to Hickey, Providence, 18 June 1920, Holy Ghost Parishioners to Hickey, Providence, 14 January 1921, and R.S. to Hickey, Providence, 12 July 1920 (trans. Hayman), HG Papers; and *Il Corriere,* 14 August 1920 (trans. Hayman). For a discussion of the religious implications of the Italian American home, or "domus," see Robert A. Orsi, *The Madonna of 115th Street: Faith and Community in Italian Harlem, 1880–1950* (New Haven: Yale University Press, 1985), chap. 4.

6. John Zuccarelli, "The Priest the Immigrants Did Not Want," *Rhode Island Echo,* 2 February 1978; Holy Ghost Parishioners to Hickey; Antonio Ciaveglio to Hickey, Providence, 2 August 1920, HG Papers; Hayman, *Catholicism, 1886–1921,* 211, 213; and Linda Perrotta, conversation with author, 16 February 2002.

7. The sample is taken from the longest surviving petition, bearing 626 names and submitted by Italian-born jeweler Mauro Corona: Mauro M. Corona et al. to Hickey, Providence, 17 January 1921, HG Papers.

8. Peter D'Agostino, "Clerical 'Birds of Passage' in the Italian Emigrant Church" (paper pre-

sented at the annual meeting of the Organization of American Historians, Indianapolis, Ind., April 1998), 16.

9. *L'Eco del Rhode Island*, 18 November 1920 (trans. Hayman); *Il Corriere*, 17 July 1920 (trans. Hayman); and Jon Gjerde, *The Minds of the West: Ethnocultural Evolution in the Rural Middle West, 1830–1917* (Chapel Hill: University of North Carolina Press, 1997), 127.

10. Charles R. Morris, *American Catholic: The Saints and Sinners Who Built America's Most Powerful Church* (New York: Vintage, 1997), 135; and Douglas J. Slawson, "National Catholic Welfare Conference," in *The Encyclopedia of American Catholic History*, ed. Michael Glazier and Thomas J. Shelley (Collegeville, Minn.: Liturgical Press, 1997), 1005–7. In 1967 the NCWC was reorganized as the United States Catholic Conference. For more on the NCWC's early years, see Douglas J. Slawson, *The Foundation and First Decade of the National Catholic Welfare Council* (Washington, D.C.: Catholic University of America Press, 1992).

11. Jay P. Dolan, *The American Catholic Experience: A History from Colonial Times to the Present* (Notre Dame: University of Notre Dame Press, 1992), 352; and Morris, *American Catholic*, 162–64.

12. *Handbook of the National Catholic War Council* (Washington, D.C.: National Catholic War Council, 1918), 24; Michael J. Slattery to Edward Joseph Hanna, San Francisco, 14 November 1918, "Correspondence, Social Reconstruction Program," Burke-Muldoon Papers, "The Church and Reconstruction," *Reconstruction Pamphlets*, March 1920, 4–5, RC Papers; and *Visitor*, 27 February 1920. For more on the bishops' postwar vision see Joseph M. McShane, *"Sufficiently Radical": Catholicism, Progressivism, and the Bishops' Program of 1919* (Washington, D.C.: Catholic University of America Press, 1986).

13. *Visitor*, 21 February, 3 April 1924.

14. D. A. McLean, "Re-Christianizing Industry," *Columbia*, January 1926, 16; *News Sheet*, December 1921, NCCW Papers, CUA; "Unemployment," *Reconstruction Pamphlets*, March 1919, 4, 10–11, 16, RC Papers; John A. Ryan and R. A. McGowan, *A Catechism of the Social Question* (New York: Missionary Society of St. Paul the Apostle, 1921), 36, 45; *Bishops' Program of Social Reconstruction* (Washington, D.C.: NCWC, n.d.), 23; and William, Cardinal O'Connell, *Religious Ideals in Industrial Relations* (1921), Pamphlet Collection, Rare Books and Special Collections, CUA, 10, 12, 19.

15. *Visitor*, 10 March 1922, 10 January 1924.

16. *Le Jean-Baptiste*, 1 April 1927; Richard S. Sorrell, "Sentinelle Affair (1924–1929)—Religion and Militant Survivance in Woonsocket, Rhode Island," *Rhode Island History* 36 (1977): 73; undated *Worcester Telegram* article (c. September 1906), Union Saint-Jean-Baptiste Papers, PCDA (hereafter cited as USJB Papers); and Dolan, *American Catholic Experience*, 183–84.

17. Undated *Worcester Telegram* article (c. September 1906); Hayman, *Catholicism, 1886–1921*, 139–43, 145–46, 165–69; Sorrell, "Sentinelle Affair," 76; and *Visitor*, 29 September 1916.

18. *Visitor*, 19 October 1917, 14 June, 27 September 1918; and *Tribune*, 20 August 1916.

19. *Handbook*, 1–2; *Report of the General Committee on Catholic Affairs and Interests* (24 September 1919), 3, "Minutes and Reports, General Committee on Catholic Affairs and Interests, 1919," Burke-Muldoon Papers; John J. Burke, *Unity Among All Catholics* (Washington, D.C.: NCWC, n.d.); *News Sheet*, 29 November 1920, 6 March 1921, NCCW Papers, CUA; and *National Council of Catholic Men: Its Functions, Its Composition and Its Constitution*, 5, General Publications, National Council of Catholic Men, NCWC Papers.

20. Michael Slattery to Hickey, Washington, 26 February 1921, National Council of Catholic Men Papers, PCDA (hereafter cited as NCCM Papers, PCDA); *Visitor*, 23 March, 12 July 1923, 8 May 1924; Joseph M. Tally to Linna Bresette, Providence, 17 October 1932, "Records of the Catholic Conference on Industrial Problems, Meetings: Providence" (November 1932), Social Action Department, NCWC Papers; *National Council of Catholic Men*, 3; and *News Sheet*, August 1922, NCCW Papers, CUA.

21. *News Sheet No. 1* (c. January 1921), 6 March 1921, NCCW Papers, CUA; and Dolan, *American Catholic Experience*, 353, 355.

22. *Visitor*, 20 April, 25 May 1923, 26 June 1924.

23. *Le Jean-Baptiste*, 14 July 1922.

24. *Report of the General Committee on Catholic Affairs*, 26; *Civics Catechism on the Rights and Duties of American Citizens* (Washington, D.C.: National Catholic War Council, 1920); and *Visitor*, 7 March 1919, 8 October 1920, 8 June 1923, 30 October 1925.

25. *How to Conduct a Study Club* (Washington, D.C.: NCWC, n.d.), 1, 7–10, 14, 17–19; and *News Sheet*, June 1921, June-July, September 1924, January 1925, January, June 1926, NCCW Papers, CUA.

26. *News Sheet*, November-December 1924, October 1929, NCCW Papers, CUA.

27. *Visitor*, 24 September 1920; "Setup of Study Club of R.I. State Circle, D. of I.," Daughters of Isabella Papers, PCDA; and Linna Bresette to Anna Fennessy, Washington, 24 August 1933, National Council of Catholic Women Papers, PCDA (hereafter cited as NCCW Papers, PCDA).

28. Paula Kane, *Separatism and Subculture: Boston Catholicism, 1900–1920* (Chapel Hill: University of North Carolina Press, 1994), 241–43; *News Sheet*, 1 May 1921, December 1926, NCCW Papers, CUA; and *Visitor*, 18 June, 24 September 1920.

29. Morris, *American Catholic*, 132; *News Sheet*, 3 March 1921, January-February 1924, January 1927, January 1928, NCCW Papers, CUA; and Dolan, *American Catholic Experience*, 364.

30. *News Sheet*, January 1927, NCCW Papers, CUA; and *United League News*, February 1921, July 1923, RILWV Papers.

31. Quoted in Nancy Cott, *The Grounding of Modern Feminism* (New Haven: Yale University Press, 1987), 101–2. For more on the nationwide decline in political engagement after the turn of the century, see Michael E. McGerr, *The Decline of Popular Politics: The American North, 1865–1928* (New York: Oxford University Press, 1986), and Frances Fox Piven and Richard A. Cloward, *Why Americans Don't Vote*, 2d ed. (New York: Pantheon, 1989).

32. William H. Chafe, *The Paradox of Change: American Women in the 20th Century* (New York: Oxford University Press, 1991), 22, 30; and Cott, *Grounding of Modern Feminism*, 110, 114.

33. *Providence Journal Almanac, 1921* (Providence: Providence Journal Co., 1921), 129; *Providence Journal Almanac, 1923* (Providence: Providence Journal Co., 1923), 161; and *Providence Journal Almanac, 1925* (Providence: Providence Journal Co., 1925), 161.

34. *News Sheet*, November-December 1922, September 1924, February 1928, NCCW Papers, CUA; and *Visitor*, 29 October 1920, 31 March, 28 April 1922, 3 April 1924, 2 March 1928.

35. Kane, *Separatism and Subculture*, 249; *News Sheet*, 29 November 1920, April 1922, NCCW Papers, CUA; and *Visitor*, 14 October 1921, 9 March 1923, 3 April, 22 May 1924.

36. *Visitor*, 3 April 1924.

37. *Visitor*, 2 June, 27 October 1922, 9 March, 18 October 1923, 12 June 1925.

38. *Tribune*, 15 June 1919; *Visitor*, 11 June 1920, 23 December 1921, 29 May 1924, 23, 30 October 1925, 17 February 1928, 27 October 1933; Agnes Regan to Agnes M. Bacon, Washington, 20 January 1931, and Bacon to Charles Mahoney, Pawtucket, 4 June 1935, NCCW Papers, PCDA; Leslie Woodcock Tentler, *Seasons of Grace: A History of the Catholic Archdiocese of Detroit* (Detroit: Wayne State University Press, 1990), 481; "Rhode Island State Circle, Daughters of Isabella, State Regent's Report," Daughters of Isabella Papers, PCDA; *News Sheet*, January 1922, NCCW Papers, CUA; and Hickey Diary (18 December 1921), Hickey Papers, PCDA.

39. Slawson, "National Catholic Welfare Conference," 1006; *News Sheet No. 1* (c. January 1921), NCCW Papers, CUA; and *Visitor*, 20 February 1920.

40. "Committee on Resolutions," 9 April 1933, HNS Papers; Elie Vezina to Hickey, Woonsocket, 4 March 1921, USJB Papers; Charles F. Dolle to Member Organizations, Washington, 9 February 1929, NCCM Papers, PCDA; *Visitor*, 8 May 1924; and Tally to "The Rev-

erend Sisters in Charge of Various Communities," Providence, 11 May 1928, NCCM Papers, PCDA.

41. "Minutes, Board of Directors" (7 September 1929), and Bacon to Hickey, Pawtucket, 2 February 1931, NCCW Papers, PCDA; and *Visitor*, 16 December 1927.

CHAPTER 10. CATHOLICS AND PROTESTANTS IN THE 1920S

1. John Higham, *Strangers in the Land: Patterns of American Nativism, 1860–1925*, 2d ed. (New York: Atheneum, 1963), 267, 269, 289, 295; William E. Leuchtenburg, *The Perils of Prosperity, 1914–32*, 2d ed. (Chicago: University of Chicago Press, 1993), 225; and Charles R. Morris, *American Catholic: The Saints and Sinners Who Built America's Most Powerful Church* (New York: Vintage, 1997), 113, 136.

2. Sara Errington, " 'The Language Question': Nativism, Politics, and Ethnicity in Rhode Island," in *New England's Disharmony: The Consequences of the Industrial Revolution*, ed. Douglas M. Reynolds and Katheryn Viens (Kingston: Rhode Island Labor History Society, 1993), 94–96.

3. Ibid., 92 n. 6, 96–97.

4. Paul Buhle, "The 1922 Textile Strike," in *A History of Rhode Island Working People*, ed. Paul Buhle, Scott Molloy, and Gail Sansbury (Providence: Regine, 1983), 45; Errington, " 'Language Question,' " 98; David Montgomery, *The Fall of the House of Labor: The Workplace, the State, and American Labor Activism, 1865–1925* (New York: Cambridge University Press, 1987), 407; and *Visitor*, 24 March 1922.

5. Gary Gerstle, *Working-Class Americanism: The Politics of Labor in a Textile City, 1914–1960* (New York: Cambridge University Press, 1989), 47; Errington, " 'Language Question,' " 93 n. 11; Dale T. Knobel, *"America for the Americans": The Nativist Movement in the United States* (New York: Twayne, 1996), 252–53; and Leslie Woodcock Tentler, *Seasons of Grace: A History of the Catholic Archdiocese of Detroit* (Detroit: Wayne State University Press, 1990), 428, 445–49.

6. Errington, " 'Language Question,' " 100, 102; and *United League News*, February 1924, 7, RILWV Papers.

7. *Le Jean-Baptiste*, 30 November 1923, 17 October 1924; and editorial reprinted from the *Woonsocket Tribune* in *Le Jean-Baptiste*, 3 December 1920.

8. *Visitor*, 11 October 1923; *Le Jean-Baptiste*, 28 April 1922; and Hickey Diary (25 April 1922), Hickey Papers, PCDA.

9. *Journal*, 11 April 1920; *Visitor*, 11 June 1920, 28 January 1921; *Le Jean-Baptiste*, 25 February 1921; and Elie Vezina to Hickey, Woonsocket, 4 March 1921, USJB Papers.

10. *Visitor*, 21 April 1922; *Le Jean-Baptiste*, 26 May 1922; and Errington, " 'Language Question,' " 102–3.

11. Errington, " 'Language Question,' " 99; Hickey Diary (25 April 1922); and *Le Jean-Baptiste*, 28 April 1922.

12. Errington, " 'Language Question,' " 100; and Buhle, "1922 Textile Strike," 46.

13. Buhle, "1922 Textile Strike," 45–46; Erwin L. Levine, *Theodore Francis Green: The Rhode Island Years, 1906–1936* (Providence: Brown University Press, 1963), 95; and *Providence Journal Almanac, 1923*, 178–79.

14. Errington, " 'Language Question,' " 101, 103–4.

15. Higham, *Strangers in the Land*, 295; Knobel, *"America for the Americans,"* 265, 269; and David H. Bennett, *The Party of Fear: The American Far Right from Nativism to the Militia Movement*, 2d ed. (New York: Vintage, 1995), 209–11, 221–22, 229.

16. Higham, *Strangers in the Land*, 291, 293; Knobel, *"America for the Americans,"* 263; and Bennett, *Party of Fear*, 210, 214–16, 222.

17. Joseph W. Sullivan, "Rhode Island's Invisible Empire: A Demographic Glimpse into the Ku Klux Klan," *Rhode Island History* 47 (1989): 74–75, 77–78.

18. Ibid., 75; and Norman W. Smith, "The Ku Klux Klan in Rhode Island," *Rhode Island History* 37 (1978): 38, 40.

19. Errington, "'Language Question,'" 102; Smith, "Ku Klux Klan," 37–38; *Le Jean-Baptiste*, 8 August 1924; Paul Buhle, ed., *Working Lives: An Oral History of Rhode Island Labor* (Providence: Rhode Island Historical Society, 1987), 26; and Sullivan, "Rhode Island's Invisible Empire," 75.

20. Smith, "Ku Klux Klan," 40; and *Visitor*, 3 April, 8 May, 19 June 1924.

21. Gainer to Hickey, 10 December 1923, and Hickey to Gainer, 11 December 1923, Ku Klux Klan Papers, PCDA; Smith, "Ku Klux Klan," 38; and Errington, "'Language Question,'" 104.

22. Smith, "Ku Klux Klan," 40; Norma LaSalle Daoust, "The Perils of Providence: Rhode Island's Capital City during the Depression and New Deal" (Ph.D. diss., University of Connecticut, 1982), 235; John K. White, "Alfred E. Smith's Rhode Island Revolution: The Election of 1928," *Rhode Island History* 42 (1983): 59; Leuchtenburg, *Perils of Prosperity*, 135–37; and Errington, "'Language Question,'" 103.

23. Levine, *Theodore Francis Green*, 97.

24. Ibid., 97–100, 102.

25. Smith, "Ku Klux Klan," 41; and *Visitor*, 28 January 1927.

26. Sullivan, "Invisible Empire," 75–77; Knobel, *"America for the Americans,"* 271–72; Higham, *Strangers in the Land*, 296–98; and Bennett, *Party of Fear*, 230–31, 235. Rhode Island's Perry claimed to be a descendant of Oliver Hazard Perry, a hero of the War of 1812, and his nephew Commodore Matthew Perry, known for opening Japan to foreign trade. Of course his mixed racial origins did not preclude this claim, as the Perrys themselves descended from an old Rhode Island slaveholding family and may have produced children with their slaves.

27. Smith, "Ku Klux Klan," 36.

28. Edward G. St.-Godard, *St. John's Parish, Pawtucket, RI, 1884–1978* (n.p., n.d.), 39–40; Richard S. Sorrell, "Sentinelle Affair (1924–1929)—Religion and Militant Survivance in Woonsocket, Rhode Island," *Rhode Island History* 36 (1977): 68; and Gerstle, *Working-Class Americanism*, 50.

29. Sorrell, "Sentinelle Affair," 67–68; *Visitor*, 7 October 1927; Robert W. Hayman, "Bishop William A. Hickey and the Sentinellists," *Visitor*, 17 April 1997; and Gerstle, *Working-Class Americanism*, 50.

30. Hayman, "Bishop William A. Hickey"; Gerstle, *Working-Class Americanism*, 52; Sorrell, "Sentinelle Affair," 69; and *Visitor*, 18 February 1927, 11 April 1928, 15 February 1929.

31. Gerstle, *Working-Class Americanism*, 56–59.

32. Sorrell, "Sentinelle Affair," 75; and Gerstle, *Working-Class Americanism*, 50.

33. Sorrell, "Sentinelle Affair," 67, 73; and Gerstle, *Working-Class Americanism*, 52.

34. Paul Buhle, "Italian-American Radicals and Labor in Rhode Island, 1905–1930," *Radical History Review* 17 (spring 1978): 144; *L'Eco*, 5 May 1927; Buhle, *Working Lives*, 24; Minutes (17 April, 1 May 1927), Providence Central Federated Union Papers, RIHS (hereafter cited as PCFU Papers); and *Visitor*, 6 May, 13 May, 12 August 1927.

35. *Journal*, 10 August 1927.

36. Timothy J. Meagher, *Inventing Irish America: Generation, Class, and Ethnic Identity in a New England City, 1880–1928* (Notre Dame: University of Notre Dame Press, 2001), 317–21; and White, "Smith's Rhode Island Revolution," 64.

37. White, "Smith's Rhode Island Revolution," 60.

38. *Visitor*, 28 September 1928.

39. Minutes (20 May 1928), PCFU Papers; *Visitor*, 8 June, 2 November 1928; White, "Smith's Rhode Island Revolution," 64; and Tally to "The Reverend Sisters in Charge of Various Communities," Providence, 11 May 1928, NCCM Papers, PCDA. Voting statistics come from the annual *Providence Journal Almanac*.

40. White, "Smith's Rhode Island Revolution," 64–65.

41. Murray S. Stedman Jr. and Susan W. Stedman, "The Rise of the Democratic Party of Rhode Island," *New England Quarterly* 24 (1951): 329; and White, "Smith's Rhode Island Revolution," 57–58. The voting statistics come from the *Providence Journal Almanac*.

42. *Providence Journal Almanac, 1929* (Providence: Providence Journal Co., 1929), 174–75, 185.

43. Daoust, "Perils of Providence," 243. In his study of voting patterns in Boston, the historian Gerald Gamm disputes the theory that the Smith election ushered in a sudden and dramatic electoral realignment. See Gerald H. Gamm, *The Making of New Deal Democrats: Voting Behavior and Realignment in Boston, 1920–1940* (Chicago: University of Chicago Press, 1986).

CHAPTER 11. SUFFRAGE REFORM AND ITS AFTERMATH

1. Erwin L. Levine, *Theodore Francis Green: The Rhode Island Years, 1906–1936* (Providence: Brown University Press, 1963), 190; *Le Jean-Baptiste*, 4 January 1924; *Jewish Review*, 3 February 1928; and *Echo*, 6 June 1930.

2. Sara M. Algeo, *The Story of a Sub-Pioneer* (Providence: Snow and Farnham, 1925), 253; *United League News*, July 1923, 5, and *Newsletter*, November 1928, RILWV Papers. Voting statistics come from the *Providence Journal Almanac*.

3. Chilton Williamson, "Rhode Island Suffrage since the Dorr War," *New England Quarterly* 28 (1955): 44–45.

4. *Visitor*, 29 October 1926.

5. Ibid., 8 December 1922.

6. Williamson, "Rhode Island Suffrage," 45–46; and *Providence News*, 29 October 1924.

7. James Quayle Dealey, *Political Situations in Rhode Island and Suggested Constitutional Changes* (Providence: Oxford Press, 1928), 8–9, 37–38, 42, 70; and Alexander Keyssar, *The Right to Vote: The Contested History of Democracy in the United States* (New York: Basic Books, 2000), 133, tables A.10 and A.11.

8. General Assembly, "Resolutions Introduced in the House" and "Resolutions Introduced in the Senate," Rhode Island State Library; *Jewish Review*, 3 February 1928; *Newsletter*, November 1928, 3; and Williamson, "Rhode Island Suffrage," 46.

9. *Newsletter*, November 1928, 2.

10. Keyssar, *Right to Vote*, 228–35, 243.

11. General Assembly, *Acts and Resolves Passed by the General Assembly of the State of Rhode Island and Providence Plantations, at the January Session,* A.D. 1927 (Pawtucket: Auto Press, 1927), 185; *United League News*, May 1927, 14; and *Newsletter*, November 1928, 6.

12. *Journal*, 7 November 1928.

13. *Bulletin* editorial reprinted in *Rhode Island Italian Echo*, 15 November 1928; and *Journal*, 7 November 1928.

14. *Journal*, 4 November 1928; *Newsletter*, November 1928, 2; Keyssar, *Right to Vote*, 230; and *Visitor*, 6 February 1936.

15. Kristi Andersen, *The Creation of a Democratic Majority, 1928–1936* (Chicago: University of Chicago Press, 1979); Gerald H. Gamm, *The Making of New Deal Democrats: Voting Behavior and Realignment in Boston, 1920–1940* (Chicago: University of Chicago Press, 1986); Samuel Lubell, *The Future of American Politics*, 2d ed. (New York: Harper and Brothers, 1952), 28–29; Lizabeth Cohen, *Making a New Deal: Industrial Workers in Chicago, 1919–1939* (New York: Cambridge University Press, 1990), chap. 6; V. O. Key Jr., "The Future of the Democratic Party," *Virginia Quarterly Review* 28 (1952): 164–66; Robert S. McElvaine, *The Great Depression: America, 1929–1941*, 2d ed. (New York: New York Times Books, 1993), chap. 5; and Ruth S. Morgenthau, *Pride without Prejudice: The Life of John O. Pastore* (Providence: Rhode Island Historical Society, 1989), 27 (Pastore quotation).

16. Murray S. Stedman Jr. and Susan W. Stedman, "The Rise of the Democratic Party of Rhode Island," *New England Quarterly* 24 (1951): 339; Norma LaSalle Daoust, "The Perils of Providence: Rhode Island's Capital City during the Depression and New Deal" (Ph.D. diss., University of Connecticut, 1982), 260; Matthew J. Smith, "The Real McCoy in the Bloodless Revolution of 1935," *Rhode Island History* 32 (1973): 72; and Levine, *Theodore Francis Green*, 175–76.

17. Levine, *Theodore Francis Green*, 177–83; and Walter H. Conser Jr., "Ethnicity and Politics in Rhode Island: The Career of Frank Licht," *Rhode Island History* 44 (1985): 102.

18. Levine, *Theodore Francis Green*, 182.

19. Ibid., 183–87.

20. Paul Buhle and Dan Georgakas, "Communist Party, USA," in *Encyclopedia of the American Left*, ed. Mari Jo Buhle, Paul Buhle, and Dan Georgakas (New York: Garland, 1990; rpt., Urbana: University of Illinois Press, 1992), 150–51; and Alan Brinkley, *Voices of Protest: Huey Long, Father Coughlin, and the Great Depression* (New York: Alfred A. Knopf, 1982).

21. David L. Davies, "Impoverished Politics: The New Deal's Impact on City Government in Providence, Rhode Island," *Rhode Island History* 42 (1983): 87–94.

22. Daoust, "Perils of Providence," 90–91; *Visitor*, 16, 23 June, 1 September 1933; and Minutes (26 April 1933), PCFU Papers.

23. *Echo*, 29 May 1931, 22 January 1932, 11 October 1935; Peter R. D'Agostino, "'Fascist Transmission Belts' or Episcopal Advisors? Italian Consuls and American Catholicism in the 1930s" (paper delivered at the Cushwa Center for the Study of American Catholicism, Notre Dame, Ind., May 1997), 22, 27, 30–31; and idem, "The Triad of Roman Authority: Fascism, the Vatican, and Italian Religious Clergy in the Italian Emigrant Church," *Journal of American Ethnic History* 17 (1998): 9, 21, 30–31.

24. D'Agostino, "'Fascist Transmission Belts,'" 6, 23; and *Echo*, 10 April, 24 July 1931, 17 April, 25 May 1936.

25. D'Agostino, "'Fascist Transmission Belts,'" 4, 6–7; *Visitor*, 1 November 1923; and *Bulletin*, 16 March 1936.

26. Paul Buhle, "Italian-American Radicals and Labor in Rhode Island, 1905–1930," *Radical History Review* 17 (spring 1978): 143; Paul Buhle, ed., *Working Lives: An Oral History of Rhode Island Labor* (Providence: Rhode Island Historical Society, 1987), 24; *Rhode Island Labor News*, 26 May 1936; and *Journal*, 26 January 1930.

27. *Echo*, 16 September 1932, 16 August, 6 September, 11, 25 October, 20 December 1935; and *Journal*, 25 May 1936.

28. Luigi Scala to Louis Metcalf Walling, Providence, 2 October 1936, Louis Metcalf Walling Papers, RIHS (hereafter cited as Walling Papers); *Echo*, 4 January 1935; and Levine, *Theodore Francis Green*, 184, 187.

29. Morgenthau, *Pride Without Prejudice*, 11–12, 14, 17–24, 27–29.

30. Ibid., 15, 33–34, 43–44, 52, 56, 116–17, 175.

31. Levine, *Theodore Francis Green*, 169–71; *Visitor*, 12 January 1934; and Minutes (14 March, 11 April 1934), PCFU Papers. For more on the 1934 textile strike, see James F. Findlay, "The Great Textile Strike of 1934: Illuminating Rhode Island History in the Thirties," *Rhode Island History* 42 (1983): 17–29.

32. *Labor News*, 30 April, 29 October 1935.

33. Ibid., 29 October 1935, 31 March, 30 June 1936.

34. Louis Metcalf Walling to John Wheeler, Providence, 2 August 1936, Walling Papers; Levine, *Theodore Francis Green*, 190–91; *Labor News*, 31 October 1938; *Visitor* 11 January 1935; Alice Hunt to Walling, Providence, 8 June 1936, and Herbert C. Parsons to Eric Stone (no location given), 5 June 1936, Walling Papers.

35. Daoust, "Perils of Providence," 281; and Frances Fox Piven and Richard A. Cloward, *Why Americans Don't Vote*, 2d ed. (New York: Pantheon, 1989), 54, 125.

36. Matthew J. Smith, "Rhode Island Politics 1956–1964: Party Realignment," *Rhode Island History* 35 (1976): 49–51.

37. Ibid., 49.

CONCLUSION

1. The historian Lizabeth Cohen finds that during the 1930s, unemployed Chicagoans turned away from community institutions such as churches and toward unions and the state because the former proved incapable of providing for them. This was not the case in Providence. Lizabeth Cohen, *Making a New Deal: Industrial Workers in Chicago, 1919–1939* (New York: Cambridge University Press, 1990), chap. 5.

2. For more about the devotion of St. Jude, see Robert A. Orsi, *Thank You, St. Jude: Women's Devotion to the Patron Saint of Hopeless Causes* (New Haven: Yale University Press, 1996). For more on the Providence church during the Depression, see Evelyn Sterne, "All Americans: The Politics of Citizenship in Providence, 1840–1940" (Ph.D. diss., Duke University, 1999), 323–34.

INDEX

Page numbers followed by *f* refer to figures.

Gorman, Charles, 61, 68, 69, 133
Grace, Lawrence, 95, 146
Granger, Daniel, 87
Greenback Labor Party, 68
Green, Theodore Francis, 163, 244, 247, 248
Grieve, Robert, 90, 96

Harkins, Matthew: Catholic unity, 206; clerical versus lay control, 124; ethnic parishes, 53, 116; as Irish American, 41, 117; politics, 75, 143, 171; religious factionalism, 195, 196, 205
Hazard, Benjamin, 16, 28
Hendricken, Thomas, 41
Hickey, William, 185, 189, 208; Catholic citizenship, 203, 212–15; Catholic unity, 208, 222, 225, 228, 230; religious factionalism, 198, 228, 229; Peck Act, 222; Smith campaign, 232
Higgins, James H., 143
Holy Ghost, 55, 123, 197 f, 221; lay organizations, 111, 118, 122, 126–27, 128; religious factionalism, 195–96, 198–201, 204, 207; World War I, 159
Holy Name Society: early twentieth century, 120–21, 122–23, 124, 128; parades, 149, 150 f, 207–8, 232; as political base, 2, 94, 95, 122, 134, 135, 143, 144, 147, 149, 150, 185, 203, 209, 215; religious factionalism, 196; World War I, 159, 170, 171
Howard, Hiram, 60, 80, 85

Immaculate Conception, 138
Immigrant Educational Bureau, 115, 162, 163, 166
immigration: communism and, 183, 185; literacy tests, 134, 177; naturalization and, 7, 243; population, 3, 28, 29, 36, 37, 48, 55, 100, 154, 217–18; restriction of, 204, 210, 214, 223, 240, 243, 254; World War I, 158, 165. *See also* Americanization; nativism; *specific ethnic groups*
Industrial Alliance, 140
Industrial Workers of the World (IWW), 6, 107, 114, 153, 184
Ireland, John, 72, 81
Irish community, 3, 14, 28, 36–43, 55, 57, 154; acculturation/naturalization, 38, 39–40, 71, 78, 155, 161, 172; Catholic Church and, 9, 29, 40–41, 43, 113–19, 125–26, 172; Catholic citizenship, 214, 215; Catholic rights movement, 146–48; Catholic unity movement, 204–8; Irish nationalists and, 39–41, 116–17, 185, 214; labor movement, 79, 85–87, 146–47; nativism and, 28–37, 62 f; occupations, 1, 37, 38;

organizations, 19, 39–40, 43, 68, 125–26; parochial schools, 112, 221; remigration, 38; World War I, 158–61, 172
Irish community, political orientation: early twentieth century, 90; late nineteenth century, 1–3, 36, 38–39, 40, 61, 63, 68–69, 77
Irish community, suffrage reform: early twentieth century, 103, 144; late nineteenth century, 61, 63, 71; post–World War I, 238; pre–Civil War, 14, 19, 20, 22, 24–25, 26, 28–31, 34–35, 39
Italian community, 3, 36, 48–55, 57, 154; Catholic Church and, 9, 52–55, 113–19, 171–72, 199, 231; Catholic rights movement, 148, 149 f; Catholic unity movement, 207; Macaroni Riots, 105–7; occupations, 48–51; parochial schools, 112, 221; publications, 118, 195, 199, 221, 246, 247; religious factionalism, 195–96, 198–201, 204, 207; remigration, 51, 165, 167–68; suffrage reform, 238; World War I, 159, 161, 165, 167–68, 184
Italian community, acculturation/naturalization: early twentieth century, 115–16; late nineteenth century, 49, 51, 52, 71–72, 78; post–World War I, 199–200, 221; World War I, 161, 167–68
Italian community, political orientation: early twentieth century, 84, 90; late nineteenth century, 51, 52, 65, 68–69, 71–72; post–World War I, 221, 223, 232, 234, 246–47, 251; World War I, 184
Italian organizations: fraternal, 51, 126–27, 167, 184, 189, 246; mutual aid, 51–52, 72, 78, 117; political, 72, 90, 107, 184, 246, 247

Jenks, Agnes M., 178
Jewish community, 6, 57, 107, 141; acculturation/naturalization, 78, 187–88, 190; nativism, 78, 225; organizations, 78, 187–88; political orientation, 8, 71, 78, 84, 93, 233, 234; publications, 184, 190; suffrage, 27, 103; World War I, 154, 165; Zionism, 185
"*Journal* ring," 63, 65

Knights of Columbus (KOC), 2, 111, 126–27, 129, 140, 143, 189
Knights of Labor, 66, 68, 81, 93, 140, 147
Know-Nothing Party, 33–34, 68
Ku Klux Klan, 218, 223–28, 230–32, 234

Labor Church, 92–93
labor movement: Americanization and, 176, 190; Catholic rights movement, 141, 145–48,

Toupin, Felix, 223, 227
Trades Union Economic League, 84, 87
Tyler, William, 41

Union of Catholic Parish Clubs, 122, 136
Union Railroad Company, 80, 83, 85–89, 146
Union Saint-Jean-Baptiste (USJB), 79, 129, 161, 205, 206, 215, 222
United Textile Workers (UTW), 181–82, 239, 250

Van Buren, Martin, 27–28
voter turnout, 7; 1928 election, 233; Bourn Amendment and, 70–71; Dorr Rebellion, 21; post–World War I, 211, 212, 233, 243; streetcar strike and, 87–89
voting restrictions: African Americans, 20–21, 24, 27, 101, 102, 211; apportionment and, 14, 241; colonial period, 26–27, 31; literacy, 100, 101; poll taxes, 211, 241; registration, 211, 237, 242; religion and, 27, 28–30; state, 26–31, 34–35, 63; women, 20, 66–70, 211–12. *See also* Dorr Rebellion; suffrage reform; woman suffrage
voting restrictions, immigrants, 1, 3, 7; early twentieth century, 100–101, 104; late nineteenth century, 61, 65, 69, 70–71, 267n. 22; post–World War I, 211–12; pre–Civil War, 14, 24–25, 27, 28–30; World War I, 179
voting restrictions, property, 1, 3; 1928 amendment, 235, 241–42; colonial, 14, 26–27; early twentieth century, 96–105, 144–45; late nineteenth century, 60–61, 63, 67, 69–70; post–World War I, 211–12, 235–42; pre–Civil War, 14–17, 24–25, 26–28; World War I, 178–79, 180, 182

Williams, Roger, 30, 31
Wilson, Woodrow, 153, 158, 185, 187, 247
woman suffrage: Americanization and, 176; civic education, 187; early twentieth century, 99, 101–5, 140; late nineteenth century, 66–67, 73; Nineteenth Amendment, 8, 178–79, 210, 211, 240; post–World War I, 210–15, 237; pre–Civil War, 20, 24; Smith campaign, 232–33; and voting, 140, 211, 212, 237; World War I, 173, 178–79, 180 f, 182
women: Americanization and, 155, 163, 175–76, 177, 188; Catholic Church, 3, 5, 120, 124–25, 130–31, 135–38, 254; as Catholic citizens, 209–15; "domestic feminism," 212–13; education, 114, 179; labor movement, 3, 6, 8; nativism, 75, 103–4; occupations, 38, 43, 45, 49, 51; organizations, 8, 51–52, 75, 91, 120–23, 124–25, 130–31, 246, 254; organizations as political base, 3, 5, 52, 135–38, 209–15; Peck Act, 220; political orientation, 3, 6, 8, 91–92, 93, 232–33, 246; religious factionalism and, 200; "separate spheres," 136–37; World War I, 160–61, 179
World War I, 153–92; Americanization, 161–73, 174–77, 182–84, 188–90, 191–92; Catholic activism, 166–73, 175–77, 188–90, 191–92; Catholic patriotism, 157–60, 170–72

Young Men's Christian Association (YMCA), 163, 168
Young Women's Christian Association (YWCA), 163, 168, 169

AUTHOR BIOGRAPHY

Evelyn Savidge Sterne is Assistant Professor of History at the University of
Rhode Island.